COLLECTED WORKS OF CHARLES BERG

Volume 6

HOMOSEXUALITY

HOMOSEXUALITY

A Subjective and Objective Investigation

CHARLES BERG

Routledge
Taylor & Francis Group

LONDON AND NEW YORK

First published in 1958 by George Allen & Unwin Ltd

This edition first published in 2022
by Routledge
4 Park Square, Milton Park, Abingdon, Oxon OX14 4RN

and by Routledge
605 Third Avenue, New York, NY 10158

Routledge is an imprint of the Taylor & Francis Group, an informa business

© 1958 George Allen & Unwin Ltd

British Library Cataloguing in Publication Data
A catalogue record for this book is available from the British Library

ISBN: 978-1-032-16970-5 (Set)
ISBN: 978-1-003-25348-8 (Set) (ebk)
ISBN: 978-1-032-17141-8 (Volume 6) (hbk)
ISBN: 978-1-032-17241-5 (Volume 6) (pbk)
ISBN: 978-1-003-25244-3 (Volume 6) (ebk)

DOI: 10.4324/9781003252443

Publisher's Note
The publisher has gone to great lengths to ensure the quality of this reprint but points out that some imperfections in the original copies may be apparent.

Disclaimer
The publisher has made every effort to trace copyright holders and would welcome correspondence from those they have been unable to trace.

This book is a re-issue originally published in 1948. The language used is a reflection of its era and no offence is meant by the Publishers to any reader by this re-publication.

HOMOSEXUALITY

A SUBJECTIVE AND OBJECTIVE

INVESTIGATION

British Edition Edited by
Dr. Charles Berg
M.D.

American Edition Edited by
A. M. Krich

Ruskin House

GEORGE ALLEN & UNWIN LTD

MUSEUM STREET LONDON

FIRST PUBLISHED IN GREAT BRITAIN
IN 1958

© George Allen and Unwin Ltd., 1958

PRINTED IN GREAT BRITAIN
in 12 pt Bembo type by
J. W. ARROWSMITH LTD.,
WINTERSTOKE ROAD, BRISTOL

CONTENTS

CONTENTS

PART TWO: CAUSE AND CURE

ACKNOWLEDGEMENTS

The editor wishes to thank the following authors, editors, publishers and copyright holders for their kind permission to reprint in this volume portions of the books and periodicals listed below:

Clarence B. Farrar, M.D., Editor, *American Journal of Psychiatry*, for 'The Homosexual Woman' by Jane McKinnon, copyright 1947 by *American Journal of Psychiatry*, and 'Varieties of Homosexual Manifestation' by George S. Sprague, M.D., copyright 1935 by *American Journal of Psychiatry*; Emerson Books, Inc. for *The Homosexual Neurosis* by Wilhelm Stekel, M.D., copyright 1922 by Richard Badger, Emerson Books, Inc., copyright renewed 1949 by Emerson Books, Inc.; The Williams & Wilkins Co. for *The Single Woman* by R. L. Dickinson, M.D. and Lura Beam, copyright 1934 by the Williams & Wilkins Co.; The Citadel Press for *New Approaches to Dream Interpretation* by Nandor Fodor, copyright 1951 by Nandor Fodor; W. W. Norton & Company, Inc., for *War in the Mind, The Case Book of a Medical Psychologist* by Charles Berg, M D., copyright 1948 by W. W. Norton & Company, Inc.; International Universities Press, Inc. for *Take Off Your Mask* by Ludwig Eidelberg, M.D., copyright 1948 by Ludwig Eidelberg, M.D., and 'An Analytic Session in a Case of Male Homosexuality' by Henri Flournoy, M.D., from *Drives, Affects, Behavior*, copyright 1953 by International Universities Press, Inc.; Dingwall-Rock, Ltd., for entries by Magnus Hirschfeld, M.D., and Gilbert Van Tassel Hamilton, M.D. in *Encyclopaedia Sexualis*, copyright 1936 by Dingwall-Rock, Ltd.; Penguin Books Ltd., for *The Psychology of Sex* by Oswald Schwarz, M.D.; Nolan D. C. Lewis, M.D., Editor, *The Journal of Nervous and Mental Disease* and *The Psychoanalytic Review* for 'Observations on Homosexuality among University Students' by Benjamin H. Glover, M.D., copyright 1951 by *The Journal of Nervous and Mental Disease*, 'On Homosexuality' by Paul Schilder, M.D., copyright 1929 by *The Psychoanalytic Review*, and 'An Analysis of the Psychosexual Development of a Female' by Morris W. Brody, M.D., copyright 1943 by *The Psychoanalytic Review*: Duncan Whitehead, Acting Editor, *The Psychiatric Quarterly* for 'Psychogenic and Constitutional Factors in Homosexuality' by George W. Henry, M.D., copyright 1934 by *The Psychiatric Quarterly*, and 'The Myth of a New National Disease: Homosexuality and the Kinsey Report' by Edmund Bergler, M.D., copyright 1948 by *The Psychiatric Quarterly*; Hermitage House, Inc. for 'Changing Concepts of Homosexuality in

7

ACKNOWLEDGEMENTS

Psychoanalysis' by Clara Thompson, M.D., from *A Study of Interpersonal Relations*, edited by Patrick Mullahy, copyright 1949 by Hermitage Press, Inc.; The Hogarth Press Ltd., for 'The Psychogenesis of a Case of Homosexuality in a Woman' by Sigmund Freud, M.D., from *Collected Papers*, Volume 11; Bollingen Foundation, Inc., for *Contributions to Analytical Psychology* by C. G. Jung; Christian Hamburger, M.D., and *The Journal of the American Medical Association* for 'Transvestism: Hormonal, Psychiatric and Surgical Treatment' by Christian Hamburger, M.D., Georg K. Sturup, M.D. and E. Dahl-Iversen, M.D., copyright 1953 by *The Journal of the American Medical Association;* Moshe Wulff, M.D., and W. Hoffer, M.D., Editor, *International Journal of Psycho-Analysis* for 'A Case of Male Homosexuality' by Moshe Wulff, M.D.

8

EDITORIAL SURVEY

WHEN the publishers asked me to edit this book, I was at first a little reluctant. There are already so many excellent books on the subject dating right back to antiquity. However, current popular interest in the subject has drawn attention to a need for whatever enlightenment psychology has to offer. The outpourings in newspapers and periodicals and the innumerable published letters, evidently emanating from people who are quite unaware of the mass of data and knowledge which science has accumulated and annotated, make one think that even a little light is better than none where all is darkness. Most of these writers do not attempt to disguise the fact that their opinions, often dogmatic, are emotionally determined—and what is more are not in any way influenced by anything other than emotion. They even boast as much! In short, our newspapers are inundated with what must be regarded as purely '*symptomatic*' opinions. It seems unlikely that if the debate were upon a natural science, such as nuclear physics, people would be so eager to display their ignorance and to assume that their opinion or bias was other than subjective.

In the light of the above public demonstration, I thought that such a book as this, which gives at least some of the facts and figures and attempts assessment of them, should certainly have every encouragement. For the psychotherapist it is particularly important to understand homosexuality, not only for its own sake as a psycho-social symptom, but also on account of its relationship to the various degrees of impairment of hetero-sexual potency so frequently encountered in almost all psycho-neuroses.

It has been said that few if any of us are capable of looking at sexual matters truly objectively. This is attributed to the power of the Oedipus complex in each of us. As an analyst I am inclined to wonder whether *any* of us can look upon *any* matter truly objectively! When one reads some of the views expressed on most subjects, and learns of some laws and legal attitudes, ancient and modern, one may well wonder. Even in the present volume the truth-seeking reader may be confused at the great variety of the more or less conflicting views expressed about homosexuality, even by the greatest authorities who have written on the subject. Nevertheless, there is a difference between incomplete knowledge with scientific hypotheses based upon it and total ignorance with emotionally determined bias.

These differences of opinion are part of the beauty and value of this catholic collection of papers. One reason for the diversity of views may be that homosexuality is not a disease, nor even a clinical entity, it is nothing more than a particular *FORM of expression*, of a psychic state which is common to all living creatures. Psychic states or emotional states, impulses and longings tend, sooner or later in the course of development, to make use of some real object to assist them to achieve gratification. They tend to express themselves in what is called '*object-relationship*'.

For instance, the psychic state of hunger expresses itself by sucking or eating—an *object*. The state of sexual 'hunger' at first expresses itself autoerotically, that is to say *without* object-relationship. Psychoanalysis has shown that every instinctual drive, every feeling or sensation, every emotional experience, gives rise to a movement in the psyche which can best be described as *unconscious phantasy*. It is a sort of dream-world, instigated principally by the sensations of physiological processes, in which the organism lives before (and after) it has very much contact with the world outside itself. Sexual feeling (like all other sensations with their accompanying unconscious phantasies), is principally autoerotic, especially early in development; but sooner or later it tends to choose some external object, usually a person, or a part of a person, in connexion with which to obtain gratification.

The *fundamental* condition is that of the sexual urge itself, emanating from the sexual instinct. A *secondary* development of this is choosing an *object* to utilize for relief of sexual tension. A further secondary development is the nature, type or sex of the '*object*' which seems most appropriate or convenient for this purpose.

Throughout the animal kingdom it is natural that if you cannot get one sort of food to eat, you eat or try to eat, whatever sort you can get, and the evidence and data in the animal kingdom show that the same rule applies more or less to the sexual appetite also. Of course, it may still be asked why, when females are available, should a male choose another male—or indeed, as all psychiatrists have seen happen, *a lock of hair, a piece of underclothing, or even a mackintosh?* The answer to this question is generally to be found in the developmental history of the individual, if not in the phylogenetic history of the species. In short, the nature of the object chosen for gratification of an instinct can be a minor aberration, inherited or acquired, operating upon a psychic state common to all. Why we make such a fuss about it (I mean when it does not infringe any individual's liberty), is to be found in the precarious balance of forces in our own repressed unconscious . . . but that is another story, to my mind even more interesting than the subject called homosexuality.

What I would like to do here, in this introductory chapter on homosexuality, is this: Having read all the literature I could find on the subject, and having spent most of my life listening to my analysands (not all of them homosexual by any means), I would like to tell the reader in a few words the nature, cause and cure of homosexuality and of all homosexuals! It would then be superfluous for him to read this or any other book on the subject. I am sorry that I cannot do this. Apparently none of the writers in this book can do it either. We would all seem to be as far from being able to do this as we are from expounding the nature, cause and cure of heterosexuality, or of love—or indeed of life and the universe itself with all its manifold phenomena. Indeed, the latter task may seem to be as near to, or as far from, solution as the former. The best we can do about all the phenomena of nature is to study them, to sift the facts from the fancies, and to go on doing this until understanding shall be thrust upon us, or so we hope. Homosexuality is a subject about which, in spite of the enormous abundance of data, there are so many divergent views, especially of its cause and cure, even amongst psychiatrists, that in a compendious study of the subject it is essential to present specimens of them all. This book attempts to do just that, and I consider that a more worth-while task than the assertion of dogmatic opinion masquerading under the guise of scientific conclusion.

Fifty years ago (1905) Freud[1] [page 19] summed up the aetiology of homosexuality as follows: 'The nature of inversion is explained neither by the hypothesis that it is innate nor by the alternative hypothesis that it is acquired. In the former case we must ask in what respect it is innate, unless we are to accept the crude explanation that everyone is born with his sexual instinct attached to a particular sexual object. In the latter case it may be questioned whether the various accidental influences would be sufficient to explain the acquisition of inversion without the co-operation of something in the subject himself. The existence of this last factor is not to be denied.'

In this summary Freud had subsumed, on his own confession, the writings of all previous authorities including those of Kraft Ebbing, Moebus, Havelock Ellis and Magnus Hirschfeld. In the same work Freud [page 26] goes on to say: 'It has been brought to our notice that we have been in the habit of regarding the connexion between the sexual instinct and the sexual object as more intimate than it in fact is. Experience of the cases that are considered abnormal has shown us that in them the sexual instinct and the sexual object are merely soldered together—a fact which we have been in danger of overlooking in consequence of the uniformity of the normal picture where the object appears to form part and parcel of the instinct. We are thus warned to loosen the bond that exists in our thoughts between instinct and object. It seems probable that the sexual instinct is in the first instance independent of its object; nor is its origin likely to be due to its object's attractions.'

We may well ask what progress in our knowledge has been made in this half century, despite increase in the data available. These data appear to be quite inexhaustible and of every variety. And yet C. H. Rolph[2] [page xv] in the year of grace 1955, can write (in the B. S. B. Council's book on female prostitution): 'I will surely show . . . that all the punitive legislation in the world could make no real impression on this problem (viz. female prostitution). It is a problem in essence of parent-and-child, its solution lies in happy homes and the manifold securities that are to be found in them. *The same is almost certainly true of that other moral outcast, the male homosexual, whose position before the law is, as I write, once more the focus of public controversy. But of that problem, and even of what is called male prostitution, still less is known.* The British Social Biology Council are now organizing, as a logical sequel to this report, a similar research into male prostitution in London, a first step towards a fuller examination of the entire social problem of homosexuality.' [My italics.]

But the data of research, if we are to avoid a misleading, narrow, parochial point of view should, like the data of anatomy, physiology, psychology and sociology, extend beyond sociology, beyond a study limited to *homo sapiens*. To obtain an adequate perspective the field of research should begin, if not with chemistry and physics, at least biologically, with the lower animals.

We have space to consider only a few excerpts from this wide field: Jenkins[3] [page 457 et seq.] found that if rats were segregated sexually so that the males and females were confined in separate places and no possible contact with the other sex allowed, then after some time homosexual behaviour would commence. This grew in proportion to the length of segregation. If later he introduced animals of the opposite sex these conditioned homosexuals showed little heterosexual interest. He found that the number which regained their heterosexuality was proportionately dependent upon the length of time they had been segregated apart. The longer the segregation the greater the number of rats which showed diminished sexuality on mixing with the other sex.

Dr. Allen[3] (1940) says: 'So strong is the instinct to copulate that an animal, and presumably a man, will attempt to perform sexual congress with unsuitable partners if no suitable ones are available.'

Margaret Mead[4] [page 131] asks: 'When human beings—or rats— are conditioned by social circumstances to respond sexually to members of their own sex as adults and in preference to members of the opposite sex, is this conditioning playing on a real bisexual base in the personality, which varies greatly in its structure as between one member of a group and another?'

It may be added that so far as human beings are concerned, homosexual 'conditioning', if of any importance, would seem to depend for its effectiveness on its being introduced before the child or infant had developed a heterosexual tendency or pattern. Yet I have known many cases where boys were seduced, even by adult males, and, though seemingly behaving homosexually, were at the most merely pseudo-homosexuals; they showed no homosexual tendencies after puberty. In normal persons heterosexual patterns are established, at least in the unconscious mind, very long before puberty, probably in babyhood, though not necessarily to the defensive exclusion of homosexual behaviour.

On the other hand, I have recently seen a young married man with a family of several children who wept to me over his compulsive addiction to lavatory meetings with unknown male seducers. He says it first happened to him unexpectedly when he was sixteen years of age and apparently exceptionally innocent.

Though he fled in terror on that occasion, he has returned to the same spot and similar spots periodically in the hope, frequently realized, that the opportunity might again present itself—and this is in spite of his evident terror of discovery. This would seem like an instance of clear-cut conditioning, but I am convinced that a deeper investigation will show other elements in his psychopathology, possibly even a fundamental homosexual trend and a current pseudo-heterosexuality. This last phenomena is more common than is generally appreciated.

It is particularly interesting that this patient originally consulted me on account of *ideas of reference*, paranoid or delusional ideas that persons in his office were looking at him suspiciously. This sort of thing is common enough in psychiatric experience and supports Freud's original view that paranoia, the insanity of delusions (from which I believe we all tend to suffer in a mild way) is psychopathologically founded upon repressed, unconscious homosexuality.

I feel that the converse mechanism suggested by Mayer-Gross[5] [page 180] where he says: 'Freud has commented on the frequency of a homosexual component in paranoid psychoses; it seems possible that for this finding social rather than constitutional or infantile psychodynamic factors are responsible', is mistaken and is putting the cart before the horse. At the most such factors, fear of social disgrace and blackmail, can act only secondarily, or as adjuvants, on the psychopathological basis of *repressed* elements in the homosexual conflict. Further, when Mayer-Gross goes on to hint that 'understanding, tolerance and sympathetic advice' can have any real influence on the course of homosexual behaviour, I feel that he is too optimistic. Homosexuality and paranoia are often comparably obstinate therapeutically—to a degree which may in itself suggest a relationship in psychopathology.

Another young man at a hospital out-patient department who told me that for many years he had been sleeping with his girl friend because he had been encouraged to do so by a doctor whom he consulted, then came out with the illuminating statement that that doctor could 'not have had a clue' of what he was talking about nor the slightest understanding of him, the patient. His grounds for this criticism of the doctor he expressed as follows: 'This sort of sex does not help me in the slightest. I am in just as awful a condition inside, if not worse. What I am thinking about and longing for all the time is sex *with a man*, and that is the only experience which brings me any satisfaction, and makes me feel at peace again.' I may mention that this patient is in appearance a healthy, normal young specimen of manhood, in spite of his acute anxiety symptoms, and his somewhat over-neat grooming.

The late Dr. Hirschfeld[6] [page 241] probably the most experienced of all sexologists, said that the diagnosis of genuine homosexuality must depend not only upon 'involuntary mental and spiritual fixation on one's own sex, striving for an outlet in sexual activity, but also upon the *absence of normal heterosexual affinity*.' (His third criterion, namely that of 'intersexual constitution', does not seem to be applicable in all cases.)

In the same way as the physical and physiological development of man can best be illuminated by such researches as those of Darwin in biology, so the fundamental nature or source of his psychological peculiarities is commonly best illuminated by a study of animal, as well as of infant, behaviour, particularly by a study of the higher mammals such as monkeys. One has the advantage here of observing Nature at work without the inhibiting and concealing effects of superimposed human culture. There have been many researchers in this field. Kinsey[7] [pages 448-9] says: 'The impression that infra-human mammals more or less confine themselves to heterosexual activities is a distortion of the fact which appears to have originated in a man-made philosophy . . . in actuality sexual contacts between individuals of the same sex are known to occur in practically every species of mammal which has been extensively studied. In many species homosexual contacts may occur with considerable frequency though never as frequently as heterosexual contacts'. . . . 'Homosexual contacts in infra-human species of mammals occur among both females and males. Homosexual contacts between females have been observed in such widely separated species as rats, mice, hamsters, guinea pigs, rabbits, porcupines, martens, cattle, antelope, goats, horses, pigs, lions, sheep, monkeys and chimpanzees.'

Apparently orgasm in the female animals is uncertain, but: 'sexual contacts between males of the lower mammalian species do proceed to the point of orgasm at least for the male that mounts another male.' However, I do not require to consult Kinsey for all the evidence in this matter, for an English farmer of sixty years standing told me that it was quite common to see cows mounting other cows, and he vouchsafed the information that the cow doing the mounting was by that act alone demonstrating that she was particularly ready for the bull. But what he considered still more curious was that the cow being mounted also showed readiness in this direction, more so than the cattle which did not partake in this. Kinsey concludes [page 450]: 'The mammalian record thus confirms our statement that any animal which is not too strongly conditioned by some special sort of experience is capable of responding to any adequate stimulus. This is what we find in the more uninhibited segments of our own human species, and this is what we find among young children who are not too rigorously restrained in their early sex play. Exclusive preferences and patterns of behaviour, heterosexual or homosexual, come only with experience, or as a result of social pressures which tend to force an individual into an exclusive pattern of one or the other sort . . . *It is more difficult to explain why each and every individual is not involved in EVERY type of sexual activity'*. [My italics.]

I think the biologist would say that the reason here is largely to do with internal secretions, endocrines and odours. On the other hand attempts to influence homosexuality by hormones has resulted in increase of erotic interest and capacity, *but without any change whatsoever in OBJECT-CHOICE*. The psychoanalyst would say that the choice of object is largely determined by a succession of early events, beginning at the breast, until the pattern is established. If we do not confine our attention to one individual life, I am convinced that, in spite of modern biological theories, we may extend this conditioning phylogenetically to the beginning of life, introducing, if we like, the Darwinian principle of natural and of sexual selection to ensure the maintenance of heterosexuality as the surviving pattern of behaviour.

Anthropological data are even more abundant than those provided by the biologists and monkey-observers, in spite of Havelock Ellis's[8] [page 8] interesting complaint that 'the travellers and others on whose records we are dependent have been so shy of touching these subjects, and so ignorant of the main points for investigation, that it is very difficult to discover sexual inversion in the proper sense in any lower race. Travellers have spoken vaguely of crimes against nature without defining the precise relationship involved nor inquiring how far any congenital impulse could be distinguished.'

Malinowski[9] [page 201] according to Reich's[9] 'summary', was not so 'shy and ignorant'. He found that 'children in the Trobriand Islands know . . . no sexual secrecy. Their sex life is allowed to develop naturally, freely and unhampered *through every stage of life, with full satisfaction*. The children engage freely in the sexual activities which correspond to their age . . . the Trobrianders know . . . no sexual perversions, no functional psychoses, no psychoneuroses, no sex murder; they have no word for theft; homosexuality and masturbation, to them, mean nothing but an unnatural and imperfect means of sexual gratification. . . The socially accepted form of sexual life is spontaneous monogamy without compulsion, a relationship which can be dissolved without difficulties; thus, there is no promiscuity.' Reich goes on to say: 'At the time when Malinowski made his studies of the Trobriand islanders, there was living a few miles away, on the Amphlett Islands, a tribe with partriarchal authoritarian family organization. The people inhabiting these islands were already showing all the traits of the European neurotic, such as distrust, anxiety, neuroses, perversion, suicide, etc.' Reich concludes [page 202]: 'The determining factor of the mental health of a population is the condition of its natural love life.'

However, there is not space in this paper to give adequate consideration to the data accumulated since Ellis's complaint, and extending beyond his survey, which covers material from ancient Egypt, Carthage, the introduction into Greece of *paiderastia* by the Dorian warriors, Persia, Constantinople, China, India, Afghanistan, American Indians from the Eskimos of Alaska to Brazil and further south, various parts of Africa, the Papuans of New Guinea, Russia, Rome, Germany and France. Every degree of homosexuality seems to have prevailed in different places and at different times, accompanied by every degree of reaction-formation, varying from 'fashion' (Havelock Ellis[8] [page 59]) in ancient Greece, official promotion, sanction or toleration, to the direst penalties, including the death sentence. As late as the eighteenth century in London, when homosexual practices were 'more prevalent ... than today,' 'the punishment for sodomy, when completely effected, was death, and it was frequently inflicted.' (Havelock Ellis[8] [page 46]). The modern equivalent of these reactive expressions is comparably savage. The Offences Against the Person Act, 1861, regarding what it calls 'the abominable crime of buggery', says, the culprit is ' ... *to be kept in penal servitude for life or for any term not less than ten years*', making it clear that the State claims monopoly of the act. Mayer-Gross[5] [page 181] says: 'In Switzerland, Scandinavia and Germany some of these offenders have been treated by castration when freely submitted to.' (One may wonder how 'free' was the submission.)

A disadvantage in such cases is that the psychiatrist may subsequently have to deal with an intractable depression.

It is noteworthy, if only as a corrective to biased conclusions, that some of the most notable persons in history were, according to Havelock Ellis,[8] [page 24] 'All charged, on more or less solid evidence, with homosexual practices'. His list includes such names as Julius Caesar, alleged to have been 'the husband of all women and the wife of all men', Augustus, Tiberius, Caligula, Claudius, Nero, Hadrian, 'many of them men of great ability, and, from a Roman standpoint, great moral worth' [page 24].

It would be interesting if we could discover whether, in accordance with Freudian psychopathology, all these could be shown to have had an exaggerated emotional attachment to their mothers, deriving from earliest Oedipus-incestuous infancy. Mayer-Gross[5] [page 177] says: 'What we have learnt about the life history of famous men such as André Gide and Marcel Proust, who were self-confessed homosexuals, certainly suggests that an intense emotional attachment to the mother may play a part in some cases.' Mayer-Gross[5] goes on to say [page 180]: 'As a matter of clinical experience it is remarkable how often homosexuals are of more than average intelligence.' Indeed, if one studies the illustrious names right up to almost modern times, one may feel that there is some excuse for the inverts' ridiculous claim of a monopoly of culture and genius. Leonardo da Vinci, perhaps the greatest artist of all time, was certainly imprisoned in his youth on account of it (Havelock Ellis[8] [page 32]). Freud[10] [page 14] points out that Leonardo was 'disgusted' with everything heterosexual, and concludes that his temperament was marked by 'ideal homosexuality'—'it may be thought by far more probable that the affectionate relationships of Leonardo to the young men did not result in sexual activity' [page 16].

'Michelangelo, one of the very chief artists of the Renaissance period, we cannot now doubt, was sexually inverted' (Havelock Ellis[8] [page 32]). The list goes on to include such august names as Virgil, Sophocles, Alexander the Great, Frederick the Great, Wagner; and in England, William Rufus, Edward II, James I, and 'Perhaps William III' [page 40]. Literary figures are not spared: Marlow and Francis Bacon are strongly suspected,

20

and even Shakespeare 'narrowly escapes' [page 44]. And so on, to include Edward Fitzgerald and Walt Whitman, until we reach 'the most famous homosexual trial of recent times in England', [page 48], that of Oscar Wilde. Concerning this trial, Ellis [page 49] says with regard to *psychopathology*: 'Although this development (Oscar Wilde's homosexual behaviour) occurred comparatively late in life, we must hesitate to describe Wilde's homosexuality as acquired. If we consider his constitution and his history, it is not difficult to suppose that homosexual germs were present in latent form from the first, and it may quite well be that Wilde's inversion was of that kind which is now described as retarded, though still congenital.' With regard to *reaction*, Ellis says: 'There arose a general howl of execration, joined in even by the Judge' (!) The same sort of thing can be witnessed in magistrates' courts today.

All this may be regarded as collateral evidence in favour of Kinsey's[11] [page 610] contention that 'perhaps the *major portion* of the male population has at least some homosexual experience between adolescence and old age.' Kinsey goes on to say 'In addition, some *sixty per cent* of pre-adolescent boys engage in homosexual activities and there is an additional group of adult males who avoid overt contacts but are quite aware of their potentialities for reacting to other males.' Kinsey, basing his conclusions upon the greatest statistical evidence yet achieved in this field, continues: [page 616] 'There is only about half of the male population whose sexual behaviour is exclusively heterosexual'. I consider his view [page 617] that 'one must learn to recognize every combination of heterosexuality and homosexuality in the histories of various individuals' as somewhat misleading—not of mere *acts*, for there he has the data, nor of the unconscious mind, which certainly contains everything—but misleading as a manifestation of *true* sexuality, that is to say of sexual behaviour which brings the fullest gratification. This is because I consider that heterosexual *activities* are *pseudo*-heterosexuality in many genuine homosexuals, and for that

21

matter homosexuality also can be *pseudo-*, particularly in boys and young people. I refer to sexual activity which is not genuinely or fully in line with the psycho-sexual phantasy and impulse, and which therefore does not achieve adequate psychosexual satisfaction. It is nevertheless commonly practised, especially in women—notably in marriage and notoriously in prostitution. A case illustrating this descrepancy between sexual phantasy and sexual practice in a married man is described later in this survey.

With regard to theory and the vexed question as to whether homosexuality is constitutional or acquired, there is every gradation of conflicting opinion from antiquity to the present day. Ellis[8] [page 59] reminds us: 'Aristotle also' [until Galileo (1564—1642) the unchallenged 'scientific' authority] 'in his fragment on physical love, though treating the whole matter with indulgence, seems to have distinguished abnormal congenital homosexuality from acquired homosexual vice'. It seems that the best course is to keep on accumulating data, and proceeding to deeper investigation of the mind, before this problem can be satisfactorily unravelled.

It is possible that Freud's theory, already quoted in this chapter, which attributes homosexuality to early experiences *combined with* congenital factors, such as bisexuality in the unconscious and personal sexual make-up, will become the most favoured. In the meantime, there are many data to reinforce the various controversial leanings regarding causation.

It is commonly held, as Krich points out in his preface to this book, that 'the chief arguments *against* the psychogenic explanation of homosexuality centre around the undeniable fact that some persons subjected to a particular set of pressures become homosexuals, while others *in the same circumstances* do not'. In my own professional experience I have often been, as it were, startled into the environmentalists' point of view by clinical evidence of some homosexual event thrust upon a person, especially at puberty or adolescence, which he subsequently appears to be compulsively re-seeking in surprisingly detailed exactitude. I have already referred to this in the case of the young married man who waited for a repetition of the identical event which he experienced in a lavatory at the age of sixteen. Magistrates and judges and perhaps the public at large appear to be 'sold' to this aetiological idea, but the facts of a wider experience certainly fail to support it. I have *also* heard much clinical detail of patients who were homosexually seduced in a variety of circumstances, particularly at school, and who subsequently emerged as heterosexual and as normal as anyone. So the problem of causation is not solved by such clinical instances.

I am convinced that an important determinant in the causation of homosexuality is, at least in many cases, similar to that of fetishism. Here it would seem that the sexual object, or rather the object that stimulates sexuality, must have a purely symbolical significance, and that such symbolic significance must have been acquired at an extremely early age, usually during the period of infantile amnesia.

How else, for instance, can one account for such an incident as the following, told me by a mackintosh fetishist? At the age of nineteen he was taken by his rather 'fast' young girl friend into her bedroom presumably for some love-making; but in spite of her passes he was and remained quite unaware of any desire for the girl. Instead, he was all eyes for a mackintosh of hers which hung on the doorpeg! This he stared at with rapt attention; he clearly remembers his mounting sexual excitement and tumescence. He was not conscious of any tendency to connect this with the girl herself. It is difficult to think of such a peculiar proclivity as being inherited. Can one possibly assume an *inherited* prediliction for mackintoshes as one's sexual object? They are obviously in such cases a *symbol* for something sexually exciting that has itself been completely repressed from consciousness. Freud[1] [page 33, footnote] says 'The true explanation (of fetishism) is that behind the first recollection of the fetish's appearance there lies a submerged and forgotten phase of sexual development.

23

The fetish, like a 'screen-memory', represents this phase and is thus a remnant and precipitate of it. The fact that this early infantile phase turns in the direction of fetishism, as well as the choice of the fetish itself, are constitutionally determined.' I may mention that the mackintosh fetishist above referred to improved to the degree of marrying and having children and enjoying his marital sexual experience, but I am still convinced that some of the potentialities for heterosexual enjoyment remain unconscious. Mackintoshes still augment his sexual pleasure.

May not the difficulty in recognizing some of the acquired causes of homosexuality be laid at the door of some such mechanisms as those responsible for fetishism. In other words there appears to me to be evidence that, at least in some cases, perhaps in many if not in all, the 'object' of the sexual excitement, be it man or mackintosh, is stimulating an unconscious mechanism in the mind similar to that responsible for fetishism. When we find a man using another man as though he were a female may he not be making a similar 'mistake' to that made by our mackintosh fetishist; and similarly perhaps when a feminine woman chooses as her lover a person of her own sex? The question may be more difficult to answer in the case of the passive male homosexual and the active, or masculine female homosexual. It seems to me possible that these latter are more constitutionally determined, whereas the aforementioned may be fetishistically determined. Nevertheless, as many writers have pointed out, in homosexuals the role is usually inter-changeable.

However, I should admit that in my opinion the strongest arguments against the psychogenic explanation of homosexuality are not in accordance with the views above referred to by Krich. It would seem to me that the strongest proof of hereditary factors in homosexuality, as in many other abnormalities, could be provided by a study of uniovular twins, or to use the American term, 'monozygotic pairs'. In a study of a consecutive series of eighty-five plainly homosexual twin index cases, Dr. Franz J. Kallmann[12] found that 'in every case of forty homosexuals who had a monozygotic twin, the twin, after adolescence, was found to have exactly the same overt homosexual practice and with the same quantitative reading of homosexual behaviour'. In other words, like all uniovular twins, they were as like as two peas in the nature and quantity of their homosexual practices. The author claims that all these pairs, forty in number, denied any mutual sexual relationship and claimed to have developed the homosexual pattern independently of each other and far apart from each other. What is more, he says that the individuals of each pair had so marked a sexual taboo between them that each disclaimed knowledge of any intimate details of his co-twin's sex life.

The remaining forty-five twin pairs of the eighty-five pairs investigated were dizygotic, or binovular, twins and the co-twin of each of these homosexual subjects did not generally show any homosexual leanings. There were homosexuals amongst them but 'only slightly in excess of Kinsey's rating for the total male population'. It certainly would seem that this investigation diminishes the plausibility of environmental causes, such as parental incompetence, for in both these groups, the forty pairs and the forty-five pairs, the childhood of each of each pair was spent in a similar environment to that of his twin, parentally and otherwise. Only the uniovular twins developed identical patterns as regards their overt homosexual practice and the quantity of it. Corroborating these findings, Mayer-Gross[5] [page 177] tells us that: 'Sanders (1934) has reported seven uniovular pairs with one member homosexual; in six of these the other twin was homosexual also. Similar observations have been made by Lange, Hirschfeld, Spiro, etc.'

In addition to mental and behaviouristic deviations we are reminded that (Mayer-Gross[5] [page 179]) 'A certain proportion of male homosexuals . . . show a deficient growth of hair on face and body, tend to have high voices, to show a more feminine type of distribution of body fat. According to Henry measurements of the bony pelvis also tend to deviate similarly from the norm in homosexuals of either sex.' Of course this is true only of 'a certain proportion' of homosexuals. A suggestion has been made by Myerson and Neustadt (1942) that 'androgen concentration (in the urine) determines the vigour of sex drive, the absolute or proportionate amount of oestrogens its direction'. (Mayer-Gross[5] [page 179]). The authors of *Clinical Psychiatry*[5] think that [page 179] 'it would be surprising if adequate further research did not lay a sure basis in a physical and most probably endocrine deviation'.

Nevertheless, I am of the opinion that these considerations do not put an end to the importance of psychological factors in this problem any more than Mendelian laws and other discoveries regarding hereditary and congenital factors put an end to the importance of psychological and environmental factors in the finer details of human behaviour and beliefs. For instance in the choice of love-object or sex-object it has been abundantly demonstrated that, from rats to mankind, in the absence of the opposite sex one's own sex is liable to be utilized, and a homosexual conditioning more or less established, if only temporarily. There is no doubt that whatever we inherit—and it may well be the foundation of everything that is us—including all our instinctual tendencies, at least the finer details of our reactions, thoughts and attitudes are profoundly influenced by environment, and particularly, as psychoanalysis has discovered, by our earliest experiences in the first few days, weeks, months and years of our individual life. Agreed that if two people are different to start with, they will react differently to similar environmental experiences. Indeed, one of a pair may collect within his psyche certain of these experiences, excluding others; and the other may collect other experiences and *block* many of those which impressed his opposite number. This is where the uniovular twin investigation comes in, because here each individual was from the identical egg and therefore, unlike a binovular twin, reacted identically in babyhood to presumably identical stimulation. The advocates of the congenital theory tell us that what we start with biologically pre-disposes us to certain reactive patterns; but there is no doubt that individual experience has some effect or influence upon the modification of inherited patterns, the formation of new reactive patterns, and upon the continuation or otherwise of patterns acquired after birth.

The congenitalists have a mass of evidence in favour of their contentions, and we look for still more evidence and enlightenment from them. Psychology and psychoanalysis should not, and do not, deny congenital and physical factors, somatic and instinctual. Indeed, they insist that instinct (by definition inherited) is the basis of all our behaviour. Psychology and psychoanalysis investigate mental mechanisms, the mind's reaction to instinctual gratifications and frustrations, and the production and development of the mental process of unconscious phantasy on these bases. Psychoanalysis has shown that these unconscious phantasies activate or influence our behaviour and beliefs. Finer details such as fetishism, for instance the mackintosh fetishism above referred to, must have their source in acquired reactive patterns rather than in inheritance. I have hinted also that such 'minor' aberrations as other object-choice, including the homosexual, may well belong to the finesse of acquired reactive patterns with their utilization of the mechanism of symbolism, than to anything more in the congenital department than some hereditary predisposition.

There is no doubt in my mind that fetishistic mechanisms play a part in all sexual object-choice whether heterosexual or homosexual. Ferenczi's paper[13] in 1916, part of which is printed in this book [page 196], points out that the buttocks can unconsciously symbolize the woman's breasts. This would be applicable for the buttocks of either sex. In the same paper he mentions also that sadistic and anal erotic impulses can be replaced by reaction formations resulting in 'sublimated or over-refined boys' love with an anxious shunning of all indecent contacts'. In other words what enters consciousness is determined by a balance of conflicting forces, impulses and repressing mechanisms from the unconscious. These are very fine adjustments of a mixture of acquired and inherited forces the results of which, though, as it were, hanging on a thread, may appear to be so very different in the reality and social world. As Dr. Kallmann[12] says 'The most plausible explanation for this (homosexual) finding is that the axis around which the organization of personality and sex function takes place is *so easily dislocated* that attainment of a maturational balance may be disarranged at different developmental stages and by a *variety of disturbing mechanisms*' (my italics). We cannot therefore afford to exclude a study of psychological considerations even if we do accept the congenitalists' point of view. Heredity directly affects mainly trends or tendencies and the balance of instincts. Such considerations help us to understand the different, and, at first sight, apparently antithetical, points of view.

Dr. Clara Thompson[14] in her *Study of Interpersonal Relations*—in this book page 308—emphasizes that 'homosexuality is not a clinical entity but a symptom with different meanings in different personality set-ups'. Like any human action, homosexuality—like heterosexuality—*means* something different in each individual . . . and in the same individual at different times and in different contexts. A handshake, or the touch of another person's hand, or having one's own hand touched by another person, may have a thousand different meanings and carry with it a thousand different subjective experiences. Apparently homosexual acts of the same, or different, variety can have many different meanings. Therefore, it is often erroneous to extract a common denominator even for acts which appear to be identical. Here, for instance, is a clinical excerpt which may cause the clinician to make different guesses at different stages of enlightenment:

I was once consulted by a deformed male midget, aged forty and about the size of a boy of eight. He came to me because he was very distressed, depressed and suicidal. The story that unfolded was this. For a decade and a half he had been living with a married couple who were childless. They had, as it were, 'adopted' him; for though intellectually adult, he was emotionally very immature. Now this dwarf was in the habit of sitting in the lap of his adopted father, who presumably was a hetero-sexual man. At this stage of the story the psychological meaning was evidently that the dwarf was experiencing the feelings of a little boy being loved by Daddy. Was there anything homo-sexual in this? Every little boy, and that was the degree of im-maturity the dwarf possessed, likes to sit in Daddy's lap. However, in due course, the patient confessed to me that this experience of sitting in his foster-father's lap was usually, though not always, accompanied by his having some degree of erection. Still later he confessed that his erotic feeling was accompanied by a desire to fondle 'father's' penis. Eventually it came about that desire was implemented by action. For very many years this had been the only alloerotic-life which this dwarf had found available. When finally it had been ended by the wife's intervention, my patient had a nervous breakdown with all the sensations of the most devastating bereavement—mourning, melancholia, and death wishes. Analytical transference appeared to rescue him only just in time. If he had needed the sexual outlet to reduce tension and anxiety, it seemed that the re-living of childhood with a good-parent-figure was even more important for his health and happiness. Not every infant is treated to *overt* incestuous relation-ships (!), but analysis reveals that a greater or lesser degree of this is experienced as an *unconscious* accompaniment of normal contact with parents and parent surrogates, together with defensive reactions against it. Unconscious phantasy supplies that which reality frustrates and denies.

In passing from the theory of congenital to that of environ-mental causes of homosexuality, we should perhaps pause for a moment, but only for a moment, at that term 'bi-sexual' which has evidently been invented in the hope of clarifying the problem. I think it leads to more confusion and misconception than to clarification. Admittedly, in the *unconscious* mind there is room for every contradiction to live side by side, and room for every variety or level of sexuality and every variety of object-choice. Jung says normal men cover the feminine component of their psyche ('anima') with a masculine mask and normal women cover their masculine component ('animus') with a feminine mask. Ernest Jones[15] [page 486] seems to have a lingering doubt about the matter. Although he says, 'the assumption of inborn bisexuality seems to me a very probable one, in favour of which many biological facts can be quoted,' he adds later, 'I do not think we should take it absolutely for granted.' Stekel[16] appears to solve the problem to his satisfaction when he says: 'There is no inborn homosexuality and no inborn heterosexuality. There is only *bisexuality*. Mono-sexuality already involves a predisposition to neurosis and in many cases stands for the neurosis proper.' I think he is dead right for the unconscious mind, and probably in his concluding remark.

The following case vividly illustrates this sort of thing: a married man consulted me on account of a variety of acute and chronic anxiety symptoms accompanied by despondency, depression, lack of concentration, lassitude, incapacity for work and the familiar polysymptomatology. He told me that his wife had just returned from the nursing home where she had had their baby. He felt he could not bear her presence in his house. Questioning elicited the fact that he had been psychosexually impotent until she, out of her love for him, had painstakingly taught him to have coitus. The degree of 'proficiency' he had acquired certainly left much, indeed everything, to be desired. In fact his so-called coitus amounted to a succession of effortful manual endeavours with an unwilling, detumescing orgasm. The result was usually total failure leaving him exhausted and irritable. I asked him what was his *natural* sexual life, and he replied, 'Masturbation'. He declared that this was without phantasy. Oh no, he certainly never had phantasies of a female, in whole or in part. This he said would have resulted in the immediate subsidence of his erection. Then he confessed that, during masturbation, he did occasionally phantasy a young man. The phantasy was that he would seek the young man's penis, make it erect and admire it. No, he had never tried this. It would be just 'too exciting'. He added: 'I would throw myself in the river, if I thought I were a homosexual.' The conclusion is inescapable, that in his unconscious phantasy this married man is terrified of the female genitals. It is possible to say two things about the aetiology of his anxiety neurosis: one, that his libido is being frustrated and inhibited from any adequate gratifying outlet, and two, that attempts to coerce it, in the face of his phobia, into a heterosexual channel, is increasing his nervous strain and exacerbating his neurosis. Further, one may ask whether what this case shows up in such strong relief is not (in a lesser degree and in a relatively inconspicuous way) common to all members of civilized communities, namely a sexual outlet which does not exactly coincide with the individual's unconscious phantasy, or a more or less effortful sexual behaviour contrary to that phantasy.

Is this the sort of thing that Stekel[16] means when he says that monosexuality' (heterosexuality *or* homosexuality) 'already involves a predisposition to neurosis and in many cases stands for the neurosis proper'? I think it is certainly in keeping with Reich's[9] [page 360] tenet that neurosis is always formed out of the residue of inadequately relieved libido. 'Orgastic impotence . . . provides the source of energy for all kinds of psychic and somatic symptoms.' 'The basis of the disturbances is a deviation from the natural modes of discharge' [page 337]. ('Natural' for that particular individual). 'Relapse into neurosis after psychoanalytic cure may be averted to the extent to which orgastic satisfaction in the sexual act is assured' [page 106]. 'The essence of a neurosis is the inability of the patient to obtain gratification' [page 128].

If we add to this ' . . . to obtain gratification in his object-relationships in adequate co-incidence with the wishes of his unconscious phantasy', then perhaps we have the essence of the immediate factor in the above mentioned case of anxiety neurosis. I would add that, *in so far as reality and unconscious phantasy do not coincide, to that degree will a corresponding quantity and quality of reactive, perverse or neurotic character traits, symptoms or behaviour be inevitable.*

According to psychoanalysis the newly born baby begins its sexual life at the oral level, its object-choice being the breast, nipple or teat. Subsequently, when through development, the genital level has acquired erotic primacy, the object-choice is not necessarily or totally the whole-object-personality, as well as body, of a person of the opposite sex. Even in the most normal a certain amount of libido is left by the wayside or taken up with part-objects—and what I call minor degrees of fetishism— whether these relate to breasts, hair, legs, figure or clothes. Symbolism, fetishism proper and homosexuality are only extreme degrees of this. The term 'bi-sexual' is misleading because, on a *conscious* level, that is to say a behaviouristic level (unlike at an unconscious level), there is a tendency for the mind to be more integrated and to reject one or other of two opposing impulses, objects or phantasies. As Bergler[17] says in this book [page 291] and in his paper in the New York *Psychiatric Quarterly* in 1948, 'Nobody can dance at two weddings at the same time, not even the wizard of a homosexual.' Although, as he admits, it *is* possible for some homosexuals to have 'erective potency in a lustless coitus', it would be misleading to call them bi-sexual on this account. I think the truth is that, if one sex is associated with gratification, the other sex tends to be associated with castration. The degree or intensity of this antithesis may vary from one individual to another.

Even Kinsey[11] [pages 656-7] with his seven point scale based upon relative frequency of 'outlet' between homosexuality and heterosexuality, deprecates the term 'bi-sexual' as untenable. Similarly with the term 'intersex': 'In spite of the fact that Goldschmidt himself (1916) accepted the idea that the homosexual human male or female was an intersex, there is no adequate basis for reaching any such conclusion' [page 658]. In biology the term would mean an individual with a portion or a whole of its structure intermediate in character between the structure of the typical male and that of the typical female of the species.

Nevertheless the fact cannot be denied that individuals do exist who both physically and mentally exhibit strikingly marked characteristics of the opposite sex. It should be remembered that such persons are not necessarily homosexual, in the correct clinical or behaviouristic sense. In spite of their contra-sexual characteristics they may actually have no sexual attraction towards members of their own sex. Although it may be true to say that the two sexes are on a mental plane not sharply differentiated and that on a physical plane each shows many physical characteristics of the other, and that these are subject to every degree and variation, nevertheless pronounced anomalies do exist and give some justification or excuse for Lang's[18] *intersex* theory. One of our latest text books on Psychiatry (Mayer-Gross[5]) appears to favour this theory of homosexuality and goes so far as to emphasize the possibility from the fact that [page 176] 'sex is determined, not by a gene or group of genes, but by a *balance being struck between opposing groups of genes*'. This may be very interesting and true, but it may not have as much bearing on homosexuality as would appear at first sight. This is because as the authors (Mayer-Gross[5], Slater and Roth [page 177]) themselves admit: '*Physical constitution and mental attitude are not closely connected*' [my italics]. And 'Homosexuality' is a term that applies to a mental attitude and not to physical constitution. Indeed, it might be true to say that a 'diagnosis' based on characteristics no deeper than the *unconscious* mind (even without morphology and genetics) would have to declare everybody bisexual *and* less or more of an *intersex*. As I have said, diagnosis has to be based on conscious and manifest trends and on behaviour. This level alone is appropriate for the clinical diagnosis of any and every condition. These terms, bisexual and intersex, though not negligible by any means, are misleading because they imply desires and behaviour that are contrary to the facts, because it seems that at conscious and manifest levels one *form* of sexuality is preferred. If this form does not absolutely exclude all others (which it often does) it tends at least to result in a marked preferential presidence of itself over all others. 'Nobody can dance at two weddings at the same time, not even the wizard of a homosexual.'

With reference to the above material in general, I would like to express my doubts as to whether the physical mechanisms of any process can provide us with anything more than an illusion of the solution of a problem. I have always felt this about the biological theory of *mutations* as an 'explanation' of the evolutionary process. Genes do not explain mutations; and mutations (even with the aid of natural-selection) do not explain evolution. Admittedly the concept of 'a balance being struck between opposing groups of genes' is a little more plausible. If 'accidents' do happen in nature they cannot be regarded as accidental but only as an aspect of the operation of the law of cause and effect. Might this balance or imbalance of genes be just another such instance of the law of cause and effect, resulting in variants that may perform functions other than those of reproduction. A neuter sex has proved helpful to survival of the Hymenoptera. A species progresses as does a multicellular organism, by the development of devious capacities for adjustment to its environment apart from those of reproduction. The conception of bisexuality and intersex may be very useful in a biological study but may prove more misleading than helpful in solving the behaviouristic problem of homosexuality.

We are left then with the two aetiological theories, the congenital and the acquired, the first being the province of biology and the second of psychology, the first relating to all that is inherited including hereditary pre-dispositions, the second concerned only with the finer adjustments of reactive pattern to individual experiences and environment. Neither of these can by itself provide a complete answer to the manifold problems presented by any behaviouristic phenomenon. They are thus mutually dependent rather than antagonistic. Let us now go a little more deeply into the environmental or psychological aspect of aetiology.

As a condensation of the *psychoanalytical* point of view a few excerpts from Fenichel's[19] [page 328] great book are representative: 'Initially, everyone is able to develop sexual feelings indiscriminately, and the search for an object is less limited by the sex of the object than is commonly supposed.' 'The fact that in a normal person the object-choice later becomes more or less limited to the opposite sex is a problem in itself' [page 329]. 'Since the homosexual, like any other human being, originally has the capacity to choose objects of either sex, what limits this capacity to objects of his own sex?' [page 329]. 'Analysis of homosexual men regularly shows that they are afraid of female genitals.' 'The female genitals, through the connection of castration anxiety with oral anxieties, may be perceived as a castrating instrument capable of biting or tearing off the penis' [page 330]. These morbid fears, arising from these unconscious phantasies, are commonly rationalized by homosexuals—for instance, into such forms as 'fear of pregnancy' and 'fear of venereal disease'.

Incidentally, Dr. T. Anwyl-Davies, the leading venereologist, tells me that venereal disease is at least as common amongst homosexuals as heterosexuals. Mayer-Gross[5] [page 180] says homosexuals 'tend to be more promiscuous than heterosexual persons', but adds 'the romantic element in passion may be as strong or stronger'.

Regarding the impression, perhaps unduly stressed by Ferenczi[13] that homosexuals can be divided into passive homosexuals or inverts on the one hand, and *object* homo-erotics, who, in the case of males, remain masculine in their behaviour, merely choosing another male as though he were a female, it is worth remembering that in the majority of homosexuals a reversal of roles is more the rule than the exception. Mayer-Gross[5] [page 179] says: 'Male homosexuals are frequently classified into the active and the passive type; female homosexuals into the

35

masculine and feminine. The active male homosexual is defined as one who in sexual relationships with another male takes the active role making his partner adopt the female position in intercourse, or to submit to, rather than to perform, sodomy, etc. The active physical role is usually accompanied by the active, seeking, courting and dominating role mentally.' . . . 'Mutatis mutandis the same may be said for female homosexuals. The active male and the passive female are frequently of fairly normal psychosomatic constitution;' . . . 'the passive male and the active female homosexual are much more likely to show contrasexual traits of physique and mind, and to be irreversibly and solely homosexually inclined.'

'There is, however, *no sharp distinction between activity and passivity*, as a lasting trait,' . . . 'Furthermore the mental and physical aspects of activity or passivity may not go together.' . . . 'reversal of roles may occur between the same partners on different occasions. Even with these reservations, however, it is broadly true that homosexuals tend to fall into one or other of these two classes and not to be unclassifiably midway between.'

Fenichel[19] [page 336] says 'Terms like subject homo-erotic and object homo-erotic have only relative significance. Active homosexuality in a man may serve to repress a deeper passive homosexual longing and vice versa . . . combinations of both types of homosexuality occur. These types constitute the majority of all male homosexualities, but occasionally other types occur.' There is a very prevalent type, originally described by Freud, as 'mild' homosexuals, which is characterized by extreme friendliness towards persons of one's own sex. Fenichel says (page 336) 'Homosexual love of this type, which according to Freud contributes largely to that which later forms 'social feelings' is mixed with characteristics of identification.' It is generally agreed that there is an element of 'identification with the object' in all homosexual love.

It may seem that the psychoanalytical theory of homosexuality is a little diffuse and perhaps vague and inconclusive, but there is no doubt that progress into a deeper understanding and clarification of it has been and is being made. In his final word Fenichel[19] [page 342] heralds this by saying: 'Homosexuality has proved to be the product of specific mechanisms of *defence* which facilitate the persistence of the repression of both the Oedipus and castration complex. At the same time, the aim of homosexual object choice is the avoidance of emotions around the castration complex, which otherwise would disturb the sexual pleasure, or at least the attainment of reassurances against them.'

Some modern psychoanalysts, particularly those of the Kleinian school, have carried the psychopathology of homosexuality a little deeper, or earlier, namely right back to what is called the *oral* phase of libidinal development. Paula Heimann and Susan Isaacs[20] [page 179] say 'The primary oral and anal anxieties are the chief factors in the homosexual fixation.' 'It is the anxiety stimulated by cannibalistic phantasies which is the most potent factor in oral fixation.' 'The dread of the destroyed internal object (devoured and therefore inside) can only be allayed by continued oral pleasure . . . it is this insatiable need which binds the libido to oral and anal forms.' 'We know that such fixations of the oral phase, with all its phantasies and anxieties, lead to profound disturbances of the genital function.'

Good, as well as bad, reactive patterns also are apparently displaced from the oral zone to the genital: 'It is now widely recognized that the earlier stages have definite and positive contributions to make to the genital phase' . . . 'Contributions from the oral phase strengthen genital impulses . . . the woman's genital impulses and phantasies take over her happy experiences at the breast' . . . 'It is not enough to say that there is a displacement of certain elements in the oral phase to the genital. This is true, but it is an incomplete statement. Those oral phantasies and aims have remained *uninterruptedly active* in the unconscious mind exerting a favourable influence and promoting genitality. The oral libido has remained labile enough to be transferred to the genital and satisfied there.'

This is rather difficult material for the non-analytical reader, especially 'the dread of the destroyed internal object (devoured and therefore inside) . . . ' A brief explanation, even if inadequate may be desirable:

Soon after the infant is born it begins to require something, some 'object' in the outside world as a necessary aid to the gratification of its oral (and hunger) instinct. It may be assumed that previously instinct gratification was in a sense physiological or auto-erotic. Now it requires *something* in its mouth to suck; it has become dependent upon this 'object', and the process of feeding, to allay its oral desires and hunger. This libidinal stage is said in psychoanalysis to be one of *oral primacy*. The 'object' which is utilized for gratification of its need is the breast, nipple or teat. With this 'object' it has established what may be called its first 'object relationship'. The point of importance is that *the pattern of its reactions to all subsequent object relationships is laid down by this first object relationship*. The external world, outside itself, when recognized as such, will tend to be '*good*' and '*bad*' in proportion to the relative amounts of gratification (pleasure) and frustration (pain) experienced orally at the breast.

The second point for consideration is the beginning of mental processes. The theory is that all sensory experiences are accompanied by what psychoanalysis calls *unconscious phantasy*. The baby knows of no world outside its sensory experiences, including the sensations of its frustrations. When oral gratification is temporarily frustrated, the infant tries to compensate for this by hallucinations of gratification. This is deduced from an observation of its sucking movements. Of course, this can provide only very temporary relief. If frustration is excessive appetite increases, the baby may become ravenous, and there is psychoanalytical evidence that it proceeds to unconscious phantasies appropriate to this ravenous condition. The phantasies include the devouring not only of the milk, but also of the breast and even subsequently of the mother! This is called 'cannibalistic phantasy.' Whatever the child feels and phantasies will, sooner or later, be *projected*, and imagined to be the state of its external world also. That is to say, if its internal world is cannibalistic it automatically assumes the existence of a cannibalistic world outside itself. This process of projection leads to fantastic fears. Thus the baby, like the wild animal, is said at this stage to live in a world of a desire to eat and a fear of being eaten.

Now, if this fantastic pattern of *object relationship* is greatly accentuated, for instance by undue oral stimulations and frustrations, the organism is apt to acquire both an undue degree of fixation to this oral phase and an undue degree of fear owing to projection of its oral hunger. Subsequently, when, in the course of development, this pattern of its first object relationship becomes inevitably *displaced* to successive zones of erotic primacy— finally to the genital zone—the object relationship at the last, or genital, zone becomes filled with the pattern acquired at the oral zone, including the unconscious phantasies and feelings of desire and *fear*. The unconscious phantasy may then include the fear of being devoured—by the vagina. This is probably the most important factor responsible for psycho-sexual impotence in men. Similar unconscious phantasies are responsible for fear of the penis and frigidity in women. A man with such an unconscious phantasy of the female genitals is liable to avoid intimate relationships with women, even to hate them, and for these reasons to be unconsciously on the defensive against any urges which might lead him towards the feared genitals. He commonly desires access to male genitals to reassure himself against his unconscious phantasies of castration associated with a female genital. He is thus pre-disposed to homosexuality.

Margaret Mead[4] [page 124] points out that amongst the peoples of the South Sea Islands those who do not wean their children early are of a placid and friendly disposition, whereas those who are in the habit of depriving the child of breast feeding are warlike, aggressive and unpleasant. Her testimony indicates at least a relationship between the oral phase and the genital pattern: 'Amongst the Arapesh, little girls share their mothers' extreme valuation of nursing, and are as unwilling as little boys to be weaned. In Manus, mothers have already communicated their lack of enthusiasm for the maternal role to their small daughters' [page 151]. 'A Manus boy . . . will not grow up to be gentle and considerate as a lover.' For an Arapesh boy 'rape and active homosexuality are outside his pattern'.

In Bergler's[17] paper (in 1948, and in this book), like Fenichel and the Kleinians, he emphasizes especially, one, that homosexuality is the result of a *defensive* mechanism, and two, that what it is on the defensive against is the acute anxieties connected with *oral and cannibalistic phantasies* and therefore against aggressive and destructive (oral) urges. Strangely enough *heterosexuality* can itself be a defence against latent homosexual tendencies. That is to say, heterosexual behaviour in the so-called 'bi-sexual' (to which category all persons *unconsciously* belong) can at least have a subsidiary function in helping to keep out of consciousness repressed and repudiated homosexual proclivities.

Many heterosexual persons, rightly so-called, are in part *potentially* homosexual without being able to admit to consciousness such a proclivity in themselves. Perhaps all normal persons, as Stekel[16] says, belong more or less to this category. To illustrate what I mean, I can quote from my clinical material a patently heterosexual man who, in the course of analysis, mentioned, in association to thoughts of having a general massage, how he would hate to be massaged by a *man* as he said *for fear* that the experience might give him an erection. At the same time, this patient anticipates with pleasure the phantasy of being massaged by a *woman*. He says he would enjoy that, especially if it *did* give him an erection. The interpretation is of course that he would feel libidinal response to such attentions from either sex irrespectively, but with the important difference that his sexual response to the stimulations of a male would be resisted, repudiated, and *feared*, or at least he would be fearful of their exposure. On the other hand, his sexual response to the stimulations of a female would not be repudiated by his super-ego and ego, *not feared*, and therefore could be enjoyed. Thus the difference in the two cases would appear to be more superficial than the sexual impulse itself. In the same way that heterosexuality can help in one's normal defences against homosexual proclivities, so homosexuality can be a defence against feared and therefore repressed heterosexual impulses. In each case an essential function is that of allaying anxiety.

It seems to me a pity that Bergler's[17] article is so confused and vitiated by a continuous and unwarranted vituperative attack upon Kinsey, who, after all, was essentially only producing statistics of *behaviour*, for not recognizing that everything depended upon the conflicts in the *unconscious* mind. Nevertheless, he reminds us how important are the repressed anxieties in connexion with pre-Oedipus, oral, cannibalistic phantasies, as a basic psychological factor in the fear of the female genital. The Oedipus conflict is, of course, a later development. The emotional patterns elaborated in the object-relationships of the Oedipus complex enter into the defences against both heterosexuality and homosexuality. The point is that both the emotional nature and intensity of the Oedipus phantasies are determined by the earlier repressed oral phantasies, with their attendant anxieties in the unconscious. These anxieties lead to heterosexual impotence and to the homosexual defence against heterosexuality and, secondarily, against a recognition of the impotence. The conscious or remembered relationships to parents are, of course, merely more superficial aspects of these unconscious patterns which were determined at such a very much earlier stage of development.

Thus, emotional reactions to parents, parent fixation to either sex and by either sex, as revealed for instance in my mother-daughter article in this book, are merely later expressions of more deeply unconscious psychic structure. They are another intermediate stage, in turn determining relationships to persons outside the family, and the choice of which sex is chosen for those relationships. What is quite inadequately appreciated by almost all of us is that, apart from overt sexual behaviour, some stimulation of unconscious sexual phantasy is an accompaniment of practically all our human relationships. This is largely the theme of my new book (1955)[21].

Overt sexual behaviour is merely the implementation by action, often crude and inaccurate, of all sorts, and every shade, of subtle emotional interaction of one person on another. Apart from the reversal of roles from active to passive, and vice versa, that commonly takes place in homosexual relationships, hetero-sexual persons are constantly reacting similarly to each other, unconsciously or consciously angling and fencing for emotional advantage in their mutual relationships. This is particularly true of married couples. Commonly they share out, or divide, their respective active or 'masculine' roles, the husband normally assuming the more dominant position in the sexual sphere and the wife in the domestic and compensatory spheres. If the husband is psychologically inadequate as a sexually dominating male, we commonly see the wife becoming more assertive and masculine, even proceeding as it were to 'emasculate' him further, and assume his role—acting, in an obscure way, much as the passive homosexual may when he becomes active towards his weakening partner. In other words, the active-passive, masculine-feminine relationship of one person to another is operative with subtle grades of variation, and even reversal, in the unconscious and in one person's emotional repercussions upon another, quite apart from overt sexual implementation. It forms the basis of inter-personal relationships.

Positions of subordination to other males (or females) on a social plane have their repercussion upon our unconscious feminine component, or upon our defences, in the same way that positions of power are stimulating to masculine elements within us, and affect our sexuality whether we know it or not. In short, homosexuality is unavoidable in the unconscious, however much it may be repudiated at conscious levels. Indeed, it may well be that the holding together of our social structure depends upon these very repudiated 'bi-sexual' potentialities within the psyche. The stone which the builders rejected . . . from consciousness . . .! What is inhibited sexually and even hidden from consciousness in civilized human beings may be apparent and overt in the behaviour of animals. In his chapter in this book, taken from his 'Incest and Homosexuality', Dr. Hamilton[22] seems to suggest this through a biological approach. He says, with regard to social behaviour in monkeys, the immature female 'is sufficiently bi-sexual to be capable of offering herself for copulation to hostile females at any age whenever there is a defensive need for doing so'. 'The readiness of the adult female to accept an invitation to play the role of copulating male, when she has directed a hostile attack against a fellow of either sex, again discloses the adaptive value of retained 'bi-sexuality', since it is in the interests of both individual and species survival'. Dr. Zuckermann[23] in his *Sexual Life of Monkeys* describes how the lesser male constantly saves itself from destruction by 'presenting' itself sexually to the angry 'overlord'. This gesture almost invariably stops the attack, whether the invitation is accepted or not. It would thus seem that the capacity for 'bi-sexuality' or homosexuality is an essential ingredient in survival of the individual and of the monkey society. Dr. Hamilton[23] goes on to say: 'If, as can be indubitably established by appropriate methods of experimentation, homosexual behaviour is at times resorted to as a purely defensive measure by the infrahuman primate, a question arises as to whether defensiveness is a factor in the determination of human homosexuality.' On the basis of my own clinical experience, while not being able to quote cases of overt practice of homosexuality as a defensive measure, I can vouch for its unconscious equivalent being very active in every department of human relationship. Therefore I have no doubt that it does actually happen. I think at the moment of a capable man patient who cannot be employed because he unconsciously equates subordination to an employer with the homosexual passive attitude; it stimulates the affects of an unconscious phantasy of emasculation, and being used as a female, and therefore provokes aggressive reactions in him. In other words, it is his defences against homosexuality which make him unemployable. This is merely a sample of the sort of thing that is going on unrecognized in the relationships of one person to another.

In accordance with psychoanalytical evidence and my own clinical experience, I am convinced that our behaviour, our compulsions, and even our beliefs, emanate from unconscious phantasies, with their emotional patterns, inherited, and acquired in infancy. Hence our *understanding* of homosexuality will never be arrived at by statistical, or conscious-level enquiry, but will be achieved only through knowledge of the unconscious phantasies revealed through deep personal analysis. The causes of the manifold effects lie within the individual's unconscious mind. Perhaps the truth is that no amount of experience will provide us with a complete answer to the riddle in the terms in which we seek it. This is because the problem as ordinarily presented is incorrectly formulated. Nevertheless experience is of value. I think it will lead us to a reorientation and a more correct formulation of the nature of the mind, of instincts, emotions and sexuality, and with this of the aetiology of hidden and overt homosexuality; and, of what may prove to be of greater practical importance, the psychopathology of our often stupid and morbid and injurious reactions against it.

The unconscious naturally contains every phantasy however fantastic, everything we can possibly think of and a great deal more that we cannot think of or cannot believe. This is because our mental censorship will not permit us to do so. Behaviour, all sexual behaviour, is merely a question of which of these innumerable sexual phantasies eludes the censorship, the internal unconscious mental censorship, and emerges in thought or in action. Anything, everything is possible—as can be proved by the fact and anything and everything *does* actually occur— including incredibly savage reactions against the repressed impulses, or rather against those who manifest them. We are none of us fundamentally different from one another. Analysis shows that all persons, normal as well as neurotic and homosexual, have an infinite variety of phantasies in their unconscious, and that these phantasies are the source from which spring their feelings, moods, thoughts and behaviour. The apparent differences between us do not lie so much in the differences in our unconscious phantasies, for as I have said we all have similar unconscious phantasies, though admittedly of different degrees of intensity. The apparent differences between one person and another lie mainly in something relatively superficial, a defensive mechanism that depends more upon the nature and intensity of the repressing forces (censorship and super-ego) than upon the nature and intensity of the impulses which they are repressing. In short, what emerges into consciousness or into action is the outcome of the conflict between super-ego and instinctual pressure. The ego may attach itself to one or other of these antagonists, but it is commonly buffeted about from one side to the other in the course of the conflict, and always in varying proportions divided or split between them. In any case, the outcome commonly depends to a lesser degree than we suppose upon the part the ego plays, though it is usually more on the side of the repressing forces. ·The trouble, if trouble there be, lies in the degree to which the relatively feeble ego is overwhelmed by the strength of the forces on one side or the other.

With most so-called normal people, it may be that the ego is more frequently overwhelmed by super-ego forces resulting in harsh or sadistic reaction formations, instigated by our own intrapsychic insecurity and consequent fear of the repressed. In this field, reaction formations are commonly too severe to be borne by oneself and are therefore projected on to a scapegoat, resulting in punishments being practically always worse, or causing more misery, than the crime. We find in the course of our analysis that denials, particularly emotionally charged denials, show the existence in the unconscious of that which is denied. In the same way that there is every variety of erotic and fetishistic mania of active and passive homosexuality and perversion, there is similarly every variety and degree of antipathy. Indeed, the latter is but the denial and repression of the former. It may be said that the antipathies, being more characteristic of the super-ego, however aggressive and destructive, are generally more freely revealed, and even advertised, than are the impulses and mania which they deny. Few people would display their perversions with the freedom and readiness with which they exhibit their moral prejudices, not suspecting that the latter prove beyond doubt the (repressed) existence within them of the former. Behaviour itself emerges only after an unconscious struggle.

The behaviouristic *form* sexuality takes (e.g. homosexuality) may be compared to the manifest content of a dream, or the appearance of a symptom. All these manifestations are merely the end product of innumerable determinants, some of which (like the latent content of the dream from which the manifest content emerges) may be very different indeed from the manifest form. Indeed, the main determinant for a manifestation may be, and often is, the diametrical opposite to that which is expressed; the manifest symptom may contain more denial than exhibition of its chief determinant. It may be a reversal for the purpose of defence, disguise or denial. Civilization is a denial of the savage within. Polite social conduct, our *mores*, is a denial of aggression and of sexuality. At best our manifest behaviour contains more resisting or repressing forces, at worst it may appear to concern itself with these alone. Thus manifest homosexuality may be *essentially* a denial (unconsciously determined) of heterosexuality. I am convinced that it is sometimes, though much more rarely than the converse situation, nothing more or less than just this. A factor determining this proclivity is often excessive fear of the uncontrollable power of the repressed heterosexual urges. As we see when we expose the transference during an analysis, in the unconscious it would be as though at all costs incest with mother must be prevented and denied. This is because it is associated with rebellion, murder and destruction, and, at an oral level, with cannibalism and the fear of being eaten. Ernest Jones[15] [page 359] says, 'The central content of the repressed impulses may be summed up in two words: incest and murder.'

Beliefs and behaviour are merely *expressions* of the various ingredients of unconscious phantasies and conflicts. No behaviour is amazing, incredible or mysterious, for in the unconscious we are accustomed to finding every ingredient, conceivable and inconceivable. Indeed, 'inconceivable' merely means repressed from consciousness. The canon of all science, cause and effect, operates just as truly and implacably in the psychological sphere as in every other, and this holds as true of the repressive reactions to instinctual behaviour as it does of this behaviour itself. I allude to the fact that whereas some persons express their emotional pressure in various forms of instinctual behaviour, and whereas others, repressing these impulses, suffer from a consequent or accompanying neurosis, still other persons, perhaps the most 'normal', express the super-ego side of their conflict in even more cruel intolerances and destructive reactions. The latter forms of expression are often designated as righteous indignation or even as justice and punishment. They commonly have no more reality basis or justification than the former. Homosexuals can be just as intolerant of heterosexuality as heterosexuals of homosexuality . . . and paranoics of everything. Such intolerances only show that each has specialized in his own particular form of defence against the opposite tendencies within himself. Stekel[16] says 'The heterosexual is inspired with disgust at any homosexual acts. That proves his affectively determined negative attitude. For disgust is but the obverse of attraction. The homosexual manifests the same feeling of disgust for woman.' From a sociological standpoint it could be argued, though maybe in Machiavellian fashion, that if unlimited expansion of homosexuality could destroy the human race through lack of population, heterosexuality may destroy it by excess of population—which latter, incidentally, is the greatest human problem.

From the point of view of a scientific study of nature it should be remembered that although homosexuality is prevalent in all mammals ('Kierman in 1888 observed that all lower animals are bisexual') (Caprio, 1954, page 114), and indeed in all living organisms, it is never in excess of heterosexuality. To imagine that laws or penalties could put an end to it is evidently to place man-made laws above those of nature. It may be that we might as well, in the fashion of King Canute, make laws forbidding the tide to come in from the sea. From a legislative point of view it should be recognized that we are dealing with *two* psychological conditions. One is homosexuality and the other is a reaction of horror against it. Each may express itself behaviouristically, the first in the phenomenon of homosexual activity and the second in the phenomenon of senseless prohibition, often with savage penalties. I fancy that the second phenomenon is worse, more serious, than the first, and even more morbid. Unlike the first, however, the second phenomenon *may* be remediable through the medium of replacing ignorance by knowledge and a proper assessment of the facts and an understanding that nature's ways have not destroyed our species and are in no danger of doing so. Knowledge and understanding may do more than this, they may enable us to prevent or limit the development of homosexual tendencies—for example by ceasing excessive frustration of heterosexual tendencies when these are developmentally ripe, or by not waiting until they are too over-ripe to function healthily. Kinsey[7] [page 460] says: 'We are inclined to believe that moral restraint of pre-marital heterosexual activity is the most important single factor contributing to the development of a homosexual history.' Those who would abolish homosexuality please note that even statistics incline the investigator to believe that this restraint is '*the most important single factor*'. Reich[9] [page 203] wrote: 'The alternative . . . is

48

not: *sexuality or abstinence*; but: *natural and healthy*, or *perverse and neurotic sexual life*'.

It seems to me that law-makers should be careful to confine themselves to their very proper concern for social and individual welfare, and should be particularly careful to exclude from the legal code *unnecessary* interferences with the liberty of the individual lest with this denial they prevent or destroy necessary adjustments—or worse—and give expression merely to emotional prejudice and their morbid anxiety or personal gratification without serving any useful purpose. Homosexuality is not necessarily a crime against the person any more than is heterosexuality, *but* assault, rape or violence *are* crimes against the person, irrespective of whether they be homosexual or heterosexual, or asexual. The law as it exists on all matters of this nature leads to a lot of indirect, as well as direct, useless misery. I shall never forget the homosexual barrister who was once a patient of mine whose defence against his own (recognized) tendencies to homosexuality and sadism was to 'sublimate' them into a professional zeal in prosecuting and persecuting homosexuals. He was prosecuting his own guilt, *in others*, and earning his living by so doing. Was this a sublimation or the perversion of a perversion.

Dr. Clifford Allen[3] says [page 137]: 'Henry and Gross draw attention to the fact that the homosexual lives in fear of being blackmailed. His mind is so perpetually haunted by the thought of falling into the hands of the authorities that he is an easy subject for the blackmailer. We have pointed out that homosexuals may be driven to violence by threat of exposure.'

The only proper approach to this problem is knowledge, knowledge of the facts, and understanding. Emotional reactions are morbid symptoms whether they manifest themselves in the positive acts of perversions, such as homosexuality, or in the reactive forms of rage and sadistic punishment against perversions and homosexuality. Both perversions and emotional reactions against them are symptoms. *Symptoms are not appropriate therapeutic agents, nor are they sound judgment.* Scientific approach demands knowledge; that is where books such as this are the appropriate weapon for dealing with the problem; nothing is achieved by an ostrich policy of ignorance, nor by emotional biases of a positive or negative nature. Nobody should be permitted to judge or to punish or to prescribe treatment until he has not only read and understood the literature on the subject, but what is far more important, until he has read and understood the 'book' of his own repressed and unconscious conflicts. That is to say until he has submitted himself to a personal analysis and become fully aware of the repressed and denied homosexuality within himself. 'He that is without sin among you, let him cast a stone.' A denial of 'sin' on a conscious plane is evidence of nothing more than denial. Analysis reveals that everyone is perjurer as well as sinner!

The unrealistic attitude of the law on homosexuality can apparently be demonstrated by statistical evidence, apart from psychological exposition. After telling us that thirty-seven per cent of the male population has some homosexual experience, and the surprising fact that 'seventeen per cent of the farm boys have animal intercourse', Kinsey[11] [page 392], by the simple process of adding percentages, concludes: 'All of these, and still other types of sexual behaviour are illicit activities, each performance of which is punishable as a crime under the law. The persons involved in these activities, taken as a whole, constitute more than ninety-five per cent of the total male population . . . It is the total ninety-five per cent of the male population for which the judge, or board of public safety, or church, or civic group demands apprehension, arrest, and conviction, when they call for a clean-up of the sex offenders in a community. *It is, in fine, a proposal that five per cent of the population should support the other ninety-five per cent in penal institutions'!* [My italics.]

Legal attitudes, like most human belief and behaviour—like homosexuality itself—may thus be seen to be more emotionally determined (i.e. letting out the tension of those unconscious conflicts) than realistic.

In conclusion I should like to summarize a personal theory which I have regarding this vexed question of the alleged antithesis between the hypotheses of congenital and acquired factors in the causation of homosexuality, and for that matter in the aetiology of all other reactive patterns, behaviour and belief. My theory, which I have worked out much more fully than here suggested, is that the antithesis is illusionary and is due to the mistake, fostered by the current, to my mind, erroneous, attitude of biologists, of assuming that old instincts alone are inherited and that acquired patterns of behaviour, however long established, are not, that life begins anew with each individual birth, instead of regarding it as the continuity which to me it obviously is.

I will begin with a little story merely to *illustrate* my theory: When I was in the London Zoo recently a young tiger in an outside cage suddenly, for no reason that I could see, became extremely excited, crouching and weaving as though getting ready to spring, with eyes fixed upon some object beyond me. Turning round I saw a baby elephant in the distance being led through the grounds by a keeper. The tiger had not shown any such excitement at the presence of human children or of any other animals, and, knowing that it came from the Bengal jungle where tigers do occasionally prey upon young elephants, I assumed at first that it must itself, at some period of its jungle career, have killed and tasted a baby elephant. However, on reading the plaque on its cage I learnt that not it, but only its parents had been captured in the Bengal jungle. This particular young tiger had been born in captivity in the Whipsnade Zoo! There is no doubt that given the opportunity it would have followed the behaviour of its ancestors in selecting for its prey the somewhat unusual diet of baby elephant. The flavour of baby elephant resided presumably in its constitutional (inherited) reactive pattern.

Can we draw a line and say *when* an acquired pattern of behaviour becomes inheritable—like an 'instinct'? The biologists say 'never'. Yet I am convinced that my own experience as a scientist and an analyst tell me differently.

Perhaps this 'dogma' of current biology is the worthy successor of its previous die-hard dogma of the immutability of species, and even of their separate creation. Less than a hundred years ago (1859), Darwin[24] began his revolutionary work, *The Origin of Species* with the following words: 'The great majority of naturalists believe that species are immutable productions, and have been separately created.'

I am convinced that instincts, *like species*, were not created separately—not even by the indirect independent-of-environment or magical process of mutations. Throughout the individual's life, instincts are being modified, however slightly, and new reactive patterns are being formed. This is a process of reactive adaptation to environment, and I am convinced that this is the process whereby new adaptations, new adaptations of old instincts *and the evolution of new instincts* are in process of being brought about however gradually and imperceptibly throughout the ages. I am convinced that this is not just simply a question of acquired reactions in antithesis to inherited ones; this is *how* the inherited ones were originally acquired and how fresh patterns of reaction are being acquired and new modifications and new instincts evolved. To my mind *this* is evolution and every other concept of it makes nonsense. Processes other than adaptation to environment, can be no more than subsidiary to this main determinant. Otherwise life and environment *would not fit together*; life, and evolution, would be impossible.

Thus my contention is that the current aetiological antithesis, between inherited and acquired, is no antithesis at all, is created purely out of a misconception as to how all behaviouristic reactions, how all instincts, are formed. Congenital and environmental, inherited and acquired, are to my mind only different terms for the same process of reactive adaptation to environment; they differ only in regard to the Time when the adaptation took place and the Depth of the modification in the mind or body. That body and that mind is a continuum hereditarily, only apparently, but not actually, broken by the phenomenon of reproduction with its Mendelian laws of averages. Hence my conclusion is that the argument about whether homosexuality is congenital *or* acquired is based on a misconception. The truth is that 'congenital' and 'acquired' are merely different operational stages of the self-same process, and the one has no meaning without the other. Thus, I am convinced that homosexuality, *like everything else*, is *both* congenital *and* acquired, with relative quantitative variations of each aetiological factor.

Some chapters in this book, even some of the case material, may strike the reader unversed in psychoanalysis as rather difficult to understand. Nevertheless, I have decided to leave almost everything that may not unduly offend the uninitiated very much as the American compiler arranged it. The plan is that of giving a certain amount of data before embarking upon theory, and for this purpose the book includes anonymous, verbatim extracts, allowing some homosexual persons to say a few words about themselves.

DR. CHARLES BERG
Harley Street
London, W.1

REFERENCES

[1] Freud: *Three Essays on the Theory of Sexuality* (1905). First English Edition 1949.
[2] C. H. Rolph: *Women of the Streets* (1955).
[3] Jenkins: *Genetic Psychological Monographs*, 3 (1928), *from* Clifford Allen's *Sexual Perversions and Abnormalities* (1940).
[4] Mead: *Male and Female* (1949).
[5] Mayer-Gross, Slater and Roth: *Clinical Psychiatry* (1954).
[6] Hirschfeld: *Sexual Anomalies and Perversions* (1938, reprint 1953).
[7] Kinsey: *Sexual Behaviour in the Human Female* (1953).
[8] Havelock Ellis: *Studies in the Psychology of Sex* (1901, reprint 1926), Vol. II, *Sexual Inversion*.

[9] Reich: *The Function of the Orgasm* (1942), quotes Malinowski: *Sexual Life of Savages* (1929).

[10] Freud: *Leonardo da Vinci* (1916), English Edition 1922.

[11] Kinsey: *Sexual Behaviour in the Human Male* (1948).

[12] Franz J. Kallmann, M.D.: 'Comparative Twin Study on the Genetic Aspects of Male Homosexuality' (April, 1952), *J. Nerv. Ment. Dis.*, New York.

[13] Ferenczi: *On the Nosology of Male Homosexuality* (1916) (Homoeroticism).

[14] Thompson: *A Study of Interpersonal Relations* (1949).

[15] Jones: *Papers on Psycho-Analysis* (1912), Fifth Edition 1948.

[16] Stekel: *Bisexual Love* (1922), also printed in Frank S. Caprio's *Female Homosexuality* (1954).

[17] Bergler: *The Myth of a New National Disease: Homosexuality and the Kinsey Report* (1948).

[18] Lang: 'Genetic Determination of Homosexuality' (1940), *J. Nerv. Ment. Dis.*, *92*, 55.

[19] Fenichel: *The Psychoanalytic Theory of Neurosis* (1946).

[20] Klein, Heimann, Isaacs and Riviere: *Developments in Psycho-Analysis* (1952).

[21] Berg: *The First Interview with a Psychiatrist* (1955), published by Allen & Unwin.

[22] Hamilton: 'Incest and Homosexuality' from *Encyclopaedia Sexualis* (1936).

[23] Zuckermann: *Sexual Life of Monkeys* (1932).

[24] Darwin: *On the Origin of Species* (1859).

PREFACE

'THE human being seems destined by his nature,' the social psychologist, Hadley Cantril, has written, 'never to enjoy the full satisfaction of sexual behaviour unless it is an interdependent aspect of that relationship between people we call "love"—a situation which exists when the satisfaction *another* person derives from his experience is a crucially important and necessary aspect of the satisfaction you derive from *your own* experience.' The overtones of this experience when the relationship is between two persons of the same sex is the subject of this book. Its purpose is to call to attention knowledge about the cause and cure of homosexuality which has come with a more intimate understanding of the homosexual as a person.

As one reads in the pages which follow the thoughtful studies of more than thirty authorities on the subject, it becomes apparent that new insights about homosexuality concern its complexity as an aspect of impulses which are present in the lives of every man and woman. Specialists from a number of divergent schools of thought share the belief that homosexual love and heterosexual love involve extremes of the same experience. They are convinced that at its deepest level, homosexuality is a failure of intimacy, a self-sexedness which throws the individual completely on his own resources without hope of renewing his powers in the partnership symbolized by the sexual union of male and female.

Seen in this light, homosexuality is an all too human confusion of the motives which are found in the sex life of normally heterosexual men and women. And the fact that homosexuality exists in latent as well as overt forms makes it even more difficult to define. It is an erotic element in human life which, to quote

Oswald Schwarz, 'is as intangible, elusive, indescribable as all real emotional archphenomena are.' Protean and pervasive, the manifestations of homosexuality in our affairs have been likened by Karl Menninger to the presence of the strings in a symphony orchestra. Not too long ago, however, homosexuality was studied as a bizarre anomaly. The homosexual was looked upon as a shadowy figure tainted by heredity and ridden by the vice of excessive masturbation, or—and this would seem to have been adding insult to injury—as a jaded roué satiated with heterosexual dissipation. Today, homosexuality is approached as a symptom; but whether the disorder it signals is congenital or acquired remains a matter of some dispute.

Are homosexuals born or made? The discovery by biologists, in the latter half of the nineteenth century, that the genital systems of both sexes develop out of a common embryonic origin which contains cellular material of both sexes, gave rise to the theories of sexual intermediacy for which Magnus Hirschfeld was so eloquent a spokesman. But proof that homosexuality is an inborn characteristic must come from the geneticists. It is not yet available. Nor does the work of the endocrinologists offer much more than a reminder that what we call male and female according to our impression of external characteristics is only a dimorphism in the species. How transitory these differences are is strikingly illustrated by the report of the Danish physicians, Hamburger, Sturup and Dahl-Iversen, of their feminization of a male transvestite. In contrast, attempts to redirect the choice of a sexual partner by shifting the weight of hormonal balance in favour of the homosexual's actual anatomical sex have been unsuccessful. Injections of testosterone in male homosexuals, for example, increase sexual response; the stimulus remains another male.

Psychoanalytic theory, while it does not disregard the individual's physiological endowment, emphasizes the effects of the environment as they are reflected in emotional and mental conflicts which arise in the bosom of the family. How the Oedipus complex is resolved is held to be crucial. Since for both boy and girl the first attachment is to the mother, the genesis of male and female homosexuality is considered to be essentially the same. But, while the road to heterosexuality for the boy leads from narcissistic self-love through dependent love of the mother to final identification with the maleness of the father, for the girl there is a detour on the way. She must identify with the mother as a receiver, not as a giver of physical love. In becoming a man, the boy returns to a first love which the girl must give up to become a woman. This, in broad outline, is the solution of the Oedipus situation when there is no fixation on either parent.

It must be pointed out, however, that there is no universal agreement on the aetiology of homosexuality even within psycho-analysis. It is significant, though, that neurotic patterns developed in early childhood have been widely accepted as causative factors. Coming at a time when the human being is most vulnerable, childish guilt and anxiety produce a host of defence mechan-isms which, as the late Fritz Wittels has shown, are not adequately appreciated by our culture until they burgeon as complicated neuroses and psychoses. Yet, the fact of the matter seems to be that human beings persist in seeking the kind of experience which has been least threatening to them in the past. Our jocular acceptance of 'tomboy' and 'sissy' stereotypes is an unconscious recognition that psychosexual development must have a model of its eventual goal. We are less aware of the confusion created when cross-sex identifications with significant adults are in-hibited or overdetermined.

The chief arguments against the psychogenic explanation of homosexuality centre around the undeniable fact that some persons subjected to a particular set of pressures become homo-sexuals, while others in the same circumstances do not. Though the environmentalists point out that no two individuals, twins included, are really raised in the same psychological climate, their opponents maintain that there must be certain predisposing factors present in the homosexual from birth. The question boils down to whether the homosexual is a person with a special kind of body which makes up his mind or a person with a special kind of mind which makes him use his body in ways we call homosexual.

That homosexuality is a state of mind would appear to be borne out by the great discrepancy between the number of persons who have reported homoerotic response (50 per cent of Kinsey's males, 28 per cent of the females) and the small minority (4 per cent of the males, 3 per cent of the females in the same population) who are exclusively homosexual. We tend to forget that the homosexual affair is never between a man and a man or a woman and a woman. The assumption behind the homosexual relationship is always that one of the partners belongs to the other sex. Though all human beings share a common mammalian background, only a few, it seems, have this capacity for self-deception.

An exception to prevalent viewpoints must be made for the Kinsey research team who believe that it is more difficult to explain why 'each and every individual is not involved in every type of sexual activity' than it is to explain homosexuality. In an admirably methodical footnote in *Sexual Behaviour in the Human Female*, practically all the theories and hypotheses ever offered on the causes of homosexuality are dismissed. Professor Kinsey and his associates insist that preference for homoerotic behaviour is the result of the conditioning effects of the first accidental experience and the failure of social pressure to convince the individual that he should reject one pattern of response in favour of another. This leaves to others the complex task of determining why, in the face of tremendous social pressure, the homosexual rejects or is incapable of gratification with a member of the opposite sex.

The contributors to this volume offer, if only tentatively and from case to case, such explanations. As the numerous personal and clinical histories in this volume attest, there are revealing relationships between cause and effect and, occasionally, between cause and cure, in the lives of those homosexuals who have come under the scrutiny of several psychotherapies. The search for the inner meaning of homosexuality governs this book's presentation of a variegated group of autobiographical and first-hand accounts of homosexual concerns and conflicts against a background of clinical and theoretical analysis. To avoid biases inevitable within the limited practice even of specialists, representatives of several orientations are heard from. The span of time covered by the material affords an added check on parochiality, for the selections are characteristic of the half-century during which we have learned that 'the riddle of homosexuality' has been, in many ways, one of our own making.

In organizing the material which follows, an attempt has been made to approximate a life situation. In Part I, we meet men and women whose existence is dominated by some aspect of homosexuality. They may, like Dr. Eidelberg's artist-patient, be engaged in an openly homosexual love life. Some, like the woman whose dreams are interpreted by Dr. Fodor, may be struggling with the bisexual components of their personalities. Or they may, like Dr. Berg's young Englishwoman be driven by guilt into feelings of unreality and 'sexual deadness.' The patterns vary but the problems presented are usually pressing. Part II presents an overview of major trends in treatment. But, because of the ambiguous nature of homosexuality treatment is determined by the theoretical position of the therapist, a basic division becomes apparent in the amount of emphasis placed on congenital or psychic factors. 'The Psychobiological Approach' ranges from Hirschfeld's conviction of innateness to Dr. Sprague's eclectic compromise between psychiatry and psychoanalysis. 'The Psychoanalytical Approach' surveys classical concepts of orthodox analysis (Ferenczi), recent extensions (Bergler) and views of the interpersonal school (Thompson). Finally, six extended reports of individual treatment—including the controversial surgical and hormonal transformation of man into 'woman'— round out the picture of cause and cure.

Despite differences of emphasis in prevailing approaches to the deviant personality, there is a confluence of theory that homosexuality is rarely a matter of choice, always an intricate genetic process. As observed in treatment, the life history of the homosexual reveals a constellation of causes, real or fancied, which make sexual relations with the opposite sex unrewarding, if not unthinkable. With new techniques of self-exploration we are beginning to understand why this is so. This is not to say that all the questions raised by homosexuality have been answered by psychiatry or psychoanalysis. Homosexuality is one of a number of importunate questions involving man's image of himself on which we remain in perplexity. The beginning of knowledge is to know what we do not know.

A. M. KRICH

New York, 1954

PART ONE

AS SEEN BY THEMSELVES

THE WOMEN

I am a homosexual woman

REPORTED BY JANE MCKINNON

REPRESENTING as it does an entirely different way of thinking and living, it is odd how easy it is to conceal homosexual tendencies. This holds particularly true where women are concerned because a masculine woman attracts less attention than an effeminate man. In many cases, she is respected and admired for her manly qualities. As a woman who is at the same time a homosexual and a member in good standing in her community and profession, I can vouch for the truth of this.

No doubt one reason for the ease with which we can conceal our attitude is that so few people are at all conscious of our existence. Homosexuality in men has been studied so fully that the general public is more aware of their problem.

To those whose sex life is based on heterosexual relationships, the homosexual is a grotesque, shadowy creature—a person spoken of with scorn, pity or lasciviousness. The person so spoken of is often in the audience. If you are not one of us, it is impossible to realize our feelings when this occurs. It is incredible to us that a well-educated girl would make the following remark: 'What do they look like? I wonder if I've ever seen one?' It is a perfect example of what the average person thinks, the few times he thinks about homosexuality at all. Fortunately for us, there is no identifying mark. Contrary to what some may think, we have no secret means of recognizing one another. Many women, not homosexual at all, wear suits a lot, cut their hair short and seem, on the whole, very unfeminine. The active homosexual often makes herself look very attractive in order to please the person she is trying to charm. Appearances have much less to do with it than most people assume they do.

What is it like to be this way?

You are always lonely. It makes no difference how many friends you have or how nice they are. Between you and other women friends is a wall which they cannot see, but which is terribly apparent to you. This wall represents the difference in the workings of your minds.

Between you and men friends is another difficult misunderstanding. Very few men desire platonic friendships, the only kind of which you are capable so far as they are concerned. The endless bitter disagreements with them cause many of us to renounce their companionship entirely. Very few men understand the need we have for their friendship and the aversion we feel for sexual love. Unable to find love or its most acceptable substitute friendship, we frequently become psychiatric cases. You cannot keep a healthy state of mind if you are very lonely.

The inability to present an honest face to those you know eventually develops a certain deviousness which is injurious to whatever basic character you may possess. Always pretending to be something you are not, moral laws lose their significance. What *is* right and wrong for you when your every effort is toward establishing a relationship with another which is completely right to you, but appallingly wrong to others?

How do homosexuals feel about one another?

One of the saddest facts in this entire picture is that we seldom like one another. On the surface this appears ridiculous, but there are good reasons for it. In order to make it more clear, let me describe the general categories into which we fall.

There are certain things which are characteristic of each type. However, it is important to remember that merely because a woman may have some of the following characteristics, she is by no means to be considered a homosexual or even one who has such tendencies. This is because the intelligent homosexual always adopts the manners and customs of the group to which she belongs. Physical build plays a large part in determining what type you are.

Type I is a large person, that is, tall although not necessarily heavy. She is successful in the business world. She is intelligent and uses her manly qualities to advance her in her work. Her clothes are good, she frequently wears tailored suits and dresses and does not care for fussy hair styles or frills of any kind. She is not drawn to another like herself because she is the aggressive sort whose efficiency and capability make her desire a partner who would be emotionally dependent on her. In many cases her behaviour with her friend can be likened to that of a mother with a helpless child.

Type II is small, feminine in appearance. She can be just as aggressive as the woman described above and, although the two types do mix, the relationship is not entirely satisfactory to either. This is because both would want to dominate.

Types I and II have certain things in common. They are both completely homosexual in their desires. They are always the active, aggressive partner. They cannot be satisfied unless they dominate, that is, assume the role of the man. That they associate at all is usually due to the inability to find another partner. There is another more delicate factor to be mentioned. What we are considering here is something so intimate that few people have any idea of the contradictory elements present. To a homosexual there is something incongruous, embarrassing, about making love to another like herself. The entire basis of the friendship is the pretence that one of the women is a man. It is uncomfortable to have in the back of your mind the idea that your associate feels just as you do instead of as a woman would. It is so much a business arrangement that it seems rather indecent.

Type III is not a real homosexual, but has strong tendencies that way. This type of girl is a natural object for the attentions of the types described above. No homosexual woman would force her attentions upon another who was completely unwilling.

This third type is almost without exception a weak individual. She may have some strong characteristics but her craving for sexual gratification is so great that she will accept it from the homosexual woman if there is no man to satisfy her.

The fact that many of these women would be heterosexual if we let them alone is no deterrent to us if they appear at all amenable to our suggestions. Education, breeding, all those things do not prevent the homosexual from drawing such a woman into her orbit of dominance if she possibly can. Her need for relief from sexual tension and loneliness is too great. Yet, so weak are most women who yield to an aggressive homosexual, that this situation often becomes a tormenting one for the latter. This is because the weaker individual cannot break off the relationship nor can she reconcile her conscience to it. Unlike the complete invert, she often feels it is wrong but can neither accept it nor end it.

Who is aggressive and who is passive?

The active homosexual always initiates the relationship. Usually the other woman is too shy to do so. However, when the two are finally on terms with one another, the aggressive type does not always take the active part. With another like herself, she would feel she had to dominate. With one whom she had drawn into it, she knows that she has the stronger personality and, therefore, can permit the other to assume the aggressive role. Some homosexuals retain just enough femininity to want to surrender themselves to another from time to time.

On the whole, the Type III individual becomes involved without realizing just what her friend wants. Needing the sexual relief, she permits the homosexual to love her. Type III's entire background having produced the feeling that this sort of behaviour is wrong, and, lacking the more urgent drive of a completely homosexual development, she seldom wants to take the initiative. The feeling that it may not be wrong if she doesn't take an active part comforts her and makes her unwilling to assume such a role unless she is implored to do so.

What happened to me? Why do I have to be this way?

No doubt every homosexual has pondered these questions, searching for an answer that will bring her peace of mind. Realization of the tendency comes slowly. It is not a question of waking up some morning and thinking: 'Why, I'm a homosexual.' I was nineteen before I ever heard the word, a sophomore in college at the time. The way in which it was mentioned in a conversation made me wonder if that was what was wrong with me. A quick look at the dictionary told me immediately that not only was I a homosexual, but that I was a most unpleasant individual, a person whom anyone decent would avoid like the plague. The next impressions I received of myself through reading were equally terrifying. I had heard of degenerates, but never realized that many would think me one if they knew a little more about me. Puzzled, bewildered, I could find nowhere a single kind word being said. Most of the writers of the books could not seem to understand that a homosexual is not a *term*, but a *person*. She has feelings just as anyone else. She has an additional burden—the necessity of being quiet about her troubles, the inability to tell her friends anything about herself. What is her position? She must occasionally be present when her friends talk about her and those like her in the most unpleasant terms you can conceive. Yet her friends and her employer, not knowing, like her a lot. If she were to say—and it is often a temptation—'I am a homosexual', the repercussions would be all that anyone could imagine.

I was unhappy in my high school years. I did not know just why at the time, but I was. I never had dates because I did not bother to make myself attractive to boys. I never thought about them at all. If I didn't like them, neither did I really dislike them. They just failed to interest me.

My parents were in their fifties at this time. Instead of

67

wondering why I never complained about not having dates, they were very thankful that I wasn't 'boy-crazy'.

In college I lived in a dormitory for four years. I was content most of the time. I became more reasonable about my appearance and conformed more to current fads. Every year I developed a terrific crush on some new girl, always an older one. My raving about her at home only provoked my mother into saying that she wished I wouldn't idealize my friends so much. She never thought that there might be more than met the eye in my behaviour.

Almost without exception, I lost these friends because I did too much for them. I would have waited on them hand and foot if I dared. Before friends, I restrained myself just enough and talked about boys just enough, to keep them from being too suspicious. Had we known more about homosexuality, my friends probably would have recognized my situation. As it was, they never did, any more than my parents did. The girls on whom I had the crushes enjoyed my infantile adoration and, realizing that to say anything would be to draw themselves into it, they made no remarks. When they became tired of it, they dropped me. Some of my blackest hours were those in which I realized that they no longer wanted me around. It was several years, however, before I ceased to rush headlong into such situations.

When I became a senior, I met a boy whom I liked rather well. We went together for three months, the longest I have ever gone 'steady' with any man. At the end of that time we were both bored and so broke it off. I felt a definite relief from the strain.

This made me realize something very fundamental. In the back of my mind, I knew I should not feel as I did about other women. However, and this is important, I was convinced that it was only because I had not met the right man. Who is the right man? Knowing now how odd my conception of this man was, I can still reproduce him in all his unreality because the concept has changed very little.

His outward appearance does not matter. The thing I wanted most was friendship; definitely not a sexual relationship. The readers of this article will have no delusions about a homosexual being prudish. The fact of the matter is that a man's attentions bore us to such a point that we cannot even pretend to enjoy them. The necessity of kissing a date several times during the evening becomes a real ordeal.

The search for a perfect man is part of the psychology of homosexuals who marry. The woman who does this brings only misery to herself and her husband. She is invariably a cold wife and frequently her nerves go to pieces under the strain. Probably many who marry never had relations with another woman, and therefore do not realize how strong the homosexual tendency is. There is one exception to this: the few times that the woman marries a man who is also homosexual. Many men can obtain more satisfaction out of this sort of arrangement than they could from the other type of marriage. This would give both the companionship they crave without the sexual obligations they cannot fulfil.

I kept thinking I had not enough experience with men, had not really given them a chance. After I left college, however, I became more attractive to them and learned how to handle them better. It just didn't work. I froze up after a while, became bored because none of them offered me friendship—only sexual love. When I had proved to myself that there was nothing in it for me, I decided to have no more dates. I have had very few since then.

How do I fill my life?

I am well-to-do financially and can go places and travel. I take underprivileged children on outings, to circuses, &c. This satisfies my need for someone to be dependent on me. My energies, thus diverted, do not travel always in the same channel: that which develops sexual tension.

Do we feel we have an advantage over the heterosexual person?

From the point of view of leading a full and happy life, we are definitely at a disadvantage. No one is content who is so very lonely. No one is content who has to exercise so much will power to subdue sexual desire.

However, there are advantages. We are frequently able to build successful careers in professions that are concerned with working with people. We are two-sided, often understand others better. Many of us are artistic, can act or write.

The moods of depression to which I am subject may be brought on by seeing someone very attractive who is equally unattainable. Then I feel frustrated and at a disadvantage. On the other hand, when feeling good, I am more than equal to anyone else, not at a disadvantage at all.

One pitfall to be guarded against is alcohol. If you are lonely, depressed, it is very easy to cure the feeling with some drinks. It is easy to feel sorry for yourself, to convince yourself that no one is as unhappy as you. The liquor always puts you on top of the world. This is no problem that can be easily solved. You have moments of introspection in which you see your life dragging out and you worry for fear you will not always be able to control yourself. It scares you to think that your physical requirements might become such that you would do something terrible or degrading in order to satisfy them. If you do not act in some way to help yourself, your mind may not be able to bear the strain and you will wake up some day in a psychiatrist's office. Liquor helps us fight down the urgent needs of our personality. If you can limit yourself in what you drink, it is better to relax this way than to try to fight it alone. It is something that must be watched, of course, and I know that not all of us watch it carefully enough.

What can be done to correct our situation?

Hardly anything has appeared in print which would warn parents of such tendencies in their children. Almost without exception, they ignore any warnings which appear in puberty. Instead, like venereal disease and other hush-hush subjects, publications that deal with this problem are often banned. Therefore, many are almost completely unaware of its existence.

The rapidly developing science of psychiatry, by bringing this out into the light, could help us by making available more facts of why we are as we are. Some of us torment ourselves with the idea that we are 'evil'. We are not degenerates, yet many refer to us in such terms. We are considered a sort of sex criminal. Not only should people realize that there are lots of us, but they should have their attitudes towards us changed. Then the parent, instead of being horrified, will be able to help his child to adjust to a rather hard world.

Self-examination is not enough to resolve the confusion in our minds, a confusion arising from our idea of ourselves versus the idea voiced by the heterosexual person. The best way to keep us from compensating our loneliness and sense of inadequacy at the expense of weaker individuals to is provide us with knowledge about our place in the order of things. There will be fewer homosexual women in mental hospitals and psychiatric offices if we are recognized as human beings instead of as material for a chapter in a book on abnormal psychology.

While being grateful to this patient for many first-hand revelations about homosexuality and indeed about sexuality and psychology in general, I think we should realize that she is more than homosexual. She is suffering from a psychoneurosis. Her unconscious phantasy is riddled with morbid guilt feelings. Indeed this guilt emanating from her Oedipus complex may be the very factor responsible for the repression of heterosexual patterns and the diversion of libido into homosexual channels. The guilt is then displaced onto the conscious homosexual tendencies in the familiar manner.

C.B.

The case of Miss Ilse

REPORTED BY WILHELM STEKEL, M.D.

MISS Ilse—we shall call her by that name—after a series of various exciting episodes has fallen a victim to depression, during which she lost a great deal of weight, but in spite of a successful fattening régime her stay at a sanatorium did not effect a complete cure. She is an impressively attractive girl, 24 years of age, voluptuous, feminine in every way up to her angular, somewhat energetic nose and prominent, curved eyebrows. Her mother, of whom the girl speaks with much feeling, believes that the girl's breakdown dates from the death of the father. Ilse irritatedly contradicts the mother several times, breaking into a quarrelsome attitude towards her mother over trifles. Reprimanded by her mother, she falls into her depression and speaks no word. I take her under treatment and for a week I have in her a heavy burden on my hands. She hardly says anything, is very negativistic in her attitude, only muttering from time to time: 'Don't trouble yourself. It will never be any different. Better give me something that will put me quickly out of the way.' She livens up somewhat only when referring to her father—thinks he should have not passed away. The mother should have called in a specialist. In fact, it was as much her fault as anybody's, for she had failed to insist on calling the best aid while there was time.

Gradually she extends me her confidence and one day she appears—like a changed person. She must tell me the truth. She is not a normal person. Since childhood she has been homosexual and had never cared for men. Her mother had implied as much when she said to me :'I cannot understand the girl. She always fled from the room when young men called on Alfred (her brother). The girl is a man hater.' This fact the girl had denied during the first visit, but now she herself admitted. She had

never cared for men. On the other hand, at 11 years of age she
had already fallen passionately in love with a woman school-
teacher. She was a frolicsome girl, often wore her brother's
clothes, and played with all the young boys of the neighbourhood.
At 14 years of age she again fell in love with a girl friend.

Her current depression is due to a terrible disappointment.
She had maintained a love affair with a French woman and was
happy. She said nothing about the character of the relations, but
admitted that they were very intimate. Suddenly she found out
that the French woman was not true to her, but was keeping up
intimate relations more often with other girls than with her.
She suffered tremendously on account of her jealousy. She began
to feel a disgust against all women not unlike her former aversion
to men. Asked why she was so antagonistic to men, she answered:
'Because they are, all, without exception, disgusting brutes . . .'

At this point Ilse begins to relate her past experiences. She
was seven years of age when she visited an uncle. . . . She did . . .
things he requested. 'How shall I have any respect for men when
they don't hesitate to poison the innocent soul of a child?' The
uncle is still living. . . . She has since thought that it must be some
morbid tendency and has forgiven him. 'It happened only a
few times and the uncle believes I have forgotten it. . .'

Another traumatic incident impressed her more seriously:
it was, in fact, a series of traumas. Her mother was a light-minded
person and is so to this day, despite her 50 years. But she knows
enough to dress herself so attractively and with such a display
of refinement that she is still capable of achieving conquests.
There follow a number of serious complaints against the mother,
which must have been true, for I have had opportunity to convince myself of the truth of some of the statements. The mother
always kept on the string a number of lovers who gratified her
extravagant requirements. As a child Ilse had been taken along
to a number of rendezvous and has repeatedly witnessed the
display of tendernesses between the lovers. She also recalled
various household scenes from her early childhood. As a child

she was already very sensuous and masturbated jointly with the sister and the brother. She was precocious as well as prematurely spoiled and every one thought she would early turn out to be like her mother. Then her sister underwent a great change in character. She became religious and wanted to join a nunnery. Ilse made fun of her religious-minded sister but secretly admired her for her chastity. She was 14 years of age at the time. She now knows that she was in love with the family physician and that she was interested in men, but at the same time she was in love at different times with various teachers and girl friends. When her sister was 16 years of age she had a love affair with an army lieutenant and had to go to a sanatorium to be curetted, fever set in after the operation, and for several weeks the girl was seriously ill.

Her sister's experience shook her to pieces. Inwardly she had been proud that there was such a pure, innocent girl in the family. Now that her sister followed the example of her mother it seemed to her that she, too, was fated to follow in the same path and that there could be no escape for her. During that period her character underwent a change and she acquired a tremendous dislike for all small children. She could not suffer to see a small child. She thought to herself, if she were its mother she would strangle it. The feeling was so horrible that she could not sleep. In time she improved somewhat, but the dislike of children or, rather, the fear of them, that is, the fear that she might do some harm to them, never left her.

I suspected that back of this feeling-attitude towards the children might be found the solution of her problem. I reverted back to her sixteenth year, for it was at that period that she turned definitely against all men.

'Why do you hate children?'

'Not that, exactly . . . In fact, I was at one time foolish over them. I have always wanted children. When I told you that I always played boyish games it was not exactly the truth. I remember now that I played nurse to my doll and that we often played the game of childbirth. Brother was the doctor and I was the pregnant lady in bed.'

'Did you happen to witness childbirth as a little girl?'

'Yes, everything . . . Our aunt gave birth to a child in our home —a romantic story. An illegitimate child; her parents were not to know anything about the birth, or they would have disowned her. But we children knew everything. Afterwards she married the man but was very unhappy with him. The little baby was with us for a time. I was very fond of it and carried it around . . .'

'Have you other such aunts in the family?'

'Between us: mother's family has a poor reputation. There were six sisters, each more flighty than the next. None was a virgin at marriage. Things were always happening and there was never any peace. That is why I was so shocked over sister's experience. I was getting to think it was my fate also to become . . . merely a prostitute. You will pardon me for speaking so harshly about my own mother. But unfortunately it is the truth . . .'

'A prostitute is purchasable . . . There is some difference whether one is light-minded through passion or for gain.'

(After a lengthy pause.) 'Just what I did find out at the time. Mother was to be had for money. Father was a humble employee, an unsuccessful jurist, who eked out a living doing secretarial service for an attorney. He could not keep up with the large household expenses even though he occasionally transacted a business deal on the side which netted him a considerable sum. Mother always had a friend who took care of our needs. Thus we were brought up rather well educated, my brother could afford to study, we did everything.'

'Did you know all that already as a child?'

'I knew it at a very early age . . .'

'You think, then, that your sister was also paid and that she sold herself?'

'No, nothing like that. In addition to the paying lover mother always had one, a purely heart affair, on the side. It was funny!

The men always brought us candies and all sorts of presents. When we grew older mother became a little more careful. Still, there was enough going on to bring shame as I look back. And so there came into our house also a young lieutenant mother had picked up—God knows where. This fellow was mother's avowed lover and could do as he pleased. The terrible thing was that he also began to pursue my sister and after a few jealousy quarrels mother had to put up with it—she perhaps even encouraged the affair. For I overheard once a talk between them and heard mother reproach 'Shikki'—that was the lieutenant's nickname—that he had used sister. She could have obtained a large sum of money for the girl because she was a virgin and the girl would have been provided for. Then there followed bitter quarrels between mother and sister.'

I interrupt the conversation at this point. It turns out that she, too, was in love with the lieutenant, and so were the others of the household, including the father and the brother; she was also jealous of her mother. Her jealousy opened her eyes. That is how it happened that she heard the unpleasant rumours about her mother circulating among the neighbours. She began hating her mother, but that continued only for a short time. Then her hatred turned to children. She hated first herself, the child who bore no respect for the mother. She did not want to be like her mother and her sister. She knew that she would have to submit to similar experiences; that her fate was sealed. She strove against her feminine and motherly instincts. But the analysis disclosed that she really entertained one supreme wish which she was unwilling to countenance openly: she wanted to be a mother and to bear many, many children. But the neurotic reaction thwarted her powerful motherly instinct. To be a mother meant identification with the despised mother. Her better feelings prompted her to draw herself far apart from the mother.

She did not want to be a woman. She did not want to be as easygoing as her mother. At that time her brother also showed a temperamental change. He became serious-minded, began to write verses, and to take an interest in all sorts of idealistic endeavours. She linked herself to him and before long she differentiated herself completely from the rest of the household, and particularly from the mother. She sought earnest-minded girl friends and came into frequent contact with her brother's companions, but was unapproachable, even though she expressed herself freely and frankly about all subjects. Her strongly sensuous temperament threw her next into the arms of the Frenchwoman and she preferred that to a love affair with a man as she was afraid of children. After the Frenchwoman's breach of loyalty she fell into her depression.

This circumstance also disclosed an interesting sidelight. She confessed to me that the Frenchwoman was also her brother's sweetheart. It had never been mentioned by the woman but she knew it even before she entered into intimate relations with her. Nevertheless it was her happiest period.

The depression is thus traceable to a second source. The brother had abandoned the Frenchwoman, having chosen another sweetheart of whom he was very fond and whom he intended to marry. The Frenchwoman was only a sensuous affair with him, the brother belonged wholly to her. They were always together and she knew all his secrets. She was never jealous when she knew that he kept up relations with some girl or woman so long as he did not love soulfully. But now the brother became acquainted with a wealthy, beautiful girl, with whom he fell in love and whom he was going actually to marry. This, for the brother, lucky event—came to nothing in the end on account of the opposition of the girl's family—left her cool. All she saw was that she was losing her brother, and that he no longer belonged to her. He could not marry the girl because her parents required that he should first prove his ability to support her. But the two lovers agreed to wait for one another and the brother had already gone pretty far and he may yet succeed to marry the girl, despite the mother's deplorable reputation. He no longer lives with his family and avoids the old home. He only sees Ilse from time to time and they are still good old pals, whenever they meet . . .

This interesting analysis illustrates all the chief points to be found in the psychogenesis of female homosexuality. In fact the girl was on the point of becoming as fond of men as her mother, perhaps of indulging in bisexual activities. Her sister's experience opened her eyes and acted as a terrible warning. The yearning for purity which animates every soul and is the polar counterpart of the desire for tasting every sort of experience, became uppermost in her case, the fear of becoming like the sister, or like the mother, and her hatred of the mother, jointly, had the effect of shaping her into a different being. She probably would have not yielded to the homosexual love of the French-woman had she not been overcome by the fact that the woman was her brother's sweetheart. It was a case of incest through a third person . . . . She hated her mother and had to protect herself against the danger of having children who grow up to be one's enemies. Thus children became her enemies. The father played a negligible role in her life and had no influence on the development of her homosexuality.

I do not know well her subsequent history. Her depression was soon relieved and her hatred of children disappeared entirely. But she left Vienna and went to another country, obviously to get away from her family and to forget her whole past. I had advised her to do so and the fact that she had followed my advice permits us to hope that, after the tempestuous course of her past life, she may have succeeded, at last, in finding a friendlier harbour.

From the casebook of a gynaecologist

CASE 1137

A YOUNG professional woman of twenty-six, tall and serious, is referred by a friend about some matter of personal adjustment which turns out to be homosexuality.

She has good health, strong, healthy long-lived family, menstruation since ten or eleven regular, first at twenty-eight now twenty-four day intervals, always clots, no pain, no pelvic examination.

Family connections are good, youngest of six children, admired father very much, mother somewhat hard on her. After college she had two years postgraduate work, now has excellent position.

She is fine looking, well built, not masculine, gaze a little weak and indirect, rather low neck exposing edges of small breasts.

'I am too keen on girls . . . I was used to my brothers and to boys at home, I had rather a crush on a teacher in high school; at college there was a girl I was crazy about and jealous of; afterward I was falling in love with a man who turned out to be a hard drinker so I couldn't marry him. He asked me to live with him instead and it was awfully hard not to, he used to get me so nervous I couldn't sleep all night. Later another man with whom I motored a good deal made proposals, but we stopped at kissing and hugging.

'The first physical experience beyond this point was with a younger girl and I was twenty-three. I loved my friend and we knew each other nearly a year first. It wore us both out, we fought it so, and it was so tremendous when it came. We would stop and then we couldn't stop. Finally she broke away.

79

It left me so I had to relieve myself. I found out what had given me a lot of wakefulness and nervousness.'

After this a third man: 'We both wanted intercourse but refrained because it wasn't right. Dancing and petting excite, cannot sleep afterward except after self-relief.'

At about twenty-five, a lifelong friend a few years older, of whom she had been seeing a good deal of late, showed that she was excitable. After that, once or twice a week, two or three orgasms for each, both stimulated by it but her friend thinks she has done wrong and they have broken off physical relations.

Woman to woman: homosexual letters

ANONYMOUS*

Sweetheart:

Why didn't I love you and pet you and say fifty different things to you before you left me, now I have to be away from you for so many hours and I will think of so many things that I wanted to say and do to you, but I suppose ten years from now, it would be the same for I can't seem to say all that I feel, if I create beautiful music, it might bring to you some of the beautiful and wonderful things I do feel for you.

Dearest, please remember that this is not a passing fancy or infatuation for you, no dear, it is something much bigger and goes much deeper and I have thought it all over seriously, and cannot picture any happiness without you.

Your letter said, 'If I fail you,' oh! my dear, (I cannot picture such a thing) but it is the other way, if you fail me or don't treat me right. I don't know what I would do, for the love I have for you has gotten out of my control, I never tire just looking at you, every caress and kiss is like electricity and when away from you, I am so unhappy longing to be back with you again, I guess I would even try to kill myself if our plans went amiss, for I am that bad off, yes, dear, I really love you that much.

When I leave here I shall be thinking of you constantly, and shall write you every day, and in that way, I shall be sure that I am not forgotten by you, and I will be brought before you each night through my letter. Please *never* think that any outside attractions could ever erase your image or in any way lessen the love I have for you, no, dear, you have won me too completely

*Homosexual letters gathered by Dr. Samuel Kahn in his capacity as psychiatrist to the Department of Correction of New York City.

F

for that, I shall play many sad songs and live in the dreams of the day we shall really be with each other, as I long to be always yours and only yours. All my love and goodnight kiss sixty minutes long.

(Signed)
Bubbles

P.S. Please answer dearest, for at night your letters are my one pleasure. I am sending paper and sing something pretty just to me, just me.

Just Sweetheart:

I am sitting here all alone thinking of the one I love most in the world and it came to me just how dearly I care for you, for if I had to make a choice I'd give up my sisters for you dear, thank God it isn't necessary, I can have both. (That's a broad assertion) and remember, my sister in New York (Marion) is the only one I have who really loves me and understands me and really cares what becomes of me, nevertheless my choice would be for you for how would anything in the world make up to me your loss.

Besides loving you as I do, you have me so much in your power, you could really do as you please with me because once you are close to me or put your arms around me, all I know is love for you dear, but why am I raving on because when you are away from me it's the same thing, the only difference is that I am longing for your touch, gee, if you did anything now to hurt me what would I do?

This afternoon I lay on my cot with my eyes closed and oh! I was in such a loving mood and had looked forward to our hour together that I really suffered and was really burning up.

Now do you realize what you have done? You have won me so completely that I cannot even master my thoughts when I am away from you—you are an obsession with me: I can think of nothing else and the big thing is, I don't want to.

Sweetie, right now I would make any sacrifice just to be down there with you, oh! just one whole night before leaving you for two long months, but the day I meet you on the bridge I shall go right to our home and when I get you *inside* I shall lock the door and throw the key away.

Now, lover, see what you have done, you have made a nut out of me, but if this is crazy, I don't want ever to be sane again.

I wonder what the girls around here think for I have my eyes on *you* all the time, and they must see love and admiration for you shining in my eyes.

Sweetheart, please sing to me tonight, I live every word you sing, in the jail and what's in it all vanished and just you remain, and your voice sounds so beautiful and I just swell up with pride when I realize that it's my sweetie singing just to me.

Lover, Lillie just came to the gate with your dear little note: oh! if I was celling with you, if I was only with you now I wouldn't move an inch away from you until I had to in the morning, and even then I'd sit close to you so I could feel you near me.

As I sat here writing, Cliff just came to the gate and handed me a 'comfritter,' oh! please, lover, don't be angry at me for anything, I wish she hadn't brought it. Please dear, don't think I would do anything, dear, that I wouldn't want you to do, damn it, I'd like to crawl right inside of you into your heart and stay there.

We do think of the same things for I was thinking of our dear little home outside and wrote about it, then I got your letter, lover please answer this and sing so I will know you are not angry, I am yours with all my heart.

(Signed)

Dreams of masculine regret

REPORTED BY NANDOR FODOR

This excerpt of advanced dream analysis may help to remind us that homosexuality, like all human thought and behaviour, emanates from Unconscious phantasy. C.B.

A WOMAN of 26, who is married and is the mother of a three-and-one-half-year-old boy, dreams of seeing a girl dressing a wooden doll, putting wadding on the chest and binding it with strings. It is the figure of a boy, and she has a feeling of frustration at the sight.

The immediate query which the dream prompts is, Was she sorry that she was not born as a boy? She was. Her mother wanted a boy; the girl always played with boys and to this day likes heavy work and masculine jobs. Six months ago, through stillbirth, she lost a boy child. She still had milk, had had too much with her first boy; and her breasts are of fair proportion. By the wadding, the dream girl (who was herself) was making a bisexual figure out of the boy doll. 'Bi' means two. She always wanted to have two children, and in her dreams people who had twins or two children figured abundantly. She was an only child and had suffered in infancy from love starvation. Was her twin fantasy an attempt to give a loving companion to the child in herself? Or was the fantasy only due to the male-female preoccupation?

She dreamed of going uphill, seeing water or a dam. Then, in a bright room, she opened a very large book about two worlds and something between them. She was thinking of an atlas and of separating. She seemed to be a boy, 10 years old, and she explained to 'another' 10-year-old boy that she was accomplished

84

in love because she had a nursemaid who was left unsatisfied with her lover, and she took his place. The book was filled with holly, the sharp edges of which fitted together. The pattern suggested drawings of spermatozoa.

Here we have proof of masculine regret and also of a split. She is two boys; the book speaks of two worlds: separation and a fitting together are mentioned with references to spermatozoa; a double number (10) is given which, from the phallic viewpoint, hints at the male and female shapes. Going uphill may indicate progress; and, from the book, she apparently wishes to learn something; perhaps separation and fitting together are not antithetic terms; perhaps her integration is dependent on the clarification of her male and female status in life. She admitted frigidity and general restlessness and dissatisfaction without knowing why. But women did not attract her and she had no sexual interest in them.

Her son had an attack of convulsions, and she took him to the hospital in the middle of the night.

'When I came home, it was early morning. It was misty. Steam came up from the manholes in the street and I experienced a wonderful feeling of elation as if walking into the complete unknown, as if I were going out of this world. It reminded me of Dante's *Inferno*. I have seen such misty mornings on Long Island, when the contours are lost; you are alone and, in the distance, faint lights twinkle in big buildings. At the head of the Eighth Avenue subway, the feeling of hurtling down into a tunnel of flickering lights gave me a similar sensation. I also experience it sometimes in the morning on Washington Square and on ferryboats to Long Island.'

The description fits the vague feelings which well up occasionally from the prenatal levels of our minds.

'I dreamed of being in the house of an unpleasant neighbour woman who is always getting involved with everybody. My husband had a mink coat on and looked fine in it. I thought I could cut it down to fit me. I tried it on, but as I kept arranging my bag and coat, the fur was gone, the coat was threadbare, a wreck.'

Men do not wear mink coats. It is a mistake to wrap her own femininity around her husband. He is not the lost Adam; he must be permitted to be himself. As long as she keeps on objectifying her masculinity in him, her marriage will be a wreck.

The same night she dreamed:

'We made our double bed into a single bed by pushing it together. I thought I could pull it apart again if I wanted to. Then I looked under the bed and saw that I wouldn't be able to reach the gas hole for light.'

Here is proof that she is attempting to fuse the male and female but that she is doubtful of its practicability. The gas in her apartment is not for light, but for heat. She is confused about both—the heat of passion and the light of understanding.

But she was progressing fast, and her relationship to her husband underwent a wholesome change.

'I am riding in the prow of a boat and see Archie, my boss, swimming in the water. He is carrying my son and a little girl on his back. My son fell off but was all right.'

This completes beautifully the prenatal bisexual picture. Her masculinity is now represented by her son. It fell off in the waters of birth. Her femininity stands out as conspicuously as the little girl on the back of Archie. His name contains an allusion to the pubic arch, and, as her boss, he represents in himself both parents fused. As she had heard some gossip regarding his homo-sexuality, no doubts can be entertained about the correctness of this interpretation. The dream continues:

'Upstairs in a closed-in sun porch, tomatoes are growing in large sandboxes. It is bright and sunny and I have a vision of water. Then comes the feeling of uselessness; the New York soil is bad; you cannot raise plants in it.'

When the patient was pregnant with her son, the only thing she could keep on her stomach was tomatoes. This association, and the vision of water, confirms that the closed-in sun porch is her own womb. She is striving for bisexual balance, but is still sceptical.

A few days later, she dreamed of being in a hospital with her husband and her son, who was in the baby carriage. Then her son ceased to be a baby. In his place, there was garden soil in the baby carriage and she was stirring it up, being conscious that she had to finish something. The hospital was composite picture of hospital, art gallery and a bank.

Stirring up the soil hints at some basic biological adjustment. The bank is another womb symbol, a place for valuables and the most valuable thing is the seed locked up in the vault of the womb. Proof of the symbolism came the same night in this dream:

'I heard a siren. It suggested a combination of fire, air raid and earthquake. I fell down and got my hands dirty in a mixture of sand and oil, such as you find on garage floors. Then I got up to put my son to sleep in another room. It turned out that they had put him to sleep in the bank vault. They had to open it to get him out. I was told I should get a letter, in order that he should be able to get a job when he grows up.'

Not only is the patient putting her masculinity in another room after it is brought to the light of the day, but she is setting out to prepare an outlet for it in adult life. The repressed male, represented by her son, is given birth, and the time is envisioned when he will have an equal place in the sun. Then, alone, will her sexual balance be complete, and she will rise up and forget about the cosmic catastrophe which knocked her down at the very beginning of life.

Mother and daughter

REPORTED BY CHARLES BERG, M.D.

THIS is a case of a single woman in the early thirties who, rather characteristically, was brought to me by her mother.

Having ascertained that the patient could speak for herself, I insisted upon seeing her alone. She complained of a curious vague symptom . . . At her first interview the new patient says:

'It is very difficult to describe these extraordinary feelings. All I can say is that they come in attacks, often when I am least expecting them. It is a feeling as though I am not here at all. Everything seems to go dim or black. I struggle against it without effect, and then the feeling works up into a sort of panic.

'It is as though it were something that I must fight or I would be overwhelmed. But my fighting is of no avail; I feel myself getting more and more lost, and then the panic gets worse and worse. I get an attack of these feelings almost every day; they have become more frequent and severe. They make the whole of my life utterly miserable.'

Analyst: 'Is your life in general satisfactory and happy?'

'Yes, I think so, apart from these feelings. I live at home with my mother. It is not frightfully exciting, of course. We do not always agree. She is difficult and I feel she is watching me all the time. But recently I have decided to accept the situation as it is. For years I'd have done anything to have left home, but that is rather impracticable, and so recently I have decided to settle down to it.'

Later on in the session she tells a curious dream she had: 'I dreamed there was somebody in jail whom I had to go and visit. I knew that if I went I would be arrested and yet I felt I must go. I talked to the woman personally, and someone came up and arrested me. I thought to myself, "well, I did this with my eyes open so I have just got to put up with it and stay here." It was a most depressing dream.'

Analyst: 'What thoughts pass through your mind if you think of this dream and the depressing feelings it provoked?'

'Well, I did not think of it before, but now the thought comes to me that I have accepted the unsatisfactory situation at home and decided that I have just got to stay there. It is similarly depressing. Mother watches me all the time like a jailer, and I suppose I do feel as if I am in prison.'

As we found in subsequent sessions, this patient usually dreams of herself as two persons. Often they each symbolize one half of her conflict. The person already in jail is her dutiful self which has throughout accepted mother-domination. The visiting self is the part of her which would rather have been free and live her own life, but which decides that it must join the other half in 'jail'.

She says these unreality feelings first started when she was thirteen; but at another session she remembers that she occasionally had 'far-away' feelings at a much younger age.

'I can remember now sitting in a cinema at about the age of eleven. I got this feeling of unreality only it had quite a different effect upon me then. *I found it rather exciting and pleasant.* I used to give myself up to it and enjoy it. And then as a young child I used to get a very pleasant thrill when in bed. I couldn't have been more than seven. Since I grew up I have had the same thrill in connexion with a woman [older than herself] with whom I was infatuated. In this connexion I found that it was sexual, though of course I did not recognize it as that when I was seven.

'As a child I simply adored my mother and was terrified of anything happening to her. Then it was love of mother and it was a pleasure: now my devotion to her is purely duty and it is the forgoing of all pleasure. It is misery.'

These last remarks should remind us that, to the infant, mother is *the* source of gratification, including especially sensuous gratification. Originally, pleasure is at the oral (mouth) level during the period of suckling; but later with the development of maturity mother comes to stand for the opposite of gratification (frustration), for the sensuous pleasure-giving zone has shifted from the oral to the genital region and mother is an obstacle to the natural fulfilment of this urge.

That this reversal of our patient's feelings towards her mother has deep-seated emotional causes is revealed by the following dream. Incidentally it shows also the marked, if totally unconscious, homosexual streak in her make-up. Homosexuality, like all other relationships of persons, has its source in the original infant-parent relationship.

She dreams: 'I was looking for a particular, most fascinating woman, older than myself, whom I had heard about and whom I wanted to make love to. Then suddenly I got terribly frightened at the thought of meeting her. I rushed away in a panic and found myself all alone in a big open space with this terrible far-away feeling.'

Free association of thought to this dream reminds her of a recent emotional scene with her mother when, after quarrelling, they both wept passionately, her mother putting her arms around her and beginning to kiss her with so much emotion that suddenly the patient got an acute revulsion. She felt somehow that her mother was becoming sexual towards her. She felt utter disgust and horror.

It transpired, too, that her life with her mother consisted largely in her assuming a defensive wariness, seemingly against the possibility of her mother's attentions to her.

Thus the older woman in the dream is the mother. The child is now more mature and its love requirements, however much they may originally have been directed towards the mother, are now sexually genital: the idea of the mother in this connexion is felt to be disgusting. Nevertheless, the mother is still regarded as the opponent of her sexual life.

It is noteworthy that in the course of repression of infantile sexuality, the original object or recipient of it, namely the parent, is evermore most strongly repressed or forgotten. The following material is perhaps even more significant:

'As a very little girl I was always fussing round my father, climbing on his knee and trying to get close to him. I could never have enough of him. Then suddenly, at some period of my life, a feeling of great awkwardness arose with him, something like the awkwardness I have felt with you, but it was much worse with him.

'I think it occurred from the time my elder brother took me into the garden and did something to me. He must have aroused some feelings in me. I know I felt awfully guilty and very self-conscious after that. I not only felt awkward with my father, until he died a few years later, but I went on feeling awkward with my brother until I was twenty.

'Shortly after this feeling of awkwardness first arose—I know it was as early as the age of thirteen—I began to get worried feelings, feelings that everything in life was futile. There seemed to be something I wanted to do but I could not think what it was. It occurs to me now that perhaps what I wanted to do was something sexual, only I did not know it. But that seems absurd at thirteen! On the contrary, I decided, shortly afterwards, that what I wanted was to be very, very good indeed.

'In addition to feeling awkward with my father and brother I became very devoted to my mother from a sense of duty. I have stuck to that duty ever since, though I have felt most miserable in it.

'It was about the same time that the far-away feelings which had previously been only rare, and always pleasant, now became very frequent and most terribly unpleasant. They were accompanied by dull misery. Sometimes they were agony, and when I couldn't stop them I would get into a panic.

'In early days I had plenty of respite from them; now they are much worse and much more frequent I think. I must have begun at thirteen a strenuous campaign against relaxing for fear I should get forbidden feelings that were not in keeping with my high ideals of perfection and my duty to my mother. But in spite of the stress and strain, or perhaps because of it, I could not prevent these terrible far-away feelings from getting into my daily life.'

Later on it transpires: 'They come most particularly when I make myself do tasks which are against my inclination. For instance, if I pick up and read the paper because I want to know the news I do not get an attack, but I can bring on the feeling by setting myself to read something in which I am not interested.

'You see, I have always had the idea that I ought to read serious things and fill up every moment of my time. I started that idea about the same time as I started these bad feelings. I do not think I have ever really relaxed from that day to this.'

At another session she says: 'You see I *had* to do something of this sort because if ever I did anything I *wanted* to do, I was always unhappy afterwards as if I had done wrong. Was it because I really wanted to do wrong?

'There are two very wrong things I have done in my life and I have been too ashamed to tell you, although after I had told you that dream the other day, I guessed the meaning of it, and I guessed too, that you knew . . . . and yet I couldn't tell you.

'When in the dream my brother told me that I need not tell you about the money I had picked up in the garden, but that I ought to tell you about the raspberries, I did tell you about his touching me in the garden, but I did not tell you about my touching myself.

'But even that is not so difficult as telling you that once I stole money from my mother, and went on stealing it for some time. It had to do with the touching somehow. I think I had some vague feeling that mother was herself getting away with similar things. I felt she was getting all the nice things and watching me and preventing me from getting anything nice. So I took her money *and* touched myself.

'I got a terrible reaction shortly afterwards: I thought, "Good God! I'm a thief." And then it was that I suppressed all my tendencies and became such a dutiful, devoted daughter.'

The reference here to the psychology of stealing is of particular interest. I have discovered from previous cases that the usual sequence of events is as follows:

First the child loses its mother as a source of satisfaction. Fundamentally, this would be the equivalent of losing the nipple as a pleasure-organ. If we skip such intermediate steps as thumb-sucking, we arrive at the second stage. This is the stage at which he discovers his own sex organs as an alternative source of self-consolation. Eventually, this is repressed with the general repression of sensuality, and in the course of a process analogous to sublimation, he looks for cultural substitutes with which to console himself. At this third stage the impulse, still very compulsive, becomes one of seizing pleasure in the shape of goods or money. It is not without significance when these are robbed from the rival parent.

Perhaps these further remarks of the patient will help to elucidate the superficial aspects of her illness.

'Almost throughout my life, at least from the age of thirteen, I have always felt pulled in two opposite directions. On the one hand I have felt I wanted to let myself go, defy my mother, clear out and do as I liked. I've felt I did not want these stupid restrictions. The impulse has been very strong to go to the opposite extreme. Then there is the other part of me which will not allow the slightest concession to the bad half of me. It can only be satisfied with 100 per cent spiritual life.

'This is the half of me which has made me cling most dutifully to my mother all these years. If I ever yielded in the slightest degree to the other half, I have only been all the more unhappy after it. Therefore, the only course for me is to resign myself to living with mother and being all good—even if it does feel like jail all the time. It is only by the success of my ideals that I can be happy. That is why the spiritual side of me always wins in the conflict between conscience and sex.'

Analyst: 'What is it that wins when you get the unreality feeling?'

93

Silence.

'Is that sex? Or is it something which is not me? It cannot be not me; it must be some part of me which I will not admit as a part of myself. When I find I cannot stop it or conquer it in spite of all my effort, then I get this miserable panic, as though something stronger than me, stronger than my will, were going to take possession of me.

'Is all my trouble due to trying to ignore absolutely something which cannot be ignored? Is it due to my conscience being too uncompromising and my passionate impulses or instincts being too strong to be subdued? Is it as though something which I have slammed the front door on forces itself back through a side door unannounced, and in spite of all my opposition?'

At a more advanced session the patient says:

'I feel very awkward and uncomfortable here with you, like I used to feel with my father at the age of fifteen. He was awkward, too. We could not bear to be alone together.

'When I first lay down here I began to feel sexual, then my panic feeling came, and now I have the horrible dead feeling,'

Analyst: 'What stopped the sexual feeling?'

'Mother's face. Mother's face when I came in from the garden after my brother had touched me. I felt she knew. I felt she was going to pounce on me, and cut my inside out. I have gone dead to stop it. I have gone dead in anticipation.'

At a later session she says:

'No sooner do I lie down on this settee than I go completely dead. It is agony. I only get it here. And yet when I'm away from here I have intense anxiety lest something, for instance an air raid, will stop me from coming to you. It isn't the air raid that I'm frightened of, not a bit, it's being prevented from getting to you. Away from here it is all pleasurable anticipation of coming to you and no sooner do I get here but I go dead all over, and simply want to get away at once.

'I do not want to be sexual with you. On the contrary, I dislike you. I feel intense hostility towards you.

'I would like to go into a convent. I suppose I will have to resign myself to living with mother and getting these bad feelings all my life.'

The interpretation of the above material is that father watches her starve (for him) and does nothing to relieve her agony. Would not any starving child feel hostility towards such a parent?

Mother, on the other hand—mother, who would destroy her for incest—offers her the consolation of martyrdom. She embraces her cross (the bad feelings) and becomes mother's good girl.

Incidentally, the patient went home and wrote a successful article on the Crucifixion. It appears that she had chosen crucifixion in place of father.

Although this case is essentially one of hysteria, it has a streak of obsessional neurosis mixed with it. The source of hysteria is conflict at the genital level, in the course of which the anti-sexual (or anti-incestuous) opposition succeeds in displacing genital affects to any and every nongenital locus, at the same time forcing them to change their emotional tone.

The 'locus' here, unlike that in most cases of hysteria, was principally away from the *reality of bodily feeling*. This attempt to escape from sexuality (more specifically from 'incest') was not altogether successful. For although the patient occasionally succeeded in 'going dead', more frequently she achieved only a feeling of unreality which was accompanied by all the agony of the conflict. More accurately this agony should be regarded as having its source in sexual feeling whose feeling-tone has been *altered* by the opposition.

It only remains to be added that the psychopathology of the obsessional element in her neurosis goes deeper than the genital level of sexual conflict. The patient is still working out her conflict in terms of genital sexuality and conscience, but it would be a mistake to suppose that some such solution as marriage would cure all her troubles.

The infantile superego (conscience acquired in infancy and still unconsciously active) would not be placated by such a superficial and reasonable solution, although admittedly marriage might help after analysis had been carried to a deeper level.

Although in obsessional cases the conflict is commonly *expressed* in terms of genital sexual impulses versus conscience, nevertheless, its real origin lies in infancy at an even earlier level than the development of genital sexuality. Deeper analysis will reveal that this same conflict had its roots at a very early age when aggressive impulses tended to have their phantasied expression in connexion with pleasurable excretory activities.

In all such cases there is precocity in the development of particularly strong passionate urges, coupled with an equal and opposite overstrong resistance. This resistance is built up by the extraordinary energy of the aggressive impulse itself going over, as it were, to the opposite side and becoming equally aggressive towards the impulse itself.

Thus it is that an unrelenting conscience is brought into being. The fight is a particularly strong one between particularly strong opponents and it can absorb a considerable proportion of the mental energy, thus rendering the ego (or reality principle) relatively impoverished. Unreality feelings are the sequel to this impoverishment. The panic is largely the fear of losing touch with reality or, in other words, of going mad. This 'madness' which is so feared may prove, as it did in this case, to be nothing more than the momentary 'madness' which occurs normally during orgasm.

If the deadlock (between the instincts on the one hand and the opposing conscience on the other) can be overcome, some of the mental energy absorbed in this struggle will be available for the use of the ego.

In such cases as the above it is only by a long and patient process of analysis, carefully conducted, that real benefit is achieved.

A jealous wife

REPORTED BY SANDOR FERENCZI, M.D.

TRANSLATED BY ERNEST JONES, M.D.

I SHALL cite as a (second) case* that of a lady, still young, who after living for years in moderate harmony with her husband, and bearing him daughters, began to suffer from delusions of jealousy not long after giving birth to a son; alcohol played no part in her case.

She began to find everything in her husband suspicious. A cook and one chambermaid after another were dismissed, and finally she got her way and had only male servants in the house. Even that didn't help. The man, who was everywhere regarded as a model husband, and who assured me on his word of honour that he had never been unfaithful to her, could not go a step or write a line without being watched, suspected, and even abused by his wife. Curiously enough she was suspicious of her husband only with either very young females, about twelve or thirteen years old, or quite old, ugly ones, while she was not jealous of society women, friends, or good-class governesses, even when they were attractive or pretty.

Her conduct at home became more and more odd, and her threats more dangerous, so that she had to be taken to a sanatorium. (Before doing this I got the patient to consult Professor Freud, who agreed with my diagnosis and approved of psychoanalysis being tried.)

The patient was so remarkably distrustful and perspicacious

---

*See 'The Perfect Servant' in the following section for the first case which deals with the relationship between homosexuality and paranoia. Both cases are taken from *On the Part Played by Homosexuality in the Pathogenesis of Paranoia* originally published in the Jahrbuch der Psychoanalyse, Vol. III, 1912.

that it was not easy to establish a *rapport* with her. I had to take the ground that I was not quite convinced of her husband's innocence and in this way induced the otherwise inaccessible patient to part with the delusional ideas that she had till then kept to herself.

Among these were pronounced delusions of grandeur and of connexion. Between the lines of the local newspaper were innumerable insinuations of her supposed moral depravity; and of her ridiculous position as a betrayed wife; the articles were written by journalists at the orders of her enemies. Personalities of the highest standing (e.g. of the episcopal court) knew of these goings on, and the fact that the royal manoeuvres took place every year just in the neighbourhood of her home was not unconnected with certain secret intentions of her enemies. The enemies turned out in the course of further conversation to be the dismissed servants.

I then gradually learned from her that it was against her will, and only at her parents' wish, especially her father's, that she had looked favourably on her husband's courtship. He seemed to her at the time too common, too coarse. After the marriage, however, she said she got used to him. A curious scene took place in the house after the birth of the first daughter. The husband was supposed to have been dissatisfied that she had not borne a son, and she felt quite conscience-pricked about it also; on this she began to doubt whether she had done right to marry this man. At this time she began to be jealous of an extra servant girl, aged thirteen and said to be very pretty. She was still in bed after the confinement when she summoned the little girl and made her kneel down and swear by her father's life that the master had done nothing to her. This oath calmed her at the time, and she thought she might have made a mistake.

After a son was at last born, she felt she had fulfilled her duty to her husband and was now free. She began to behave discordantly. She became jealous of her husband again, and on the other hand would behave towards men in a remarkable manner.

'Only with the eyes, however,' she said, and if anyone took the hints she gave, she always vigorously rebuffed him.

This 'harmless playfulness', on which her enemies similarly put a false construction, soon disappeared from view, however, behind the jealousy scenes, which went from bad to worse.

In order to make her husband impotent as regards other women, she got him to perform coitus several times every night. Even so, when she left the bedroom for a moment (to attend to bodily needs) she locked the room behind her. She hurried back at once, but if she found any disarrangement of the bedclothes she became suspicious that the discharged cook, who might have got a key made, had been with him in the interval.

The patient, as we see, realized the sexual insatiability that the alcoholic paranoiac mentioned above had only invented and could not carry out. (A woman can, to be sure, increase sexual relations at will, even without real pleasure, much more easily than a man.) The sharp watching of the state of the bedclothes was also repeated here.

The patient's behaviour in the sanatorium was full of contradictions. She coquetted with all the men, but would not let any of them approach her. On the other hand she made close friendships and enmities with all the female inhabitants of the house, and her conversations with me turned for the most part on these. She willingly took the lukewarm baths prescribed for her, but used the opportunity given by the bathing to collect detailed observations on the shapes and figures of the other female patients. She described to me with every sign of disgust and abhorrence the wrinkled abdomen of an elderly patient who was very ill. As she narrated her observations on prettier patients, however, the lascivious expression of her face was unmistakable. One day when she was alone with these younger ones she got up a 'calf exhibition'; she stated that she won the first prize in the competition (narcissism).

I tried with great circumspection, to learn something about the homosexual component of her sexual development by asking her whether, like so many young girls, she had been passionately fond of her girl friends. She divined my intention immediately, however, snubbed me severely, and maintained that I wanted to talk her into all sorts of abominations. I managed to calm her, whereupon she confessed to me under a pledge of secrecy that when she was a child she performed mutual masturbation for years with a little girl, whom she had seduced. (The patient had only sisters, no brothers.) More than this, indications of over-strong sexual fixations to the mother and nurses could be inferred from the patient's communications, which were becoming more and more scanty.

The comparative peacefulness of the patient was for the first time seriously disturbed by her husband's visit, and the delusions of jealousy flared up anew. She accused her husband of having used her absence to do all sorts of disgraceful things, and her suspicion was particularly directed against the aged house porteress, who, as she had heard, had helped in the house-cleaning. In sexual relations she became more insatiable than ever. If her husband refused this, she threatened to kill him, and on one occasion actually threw a knife at him.

The slight traces of transference to the physician, which were present at the beginning, also gave way in these stormy times to a more and more vehement resistance, so that the prospects of the analysis sank to nothing. We found ourselves compelled, therefore, to provide for her in a more distant institution where she could be more strictly watched.

This case also of a delusional jealousy only becomes clear when we assume that it was a question of the projection onto the husband of her pleasure in her own sex. A girl who had grown up in almost exclusively feminine surroundings, who as a child was too strongly attached to the female nurses and servants and in addition to this had for years enjoyed sexual relations with a girl friend of her own age, is suddenly forced into a *marriage de convenance* with a 'coarse man'. She reconciles herself to it, however, and only once shows indignation against an especially crude piece of unkindness on her husband's part, by letting her desires turn towards her childhood ideal (a little servant girl). The attempt fails, she cannot endure the homosexuality any longer, and has to project it onto her husband. That was the first, temporary attack of jealousy. Finally, when she had done her 'duty' and borne her husband the son he demanded, she felt herself free. The homosexuality that had been kept in bounds until then takes stormy possession in a crude erotic way of all the objects that offer no possibility for sublimation (quite young girls, old women and servants), though all this eroticism, with the exception of the cases where she can hide it under the mask of harmless play, is imputed to the husband. In order to support herself in this lie, the patient is compelled to show increased coquetry towards the male sex, to whom she had become pretty indifferent, and indeed to demean herself like a nymphomaniac.

THE MEN

'Better than the love of women. . .'

REPORTED BY LUDWIG EIDELBERG, M.D.

The next hour was to be my first session with Mr. Dorian Germaine, my next patient.* I knew him by reputation. He was a young man in his middle thirties, who came from a very wealthy family. The death of his parents, some years before, had left him with a large inheritance, which he had used to gratify his every wish. He was, I knew, one of America's outstanding painters, whose work had been exhibited in many museums and private galleries. I also knew, from the gossip of art circles, that he was reputed to be a homosexual.

He entered my office, and I found myself shaking hands with a slight, pleasant-looking young man, flat and sibilant. I took particular notice of his attire. It was hard not to do so. He had on a green double-breasted suit which buttoned on the left, or feminine, side, a cerise shirt, a green bow tie, cerise socks, and a bright yellow pocket handkerchief! He was blond, green-eyed, and, as he walked across the room to sit in the chair I indicated, I noticed a certain femininity in his walk and carriage. This is not at all indicative of homosexuality, for there are many normal men who bear themselves somewhat effeminately.

Mr. Germaine stopped at the couch before he reached the chair. I noticed he was looking at the Van Gogh reproductions on the wall.

*Dorian Germaine is a fictional composite portrait drawn from Dr. Eidelberg's practice (Editor's note).

'I see you have a nice taste in paintings,' he said. 'The room of Van Gogh at Arles, the "Cypresses"—very good!' He looked about him at the room. Apparently, what he saw did not displease him, for a certain strained expression left his face. He walked to the chair, sat down, and produced a gold cigarette case. 'Smoke?' he asked, offering it to me. I took the cigarette, and, as we lit up, I felt his eyes upon my face. He studied me intently for a moment, then leaned back in his chair, and said:

'I'm not sure, Doctor, that you're the man I'm looking for!'

I looked at him questioningly. He continued, 'I know how busy you are, and I apologize for taking up your time. I'm afraid that I'm not the kind of patient to whom you're accustomed .... I have, of course, some friends who were analysed, and I've read a few books about Freud. I know what you consider normal, and how you try to help those who've lost their bearings to return to their place in the community. However, the trouble with me is that I'm not a joiner—and I don't intend to become one! *Odi profanum vulgus*—I like being different . . .'

'I see,' I nodded, 'but there must be something about yourself which you don't like, or you wouldn't be here.'

He settled himself more deeply in his chair, and replied, 'Oh, certainly! There *is* something I dislike, although you'll probably consider it a small detail—of secondary importance.' He toyed with the gold identification bracelet on his left wrist.

'Something connected with your sex life?' I asked.

He looked annoyed. 'Why use such a vulgar phrase? Why not call it my "love life"? Or do you consider love passé—a romantic dream of adolescence? Does the great professor recognize only glands and their discharge?'

I smiled. 'I hate to disappoint you by saying that the discovery of glands and their functions didn't change love into a hackneyed matter. At least, not for me . . . However, I feel that you're not concerned with my views about love, but would prefer—shall we say?—some help for *your* glands.'

He sat up. His expressive eyebrows fluttered. 'You've hit the bull's eye, Doctor,' he said. 'My love life is perfect. I love, and am loved, as few men are. However, there is a certain element of frustration—or shall I say, disappointment—in the execution of my love which, by its short duration, interferes with my happiness. If you could help me to eliminate this little weakness of mine, I'd be very grateful.'

I looked at him closely. His confession was one which no man likes to make. Premature ejaculation is not a symptom to boast about. But Mr. Germaine seemed quite at ease. He puffed at his cigarette and watched the smoke's lazy ascent to the ceiling.

'If you want my help, you'll have to be more precise,' I told him.

He confessed that his easy air was only a pretence with, 'I know that I'll have to, but it's rather painful and humiliating. But there's no reason to beat around the bush. After all, you *are* a doctor, aren't you? So I might as well get it over with . . .

'I assume that my name is familiar to you. I was born in Virginia, May 1, 1911. You know that I'm a well-known painter. Perhaps you've seen some of my paintings?' I nodded. He looked pleased and continued, 'My last painting shows a young and very pretty boy looking into a mirror, from which he sees his image emerging somewhat changed and somewhat more feminine. Well, this pretty boy loves me.'

I nodded, and put out my cigarette. 'Perhaps you ought to tell me something more about him,' I suggested.

He shrugged. 'He himself is of as little importance as the original yellow chair that Van Gogh used as his model.' He gestured at the picture on the wall. 'As Altenberg says,

"*Du bist nur das, was er von Dir singt,*
Und singt er nicht, so bist Du nie gewesen . . ."

(You are only what he sings about you,
And if he had never sung, you would never be . . .)

'For your records, in which, I presume, figures are more important than ideas, you may note that he is eighteen, looks twenty, and acts like a six-year-old. This pretty little boy loves me, but my ability to express my own love—*hlas!*—is impaired. I'd like to remove this ridiculous weakness, that's all . . . . I know that you analysts don't consider my love as love, but as a perversion—and that you'll probably advise me to do something about it. It's ridiculous, of course, to treat my love, just because its object happens to be a boy instead of a girl, as if it were an illness! What's so marvellous about girls?' He shuddered with fastidious repulsion, and adjusted the wings of his bow tie, although it was a miracle of neatness. 'Why should an intelligent man waste his time, his ideas, and his love on those feeble-minded creatures? How can women be expected to understand a man, since they're so different, so alien to him? And how can a man love creatures so dissimilar, or expect to be loved by them? All the things that seem so dear to me—honour, dignity, truth, courage, and loyalty—have no meaning to women. So what's wrong with my being happy in my own way?'

Having delivered himself of this oration, he sat back with a satisfied expression on his face, an expression which changed suddenly to one of pain. He hastily removed his hand from the ash tray beside him, and licked the burnt spot on his fingertip, where a glowing cigarette butt had touched him. He looked at me as I asked, 'But are you happy?'

'Certainly!' he replied, 'I am as happy, and as unhappy, as the usual human being . . . . If Barry—oh, that's his name—'he explained, '—if Barry's with me, I'm happy. Without him, I suffer. *Voila!* But I'm *not* unhappy because I'm in love with a boy instead of a girl!'

'Why do you assume that I'm against your choice of a love object?' I asked.

He shrugged again. 'Oh, I've read some analytical books, and I know that you would call me a pervert.'

105

'Never mind the name. That's purely a problem in terminology. As a doctor, I'm only interested in helping the patient.'

'Does that mean that you can cure me of my sexual weakness without interfering with my ideas about life and love?'

'It means that I would try to help you to the extent you *want* to be helped. But I can't guarantee that analysis won't interfere with your other problems.'

He got up from his chair and paced around the room. He paused, and looked at a picture on the wall. Finally, his back still toward me, he said, 'That sounds tricky to me.'

'It's really an honest warning. When we start an analysis, we can't predict how much the patient will decide to change.'

He returned to his chair, but didn't sit down. 'But I know what it is I want to change,' he said. 'I'm sure nothing you could tell me, nothing you could discover in my dreams, would influence me in any other way.'

'Oh?'

'But I know that I may be forced to change my mind against my will. I know that, in analysis, we become dependent upon the analyst.'

'Then how do you expect me to change you?' I asked.

'Well, I'm not so naïve as to expect you to do it merely by ordering me to change. I told you I've read some books on analysis. Now, the case history of Zeltner, whom you described in your paper on perversion, made a deep impression on me. Let's see. . . . As I recall, when he came to see you, he had merely fantasies about pretty boys, without daring to approach them. But, as he progressed in his treatment, he actually embarked on his first affair with a man. That shows how smart you were. For while he enjoyed this affair, he continued to come to you. He kept up the analytical treatment, reporting his dreams, saying what went through his mind, and so forth . . . .' I could see that Mr. Germaine was becoming more agitated, and waited for the reason to assert itself.

'He kept on with his analysis because you were helping him

with some other difficulties—I think it was with a phobia of
some kind—and he was confident that you wouldn't interfere
with his new love life. Then you surprised him! First you showed
him that the people he was afraid of represented his father, and
then you shocked him by proving that his boy friend really
represented his mother! He thought that he had succeeded in
freeing himself from females, only to find that the man he loved
was not a man at all!'

He began his pacing once more. Again, he stopped before the
Van Goghs, looked at them intently, then wheeled on me.

'Since reading that case, I've lost my self-confidence. I've
begun to doubt . . . Can it be that Barry, my pretty little curly-
head, isn't a boy, but a girl—to me? That, in spite of the anatomical facts which I see and enjoy, it's—well, shall I say "his soul,"
because it's not his mind—which makes me crazy about him?'
He walked over to confront me. 'Do you know why you love
your wife? Do you know the real reason why you spend half of
your life and three-quarters of your income on that gorgeous
bitch I met in the elevator? I hope you don't—or you may find
that she isn't a woman at all, but your father, or your grand-
father!'

I looked interested, but something must have made him feel
foolish, for he turned away, and returned to his chair. He sat
there, looking out of the window at the gently waving treetops
in the park below. Finally, he continued, 'I'm sure you don't
bother about *your Unconscious*. You couldn't afford to, not at
your fees—not with the kind of hats your wife wears!'

I waited, watching him.

He turned to face me. 'What did you mean, when you said
that Zeltner's boy friend represented his mother?'

'I meant that the feeling he had for his friend was, in part,
the emotion he felt for his mother when he was a child.'

'How were you able to discover that?'

'Well, since you've read my paper, you should be able to
answer your own question. It was possible to see what Zeltner

wanted from his friend through his own dreams and associations. The desires expressed in them not only reminded him of the caresses he had received in childhood from his mother, but were actual repetitions of his early experiences. However, there was one important difference. In his relationship with his friend, Zeltner not only played the role of the infant who is nursed by his mother, but also cast himself in the part of his mother, nursing a child—his friend. He not only insisted on being loved as an infant is, but also on the fulfilment of all his wishes at one and the same time.'

He nodded. '—"intolerant of any delay, and playing both roles simultaneously".... Yes, your description—or shall I say, your analysis?—was correct. I know from my own experience ... But what's wrong with my love, as long as it makes me happy?'

'As long as your way makes you happy, there's no reason for me to interfere. But the fact that you're here today, shows that it doesn't.'

'Well, a normal man isn't always happy!' I took note of his use of the word, 'normal.' 'Disappointments can't be avoided. You certainly can't assert that being in love with a woman, instead of a pretty boy, is a guarantee against conflicts, unhappiness, and misery!'

'There are different kinds of women,' I said.

He sneered. 'But your own, I suppose, is perfect! She loves only you. She has only one wish—to make you happy!'

I could see that he loved to argue, and to display the peculiar type of malevolence characteristic of some homosexuals.

'I suppose she's as glamorous, and as seductive, as she was the first day you met her! I suppose you never get irritated because this brainless creature is unable to discuss a problem intelligently! I suppose you've never suffered from the agonies of jealousy, because she is attracted to some feeble-minded, good-looking moron, whom she'll desert as soon as a man with more money makes her an offer!'

I waited a few moments to give him time to simmer down. 'So your pretty boy is really a bad boy, isn't he?' I said.

He looked miserably at his hands, which he had clasped together tightly in his lap. 'He's neither good, nor bad. He can't be, because he's unable to differentiate between right and wrong. He's a child . . . He takes what he likes, and what's worse, he doesn't mind if I do the same. . . .'

'But you mind, don't you?'

He lifted his left hand, and again stared at his gold identification bracelet. 'I do,' he said.

'I suppose it is difficult for an adult to play the role of an infant.'

'It's humiliating, degrading! Can't you teach me to take it as lightly as Barry does?'

'I'm afraid that I can't. Because I find your reaction to your friend's behaviour justified.'

His poses were forgotten. 'Then what shall I do?'

'Mm—perhaps take another friend.'

'But they're all like that. You don't know them, or you wouldn't suggest . . . After all, I've had some experience with them, with their instability, their fluctuations of affection, their promiscuity...' He sighed. '. . . But that's why they attract me.'

'Exactly. Now, in analysis you may discover that this attraction is based on some sort of misunderstanding, that you stick to this attraction because you're afraid of another, and that, while this fear was justified when you were a child, it's senseless at the present time. As a result, you may decide to act as an adult, to cease repeating your childhood experiences, and to accept the fact that you're no longer an infant. You may even fall in love with a mature woman. You see, that's why I can't guarantee that analysis will affect only your sexual weakness. It may change your whole personality.'

'But what about my painting? Will I stop painting when I discover what art means to me—unconsciously? "*Noli tangere circulos meos*" . . . . You may be an excellent analyst, and an expert in cleaning the sewers of the soul; you may know, exactly to the minute, how long love should last, and how much a man should pay to make it last longer; but, to quote my friend Oscar Wilde, "You know the price of everything, and the value of nothing. . . ." '

I started to say, 'But——' He interrupted me.

'Don't be offended. I really like you, as I like all people who live by their wits. You're not like those foreign-born analysts who explain all things by sex, and who can't understand that there are two worlds: one of hunger and hatred, in which everyone wants to have what he sees, and to destroy whatever offers resistance; and the second, in which frustration becomes a pleasure, and defeat turns into victory. The latter is that world in which we stop living as animals, and become demi-gods whose lives are above the ridiculous limitations of reality. . .

'I assume that, in spite of being a psychoanalyst, you don't share in the materialistic outlook of Freud, and don't try to reduce the infinite variations of our thoughts to symbolic representations of the genitals . . . . Nobody denies the existence of the sex drive, but for God's sake, let's admit that there are additional drives, desires, and tendencies!'

'I don't know why you accuse Freud of being a kind of sex maniac,' I said. 'Even if you haven't bothered to read his books, you must admit that his standing, as well as the results he achieved, should show that he wasn't interested solely in sexual intercourse!'

'But doesn't Freud preach that all neuroses are caused by the lack of sexual intercourse? Isn't psychoanalysis based on the dogma that the human being is impelled by the desire to copulate?'

I was a little sharp with him as I replied, 'If that's the impression you got from reading psychoanalytic books, then there must be something wrong with your ability to read! First of all, Freud never preached. Psychoanalysis is not a religion. On the basis of facts he collected in treating neurotics, Freud developed a theory in which two instincts were suggested: the sexual, and the narcissistic. After more years of work, he changed that theory into one in which he defined the two main instincts as sexual and aggressive. But he never insisted that his theory was the only possible approach to the problem of the instinctual drives. He even referred to his theory as a sort of "mythology," and always stressed the difference between the actual facts he collected, and the assumptions he made. The theory of instincts, far from being a psychoanalytic credo, is a sort of filing system for the collection and organization of the material we get from the patients' Unconscious.'

I spoke vehemently. It irked me that so intelligent a man as Mr. Germaine should be influenced by the purveyors of sensationalism and sex.

Mr. Germaine was apologetic. 'You may be right, Doctor. You see, I'm not a scientist. I'm an artist and, I hope, a great one. When I read Freud, I wasn't interested in ascertaining whether his books contained truths, but wanted to obtain a certain aesthetic pleasure from them—and I did receive that, to a degree. Many of his ideas appeared highly stimulating, while others sounded exaggerated. But as an artist, I know that, in creating new things, we all exaggerate. Without the feeling that what we've produced is the most important thing in the world, we would never disturb the peace of our fellow men. You see, I know that we all prefer to be unperturbed; we all like the *status quo*. But some of us are forced at times, to interrupt our monotonous lives. Something penetrates our defences, explodes in our hearts and our brains, and we have to rise and give testimony as to what's happened. We discover new continents, tame Nature, and change Man's thoughts about himself and his universe. . . They jail us, burn us, crucify us—but we have no choice. . .

'You see, you shouldn't compare me to your other patients. You would admire me too much, and, after all, I'm not here to be admired. I want your help. I want it, that is, on the condition that you won't interfere with my love life, or try to destroy my work. You must understand that it would make me miserable to be deprived of my ability to paint and to love, just to be cured of a sexual weakness. I'm not the ordinary patient . . . You'll have to treat me in a different way. Compare me with everyone, mix me with no one. . . .'

'Now I'm confused,' I said, with a slight smile. 'Am I supposed to compare you with other patients to see how different you are, or shall I abstain from comparisons, lest I admire you too much?'

He grinned back, and gave me a mocking salute, the kind a fencer gives his opponent. '*Touché!*' he cried. 'Next time, I must not forget my riposte! I have an idea . . . . Would you like to dine at my club with me, and meet my pretty Barry?'

'I'm sorry. We don't meet our patients socially, and you may become one. You see, it would interfere with your treatment.'

'Now, really! I must salute you! In order to help me—that is, if I decide to start my treatment—you're willing to give up an opportunity to meet me socially!'

I was curious. How much of this bravado was real? 'And how do you know that my refusal is a sacrifice?' I asked. 'How do you know that I would like to dine with you, even if you weren't my patient?'

He covered his face with his slender hands. 'Why, this is preposterous! Is it possible that you don't like me? That you even despise me? But why?'

I leaned back in my chair, and folded my hands in my lap. 'Why should a lack of interest in dining with you indicate that I despise you?'

He paid no attention to my last statement. His hands still over his face, he said, softly, 'Oh, this is terrible! You should never have said that! I'll never get over it!'

'Well, if you want to be analysed, many such blows will have to fall. To be cured, you must be able to give up the idea that everyone despises you, and that the lack of admiration means disaster.' He looked up from his hands, and I noted that he really seemed to feel my 'rejection' keenly. 'Now don't be ridiculous,' I said. 'You're not an infant, and you don't need exaggerated care and attention. You're strong enough to take rejections, indifference, even——' He interrupted me.

'But you don't understand! An artist who gives so much to others, must get something in exchange, or he freezes to death! After creating, I feel empty, and I need love!'

'We all need love,' I said, dryly. 'However, you may be right. A creative man may need more than others. But don't you get enough love from Barry?'

'I've never had enough. The more I get, the more I want. Even when I'm with him, when I'm happy, I'm not fully satisfied. When I hear my doorbell ring at last, and the tension inside me, which mounts until it hurts like hell while I wait for him, begins to disappear, even then . . . When I open the door, and see it's Barry, I begin to breathe more freely, and life magically becomes a joy! I feel happy, satisfied, in the first few moments of reunion. But those minutes pass, and his words, his caresses, the way he looks at me and the way I look at him— all these, which helped me to release my tension, now begin to produce a new desire. My lips, which quenched my thirst when I kissed him, grow fiery, and the fire spreads. . . . While Barry—'

'—seems to be different?'

'Yes. You see, when I love someone, just the fact that I love him makes him the most desirable, the most beautiful person in the world! Barry, on the other hand, feels that anyone who loves him must be inferior. Knowing how worthless he is, he has contempt for anyone who admires him.'

'Then your relationship isn't so happy, after all.'

'It isn't. Yesterday, I spent three boring hours at a cocktail party, forced to answer all sorts of silly questions. And why was I there? Because I hoped that he would show up, and I'd be able to talk to him, light his cigarette, touch his hand . . . ' His mouth twitched. 'But he didn't show up. . . .'

'Perhaps he doesn't love you.'

Mr. Germaine looked at his nicely polished nails. 'Oh, he does. These brainless brats all fall for brains. He loves me in the way an infant loves its wet-nurse. He loves me because he needs my love, my protection: when I paint him, he becomes beautiful; talking to me, he feels witty; going out with me, he is rich. Without me, he is no longer distinctive. He returns to the anonymous mass. So he loves me—and I think that's why he hates me. Why—he tries continuously to hurt, humiliate, and escape me!'

'Why don't you let him go?'

'It's not as simple as that. By seeing him, I don't have to think about him. You see, I need him, too! Once, someone told me that a German poet, whose name I forgot, used to keep rotten apples in his desk drawer so that their smell would stimulate him and help him to write. Barry does the same to me—this creature without a brain! This incarnation of beauty, without memory, without conscience, completely inhuman, half-animal and half-god, is my twin brother! We understand each other, and agree on practically everything—with the exception of those few points on which he is wrong. Without him, I'm bored: I have no ideas, and can't paint. I need my rotten apples, too. I need Barry, and I need the pain, the frustration he brings me. Don't misunderstand me. I'm not a masochist. I don't like to suffer, but I can't create without it. My brain is—like the womb of a woman. I hate to say it, but unfortunately, it's true. My ideas are like ovula. They must be fertilized to multiply, develop, and grow. I'm like the oyster which, to produce a pearl, must be irritated by a grain of sand. "*Margaritas ante porcos iactamus*"— I throw pearls before swine. . . .'

'Ah, you will never understand what I mean! But if Barry, who can't distinguish a Rubens from a Rembrandt, can sometimes guess what my paintings try to say, then, by a similar miracle, you too may get what I feel.' He drew a deep breath, and looked at me anxiously.

I said, 'I'm glad you've given me a sporting chance. In reply,

I'd like to assure you about your work. As a rule, I don't reassure my patients. Rather, I stimulate their self-criticism, and increase their worries. But in this case, I don't mind telling you that my experience, and that of my colleagues, indicated that analysis does not destroy artistic ability—even in the case of geniuses. To be sure, the neurotic defence mechanism and the artistic creation are based on similar drives. But if an individual has the ability to produce a work of art, he usually avoids becoming neurotic. We don't touch that part of your Unconscious which forces you to create. Therefore, I think I can promise that, should you start your analysis and be cured, your work won't suffer. In fact, it might even improve.'

'But what about Barry? As I've explained, I'm unable to work without him.'

'You worked before you met him, didn't you?'

'Yes. But there was always some Barry on hand.'

'Was it always a boy?'

'Always. Girls just don't appeal to me.'

'Did you ever try to discover why?'

'Yes, I did. First of all, women are frigid. That is practically all of them.'

'*Practically* all? Then you admit there are some exceptions?'

He pursed his full lips. 'Mmmm. . . I just thought of Nina.'

'Nina? Who's she?'

He waved his hand languidly. 'Oh, a nice girl who's in love with me.'

'Oh? Who's not frigid?'

'Neither frigid, nor a nymphomaniac, nor inhibited, nor vulgar. Just a nice, normal girl. Well. . . .not quite normal, or she wouldn't have fallen in love with me.'

'Does she know. . . .?'

He sighed. 'Yes, she does. A few days ago, we had it out. I'd begun to notice that she was getting a little too interested in my paintings . . . You see, she's a pupil of mine . . . and I began to feel embarrassed.' He stared down at his fingernails.

'Perhaps—even annoyed?'

'No, not annoyed. Just embarrassed. A little scared, perhaps. She's just a kid. She wouldn't rape me, but I didn't want her to waste her time. After all, there are plenty of normal boys around just waiting for her. So a few days ago, while we were sitting in a tiny French restaurant sipping vermouth, I asked her rather bluntly what she expected of me. Her answer was just as blunt —"You." Providentially, some friends arrived just then, and we interrupted our conversation. The next day, I received an enormous bunch of mimosa, with a letter—a nice one. She writes well. She ought to be a writer, not a painter; there's no money in painting. . . .' He looked up at me and, putting his hand into the inside pocket of his smart jacket, he said. 'I have the letter here. Would you like me to read it to you?'

I nodded. He pulled out a plain white envelope, removed the letter, unfolded it, and read—' "I want you. As simple as that. It's not too much, because less wouldn't satisfy me. And it's not too little, because you're so much to me. . ." ' He looked down at the letter after he finished reading it, and smiled. He folded it carefully, and replaced it in its envelope. Gently, tenderly, he put it back into his pocket.

I asked, 'And what was your response?'

'Oh, I felt flattered, of course. Who wouldn't? Well perhaps you wouldn't, because all your patients are in love with you. At least, so they tell me . . . But my patie—my pupils, have better taste, on the whole. They fall in love with each other.' He was silent for a while, then said, smiling to take the sting out of the words, 'Really, I wonder what your patients see in you. I'm not impressed. But maybe it's just because you're not my type.'

I, too, smiled. 'You see, the patients begin to fall in love with me only after they've spent a few weeks on the couch.'

'Oh? The couch has some magic power?'

'No. But when they lie on it, they can't see me.'

He laughed. 'Good. . . .rather good! I really should keep a

score of your sallies. . . . But, to return to Nina, if I may—I
wish you'd advise me how to handle her. You see, I do like her.
I think I like her a great deal. But she doesn't induce the flaming
response, the heart palpitations, the drying lips, that I get just by
thinking of Barry!'

'What kind of emotion does Nina produce in you?'

He shrugged. 'Oh, I feel pleasantly relaxed.'

'But sometimes you do get embarrassed?'

'Only if sex is mentioned.'

'Does she know about Barry?'

'Yes.'

'Is she jealous?'

'Curiously enough, she isn't.'

'How come?'

'She's convinced that I'll finally drop him.'

'—and fall for her?'

'Exactly. When I told her to look for someone else because I
couldn't love her, she just laughed, and said, "But you do love
me. . . . You're just not aware of it!" '

I raised my eyebrows. 'Quite a smart girl!'

'I knew she—you—would like her. . . .' He stared out of the
window, turned back to look at me, stroked the arm of his
chair, and was silent. Then he jingled his bracelet, and, looking
up at me, blurted, 'I might as well admit it. She's really responsible for my being here. She said, "I think you love me, but
you're afraid to recognize it. Why don't you go to a psychoanalyst, and find out for sure? I know a nice one——" She meant
you.'

'I see. Are you disappointed?'

'I really don't know. You don't seem so bad. You're not like
the stuffy analysts one sees in the cartoons. But that's beside the
point. . . . What do you think I should do about Nina?'

'Mmmm. . . . She seems to be very alert.'

'Do you think that she could be right?'

'Well, you did what she wanted, and you—'

He interrupted again. 'Only to prove how wrong she was! At first, I refused to come to see you, but she said that my refusal was a sign of fear. That sounded like some sort of double talk to me, but after all, I could spare a few hours, and I had a few questions I wanted answered, so I came to the oracle. Now, what's your advice?'

'You'd better stay away from both Nina and myself, or you may discover that she's right. You may find out, that your lack of interest in women isn't genuine!'

He grew pale, and glared at me. 'Do you think that I'm a liar? That my love for Barry is just an act?' Getting up from his chair, he strode restlessly about the room.

'By no means. But your embarrassment whenever Nina mentioned sex, may not be as simple as it appears. . . .It may well be that you're concerned not only with *her* falling in love, and its resulting disappointments. . . .Obviously, her emotion represents no danger, or, as you aptly put it, she wouldn't rape you. But your own emotions may overpower your defences, and force you to admit that you're not as—shall we say "different"?—as you would like to be.'

He returned, and stood over my chair as he fumed, 'That's nonsense! Are you suggesting that I'm afraid of my emotions? I who regard myself as the mere executor of my desires, who preach that an artist should disregard all inhibitions, in order to express the eternal truths?' His soft voice began to tremble, and he dropped his cigarette case as he brought it out of his pocket. He retrieved it, and, glaring at me, picked up a folder of matches from my desk. Tearing a match from the folder, he put it into his mouth, instead of a cigarette. His recognition of his error made him feel ridiculous, and, as he tried to correct it, he dropped the match.

I came to the rescue, and said, as I lit another match and held it to the cigarette in his shaking hand, 'Now, calm down. There's no use getting excited—at least, as long as you're not on the analytical couch. Scientific problems aren't solved that way.

You asked my advice, and I expressed my opinion. I didn't say that you *did* love Nina and repressed your love for her. I merely said that I have a suspicion that such is the case. If you're interested in proving that I'm wrong, I'm ready to help you.'

He sat down. 'How long would that take? he asked.

'Oh, a few weeks, or a few months.'

'Just to unearth what I feel? And how long would it take to change me, just in case you're. . . .?'

'A year, perhaps two—perhaps more.'

He was shocked. 'But that's far too long!'

'Didn't Nina warn you?'

'She did, but I couldn't believe it! She said she would wait for me, even if the cure took five years.'

I smiled. 'That sounds like her five-year plan.'

'To me, it sounds like a five-year sentence to jail! Damn that girl!'

'At least, she knows what she wants.'

He grimaced. 'That's why I prefer Barry. He's more flexible.'

'And less serious.'

'You doubt that I love him?'

'No. I'm convinced that Barry sometimes makes you happy, then again makes you miserable, and I certainly won't deny that he may have stimulated your work. But the emotions you have for him—are they the only ones you can produce? Or do you use these emotions to repress others—like the man who hires one gangster to protect him against another?'

'Thanks for the flattering simile,' he scowled. 'Why don't you stick to your biology, and speak of toxins and antitoxins?'

'I'm sorry. Anyhow, you get what I mean. The fact that you're so tolerant with your feelings, so interested in their expression and satisfaction, doesn't mean that you're not using them to keep other emotions behind an iron curtain of repression.'

'Why should I be afraid of them?'

'Because they caused you so much trouble when you were an infant, and because you believe that they're as powerful now as they were at that time. Your love for Barry is like his love for you—love *and* hatred!'

He grew almost pugnacious. 'Who says so?'

'You did. You told me that Barry continuously tried to hurt and humiliate you. You paid him back by calling him a "creature without memory and conscience, a brainless brat—" '

'But is it possible to love without hating? Don't you hate the person who rejects and frustrates you?'

I leaned back in my chair and drew a deep breath. 'Your hate is not the result of your being in love, but of your choice of Barry as its object.'

'You mean—if Barry were someone else, I'd be able to love without frustration, and without hate?'

I nodded. He fidgeted in his seat, and exclaimed, 'You may be right. But if Barry would love me as I want him to, I'd never paint. Since he doesn't, I want the whole world to give me that love.'

'Perhaps you wouldn't paint, but you'd be a happier man.'

He stared out over the park. 'I don't want to be happy,' he said. 'Not at that price. No real artist would sell his work for a cheap romance. You'll never understand me. . . . To me, painting is more important than happiness, than life!'

'Some artists', I reminded him, 'are able to love *and* to paint.'

He turned away from the window, and looked directly at me. 'I doubt it,' he said. 'Most of them are like me—more interested in love, than in the boys they love.'

'I know many artists who prefer girls. In fact, I understand that most of them do.'

'Let's not quarrel about it,' he said wearily. 'I'm prepared to concede that a few do. But their love for women is no different from my love for Barry. They too "love what they hate, and hate what they love. . . ." I think I am quoting correctly from your paper, "A Contribution to the Study of Art" '.

'You are. But you forget to add that I point out something else. There are artists who have quite normal relationships with their love-objects,'

'What do you mean by—"normal"?'

' "A relationship in which the object does not unconsciously represent the father or mother, and is not regarded as a part of one's body, but as another human being..." That's a quotation, and I'm not good at quotations, but you'll find it in the paper you mentioned, if you're interested,' I looked at the clock on my desk. 'We have no more time for this kind of discussion ... Mr. Germaine, although I'm no artist myself, I'm aware of the difference between your approach to reality, and my own. But you aren't the only painter in the world, as I'm not the only scientist. In addition to your work, you're entitled to a normal life. The happiness of a normal life is certainly not reserved solely for the uncreative masses. We may both spend a few happy hours looking at that yellow chair of Van Gogh's ...' I waved my hand at the picture, '... but we don't have to try to sit on it. I prefer something more comfortable.'

'Well, I don't. At least, I think I don't. But you're a dangerous man, Doctor. A few more hours with you, and I'd fail to differentiate between right and wrong. I'd begin to doubt—am I a coward or a hero? ... You're like a married woman, who can make a genius feel like a heel!'

'Some married women make a heel feel like a genius.'

'That may be your own experience,' he said, 'but I don't care for the type. If there were only a woman who could make a genius feel like one ... I'm afraid that, if there *is* such a woman, she's already somebody's wife. You assume, don't you, that I'm talking about your own wife now. That's the trouble with you. You take everything so personally, and you behave as if the patient were interested solely in you!'

He got up from his chair, and moved to the door. I looked at the clock, saw the hour was almost up, and accompanied him. At the door, he turned to face me, and a glint of—what was it—anger, self-pity, desire?—was in his eye, as he said, 'No, I'm afraid that you're not the man I'm looking for, Doctor. You may succeed in curing my sexual weakness, but your price is too high.' I looked at him, and he added, hastily, 'At least, I'm so busy right now, that I couldn't spare five hours a week, even if I wanted to. Perhaps I'll be able to, when I finish my present work.'

'Perhaps . . . ' I said quietly.

He grew quite gay and charming. It may have been the prospect of imminent release from this place where embarrassing truths were the topics of conversation, where candour made ideas too uncomfortable

'But really, Doctor—I'd like to paint you. In a way, I do find you stimulating. Or would painting you be considered a sacrilege? After all, the Commandments say, "Thou shalt not make a picture of thy Lord!" Would you care to sit for me?'

Gravely, I replied, 'I'd like to, very much—but I'm so busy right now, that I can't. Perhaps some other day . . .'

The doorknob turned under his hand, and the door opened.

'Thank you so much, Doctor,' said Mr. Germaine. 'Thank you for your kindness. But I can't give Barry up. I like pretty boys, and I don't want to change. I hope you have no hard feelings because I don't . . .'

'Of course not,' I said, and we shook hands. The door closed behind him, and I stood staring at it for a long moment. Then I sighed. I hoped he would be back . . .

Autobiography of a homosexual writer

ANONYMOUS*

FROM my earliest childhood there was something girlish in my whole nature, both outwardly and (more especially) inwardly. I was very quiet, obedient, diligent, sensitive to praise and blame, rather bright. I associated chiefly with adults, and was generally beloved. Sexual activity began unusually early.

At school, where I always distinguished myself by my application and success, I sometimes enjoyed mutual 'feeling' with several other boys. From which side I inherited the unusual intensity of the sexual impulse I do not know, but I remember that when I was about twelve years old I already suffered a good deal from sexual desire, and that it came to me as a solution of a great difficulty when a friend instructed me in the practice of masturbation. It is remarkable that for some time afterwards there was evacuation of semen. When this first appeared I was very much alarmed and disquieted, but I soon became accustomed to it, and this the more readily because I had no doubt whatever that all men regularly indulged in the same pleasure. This 'Paradisaical' state did not, however, last for long; and after a time, when I recognized the unnatural and dangerous nature of my conduct, I conducted a severe and unsuccessful contest against my desires. In my life generally I had a good deal to bear, and I can say that I have hardly preserved a single really pleasant memory of my past; and yet I could look back to this past with a certain pride and satisfaction if it had not been that the sexual side of my life has left such gloomy shadows in my soul.

I remember that from very early days my eyes involuntarily turned with longing towards elderly vigorous men, but I did not pay much attention to this fact. I believed that I only practised

*From *The Sexual Life of Our Time*, by Ivan Bloch, M.D.

masturbation (the influence of which I doubtless exaggerate in memory to some extent) because it was not possible for me to have sexual intercourse with women. I was accustomed some-times to have friendly association with young girls, who appeared to be extremely attracted towards me. I always took care, how-ever, that such love tendencies were nipped in the bud, because I felt that it was impossible for me to go any further with them. Ultimately I determined to seek salvation in intercourse with prostitutes, although they were disagreeable to my aesthetic and moral feelings: but I got no help here: either I was unable to complete the normal sexual act, or in other cases it was com-pleted without any particular pleasure, and I was always consumed with anxiety with respect to infection. I had, indeed, often the opportunity of forming an 'intimacy' with a woman, but I did not do it, and always supposed that my failure to do so depended upon my ridiculous bashfulness and upon the excessive sensitiveness of my conscience. But though there is some truth in both of these suggestions, I have not taken into account the principal grounds—namely, that I am congenitally homosexual, and that I feel no physical attraction, or almost none, towards the other sex. This suffices to explain the fact (which can be explained in no other way) that when masturbating I almost always represented in imagination handsome elderly men. In my lascivious dreams, also, such men play the principal role.

These longings were so powerful that it was impossible that I should not soon have my attention directed to them: but as I could not understand them and would not take the matter seriously (I knew, indeed, that man *must* feel drawn towards woman, and not towards man), I continued unceasingly and despairingly to fight against these fixed ideas, while at the same time with varying success I endeavoured to cure myself of mastur-bation; for in the first place it now gave very little satisfaction, and in the second place it destroyed my hopes of eventually procreating healthy children. I had almost come to believe myself no longer competent for the sexual life when I noticed one day that the view of a male organ set my blood flowing fiercely. I then remembered that this had sometimes happened before, although to a less marked extent. I was now compelled to recognize that I was not the same as everyone else. This fact, which I had before suspected, and of which I now became more and more firmly convinced, reduced me to despair, which was all the greater because in other ways I felt extremely unhappy, and because I did not dare to speak of it to any human being. Sometimes I still thought that there must be some 'misunderstanding,' and that there must be some salvation for me. Then it happened that a simple girl fell in love with me, and I went so far as to enter into an intimacy with her, although I openly assured her that as far as I was concerned it was simply a matter of physical enjoyment, and that I could not in any way make myself responsible for her future. During this intimacy, which lasted several months, I sometimes overcame my enduring inclinations towards men, but completely to suppress them was impossible.

My association with the girl was still continuing, when one day in a public lavatory I saw an elderly gentleman whose appearance greatly pleased me. He looked at me tentatively. Cautiously he leaned over, in order to look at my organ; he gradually drew near to me, moved his shaking hand and stroked it. I was so much surprised and alarmed that I ran away, and avoided for some time afterwards passing by the same place. All the stronger, however, was the impulse to find this remarkable man once more, and this was not at all difficult. What an enigma such a man seemed to me! How could it happen that he dared to do that of which I had always been able only to think, to dream, with heart-quaking and horror? Could there, perhaps, be another man like this—perhaps several such exceptional beings? A short period convinced me that I was not quite alone in my way of feeling; but this was a weak consolation. Rather, since that time—that is to say, during the last five years—my inward battle has become more unbearable, for earlier my only battle was to reject homosexual ideas, and to overcome the habit of solitary self-abuse. Now sometimes I practise mutual onanism (to me the proper 'natural' mode of sexual gratification), and yet I cannot forgive myself for doing it because it is effected in so unaesthetic a manner, and is associated with such dangers. Notwithstanding all my endeavours, however, I have never been able to resist the temptation for a long time together; and thus I am hunted always by my impulse as by a wild animal, and can nowhere and in nothing find repose and forgetfulness. I have frequently changed my place of residence, but I always before long form new 'relationships.'

The tortures which I suffer in consequence of the incomparable power of the impulse are greater than I can possibly express in words. I can only wonder that I did not lose my reason, and that in the eyes of my friends and acquaintances I am now, as before, 'the most normal of all human beings'. In the senseless and utterly unsuccessful contest with an impulse which, as far as I am concerned, is wholly, or almost wholly, congenital, I have lost the best of my powers, although I have long recognized the fact that this impulse in and by itself is neither morbid nor sinful, for a divergence from the norm is not a disease, and the gratification of a natural impulse, which in no respect and for no human being leads to evil consequences, cannot be regarded as sinful. Why, then, must I continue to strive against this impulse like a madman? Because it is very generally misunderstood, so unpardonably condemned. What help is it that I am now surrounded by love and respect? I know that so many would turn away from me with horror if they were to learn my sexual constitution, although it is a matter which does not concern them at all. Scorn and contempt would then be my lot. I should be regarded by the majority of human beings as a libertine; whereas I feel and know that, notwithstanding all the sensuality of my nature, I have been created for some other purpose than simply to follow my lustful desire. Who will believe that I suffer in the struggle with myself? Who will have compassion upon me? This idea is intolerable. I am condemned to eternal solitude. I have not the moral right to found a home, to embrace a child who would give me the name of 'father.' Is not this punishment sufficiently severe for God knows what sins? Why, in addition, should I be a pariah, an outcast from society?

Owing to the opinion of society regarding the homosexual— an opinion based upon ignorance, stupidity, and ill-nature— society drives these unhappy beings to death (or to a marriage which in their case is criminal), and then triumphantly exclaims: 'Look what degenerate beings they are!' No, they are not degenerates, those whose lives you have made unbearable; they are for the most part spiritually and morally very healthy human beings. I will speak of myself. Why do I long for death? Certainly not because I am mentally abnormal. I am no morbid pessimist, and I know well enough that life can be very beautiful. But, unfortunately, it cannot be so for me; for my life is a hell; I am intolerably weary of my internal conflict; it has become horribly difficult to me to play the hypocrite, to pretend continually to be a happy man rejoicing in life; I am bending beneath the burden of my heavy iron mask. Recently I had myself hypnotized, in order to have my thoughts turned away as far as possible from sexual matters. My hypnotist said to me: 'You see, you will be at rest now,' and involuntarily in sleep I had to swallow these words, 'Be at rest'! Good God, is that possible? Does the 'normal' man know how this word sounds in our ears? Who will understand my intolerable pain? Perhaps my dear parents could have done so, as they loved me above all, as if they had a presentiment that I should be the most unhappy of their children; but they have been dead for several years, and so, notwithstanding my numerous relatives and friends, I stand quite alone in this world and vainly seek an answer to the questions 'Why?' and 'Wherefore?'.

Crisis in the life of a homosexual

ANONYMOUS*

I SHALL attempt to conform with your request and give you a cursive and true insight into my sexual and mental life. Born and raised the youngest of ten children, three of whom died early of children's diseases, I lived in the country till my fifth year, when I started going to school and I remember nothing of that period except that I was tremendously fond of *playing with fire* and that I kept up till then, more or less, the habit of bed-wetting, an act which was associated with the pleasurable feeling that I was sitting on the chamber. I know also that I envied my sisters a great deal. My unusually strict and religious parents naturally subjected me to rigorous training and thus I learned early to distinguish between mine and thine, good and evil, truth and falsehood. Continually watched over by parents and instructors—a custom contrary to the modern spirit—I was kept from many of the children's games.

When I did play, it was mostly with boys and I do not recall having preferred the company of girls. My free time was taken up a great deal with agricultural pursuits and I was about eight years of age when the first sexual episode took place which left an impression on my mind, *having witnessed that year how some boys of my own age played with their own sexual parts but without feeling on my part any desire to imitate them. With girls I came but little into contact as a child, but I remember once having been present when several boys, eleven to twelve years of age, abused a girl* but I took no part in the deed. At about that period I put on women's clothes a few times though today a man in women's clothes rather disgusts me. Two incidents concerning me personally are still vivid in my memory, namely, playing once with my privates, in the presence of other boys, and another time, warmly

*From *The Homosexual Neurosis*, by Wilhelm Stekel.

embracing the naked body of another boy while playing a 'mother and father' game.

Thirteen years thus passed with nothing eventful taking place, except a fall from a tree as the result of which I hurt myself rather seriously. It was at that period that my teacher, who considered me not only a bright boy but a model student as well, prevailed upon my struggling parents to permit me to continue my schooling. I was able to secure, in fact, a free scholarship at an Institute. Shortly after that a schoolmate grew attached to me and he *taught me to masturbate*. Although I already had erections, there was no seminal loss, probably on account of deficient development. He and another schoolmate prevailed on me to masturbate them—but nothing more. About that time other schoolmates were in the habit of speaking of some girl or other, admiring her beauty. *This talk about a 'pretty girl' struck me as strange*, so far as I remember. It was during my second high school year—I may have been just over my fourteenth year, at the time—when a teacher appeared in class with the trousers absent-mindedly unbuttoned and when I noticed it my eyes became glued on his trouser fly as though in a trance, and thus I awoke, for the first time, to the sad realization of my sexual bent. From that time on I noticed that I was extraordinarily attracted to this teacher although he did not like me in school. It was then that my first struggles, the first wishes in my awakened boyish soul, began to shape themselves. There were two boys in particular who, among others, charmed me with their attractiveness. I masturbated a great deal during that period, without indulging in any particular phantasies— occasionally in the company of other boys. But I had the feeling of being sexually attracted to boys and in my dreams appeared the wish to be their friend. But the stimuli were not of a character which I found impossible to curb.

Next I felt myself irresistibly attracted to an elderly man. Neither in the waking state nor in my dreams did I think at all of women during that time. Around my eighteenth year I experienced the first stormy upheaval which nearly unbalanced me. I came into close touch with a distant relative, an attractive, interesting and splendid intellectual man who, moreover, was happily married. I then passed through the anguish of unrequited love, kept dreaming of what was beyond my reach, and endeavoured to still my unnatural passion through excessive onanism. The keen struggle to preserve my secret, the intense mental torture, caused me one day to break down. The strict but kindhearted talk of my relative in whom, of necessity, I forced myself to confide, saved me that time from suicide. The next day the house physician was called, a cordial and kindly young man, who took a strong professional interest in me. Day after day he spoke to me and tried to influence my mind and he succeeded in shifting my sexual feelings entirely into the background and in about five months he thought I was ready to try regular intercourse. But the attempt proved a new defeat for me. *The secret aversion, the fear of infection*, made me prove myself impotent at the critical moment. But I did not tell the physician *and shortly thereafter he dismissed me as cured.*

There followed again years of struggle. Fearing mental breakdown I was driven to the idea of seeking final release through suicide. But I lacked courage for the deed. . . . Was it cowardice, was it the yearning of my sickly body that prevented me from ending then a life unblessed by a single experience of that highest yearning of a healthy body—the consummation of love? During that time my relative also died and my anguish was unbearable. For I was absorbed in that great passion of mine so deeply that I had forgotten all about the rest of the world. I was hardly reconciled to that misfortune when further anguish came into my life; several men crossed my path with whom I would have no doubt entered into intimacy if I had found any points of contact.

In my despairing mood I confided in a man I respected, who consoled me saying that my misfortune could not be very deep-rooted since I had come to him about it. He advised me to seek intimacy with girls (I came a great deal in contact with girls in the course of my daily work and also forced myself to learn dancing). In accordance with his advice I resorted to prostitutes and had intercourse a number of times but without particular pleasure or satisfaction. Yes, I went so far as to propose marriage to a girl of a good family. It was my fate not to meet with a favourable response, although secretly I was gratified at that. For I could not think that my supreme passion intimately and indissolubly linked to the nature, the appearance and form of boyhood and charming old age would ever be overcome. Springtide and autumn, boyhood and old age, evoke in me the wonders of development and suggest the soft quiet stealing in of blissful eternal peace. Although the sense of touch alone is enough to rouse in me the most wonderful feeling of bliss, contact with a woman leaves me indifferent, if it does not actually inspire me with disgust. Thus I kept up for a time longer, greatly agitated but unyielding, the fear of being discovered keeping me back. Tortured at night by the yearnings of the day while dreaming of endless bliss by conjuring up the most intimate scenes depicting contact, dreaming and thinking also of oral (lip) contact, but never of any love anal act. In terror of being found out—I blushed at the lightest pointed joke when in company—I often thought of joining the foreign legion or to migrate to some country where homosexual love is not looked upon as a crime or as something shameful.

Often I heard of places where persons of my bent may be found but I never had the courage to look them up, fearing that I would be recognized, that I would be put to shame and that I should lose my means of subsistence. I am particularly pained at the thought that I must pass for an inferior dissolute type while millions and millions of insignificant tramps are placed on a higher level in the eyes of the law, enjoy life and are even honoured and respected while I, in spite of possessing the qualities of a truer manhood, must waste my life in joyless existence.

Two women came into my life with whom I became somewhat intimate, *one attracting me temporarily because her physical appear-*

ance was like that of a boy undeveloped, the other, because I was at the time under the influence of alcohol. But I noticed in connexion with those two experiences that I felt no particular satisfaction during bodily contact with the women or while kissing them, *in fact, many women cause me nausea if I so much as take food out of their hand.* Several prostitutes have tried to rouse my sexual feelings (by playing with my penis), but in spite of erection I felt no particular pleasure, and the act was always followed by a feeling of despair—the same old story. Sometimes in my anguish I sought the church and there I broke into tears and I yearningly clasped my hands in prayer without being a believer at heart. Oftentimes I thought my mind must be affected and thought I had to go to an asylum for the insane but it would make my trouble known to do so and I feared I should have to forego contact with men forever after that. Occasionally *I dreamed also of women,* but without any particular feelings, while if I dreamed of clasping in a warm embrace or only touching or even merely looking at a boy, or at an elderly man, I felt great pleasure. I dreamed of contact with the lips.

Something more about the family: On account of father's strict discipline *I inclined more to mother who was more indulgent.* One of four sisters is married, also both brothers, happy and satisfied, I believe. (I am very bashful with all my relations, old and young.) One uncle only showed eccentricities and he remained single. All my other habits of life are not unlike those of any normal young man, I have friends who are married and who are unaware of my condition. But time after time I am tremendously agitated on account of my mental struggle. Finally, to conclude: my dear doctor, you cannot prevail upon me again to try to look you up at your office because the penetrating look of your office girl inspires me with the fear that my condition is recognized and diagnosed at a glance. If you feel inclined to advise me how best to withstand this craving or to mention some country where I may go, I should be very grateful to you—if not, I have learned to bear defeat. . . .

Letter of a homosexual husband

ANONYMOUS

THESE are notes from a letter of one husband to another, brought to the office by a patient.* They are included here as reflecting a psychological aspect of latent homosexuality:

'I have postponed answering your letter until I had some leisure and the inspiration to answer it in full. Even now I am writing only to answer it in part and to tell you how very deeply I appreciate the brotherly tone of your letter and your invitation to call on you when I feel the need. Let me tell you of something you seem to have done for me already. Before our trip, I gave practically no time to quiet story or meditation—couldn't be bothered reading Whitman's *Leaves of Grass*, Carpenter's *Towards Democracy*, etc., and was consumed with a restlessness that would not permit me to stay still an instant. Moreover, I was forever giving myself over to expressions, making coffee, drinking, sex expression and so on. Since then I have hardly touched coffee, have had no cigarettes at all, have found moderation in sex matters much easier and have derived a great deal of quiet but deep pleasure in reading Burke's *Cosmic Consciousness*, and the books previously mentioned. I have lost much of that destructive restlessness and find sitting quietly at home studying not only easy but satisfying and pleasant. Moreover, I have definitely embraced the conviction previously possessed but for a long time ignored, that it profiteth a man nothing to win the world and lose his soul. I am again definitely on the path of the spiritual quest; not so much what you said as what you are, is what fixed me.

'To get back to your letter. I am familiar with much of the
*Reported by R. L. Dickinson, M.D.

literature you mention and the psychoanalytic and psychiatric approach to the question of sex. It helped immensely to emancipate me from all the fears and phobias early training had planted within one regarding it. I am just reading a new book edited by Calverton and Schmalhausen entitled *The New Generation*. It is a challenging and thought-provoking book. Have you read it? The trouble is for me personally such books are not helpful. They help me immensely in my work, but unless I am extremely careful, they subtly become excuses for excess. For me, if I could achieve absolute continence, it would be the very best thing that could happen, but only because I know perfect mastery in the use of sex for me impossible. I think the highest ideal of all is expressed in the Bhagavad-Gita—action without attachment to the results of action—to achieve a state of desirelessness—the highest ideal that is, as a purely personal, individual aim.

'I have never written to anyone before, nor even spoken of my married life. To you I am anxious to do so, for two main reasons. First, my experience may help you to help someone else, second, you will certainly help me if only by your understanding reception of what I tell you. Regarding masturbation I want you to understand that I am no longer under the thrall of mistaken conceptions regarding the ill effects of my trouble, but I know only too well my efficiency is impaired, my will weakened, and my spiritual energy drained off into other channels. Dear friend, I am sure you can help me a lot in this matter. I think as a phase in development it is harmless, as the writers say. But as you say, when excessive and prolonged, it is devitalizing and destroying—it is a throwing away of vital energy that should be used to far better purpose. But when, as in my case, the habit begins in early childhood, there are more harmful results. It dwarfs the organ [*sic*] and causes premature ejaculation during intercourse, both of which seriously interfere with the normal satisfaction.

'You know, for weeks after seeing you this hypersensitivity seemed to leave me; I marvelled at it. But it is so wrapped up with a multitude of factors such as acidity of the system, irritation, constipation, rush, fatigue, etc. I sometimes become afraid that a sexual obsession will get me. Isn't that a hell of an admission? And somewhat contradictory of my former statement that I was free of fear complexes? I think sex is a wonderful, marvellous thing, but is it not true that the finer the thing, the greater the danger in its abuse? The results of unsatisfactory intercourse are a thwarting, a blocked, frustrated desperate feeling—a fundamental source of inferiority and all the neurotic and even psychotic effects that follow in its train. In the first years of our married life, intercourse was fairly satisfactory but spoilt by excess on my part. There were times, as I have said, when it raised us both to high spiritual levels, but after our third baby was born my wife was not properly attended to by the doctor, the handicap of a dwarfed member was exaggerated. We both felt, too, that neither was healthy and robust enough to justify our bringing another child into the world, so we practised methods of contraception that were psychologically and probably physically harmful.

'I think I have suffered most from the thought that I have done my wife harm and from a very, very bitter feeling of inferiority and a sense of helplessness against an overpowering urge that swept my puny will away as a wave would overwhelm a straw. I have over a long period toyed with the thought of suicide as a way out and for some time accepted a materialistic, fatalistic philosophy. The knowledge that this thing was sapping energies that could have been used for fine purposes (I am conscious of real ability in some directions), that whatever I did would be a third or fifth rate best because of it, and that there was seemingly no way out, gave me a tired attitude towards life.

'Hence, I not only disbelieved in a life after death, I resented the very idea of it. Don't we have to struggle enough here, and be dogged with our weaknesses enough here, without living forever? Death, a long dreamless sleep from which there shall be no wakening—that was paradise enough for me. No more defeats, no more loathing disgusts, no more neurotic digestive troubles from nervous maladjustment. Death was just a dear friend who would take care of everything for a fellow who didn't have guts enough to end it all himself. That was how I viewed it in my more pessimistic moments. Yet in spite of it all we have managed to get a good deal of helpful companionship out of each other. Nowadays, and especially since setting eyes on your radiant visage, we have been very happy together. The dear girl has always followed the Gleam more consistently than I, though I probably have greater capacity for the great experience described in *Cosmic Consciousness* than she. Fortunately for us both she is wonderfully poised sexually. One author in *The New Generation* states that happy marriage is more probable in the case of one who has had no precocious sexual awakening. I think she is the world's champion, for at twenty-four when she married she knew absolutely nothing about sex. How she accomplished that feat is still a marvel to me. It was not because she was cold sexually, she is not, but how on earth did she do it, going to a crowded public school in the city? If I had married anyone else I am quite sure the marriage would have gone on the rocks. I have written enough, I think, to answer your question about my difficulty.

'I want you to know that if there is any way in which I can be of service to you, either personally, or in some undertaking of yours, I want to have the privilege of helping. Please feel that our home is ever open to you and that we should feel honoured to have you as our guest. If you are short of funds for any project you have in mind, what I have is yours. I am selfish enough to hope that it will not be long before we can talk together again. It would mean a tremendous lot to me. I trust you will not worry overmuch about the fact that in many things you don't know what to think. I am perfectly certain that it is what you are that is more important.

'In closing, I want to tell you again that I am with you daily, earnestly wishing that some of the bitter things that have come to you will vanish completely away.'

The perfect servant

REPORTED BY SANDOR FERENCZI, M.D.

TRANSLATED BY ERNEST JONES, M.D.

The observation of (two) cases*, presently to be related seems
to justify the surmise that in the pathogenesis of paranoia, homosexuality plays not a chance part, but the most important one,
and that paranoia is perhaps nothing else at all than disguised
homosexuality.

The first case occurred in the husband of my own housekeeper, a well-built man of about thirty-eight, whom I had occasion to observe exhaustively for several months.

He and his wife (who could hardly be called pretty), who had
got married just before entering my service, occupied a part of
my flat consisting of one room and the kitchen. The husband
worked all day (he was an employee in the post office), came home
punctually in the evening, and in the first part of his time with
me gave no grounds for complaint. On the contrary, he impressed
me by his extraordinary diligence and his great politeness to
myself. He always found something in my rooms to clean and
embellish. I would come across him late at night putting fresh
polish on the doors or floors, burnishing the top windowpanes
that could hardly be reached, or arranging some ingenious
novelty in the bathroom. He was most desirous of giving me
satisfaction, obeyed all my instructions with military smartness
and punctuality, but was extremely sensitive to any criticism
on my part, for which, it is true, he rarely gave any occasion.

*From 'On the Part Played by Homosexuality in the Pathogenesis of Par-
anoia' originally published in the *Jahrbuch der Psychoanalyse*, Vol. III, 1912.
The second case is presented in the section on Women under the title 'A
Jealous Wife.' (Ed.)

One day the housekeeper sobbingly told me that she lived very unhappily with her husband. He was drinking a great deal latterly, came home late, and constantly scolded and abused her without cause. At first I did not want to interfere in this domestic affair, but when I accidentally heard that he was beating his wife (which fact the woman had concealed from me for fear of losing her place), I spoke to him seriously and insisted he should abstain from alcohol and treat his wife well, all of which he tearfully promised me. When I offered to shake hands with him I could not prevent his impetuously kissing my hand. I ascribed this at the time, however, to his emotion and to my 'paternal' attitude (although I was younger than he).

After this scene peace prevailed in the house for a time. A few weeks later, however, the same scenes were repeated, and when I now looked at the man more carefully I saw evident signs of chronic alcoholism. On this I interrogated the woman and learned from her that she was constantly being accused by her husband of marital infidelity, without the slightest ground. The suspicion naturally occurred to me at once that the husband was suffering from alcoholic delusions of jealousy, the more so since I knew the housekeeper to be a very respectable and modest person. I managed once more to get the husband to give up drinking, and to restore peace in the house for a while.

The state of affairs, however, soon changed for the worse. It became clear that we had to deal with a case of alcoholic paranoia. The man neglected his wife, and stayed in the public-house drinking till midnight. On coming home he beat his wife, abused her incessantly, and accused her of flirting with every male patient who came to see me. I learned subsequently that he was even at this time jealous also of me, but his wife, from a comprehensible anxiety, concealed this from me. I was naturally unable to keep the couple any longer, but I allowed the woman, at her request, to retain her position until the quarter was up.

It was now that I learned all the details of these domestic scenes. The husband, whom I called to account, absolutely denied having beaten his wife, although this had been confirmed by people who had witnessed it. He maintained that his wife was a lascivious woman, a sort of vampire that 'sucked out a man's force'; that he had relations with her five or six times every night, that this was never enough for her, however, so that she committed adultery with every possible man. During this explanation the emotional scene, described above, was repeated; he took possession again of my hand and kissed it amid tears. He said he had never known anyone dearer or kinder than I.

As his case began to interest me from a psychiatric point of view also, I learned from the woman that the man had had sexual relations with her only two or three times since they were married. Now and then he would make preparations in this direction—mostly *a tergo*—and then push her away, declaring in abusive language that she was a whore, and that she could do it with anyone she liked but not with him.

I began to play an increasingly important part in his delusions. He wanted to force his wife, under the threat of stabbing her, to confess she had had sexual relations with me. Every morning when I went out he burst into my bedroom, sniffed the bed-clothes, and then beat his wife, asserting he had recognized her odour in the bedding. He tore from her a head-kerchief I had brought back for her from a holiday, and stroked it several times a day; he was not to be parted from a tobacco-pipe that I had made him a present of. If I was in the watercloset he listened all the time in the ante-room, then related to his wife with obscene words what he had heard, and asked her 'if it pleased her.' He then hurried into the closet immediately after me, to see whether I had 'properly rinsed everything away'.

All this time he remained the most zealous servant you could think of, and was exaggeratedly amiable towards me. He turned to account my absence from Budapest and without instructions repainted the watercloset, even adorning the walls with coloured sketches.

The fact that they had been discharged was kept private from him for a time. When he heard of it he became sad, abused and hit his wife, and threatened that he would put her in the street and stab me, 'her darling'. Even now he remained well-behaved and devoted so far as I personally was concerned. When I learned, however, that he was sleeping at night with a well-ground kitchen knife at his side and on one occasion seriously looked like forcing his way into my bedroom, I felt I could not wait the two or three days till their notice was up. The woman notified the authorities, who took him to the insane asylum after having him medically certified.

There is no doubt that this was a case of alcoholic delusions of jealousy. The conspicuous feature of homosexual transference to myself, however, allows of the interpretation that this jealousy of men signified only the projection of his own erotic pleasure in the male sex. Also, the disinclination for sexual relations with his wife was probably not simply impotency, but was determined by his unconscious homosexuality. The alcohol for the most part (though not quite) robbed his homosexuality, which had been spiritualized into friendliness, assiduity and complaisance, of its sublimations, and so caused the crude homosexual eroticism that thus came to the surface—intolerable as such to the consciousness of a man of ethical high standing—to be simply imputed to his wife. In my opinion the alcohol played here only the part of an agent destroying sublimation, through the effect of which the man's true sexual constitution, namely the preference for a member of the same sex, became evident.

It was only subsequently that I received a complete confirmation of this. I learned that he had been married before, years ago. He lived only a short time in peace with this first wife also, began to drink soon after the wedding, and abused his wife, tormenting her with jealousy scenes, until she left him and got a divorce.

In the interval between these two marriages he was said to have been a temperate, reliable, and steady man, and to have taken again to drink only after the second marriage. Alcoholism was thus not the deeper cause of the paranoia; it was rather that in the insoluble conflict between his conscious heterosexual and unconscious homosexual desires he took to alcohol, which then by destroying the sublimations brought the homosexual eroticism to the surface, his consciousness getting rid of this by way of projection, of delusions of jealousy.

The destruction of the sublimation was not complete. He was still able to let a part of his homosexual tendency function in a spiritualized form, as a faithful, compliant servant of his master, as a smart subordinate in his office, and as a competent worker in both positions. Where the circumstances made high claims on his capacity for sublimation, however—for instance, in his occupation with the bedroom and closet—he was compelled to saddle his wife with his desires, and by jealousy scenes to assure himself that he was in love with her. The boasting about his colossal potency in regard to his wife was similarly a distortion of the facts that served to calm his mind.*

*The one-sided agitation of temperance reformers tries to veil the fact that in the large majority of cases alcoholism in not the cause of neuroses, but a result of them, and a calamitous one. Both individual and social alcoholism can be cured only by the help of psychoanalysis, which discloses the causes of the 'flight into narcosis' and neutralizes them. The eradication of alcoholism only seemingly signifies an improvement in hygiene. When alcohol is withdrawn, there remain at the disposal of the psyche numerous other paths to the flight into disease. And when then psychoneurotics suffer from anxiety-hysteria or dementia praecox instead of from alcoholism, one regrets the enormous expenditure of energy that has been applied against alcoholism but in the wrong place.

PART TWO

CAUSE AND CURE

The homosexual as an intersex

MAGNUS HIRSCHFELD, M.D.

TO avoid all misunderstanding, the question as to what I mean by homosexuality must be clear at the start. Homosexuality, or 'self-sexedness,' is a definite form from which springs certain feeling which in turn translates itself into certain acts, mostly not those ordinarily imagined. As in sex generally: first, the form (*artung*); second, feeling and inclination; third, action. An act which does not correspond to sensation produces no new form, and retroactively no new sensation. In fact, among the many thousands of homosexual men and women I have learned to know, I have never heard one seriously say that he held another responsible for his homosexual proclivities (it may then have been his progenitors).

In the following I shall briefly enumerate the twelve chief points from whose totality (even though one or another point may be less decisive) anyone whose mind is open to reason will draw the irrevocable conclusion that homosexuality is a question of a 'deeply underlying constitutional predisposition.'

I. *Spontaneous Eruption of Homosexual Feeling.* Homosexual urge breaks its path despite the glorification of love for the opposite sex in literature and in untold works of art; despite the powerful suggestion of the environment in the opposite direction. It breaks through, although the individual, still totally ignorant of the significance of the phenomenon, rejects as something

K

abhorrent that which he hears regarding the homosexual relation. The entire mode of education is directed towards making the boy a complete man; at home and in school he is treated precisely as normal boys, and that which is becoming to the opposite sex, is, at an early age, pointed out as unbecoming to him. The same is true in the education of girls.

At the age of 13 to 14, when his friends begin to enthuse over the opposite sex, the homosexual youth takes pains to emulate them; he is, so to say, embarrassed at having no 'flame'. Frequently, the first seduction takes place at this time; in Europe, often by the servant girl. A great many homosexuals declare they can definitely remember that their first excitation was caused by the opposite sex. However, a homosexual will not become a woman-lover as a result of this first sexual excitation any more than a heterosexual will become a homosexual by being seduced, as it often happens, by a person of the male sex.

II. *The Difference Already Present in the Child.* Even before reaching puberty, a child, who later becomes homosexual, shows characterological traits of being differently constituted than other children, who when grown up will have heterosexual feelings; *i.e.*, a girlish appearance in the boy and boyish appearance in the girl. Schrenck-Notzig and others see in this phenomenon 'a proof of original predisposition to contrary sexual feelings.'

III. *Child's Asexual Subconscious Urge towards the Future Sexual Object.* Already long before puberty, homosexuals are drawn towards the person resembling closely the type which will later excite them erotically; they are, however, completely in the dark that they are harbouring the germ of sexual inclination. To the question asked of 500 homosexuals, having passed the 25th year, as to when they first experienced homosexual stirrings, the following answers were given:

Between 4 and 13 years, 271   54.4 per cent.
Between 14 and 20 years, 183   36.6 per cent.

The remaining 9 per cent answered as follows: 5 in earliest childhood; 16 very early; 24 could not remember. A similar ratio resulted from an investigation of 930 other cases.

Magnan, an outstanding French psychiatrist, says: 'Inversion of sexual feeling (*inversion du sens génital*) is frequently apparent in earliest youth, which in itself is characteristic: nothing speaks more clearly for the inborn quality of this anomaly than its early appearance.'

Practically all homosexual men and women can remember that their conscious sexual urge was first awakened by persons of their own sex.

IV. *Non-Appearance of Desire for the Opposite Sex.* Potency, as such, is a reflexive process independent of the will. In average homosexuals this force is directed towards their own sex. They are entirely impotent or merely weakly potent with the opposite sex and then only with the help of phantasies centred around their own sex. It is, therefore, conclusive that the homosexual urge is independent of wish and will, and that its phenomenon lies in the individual constitution itself.

V. *Content of Sex Dreams.* It speaks for the innateness of the homosexual urge that the first erotic dreams, as well as the later ones, are centred around persons of the same sex.

VI. *Harmony between Sexual Personality and Sex Urge.* That homosexuality is constitutional is further apparent from the fact that it is closely bound up with the very essence of the personality. The homosexual man and the homosexual woman differ from the heterosexual man and woman not only in the direction of their sex urge but also by the singularity of their being. This is true not only of the feminine among the masculine; of the masculine among the feminine homosexuals; but the apparently male types among homosexual men and the apparently feminine types among homosexual women also differ from the full sex-types. These apparently homosexual types, as far as they are conscious of their anomaly, endeavour, of course, to hide their peculiarity from the world under a sort of sexual mimicry.

VII. *Physical Signs of Recognition in the Homosexual.* Even in the distant past, the gait and other motions were recognized by experts as the undeniable sign of the homosexual. His walk is distinguishable by small, tripping, dancing, often slightly undulating steps; his gait is graceful with a slight turning of the shoulders and the pelvis; his trunk inclines forward and the head seems less firm than in pronounced masculine individuals. The walk is so characteristic that, sitting in my office, I have frequently been able to recognize a homosexual as soon as he entered my waiting room. The human gait is dependent upon anatomical and psychic factors, I mean, that the somatic conditions of urnings—the breadth of the hips, the resultant strongly converging thighs, the weaker development of their bending and stretching muscles—cannot be without effect upon their walk. Psychic differences, of course, are here also significant. In order not to betray himself, the homosexual adopts quiet, grave steps. However, when excited or running, he lapses into his natural gait. A police commissioner once said to me: 'My steps were very small and hopping; but I trained myself and lost the habit. But as soon as I walk with a handsome young man it happens to me again'. Very typical are the motions of the arms, especially those called into action by writing, and which are dependent upon other physical and psychic momenta than walking.

Striking proof for the necessity of scientific methods was brought forward by later researches. Among the most significant are the recommended measurements proposed by A. Weil of our Institute in his investigation: 'Is There an Anatomical Basis for the Innateness of Homosexuality?' (Archiv für Frauenkunde und Konstitutionforschung, Vol. x., No. 1; prize conferred by the Aerztliche Gesellschaft für Sexualwissenschaft und Konstitutionforschung).

In this work, Weil assembled the results of measurements of 370 homosexuals and 1,000 heterosexual men, and arrived at the following conclusion: 'More than one-half to two-thirds of all homosexuals show deviation from the "norm"; anatomical deviation, which means that there is a different physical build and constitution than in heterosexual men.' He adds; 'In determining this, the question of homosexuality being inborn is answered.' These measurements undertaken by an earnest, reliable investigator have up to the present not been contradicted. To doubt them without inquiry or investigation must be rejected as unscientific and unwarranted.

VIII. *Ineffectiveness of Extraneous Influences on Homosexuality.* That the homosexual urge is not acquired but inborn is apparent from the phenomenon of its tenacity. Were it caused by external influences, it would be necessary to assume that it would yield to extraneous influences. In such a case, it would be possible not only for the heterosexual individual to become homosexual, but also, for a homosexual to become heterosexual, Both assumptions are at variance with the results of abundant experience. It is certain, on the other hand, that men and women of extraordinarily strong character and will-power were unable to change the direction of their sex urge in spite of great effort.

Let two instances quoted from letters on the subject confirm our statement. A homosexual writes from Switzerland: 'I have always been very strict with myself from my early youth, and taken great pains to master my tendencies. I was successful now and then; unfortunately, however, I have always had the identical experience: the longer and the more stubbornly did I suppress this urge, the more violent was its sudden return. What haven't I done! Firm resolutions, vows, medical advice, water cures, hypnosis, electricity, systematic deviation from dangerous thoughts by bodily exercises, agriculture, travels, military service, studies, etc. I sacrificed beloved objects; neither religion nor philosophy was of any use. I was morbidly tired of life. For four years I had been passionately in love with a young man of my age. He died at the age of twenty-four without my having been permitted to speak to him of my love. It was a life of hell!'

A homosexual artisan expresses himself as follows: 'My very pious mother brought me up in deeply religious faith, and when I realized my emotional state I supplicated God in fervent prayers to help me in my great need. When, despite my self-control and bitter inner struggle, I realized that my condition did not change, I lost my faith in God.' Similar letters taken from our questionnaires are legion.

IX. *Parallelism in Homosexual and Heterosexual Phenomena.* The innateness of homosexuality is further evident from the complete agreement of the homosexual and the heterosexual urge in all its accompanying spiritual phenomena, its seeking and longing, joy and sorrow, its form and consequences, in its more or less idealistic aspects, in its extraordinary differentiation and general anomalies. If we assume that love for the opposite sex is inborn in the greater part of humanity, we must deduce that analogous phenomena hold true of the lesser part of mankind and that homosexual love is also inborn.

X. *Familial Appearance of Homosexuality.* That homosexuality has a congenital basis is further apparent from the fact that among blood relations of homosexual men and women are to be found individuals who are similarly endowed and who bear the unmistakable characteristics of intermediacy.

One of the earlier research workers in the field, the Hollander, L. S. A. M. v. Römer, says: 'In at least 35% of the cases, urnanism is familial' (*The Urning Family, Researches into the Ascendancy of Uranians*). In complete agreement with this view, as with the many examples which I have quoted in my *Homosexuality in Man and Woman*, is the statement of Walter Wolf in his *Researches in the Heredity of the Problem of Homosexuality* (Archiv für Psychiatrie und Nervenkrankheiten, Vol. 75, No. 1, from the

neurological department of the Berlin Institute of Sexual Science):
'The results of family-tree study show that homosexuality is an
hereditary-biological resultant, the outgrowth of the coming
together of collective ascendants, which, though they may have
heterosexual perception, are endowed with psychic qualities
which correspond to the opposite sex. Such psychosexual tran-
sitional forms are common in families of homosexuals, less
common in normal families. Accordingly, therefore, homosexuality is not to be considered as a biological peculiarity, but
as an extreme variant of all transitory forms of sexual structure
to be found between mankind and womankind. A close theoretical
deduction would be the assumption of double psychosexus.
Perpetuation of homosexual variants is favoured and granted by
Nature herself as my family tree researches have shown, through a
special attraction tendency whereby the feminine male and the
masculine female usually enter into sexual union.'

Thus, recently, in a family of five brothers and sisters, I found
the fourth to be homosexual; two brothers and a sister had
previously consulted me. In a case of eight brothers and sisters
there were three homosexual daughters and two bisexual sons.
The parents were consanguineous. I have repeatedly been able
to observe the three homosexual brothers, two very frequently.

The constitutional character of homosexuality is especially apparent in cases of identical twins. They are always either both
masculine or feminine, but in addition to being of the same sex,
they also manifest other extensive agreements (the popular
saying is: sie gleichen sich wie ein Ei dem andern; 'they are
alike s two eggs') so that at the beginning even their own parents
have difficulty in telling them apart. Conformity in constitutional
defects is particularly startling, such as visual disturbances, for
instance, deviation in vision (myopia, etc) to the very refraction
of dioptry.

Now let us consider homosexuality in identical twins. In my
vast material I have found only two cases of male identical twins.
In both cases, the second twin brother too was homosexual.

Spiro of Recklingshausen who has given particular attention to the problem of identical twins wrote me to say that in four cases of identical twins, he ascertained that the agreements also included the homosexual urge. Similar findings were submitted by the Holland physician, J. Sanders, in his recently published *Homosexualitaet bij Zweelingen* (Tijdenschrift voor Geneskunde, 1934). Neither Spiro nor myself has thus far found a case where one sister or one brother of identical twins was homosexual and the other heterosexual. The one instance referred to by Sanders where such may be the case cannot be described as entirely unquestionable; its incidence cannot in any way nullify the strength of proof of the above cited cases.

Not only their ancestry and relations but their progeny shows the constitutional character of homosexual men and women. The more I see of homosexual men and women, whether they are entirely or preponderantly homosexual, the stronger is my conviction that—the real crime of homosexuals is their marriage. I am convinced without a shadow of a doubt that men and women who consummate marriage with the knowledge of their homosexual predisposition are guilty of grave deception, at least where they neglect to enlighten the second party in advance and in no uncertain terms.

In my article, 'Has Homosexuality a Physical or Spiritual Basis?' (Münchener Medizinische Wochenschrift, 1918), I arrived at the following conclusion: The quantitative and qualitative injury to the life of a nation is caused by homosexual marriages only in so far as they frequently eliminate the possibility of propagation by healthy women; also that possible children from such unions are rarely entirely normal.

XI. *Equal Diffusion of Homosexuality*. That homosexuality is inherent in the human organization is proven by its uniform diffusion in all centuries and under all skies, among all nations and all occupations within all cultural stages. Homosexuality is not limited to the *genus humanum*, but investigation has proven that among all sexually-divided species of the animal and plant kingdoms there exists always a group of individuals which have the intersexual form and which are attracted, not by heterosexual, but by homosexual partners.

The statement of the anonymous authority, quoted by the well-known naturalist, Gustav Jäger, is undoubtedly well-founded. For nineteen centuries, even patricide and the most audacious rape were less hateful and abhorrent than homosexuality, and for long periods homosexuals, or even those with a reputation of such leanings, were threatened with death by fire, and even later with most severe punishments, with dishonour, economic ostracism, severance of all social ties, etc. And see, not to speak of antiquity, modern history shows us plainly a considerable number of famous men—men who filled the world with idealistic concepts, who were equally fine as citizens and human beings and creators, who nevertheless were incapable of mastering themselves sufficiently not to betray their secret passion; princes, powerful and rich individuals, who could afford to keep entire harems, or who could have chosen their mistresses from all the beauties of the world and made them their slaves, yet succumbed to this branding passion. Can you imagine a more forcible argument for the inborn character of homosexuality?'

Statistical data compiled under greatest difficulties, but also with greatest care, have given comparative figures (occurring again and again in mathematical order) regarding the diffusion of homosexuality:

Among 1,000 persons, 15 declared themselves as entirely homosexual; 40, bi-sexual; 8, preponderantly homosexual. These figures show that among us every 66th person is entirely homosexual; every 45th either entirely or preponderantly homosexual; every 25th inclines towards both sexes, and every 18th predisposed to deviation from the norm; these calculations, for example, should mean there are 1,437,500 (2·3 per cent of 62,000,500) homosexuals in Germany; 10,327,000 (2·3 per cent of 449 millions) in Europe; and 41,883,000 (2·3 per cent of 1821 millions) on earth, men and women whose constitutional predisposition is largely or completely homosexual.

The extraordinarily large constancy of (homosexual) comparative figures must rest upon the identical natural laws on which the sexual proportion of boys and girls (106 male *vs*. 100 female births) is based; here too we find an imposing conformity.

XII. *Further Proof of the Innateness of Homosexuality 'per exclusionem.'* Among general theories, the one claiming that heterosexual persons may become homosexual and that their acquisition of homosexuality is the prime cause for the changed direction of their sex urge must, on the hand of abundant observation material, be considered erroneous. There are no less than one hundred causes to which the manifestation of homosexuality has been attributed. Not one of these causes, however, withstood careful probing, so that an impartial examination of these allegedly striking facts must lead to the conclusion that genuine homosexuality cannot be acquired through external conditions, but that it is an inherent quality rooted in the inborn constitution and that it is inseparably and indivisibly united with the individual's personality.

To Ivan Bloch belongs the merit of compiling in his thorough work, *Beiträge zur Aetiologie der Psychopathia Sexualis*, over sixty 'occasional factors' (*okkasionelle Momente*) from which, as was formerly supposed and still is claimed today, 'homosexual love may arise without any original predisposition' (*analge*). The insufficiency of practically all these motivations is apparent in the fact that there is probably not one individual who at one time or another in his life has not forcibly and repeatedly been confronted with these factors. Actually, however, only a negligible number of such individuals become homosexual, and only those who originally harboured the tendency. The reasons for this may be found solely in the different psychophysical make-up of the individual; a different constitution exclusively is the cause for the various reactions of people under the same circumstances.

Therefore the statement of R. Loewenfeld in 'Homosexuality and the Penal Laws' (*Homosexualität und Strafgesetz*) is singularly true to fact: 'Of the various kinds of harm which, according to current opinion, may cause the sexual urge to deviate into the homosexual path, not one has been found that was regularly followed by homosexuality. Numerous individuals in the span of life are exposed to such harmful influences, and yet their urge retains its heterosexual character. Even in persons with hereditary neuropathic tendencies, these problematical harms may remain without effect upon the direction of their sexual urge.'

According to Bloch's *Aetiologie der Psychopathia Sexualis* there is hardly anything which as a cause of homosexuality could not be drawn into consideration. Among the things which, through their effect, can produce homosexuality there is a considerable number of obvious contradictions. Thus, for instance, we find in Bloch's compilation of the literature, the following as the cause of homosexuality: too hot and too cold climate; asceticism and satiety; celibacy and polygamy; youth and senility; insufficient or excessive sex urge; adulation of and repugnance for physical beauty; the sight of the clothed and of the naked body; life in workers' quarters and in palaces, in shops and on farms. And Sadger declares (*Fragment der Psychoanalyse eines Homosexuallen*): 'the regularly to-be-found aetiology of passive pederasty is the frequent clyster-enema administered by the mother in infancy.'

Further supposed aetiological factors which may lead a normal heterosexual individual to homosexuality are occupations corresponding rather to feminine characters, such as cooking, hairdressing, dressmaking; female impersonations; very vivid or misguided phantasies, especially of artists; religious fervour, abnormalities of the genitals, such as exceptional smallness of the membrum virile; abnormal width or narrowness of the vagina; gonorrhoea; castration and eunuchism; physical hermaphrodism; masturbation; chronic alcoholism; opium addiction; use of hasheesh; effeminism in clothes and manner; need for variation in the sexual relation, which may lead to lust; debauchery; Don Juanism; idleness; boredom; seduction, especially by guardians and in brothels; also by other homosexuals; congregation of people of the same sex in barracks, schools, boarding schools, cadets' quarters, harems, monasteries and convents, prisons, large hotels, theatres and public retiring places.

Still further causes cited are; witnessing animal sexual acts as well as constant association with animals; erotic and obscene literature—even the Bible and the writings of the Church Fathers were held responsible; the sight of erotically-stimulating works of art; contemplation of one's own mirrored image; obscene photographs and pictures; obscene tattooing.

Similar effects are ascribed to the following: visits to museums of antique and modern statues, but still more responsible are anatomical museums with plastic reproductions of male and female genital organs; visits to public art exhibitions; ballets, dances, certain scenes in circus performances and variety theatres ('revues' in the modern sense were unknown in older literature); animated pictures, *poses plastique* of heroic or idyllic nature; the sight of men in women's clothes was brought forward as causing homosexuality; further, accidental sight of the male genitalia, for instance, the father's membrum virile; repellent ugliness; fear of venereal diseases; abnormal constitutional peculiarity of the anal region; anal masturbation; flagellation of the anal region; assuming masculine habits (especially by prostitutes); and vice versa, feminine habits in men; mysogyny of the high-liver: male prostitution.

As particular causes of feminine homosexuality, the following are cited: mutual masturbation of the clitoris *cum digito et lingua*; boredom with husband; repugnance of intercourse with man; and finally, the modern women's movement, which makes the woman self-reliant and cultivates in her a masculine character.

That external 'occasional factors' are insufficient for the onset of homosexuality, is easily explained. First of all, the numerous instances are too widely spread to constitute a bona fide basis.

Millions upon millions of people witness sexual acts of animals or visit retiring rooms, and as only an infinitesimal part of them are homo- or bi-sexual, then according to all rules of logic there cannot be any connexion between these facts.

If, of the multitudes who live in either torrid or frigid climates; who occupy workers' quarters or mansions; who have a vivid imagination; those deeply religious; those who visit public art exhibitions or museums, who live in schools or dormitories; who see themselves naked in the mirror or engage in ipsation, only a small (and strikingly proportionate at that) percentage are or become urnings, then the recited circumstances in comparison to the decisive causality must be considered as unimportant.

Into the second group belong the not less numerous factors in which the confusion of cause and effect is evident. Homosexual inclination in man does not spring from celibacy or impotence, but celibacy and impotence result from man's homosexual tendency; likewise, woman's feeling of repugnance for the husband is not the cause but the effect of her homosexual nature. Also, the feminine clothes do not mean modification of the inner man, but the inner man obtains such clothes as suit him. The cause of the character does not lie in the garment, but the reason of the garment lies in the character of the wearer. The same is true of chosen occupations. The homosexual does not become feminine because he acts female roles, but because he is feminine he prefers female roles.

The third rubric finally embraces that hypothesis which shows a complete lack of knowledge of homosexuals. When one has examined only 200 homosexuals he is not in a position to write that abnormalities of the genitals, an abnormal constitutional peculiarity of the anal region, repellent ugliness (even Voltaire whose ugliness is proverbial and who lived in the turmoil of the Prussian court where homosexuality was not altogether despised, did not become 'so'), or chronic alcoholism, lead to homosexuality. It is simply not true to fact that the average of homosexuals is more ugly, more addicted to drinking, more strongly handicapped with abnormalities of the anal region than the average of the normal sexuals.

It is not less incorrect, of course, to explain homosexuality on aesthetic grounds, by great physical beauty of the male sex, as had been done by artists and pseudoscientists and occasionally by homosexuals themselves.

Let us further examine more closely several of the alleged causes, which, although not as frequently as in the past are given as origins of homosexuality: satiety, ipsation and seduction. Even physicians and jurists still defend the satiety theory. Thus, Wollenberg says that homosexuality in most cases must be considered the end product of a vicious sexual life.

I have taken great pains to find those libertines and roués, and the oversatiated women, of whom it is said that they fall upon their own sex through 'raffinement' and wickedness. But I have not been successful. Among the large number of homosexuals I have observed, there was not one who had been satiated with women; most of them had not even once enjoyed one, to say nothing of having enjoyed too many. Homosexual youths having predilection for older men, undoubtedly must have chanced upon 'pederast debauchees,' though they absolutely deny their existence. But if we follow an analogy, one of these pederastic roués, driven by lust, must at one time or another have resorted to woman. This would then be a way to 'cure' them. But it does not happen. In view of my researches, I consider these oversatiated monsters fictitious, in the same way as witches of whose appearance, acts and habits, detailed descriptions were given at the time of their trials.

That ipsation* is not of decisive importance for the origin of homosexuality is proven by a simple example in arithmetic. If all of 120 orphan boys brought up under the same conditions were addicted to ipsation and later only one proves homosexual; if—another example of life—of 100 persons, 98 are ipsants and

*Hirschfeld prefers the term, ipsation (self-satisfaction), to the more limited word, masturbation [Ed.].

of these later only one turns out to be homosexual, 2 bisexual and 96 completely heterosexual, then we can hardly look upon ipsation as sufficient ground for the homosexual urge.

Of the many male and female persons who consulted the writer, there was not one whose psychic urge was altered as a result of ipsation. The heterosexual majority remains heterosexual; the homosexual minority remains homosexual. As far as I was able to ascertain, phantasies also remained the same. They were either heterosexual or homosexual in content. True it is that homosexuals in general continue self-manipulation to an age when in the life of the heterosexual it has already been replaced by intercourse with the opposite sex. This may have prophylactic reasons. Thus, a high Protestant clergyman once came to my office saying that since his 20th year—he was 54— he ipsated twice or thrice daily with homosexual images to guard himself against temptations which might become dangerous to him.

It has been said that ipsation produces homosexuality because it so undermines the will power of the ipsant that he 'loses courage to go to a woman and goes after men instead.' As though, under present conditions it required less courage to accost a male instead of a female, for example, a prostitute! But should potency here be meant, then it must not be left unsaid that as much potency is needed for homosexuals as for heterosexual intercourse.

Considering the much-feared seduction, it must be admitted that the normally sexed occasionally turn to homosexual activity for extraneous, chiefly material, reasons. But it is entirely incorrect to assume that they become homosexual. The act which they perform with a homosexual in such cases is comparable to ipsation and is to be judged as such. Just as soon as opportunity presents itself, they will follow their natural inclination. There are many instances where young men and women who had occasional homosexual intercourse between 16 and 21 were completely heterosexual later.

It has been said that if not through seduction—or more

correctly, the consummation of homosexual acts—a heterosexual feeling may be altered into homosexual, and this alteration may occur by psychic force of suggestion in associating with homosexuals; as Tarnowsky once expressed it, by 'moral contagion'. It must be admitted that fully normal people, chiefly in their youth, may temporarily assume the homosexual 'pose'. Here, however, can be no question of a lasting metamorphosis. Were it possible to acquire this tendency by suggestion, then the real suggestion which should tend to steer the homosexually predisposed into the opposite direction—autosuggestion, extraneous suggestion to which he is daily and continuously exposed in his journey through life, verbal suggestion of his immediate circle and family—would have long ago extinguished this phenomenon of Nature, the homosexual urge.

The power of suggestion in general literature—novels, epic poems, dramas and poetry—the central point of which is normal love, is not able to direct the urge of a homosexual man to a woman. When the young man becomes gradually aware that his desire greatly differs from that of his surroundings, and this happens usually at about the age of 20, he generally commences a battle against himself, the fierceness of which has hardly an equal.

And yet literature has often been held responsible for exercising a strong suggestive influence, especially those branches devoted to scientific and belletristic aspects and dealing with the problem of homosexuality. Even authors like Schrench-Notzing and Cramer believe in 'auto-suggestion' originating from perusal of such literature. In courtrooms, I have heard again and again from lawyers, judges and experts, the opinion that the accused had 'read himself' into homosexuality in Krafft-Ebing—my works too on the problem were occasionally cited as having had that effect. As though there had been no homosexuals long before the scientific investigation of the problem!

However, if many homosexuals possess more books dealing with homosexuality, be they scientific or literary, than we find in possession of others, this is explained simply by the fact that the homosexual, in his desire to enlighten himself as to his condition, tries to procure such reading. Homosexuality therefore results not from such reading, but such reading is the result of homosexuality. Furthermore, there is a large number of homosexual men and women who have never read a book on homosexuality and yet are entirely homosexual.

The much-repeated theory, first enunciated by Binet, that contrary sexual perceptions are due to 'pathological associations' in earliest childhood, a *choc fortuit*, a psychic trauma, has not been confirmed by factual material and remains, therefore, an unsupported hypothesis. Were it material whether the first erection was produced by a man or by a woman, then the number of homosexuals would be much larger, for it is a proven fact that many children are first stirred by the comrades of their own sex. How could such a shock bring about such a metamorphosis of the entire physical and mental make-up as we frequently find in the homosexual? I well remember the remark of a colleague to whom I once introduced a homosexual whose every feature, every movement, voice and manner, revealed a born homosexual. My colleague exclaimed with fine irony: 'What a strong *choc fortuit* he must have received!'

Binet's conception of the origin of homosexuality, which has found ready reception chiefly with the French, shows a certain relationship to the theory of Freud in that both ascribe decisive importance to infantile sexual influences. True, the Freudian school does not attribute compulsive homosexuality to a sudden shock, but claims it is caused by a peculiar attachment of the child to its immediate surroundings, particularly to its mother. We, on the other hand, see in the mother fixation of feminine sons and the father complex of masculine daughters certain phenomena resulting from the psychophysical peculiarity of the children; this peculiarity is constitutional, as is homosexuality, which later develops from the same basis.

It seems to me that more conclusive proofs than here assembled, bearing upon the actual existence of deeply rooted constitutional predisposition (*anlage*), cannot be advanced. As far as the statements of these persecuted persons are concerned, to believe them implicitly would perhaps be asking too much. What, however, should be demanded, in view of these unjust persecutions by law and society, is that their claims be investigated. Here then is where the lawmakers and those who influence the making of laws have a distinct duty, and in the present state of scientific knowledge it should not be difficult for them—without, however, having recourse to court proceedings which tend only to dim the clear outlook—to persuade a considerable number of homosexual men and women, in every stratum of society, to enlist in the cause of this phase of cultural progress.

The conclusions reached by us and others found their confirmation in the brilliant experiments—to alter the psychophysical sexual characteristics—of Steinach (Vienna), Pézard (Paris), and Knud Sand (Copenhagen).

Finally: Steinach's belief—opposed by Benda and other investigators of interstitial tissues—that he has actually found female cells in the sex glands of homosexual men, seems to matter less to me than the fact, proved beyond doubt, that male, female, and intersexual constitutional types can be created at will by implanting certain sex glands in diverse species of animals; in other words that, like the male and female sex type, the intersexual, in its varied stages, is dependent upon the gonads.

Homosexuality of youth

OSWALD SCHWARZ, M.D.

MASTURBATION bridges the gulf between the autoeroticism of the child and the heterosexuality of the grown-up, by way of introducing an imaginary partner; it is a normal step in our sexual development and independent of environmental influences, for which reason practically every normal boy masturbates more or less during a certain period of his life.

The homosexuality of youth, the only form of homosexuality with which we are dealing here, is another step in this development, but it is always definitely abnormal, to a very large extent induced by the environment and therefore practised by only a very small number of boys.

It consists, at any rate in its fully developed form, in mutual masturbation. In some cases these activities are a relief of a genuine physical urge which can no longer be satisfied by solitary masturbation but needs a kind of live partner. In other cases an emotional attachment which tends towards physical manifestation is the prime incentive. Thus in several respects this kind of homosexuality bears some resemblance to grown-up sexuality; it can, from the purely developmental point of view, be considered as a step towards it, but, as I said before, an unnecessary and therefore an abnormal one. In order to understand its nature it must be distinguished from friendship on the one hand and from homosexuality proper on the other. It is more than friendship, and from homosexuality proper it borrows only the gesture.

Friendship, like any other human attitude towards the world, passes through some well-defined stages of development until it reaches its final character. Friendship among children is hardly more than a rather loosely knit grouping of playmates and not before puberty does real friendship develop. Its core is a longing

163

for completion, for support, for a helper in the distress and anxious loneliness in which the growing child finds itself during the difficult period of puberty. The friend is someone we can trust, confide in, someone who understands. The purpose of these friendships is to bring about the consolidation of the personality of each of the two. Characteristically, one is always the more active, the other the more passive partner, one is the leader, the other the led; the younger looks up to the older one, and the older protects his younger friend. The friendship of grown-up men unites equals, the relationship of subordination changes into co-operation, and working together for a common purpose constitutes the unifying factor.

The second element of the emotional life of the pubescent is *erotic*. Since Plato made this concept the centre of his whole philosophy, many times through the ages attempts have been made to define this phenomenon, which is as intangible, elusive, indescribable, as all real emotional arch-phenomena are. Delight in the beauty, charm, strength of the body is at the root of eroticism; but it is not the body as such, not its material beauty but the beauty of a soul expressed in the loveliness of the body. This is the true meaning of the much misused term 'Platonic love'. It is not a pale, emaciated sentiment, but the vigorous desire to express the spiritual-emotional experience in bodily contact as well. Nearest to it comes what we call 'tenderness'. *Tenderness*, too, wants physical manifestation, such as touching, stroking, embracing, kissing. And what can already be seen from these activities, and can be conclusively proved psychologically, is that these erotic-tender relationships are essentially different from sexual ones. Later on they become a constituent part of mature sexuality, they lie at the bottom of sensuality and stand at its beginning and its end, from the moment a woman puts her arm round the neck of her friend until the lovers fall asleep in each other's arms.

All these three elements, friendship, eroticism and sensuality, contribute to the mature sexuality; from friendship comes the 'standing-up' for one another, from eroticism the tenderness, and from sensuality springs sexuality proper.

Now, this erotic tenderness forms the core of adolescent homosexuality. In practice we meet with different forms of homosexual relationships according to the different motives that lead to them. Just as we did with masturbation, we find here a primitive form established for the relief of a purely physical urge—mutual masturbation in the strict sense of the term. In a second group we find, again in perfect analogy to what we have learned in the case of masturbation, that originally nonsexual sensations are relieved through genital functions. With homosexuality this sensation is what I should call the 'tension of subordination'. There are analogies to be found in the sexual activities of animals. With male rats, for example, the weaker rat takes on the part of the female; tired cockchafers are treated as females by stronger males; birds of different species but of the same sex, kept in the same cage, copulate in a homosexual manner: in other words, all kinds of differences (physical superiority, racial difference) can be experienced in these cases as 'sexual' differences. In the case of adolescent homosexuality the same tension of subordination is operative, inasmuch as one of the partners is the older or stronger one, the leader, the master. In a third group erotic tenderness is the motive for homosexual acitvities.*

So far so good. But there is still the urgent and intriguing question, what causes a boy to turn his tender affection to another boy, instead of to a girl, as the vast majority of 'normal' boys do. In the first place it must be admitted that some external factors support this choice, such as boarding-school education and all sorts of youth clubs; the Wandervogel movement in pre-Hitler Germany, for instance, was in this respect a worthy

*This love, in the truest sense Platonic, can also be experienced by grown-up men towards adolescents without losing its emotional delicacy. Such an experience on the part of an aging man is described in Thomas Mann's classical novel, *Death in Venice*, and in Fr. Rolfe's *The Desire and Pursuit of the Whole*, one of the most fragrant and delicate love stories ever written.

forerunner of the Hitler Youth. If during these critical years boys find themselves practically cut off from the company of girls it is understandable that their often violently awakening emotions turn to the only sort of objects they can get hold of: other boys. But it is obvious that this seclusion is only a supporting and by no means the real causal factor. The true reason must be looked for elsewhere. It lies, as in all cases of sexual difficulty and aberration, not in the sexual sphere itself but in an abnormality of the whole personality of the boy. Its roots are in that abnormality of which it is but one manifestation. In order to make this quite clear we must once more revert to developmental psychology. Our life is from the beginning a continuous breaking-up of existing contacts and entering into new ones. The new-born leaves the body of his mother and after the umbilical cord has been cut he starts a semi-independent existence; semi-independent only because he still gets his food from his mother's breast. When this bodily link too is severed, the child still lives in the orbit of his mother, often enough tied to her by her notorious apron-strings. When more children arrive he enters into their group, and it is only too well known how difficult it is for many a first-born to be demoted from his unique position to being just one among many. The first real break comes when the child leaves home and goes to school, which means entering the 'world'. Brothers and sisters are separate individuals, but still of the same flesh and blood, but schoolmates are real strangers, although here again strangeness is still mitigated by their being creatures of the same sex. But when after the end of puberty the boy is expected to turn to girls, he finds himself facing utter strangeness, an individual with whom he has nothing in common, but in whom he may dimly sense an unknown danger. To take this final step needs self-reliance, determination and courage, and some hesitate on the brink. Instead of taking the ditch in one leap, they cautiously step on to a steppingstone in the midst of the water and take a rest: the steppingstone is the partner of the same sex, and the rest is adolescent homosexuality.

In other words, this kind of homosexuality is the result of timidity, a manifestation of the celebrated inferiority complex, and therefore is abnormal.

Occasionally one comes across a different variety or higher degree of the same trouble: a boy wants to be a girl and, if this desire is strong enough, adopts a female mentality which may lead to all sorts of absurdities in later life, such as homosexuality, dressing as a woman (transvestism), or even the wish to be transformed into a woman by means of operations. In all these cases, with the very rare exception of those with glandular anomalies, this tendency is due to unfortunate experiences on the part of the child attributable to his being a boy. In some such cases the parents have wanted a girl instead of a boy and make the boy feel their disappointment*, or, more frequently, the boy suffers from the successful competition of a sister. I remember a young man who gave this explanation for his 'perversion': 'My sister knew everything without learning, and I always tried hard to learn but never knew a thing, and at school the girls were always preferred by the masters.' Thus he formed the resolve to become a girl. What actually stood behind it was not the wish to change his sex, but only his tiresome life, and to get his success by a trick, as he despaired of getting it by normal means. The concept 'girl' was completely desexualized and only meant 'enviable existence'.

In other cases it means 'easier competition', as in the following story, which demonstrates the genesis of homosexuality with rare lucidity. A man, now 26 years old, was a frail and timid little boy. He went to a co-educational school in which boys and girls played games separately. He was not very good at games and was mercilessly teased about it by his schoolmates. One day it occurred to him that things might be much better if he played with the girls, which he did. The bad piece of luck which this man had at this difficult time in his life was that the headmaster

*The far-reaching results of the stubborn refusal of parents to accept facts as they are is admirably described in Radclyffe Hall's autobiographical novel, *The Well of Loneliness*.

of the school understood the situation at once and tolerated this most unusual arrangement. Thus, the boy went on playing the game of life on the other side of the fence, that is to say, when later on sex awoke in him, he expressed his timidity in sexual terms and became—homosexual.

But the most important and most frequent cause of homosexuality in youth is the desire for support and security. This is the motive of adolescents having affairs with grown-up men, the form of homosexuality most condemned by society. I knew a young man, aged 21, who had several affairs with grown-up men after he had been seduced by a schoolmaster when he was 14. What attracted the boy was maturity as such, and what he wanted was stability, security and permanency. As time went by it occurred to him that a homosexual relation was mainly based on sex because these men seemed to want only sex; the security they gave him was only incidental for them, whereas he wanted and gave passion above all. It gradually dawned on him that what he wanted could really only be given by a woman. Only a woman could be co-operative in feelings and decisions, and although sex must not be the main thing in marriage, the stability he so urgently needed, and which would so much enhance his efficiency, could derive only from a sexual relationship with a woman. This realization put an end to his 'homosexuality'.

This story needs no comment. The sexuality was hardly more than the price, as it were, which he paid for the security he wanted, and passion was the vehicle through which the proximity of these men, the source of his security, was established. The obvious cause of this whole attitude was the fact that his father had left the family when the boy was still small, and all these men had to take over the paternal function. The most remarkable feature of this development is the correct intuition of the young man that only in a proper man-woman relationship can a lasting bond between two persons be established, and that this notion eventually broke through the thin texture of his pseudo-homosexuality.

The case of girls at this stage of their development is somewhat different. The psychological situation is similar to that of boys, but one cannot speak of homosexuality, since everything remains almost exclusively in the erotic sphere. There are kisses, strokings and embracings, but no real sexual acts. Emotions, on the other hand, are very prominent and ardent, and frequently we find diaries expressing the most passionate devotion, the object of which is frequently a woman teacher. As far as we know at present this 'crush' phase is a normal one; nearly all girls pass through it.

Finally, a few words about the attitude educators should adopt towards the problem. As to the victim, the younger boy, it all depends on whether he has already reached the stage of sexual awareness. If not, he remains practically unaffected, and things may sometimes take a rather amusing turn. One day an irate father stormed into my consulting room bitterly complaining that his boy had been seduced at one of the expensive public schools. When I had an opportunity of talking to the boy himself, he quite frankly admitted the facts, and when I asked him how he felt about it at the time he said: 'Well, sir, I was so bored with all this that I went on eating my apple.' But even at a later stage, the resilience of a healthy mind is so great that most boys forget these experiences and emerge unscathed. But it must be admitted that boys predisposed by their aforementioned debility of character are exposed to risks which under more favourable circumstances they might have avoided. More complicated is the position of the older, the aggressive, partner. Here, too, Nature comes to our assistance in that most boys outgrow their physical inferiority and mental timidity, and therefore drop their sexual anomalies before they leave school and find the way to the other sex. But not all of them do so, and by far the larger proportion of all those young men who parade as homosexuals at college and later in life are nothing but overgrown schoolboys.

True, these practices cannot be tolerated in schools, but vigorous severity is just as out of date as is corporal punishment as a means of education; nor are moral exhortations much good. Experience has proved that it is practically most effective and psychologically least harmful to treat the whole thing as a matter of discipline, as something that cannot be tolerated in a school any more than smoking or talking after lights-out, supported perhaps by an appeal to the sense of responsibility of older boys towards their juniors. Boys who do not respond must have psychological treatment, not because of their homosexuality, but because of the underlying cause, as described above.

One would think that co-education is the obvious way to circumvent the whole problem of the approach to sex, of which homosexuality in youth is only one, although the most conspicuous, manifestation. And it is so in many respects: homosexuality is almost unknown in co-educational schools, and women students in Oxford or Cambridge can at once distinguish by his easy manners a co-educated male student from one coming from a tough boys' school. But there is still another aspect to this question. I remember a boy who, when I discussed this problem with him, laughingly said: 'But how can one fall in love with a girl who sweats and toils and fears and hopes in class just like oneself?' What he meant was that the close proximity of comradeship lowers the 'tension of difference' which, as we have seen before, is an essential element of sexual sentiment—or another version of the old adage that familiarity breeds contempt. But that this need not always be so has been amply demonstrated during the war, when work done and danger braved together has helped many a boy to meet girls. There is obviously no clear-cut solution to this problem, any more than of any other real problem of life, and even educators and psychologists must have experienced the unfathomable complexity of life by themselves, in order to be protected from the lure of scientific oversimplification.

Homosexuality among university students

BENJAMIN H. GLOVER, M.D.

SINCE the war there has been a noticeable increase in cases of homosexuality as well as other socially offending sex cases among the general type of psychiatric problems seen in the University of Wisconsin Student Health Department. A great majority of the cases have been veterans.

Fear, of course, is the basic mechanism which drives patients to doctors. In the case of these individuals, who are usually first seen in a homosexual panic, there is intense fear of being caught, of being noticeably different, or the fear which slowly and deeply grows to depressing proportions, that of being unable to be like other people, to be happily married and to raise a family which will be their solace in later years. This fear of an old age loneliness was found in all individuals to be more important to them than was the immediate threat of ostracism at the present time should they be discovered. Hearing of the nonjudicial psychiatric staff, these patients would make an appointment, and in interview would cautiously make inquiries as to the privacy of records and the connexion of the staff to any administrative or disciplinary body. Little was accomplished during the first two or three interviews except for inaccurate, frequently contradictory, records, which were corrected through several future visits, changing 'no affairs' to 'a few childhood experiences' to 'innumerable nights of intimacy' or a long suppressed story of incest. As the number of cases increased and the grapevine spread the news that help through the Psychiatric Department was available, it became more common for panic cases to drop in as emergencies and explode all at once in the first conference.

These were often timed with publication of some local news item concerning exhibitionism or discovery of a group of consorting individuals in town. Another cause was meeting a girl with whom they thought a future life could be enjoyable. Both situations produced the same fear of being found wanting in normal sexual concepts and activities and of being ostracized by society.

From 52 sample cases of assorted sexual deviations in male students seen by this investigator during the last year, 12 cases— all white and single—have been selected as true homosexuals— that is, overt performers of deviant sex practices with their own sex by reason of personal choice, without coercion, with enjoyment—who frequently sought the haunts and company and engaged in the activities of other homosexuals.

No psychotics were included in the original group. Of the remainder of the 52 cases 10 were involved in exhibitionism and public masturbation of the semiprivate variety; 4 were caught as 'peeping Toms'; 2 were indiscreet as fornicators; 7 were psychopathic personalities of a multisexual opportunist variety; and 17 were considered as latent homosexuals, since they were either without overt experience or were limited to a few trial episodes. Several of these latent homosexuals were so young when they experienced their homosexual activities and were still too unfixed in their sexual pattern to permit classification among the regulars.

The whole group of 52 ranged in age from 17 to 42 years. (The 12 selected were from 19 to 31, except for one individual of 42 years.) These 12 patients were especially questioned as to their age at the origin of their condition. In retrospect, many would place the groundwork for their homosexual experience in childhood; thus incidents were brought up of family characteristics of dressing and undressing in the presence of mother and sisters, of mutual masturbation in childhood, of 'horsing around' in wrestling with older boys, of old men taking an unusual interest in their clothing and urinary and bowel habits, and holding the children between their legs. Some felt it was a particularly attractive influence a person had cast over them in their late high school years. All, however, noticed they were different from others of their age group in childhood, and definitely in a different social category after puberty. None of them attributed their state to any deviant pattern in their immediate family, but only a few knew their genealogy beyond the parents, and none knew any details of the sexual patterns of their parents. In immediate families the only abnormalities noted were alcoholism in one, a promiscuous father in another, and divorce and remarriage in 2.

Socially, these patients attained a fairly significant status. Two were active in the dramatic arts; one was a professional musician in a large metropolitan symphony orchestra; one was a medical student; 3 were advanced graduate students, with one a Phi Beta Kappa. Two were teachers, another a radical politico with much publicity, and 2 were mediocre students with poorly defined future plans. None of the group had a hobby, such as woodworking, stamp collecting, radio, etc. In a few cases reading and walking were listed as hobbies. Organized sports were untouched by this group, rarely even as spectators.

Practically all said they spent their free time in deep discussion of art, drama, rights of man, and much common gossip including relation of their own past histories and their action to its retelling. This often led to segregation of couples and more intimate discussions as bedtime approached. All claimed the passive part in the initiation and continuance of homosexual activity, but later as they grew older they adopted more aggressive and daring approaches. In order of frequency and adoption of techniques, it was most common to start with mutual masturbation, then assume heterosexual positions in intercrural intercourse, or to reverse to the position of sodomy. In time one method was favoured, although all participants admitted they would tolerate another approach if they 'loved him enough'. Two members consorted regularly with Negroes. One attempted to room with a Negro, but owing to private and public reaction was prevented from doing so. The 2 who associated with Negroes favoured themselves as fellator first and sodomist second. There were no examples of transvestism or of violent masochistic supplementations, as flagellation, biting or scratching. A few of these individuals noted a progressive change in their pleasure from seeking the part of the male acting partner to a gradually increasing desire to take the female acting part. In first commencing their activities in youth all stated they were passive receivers of a repugnant act almost forced upon them. All but 2 remained relatively passive in their adult invitation to sexual activity. Two repeatedly sought out much younger individuals with little or no experience and aggressively planned their conquest.

The mechanism of meeting is elaborate and prolonged. The city square at night is often a favourite place for picking up companions. During the promenade an interested person picks up one or more followers, moves to a position where he can stand without too much attention being drawn to him, as at a railing, then waits for his followers to show up, one to make the gradual approach, usually remark on the beauty of the evening, edge up to bodily contact, and place a hand on the shoulder, thigh or more personal areas. Remarks are veiled, and usually both parties are unwilling to make the first verbal or physical entree which could be interpreted as a sexual approach, possibly for fear they may be in error and subject to immediate arrest. The next step, if familiarities are permitted, is to suggest a drink or an immediate visit to a room where activities commence. Taverns and bars were most often centres of congregation. Glances and smiles are exchanged and through several hours aggressors move toward or away from various passives until in time a selection of a mate is made. Sometimes a selection is made only after several tavern visits. Occasionally, nothing is said between two interested parties. This is particularly satisfying and is held as the highest achievement because it proves the attraction each has for the other is not based on the artificialities of speech. Movie theatre back seats are used as rendezvous for lonely and desperate consorts. Acquaintance through usual social channels is more difficult except in the group frequenting musical and dramatic performances.

Religiously, opinion in the group was liberal. None expressed religious or racial prejudice. Regarding creed, 5 protested a definite belief, 3 coming from Protestant and 2 from Catholic homes. The remaining 7 were divided into 4 of Protestant faith, including a Quaker and a Christian Scientist, 2 Jewish, and 1 who stated he could not be bound by the dogma of any faith other than a belief in a Greater Being. Only 2 attended church regularly. None felt that there was any religious taboo specifically relating to homosexuality. Only one was an active religious proselyte. This was a Quaker who was actively engaged in a socio-religious peace movement.

Six of the 12 are veterans of World War II, discharged on points with no disciplinary record. Five of the 6 were active homosexually during their service life. The other one immediately became active on discharge when he heard of the death of a nurse whom he had frequently dated, and who knew of his latent homosexual status and with whom he had planned marriage. One was specifically directed not to drink while in service because he 'did things in public' that he should not do, which were punishable by court-martial. As reported often in military psychiatry, most homosexuals are to be found in the secretarial branches, chaplain's aides, hospital assistants, photographers. Two of the 6 veterans during service were employed as hospital assistants, another in a band and a dance orchestra, another as a chaplain's aide, and one as a stenographer. None saw active combat and only one was overseas. Contrary to expectations, none were introduced to homosexuality via the service. One of the nonveterans served as a conscientious objector in camp and prison for three years. The others were excluded from service by reason of physical disqualifications, essential jobs as teacher, premedical student, aeroplane factory worker, or under age.

Among the group there was no great use of special slang terminology. Perhaps this was due to the cultured atmosphere, but the only terms used were gay, queer, queen and fan. Only 2 of the group spontaneously mentioned the pleasures of the ambiguous speech between homosexuals as contrasted with the vulgarity of any attempts at ambiguous speech in heterosexuals.

Only 4 of the group failed to experience physical revulsion approaching nausea when exposed intimately to the female body. One, while sitting in a deep hammock with a lightly clad female, experienced an erection followed by sudden nausea. None had prostituted themselves. Two had visited female prostitutes, one without resultant special feeling of any kind, the other with increasing disgust, use of repeated prophylactics and troubled dreams for some time thereafter. The likes and dislikes of the group were interesting. After careful consideration and reminder on at least two visits with a final culling on the third visit, they were asked to select their most deeply felt likes and dislikes in life, aside from active sex. The likes included: evening with family or friends, ballet, movies, plays, reading, dancing, radio, especially music and particularly the impressionistic and classical type of Debussy and Tschaikovsky. Those who cared for nonclassical modern music enjoyed Count Basie and Duke Ellington as favourites. It is interesting that both of these men are Negroes. With this list their likes stopped. Those things which were most distasteful to these patients were: chalk on hands, dirt, stepping on bugs, music out of tune, women in general (described as 'awful'), baseball, piety, required social functions, noise, police, routine or anything approaching monotony.

Love is a commonplace word in conversation with homosexuals. They are fully able to understand the unusual loves expressed by another and to entertain an excellent empathy in their relating. Thus when an overt homosexual has been told in a hypothetical case of the letters and exchanges of gifts, the philosophies and physical raptures described by another homosexual he becomes deeply touched. He may attempt to offer or even urge his own advice on the one described and to make sincere inquiry from time to time through the doctor about the progress of the lovers. Because of their casual freedom of speech on sex matters between themselves it has been difficult to discuss some of their own much involved individual case histories in the more active members of this group without implicating a large number of well-known homosexuals on the campus. Thus in the 12 included here, there was a clique of 3 who well knew the life histories of the other 2 in the group. Like heterosexuals it was perhaps significant that each deleted from his story to the other that more than one affair was in progress at or about the same time. Likewise, each homosexual among the 12 felt that his present amour was a permanent one, different from the one before him.

These people represent a parody and a paradox in emotions: in a sense they burlesque love as a heterosexual knows it and yet they are a continual tragedy of failure to find either sex grati-fication or a person through whom they may enjoy continuously that measure of sex gratification they attain. They are devoted to their loves with an expressed passion; yet they have little if any feeling for their parents and doubt that they would be upset beyond a small measure of inconvenience if death or severe illness were to involve them. There is a narcissistic selfishness in their disregard for people as a whole, no nationalistic or patriotic feeling, a general disdain of inheritance and social values of law, religion and the betterment of mankind. It is obvious that there is no interest in eugenics. All feel distinctly inferior though their façade may be one of superiority. Their periods of panic are brief interludes of near awakening to heterosexual thinking, but almost entirely on a level of childish immaturity such as the fear of being caught. Their decisiveness is lacking, from the initiation of sexual activity among their own kind to the lack of resistance to its continuance or the ability to change actively to more socially acceptable sexual performances. This is in the nature of a com-pulsion of inertia. Their indifference to fundamentals, their inertia, their fantasies and investiture of simple events with markedly exaggerated interpretation, their paranoid trends, emotional immaturity and well-known instability and suicidal ideas indicate a large schizoid element in their personality. They are preoccupied with sex gratification and largely controlled by the desire to increase their opportunities in sex activity. No critical analysis of objective tests has been attempted for this small group. However, the profiles of both overt and latent homosexuals who took the Minnesota-Multiphasic Test were above the normal in Mf (Masculine-Feminine) score and low in Pd (Psychopathic deviate), but within normal range. It is emphasized that homosexuality should not be considered as a separate entity, though it may approach such proportions in some individuals.

From earliest times the question of inheritance versus effects of the environment in producing the qualities of homosexuality has been debated. During the last century the tendency to accept homosexuality as an acquired characteristic was common and many attempts were made in treatment to control the drives of these people by psychotherapeutic methods. There have been obvious deficiencies in this concept. The present attitude is toward the congenital anomaly or inherited tendencies in this group.

In favour of the inherited aetiology, Theo Lang[4] in his studies on the genetic determination of homosexuality obtained figures which suggest strongly that many cases of homosexuality are hereditarily determined by a definite genetic mechanism. There is further evidence of the basic medical differences between homosexuals and normal individuals as seen by the work of Wright,[12] Sevringhaus[9] and Meyerson and Neustadt[5] in which the amount and proportion of oestrogens and androgens are distinctly different from similar determinations of normal individuals. Green and Johnson[2] support this view experimentally and consider the abnormal ratio as a sign of homosexuality. It is concluded by Meyerson and Neustadt[5] that the amount of androgens in the body is mainly responsible for the strength and vigour of the sex drive of the individual, while the absolute and proportionate amount of oestrogen determines its general direction. Williams[6] (at Lexington, Kentucky) has demonstrated that feminine male homosexuals differ from other males in that the usual decrease in serum cholinesterase following prostigmine injection does not occur. Clinical evidence has repeatedly demonstrated a great mass of information which tends to confirm the constitutional qualities of homosexuality by personal history and autobiographies of known homosexuals. Many of these records show practically no environmental influence to produce personality moulding toward such an aberration. All stress the very early development of homosexual idiosyncracies. In a great majority of cases extreme mother dependence is common. Silverman and Rosanoff[10] in a study of 55 homosexuals at the Springfield, Missouri, Medical Center for Federal Prisoners obtained a high incidence of neurologic signs suggestive of cerebral lesions as well as histories of neuropathic taint in the family histories of homosexual individuals. Pathologic or borderline electroencephalographic tracings were obtained from 75 per cent of the prisoners tested. It was concluded that an inherited or early acquired abnormality of the central nervous system played a contributory role in the development of homosexuality. X-ray studies of the skull and metabolic tests failed to show significant deviations from the normal in other of Rosanoff's studies[8]. Havelock Ellis[2] reported that eccentricity, alcoholism, neurasthenia, insanity, nervous disease and inversion were commonly found in the family background of homosexuals. Whether these various findings indicate a distinct third sex, a sex intergrade or sport, or an interruption in maturation producing moral, intellectual and physical alterations in the individual is far from conclusively established, but in general the theory concerning the constitutional character of homosexuality is currently popular.

The problem of treatment of homosexuality is made immensely more difficult and decidedly empirical because of the undetermined aetiology. All the techniques of psychiatry have been applied in attempting a 'cure' of homosexuality. Most textbooks gracefully evade the subject. Of the various methods now in use to correct homosexuality, the endocrine method has not proved satisfactory. Meyerson and Neustadt[6] with the use of oral methyltestosterone, 10 mg. twice daily for two months alternating with a rest period of two months, have demonstrated that the treatment may modify homosexuality, taking away the compelling drive, but basically does not change the direction of sex gratification. This is essentially the result of all other investigators in the field of endocrinology. Disciplinary measures have long been known to be unsuccessful. Hypnotherapy and narco-suggestion have failed. Conscious methods of psychotherapy involving substitution techniques, the use of sedative or depressant drugs and recommendations for heterosexual intercourse have shown no conclusively effective result in control or obliteration of the condition. Curran[1] in England states there is little hope of alteration after the age of 25, although there is better perspective and better coping with the problem. He states it is necessary for people to remove their homosexual disabilities from a special mental compartment where they are subjectively hidden. Habit formation is stressed as important and avoiding abnormally stimulating situations. Good mental hygiene is stressed. He adds that sexual perversions are often the result of boredom, using the adage, 'the Devil finds work for idle hands'.

The only person to claim real success has been Owensby of Atlanta.[7] In 1940 he reported his treatment by means of metrazol shock therapy. In 1941 he reported 15 cases treated by this method with 13 'cured' for three years and only 2 failures because of inadequate follow-up. He states that male homosexuals do not want to change except for the fear of social penalty. He accents that homosexuals are on the increase and that there are from 10 to 30 million in number in the United States. (We have seen one homosexual whose latent quality, prior to electric shock therapy given for a schizophrenic episode, has turned to overt activities on at least one occasion and possibly two since his therapy.) As yet the enthusiastic reports of Dr. Owensby are not substantiated. The method of treatment used by us here has been one of direct psychotherapy. The patient is carefully informed that the desire to make a permanent change in his habits, co-operative self-help throughout life, and the temporary cessation of all overt sexual activities, both homosexual and heterosexual, is necessary from the beginning. He is advised to consider carefully just how much he really desires to alter his way of thinking, acting and feeling. Perhaps he is given more opportunity to withdraw than to enter upon a hard and lifelong project. No guarantee of success is offered, but a possibility of reshaping his life by reconditioning and re-education is suggested. It is only fair to admit that many individuals are unwilling to accept so tenuous a security as a hope and immediately withdraw from the long term therapy plan.

If agreeable to the plan, the project is commenced by a description of the early embryologic bisexuality in the human being with stress on a late determination of individual sex characteristics in intra-uterine life. This opens the way to discussion of the many possible intergrades between 'absolute masculinity and femininity.' There are innumerable examples which can be drawn from personal acquaintances of the patient or from his knowledge of animals as cows, chickens and dogs in which one sex may undertake or assume the position and activities of the other sex at certain seasons or when in certain combinations of herd or associations. Also, many examples of the flexibility of sexual adaptation can be drawn from information on persons exposed to unusual circumstances as the conversion of an apparently stable heterosexual to overt homosexuality under stress of war, isolation, imprisonment, alcoholic intoxication or immediate social pressure. The return to heterosexual living by change of environment, change of social pressure and factors of adaptability in these people are a stimulus to the hopes and plans of the prospective patient.

As the patient is desensitized to the enormity of his problem and to the disinterested scientific attitude and terminology of the psychiatrist there is good opportunity to explain the logical development of the restrictions of society on deviant sex practices. A practical, sociologic approach sprinkled generously with present-day tribal variations and religious and superstitious influences serves to make more interesting a purely historical and ethnologic subject. Thus the early polygamy and mixed sexuality and practices of early man are brought down through history and conditions of living to the accepted monogamous and purely heterosexual practices of the present *mores* of civilized man. Emphasis is placed on bringing the description up to present-day life with examples of the practical value of adherence to the basic taboos even though it is common knowledge that some other condition as heterosexual familiarity or even promiscuity are tolerated and apparently even sanctioned publicly.

With the academic preparation finished the interviews become more practical and personal. Several sessions are devoted to questioning the patient on his concepts as to the outward appearance and manner (criteria of identification) of the commonly accepted homosexual type, then specifically those marks of homosexuality which apply to himself are determined. The patient frequently recalls conversational allusions by people unacquainted with his sexual practices which were spoken of as 'queer' patterns. These are studiously eliminated as a practical lesson of establishing confidence by manly first appearance and the development of mannerisms which are masculine in connotation or at least not doubtfully masculine. At first many patients feel that changes in hand movements, voice inflection and especially in gait and facial responses are unnatural and a false veneer, but as they continue to practise and obtain favourable reactions from their associates or at least do not find themselves under unfavourable surveillance they are increasingly eager to improve their adaptations and obtain a confident polish to their physical control. This conning in the dramatic arts is a delicate feature of the therapy. It is difficult for the patient to give up or to alter many patterns of lifelong duration or those which he has formerly cultivated to a high degree of perfection in an effort to obtain greater satisfaction in his former way of living. It is obviously very easy to antagonize by aggressive criticism at this time. Nevertheless with any slight achievement this step coming early in the programme gives great stimulus to the shaken confidence of the homosexual.

The change in the associational thinking of the homosexual commences with the first interview and continues throughout every contact thereafter. The process is a slow and often un-conscious one among those who collaborate by dropping their connexions with their homosexual friends and endeavouring to expand their interests and activities along conventional lines of psychosexual behaviour. Among those who are resistant to giving up a room-mate or friend, or unwilling to renounce completely the homosexual preoccupation with daydreaming fantasy, there is only superficial alteration with no real change in the ego image. Where there is fairly strong evidence of psycho-pathic personality there is little chance of developing an undevi-ating heterosexual response pattern to the stimuli received by these individuals who have over a long formative period attached a veiled homosexual connotation to almost everything in their environment. The whole ecology of the patient must be modified and particularly in this area of associational and conceptual thinking which in turn is dependent on the degree of adaptability and the experiences of pleasure in the new environment. Great effort is devoted to encouraging a competitive sense, beginning with sports or games with the intent of diverting a usually large amount of unbalanced paranoid feeling to the control seen in competitive fair play. The socialization and diversion of outlook in group endeavours is pushed and opportunity for acceptance by a heterosexually oriented group is constantly sought. The plan bogs down badly among the unconfident, passive and dependent individuals who must be encouraged along more organized lines such as taking courses in public speaking and debate (foregoing dramatics) rather than progressing by his own volition in seeking responsibilities.

The lassitude and inertia of homosexuals greatly contributes to the poor psychotherapeutic results. During the heat of remorse at being publicly exposed or legally punished they respond attentively to the preliminary work of preparing them for their ecological change, but the stigma of their pattern follows them in time and their socialization is a most difficult thing in even the relatively enlightened atmosphere of a university. Those who have sought help without public pressure also quickly deteriorate in the strength and vigour of their efforts.

Up to the present time only one of the selected 12 has made significant improvement during one year of this type of psychotherapy. His pattern is not yet automatic, but he has found a reality which is not without great compensation in comparison with his former fantasy and practice. There have been no scholastic or psychiatric casualties in this group.

REFERENCES

[1] Curran, D.: Perversions and Their Treatment, *Practitioner*, *158:* 343 (1947).

[2] Ellis, H.: *Psychology of Sex. Studies in the Psychology of Sex*, Vol. 22, Part II.

[3] Green and Johnson: *J. Crim. Psychopath.*, 5, 467 (1944).

[4] Lang, T.: 'Studies on the Genetic Determination of Homosexuality,' *Journal of Nervous and Mental Disease*, 92, 55 (1940).

[5] Meyerson, A., and Neustadt, R.: 'Bisexuality and Male Homosexuality. Their Biologic and Medical Aspects', *Clinics*, 1, 932 (1942).

[6] ———: 'Essential Male Homosexuality and Results of Treatment', *Arch. Neurol. & Psychait.*, 55, 291 (1946).

[7] Owensby, N. M.: 'Homosexuality and Lesbianism Treated with Metrazol', *Journal of Nervous and Mental Disease*, 92, 65 (1940).
———:'Correction of Homosexuality', *Urol. & Cutan. Rev.*, 45, 494 (1941).

[8] Rosanoff, W. R., and Murphy, F. E.: 'The Basal Metabolic Rate, Fasting Blood Sugar, Glucose Tolerance and Size of the Sella Turcica in Homosexuals'. *Am. J. Psychiat.*, 101, 97 (1944).

[9] Sevringhaus, E. L., and Chornyak, J.: 'Homosexual Adult Males', *Psychosomat. Med.*, *7*, 302 (1945).

[10] Silverman, D., and Rosanoff, W. R.: 'Electroencephalographic and Neurologic Studies of Homosexuals', *Journal of Nervous and Mental Disease*, *101*, 311 (1945).

[11] Williams, E. G.: 'Homosexuality: A Biological Anomaly', *Journal of Nervous and Mental Disease*, *99*, 65 (1944).

[12] Wright, C. A.: *M. Rec.*, *149*: 399 (1939); *ibid.*, *154*, 60 (1941).

Psychogenic and constitutional factors

GEORGE W. HENRY, M.D.

It should not be necessary to remark that the division of any group of human beings into those who are heterosexually adapted and those who are chiefly homosexual in their interests is somewhat arbitrary. Phylogenetically and embryologically it seems that we have evolved from a state of hermaphroditism and it would be unlikely if not impossible that any individual would lose all traces of bisexuality however mature he became. A predominance of maleness or femaleness, according to the sex, is all that may be expected in those who are heterosexually adjusted. In many individuals it seems that the sexual balance is so delicate that unfortunate sexual traumata occurring early in life, or the many obstacles in the pathway to sexual maturity may determine a homosexual development.*

The problem of the extent to which there may be constitutional and physiological predisposition to heterosexual or homosexual adaptation will probably always give rise to much speculation. In this particular study the basis for the selection of the two groups was the psychosexual development of each patient as noted in the clinical history and in the records of interviews with the patient.

When the actual performance of these groups is compared the differences are rather striking. All of the heterosexual patients were married and reproduced. None of them had been divorced and there were no extramarital relationships. The male hetero-

*In this study an individual was regarded as being homosexual when there was evidence of pleasure derived from repeated homosexual relationships. Such an individual also failed to make an adequate heterosexual adaptation and in illness manifested either overt homosexual desires or compensatory strivings against them.

sexual patients were the fathers of from one to four children and the female heterosexual patients had given birth to from one to seven children.

In contrast to this none of the homosexual male patients had children and only 3 of the 17 had married. Two of these three were divorced and the third was separated. Of the 16 homosexual female patients 5 had married but 2 of these were divorced and one marriage was annulled. Only 4 of this group had reproduced and none of them had more than one child.

A more searching inquiry into the relationship of the psychosexual development to unusual childhood attachments or aversions and to sexual experiences seems to add to the understanding of the general observations already stated. Such an inquiry inevitably leads to a most detailed study of individual cases but it is still possible to note general tendencies. The clinical notations to be given were obtained entirely from the records of homosexual patients because the heterosexual patients presented no such material.

Any intimate emotional relationship during childhood with a member of the family is prone to strongly influence the psychosexual development of the individual. More often this relationship involves the parents. Its effects are observable whether the reaction is one of affection, fear or antagonism.

Unusual affectionate relations and experiences tend to be perpetuated and reappear later in life with substituted persons, in dreams, in fantasies or in psychotic reconstructions. The deep affection of a devoted son for his mother, who was described as being 'full of vitality', may have been a determining factor in the sexual relations of this son with the father's secretary, an older married woman. This was followed by a profound sense of guilt and an attempt at suicide on the father's birthday. In his psychosis he referred to himself as a 'weak sister'. This in turn may have been an identification with the father who described himself as being 'a regular old woman'. This patient sought passive fellatio relations with male nurses.

A childhood characterized by fear of the father and an older brother and by peeping on female members of the family probably was related to the subsequent psychosexual events in another patient. He was boxed on the ear at the age of four by his father for not knowing the catechism. He was teased and bullied by his brother who also frightened him by dressing up as a ghost. He was in constant fear of punishment for peeping which he continued at least until puberty. In addition to homosexual love affairs he was seduced by a series of sophisticated women, most of whom were married. Finally, shortly before his psychosis a divorced woman with four children induced him to marry her. They all had to be supported by his family. In his psychosis he was fearful that he would be attacked by the male nurses.

Antagonism toward and fear of the father along with an attachment to the mother in the childhood of a third patient was followed in adult life by passive fellatio desires and an inability to make a heterosexual adjustment. During the acute stages of his illness the patient made several attacks upon women in order to try to overcome his homosexual tendencies. One of these attacks was upon an older sister who resembled his mother and to whom in fantasy he was married. He also said, 'I am so much attached to my mother I am fighting my father all of the time .... it's the father prohibition that keeps me away from women .... The strongest sexual combination is with my mother ... having my feet in her mouth and my penis in her vagina.' His most difficult task was to get the woman in him to overcome the father in him and he added, 'When you have both of them you are a child.' He gradually gave up the struggle as futile, accepted the role of being a child, wore white garments and asked to be circumcised as a symbol of purification.

There is abundant evidence that the particular variety of sexuality experienced in childhood determines the preference of later years. The conflict that arises therefrom may be terrific and may result in most vigorous denials, in distortion and projection of the libidinous interests or in acts of violence. One patient formed a morbid attachment for another boy at the age of 5 and continued this until 15 when the other boy left him. At 21 in his first heterosexual experience he expected to find a protruding genital canal. In commenting upon the experience he said, 'I went right for her breasts—kissed them—took the nipple in my mouth—I felt just like a baby . . . afterward I felt disgusted'. A second attempt two years later was less successful and the girl suggested that he get a 'fairy'. In his psychosis he felt that people regarded him as a homosexual and that they could tell this by the changes in his lips and face. He said he would rather die than be considered a homosexual.

Another patient at the age of 12 was the victim of anal relations with his father and with an older brother. In his psychosis he believed that in his sleep his brother and another man committed sodomy upon him. He said that his father always had an odour about his genitals as a result of these perverse practices.

The inability in later life to acknowledge the perverse tendencies of childhood is illustrated by a patient who was regarded as a 'model child' but who at the age of 10 had fellatio relations with another boy. In his psychosis he said that people put out their tongues at him indicating thereby that he was a c. s. Phrases of this kind kept coming to his mind and voices called him a c. s.

More careful study of the patient shows that the psychosexual history is usually much more complicated than is indicated by the illustrations thus far given. Childhood experiences may not be the only determinants of libidinous preferences. One of the homosexual patients had masturbated with other boys throughout childhood and his adult homosexual relations also consisted of mutual masturbation. At the age of 11 his mother described heterosexual intercourse to him as being disgusting and it was not until he was 20 years old that he was aware of heterosexual desires. At that time he happened to see the exposed buttocks of of an aunt and had a desire for anal relations with her. Four years later he was pursued by a married woman who obtained a divorce in order to marry him. He retreated in vain. On their honeymoon he tried to choke her and then said he would like to have sexual relations with her. He began to use cannabis indica and put cheyenne pepper on the glans. He wished his penis was larger and put pieces of rubber around it to make it fit tighter. Within a few months his chief desire was for anal relations. He pressed his genitals against the buttocks of women in elevators and embarrassed his wife by demanding anal relations from one of her female friends, old enough to be his mother. His wife then obtained a divorce. In his psychosis he went about exposing his genitals to men. He said that a certain married woman was to be his wife, his mother and his sweetheart and that she was going to treat him like a three-year-old child.

It is somewhat more difficult to establish life patterns among the female homosexuals. In general their libidinous preferences are less obvious and the attachments between females are less conspicuous.

Either passivity or devotion to the mother was observed in two-thirds of the group. Some of the members of this group wished they were boys and they readily established 'crushes' on girls in school. Passivity and the tendency to be unusually affectionate toward the mother seemed to continue. There was conspicuous failure to adjust after the mother died or when confronted with any situation in which heterosexual adaptation was required. While psychotic they either felt attracted to women and made homosexual advances or they felt that other women were doing something to arouse them sexually.

These tendencies may be illustrated by the two following cases. One was a precocious, timid child who was attached to her mother and always wished she had been a boy. She had had crushes on girls of the feminine type toward whom she used to play a masculine role. In her psychosis she had a violent attachment to another patient, got in bed with her and wrote ecstatic love verses to her.

The other patient illustrating these tendencies was shy with women before puberty but had a crush on a female professor in college. She talked a good deal about homosexuality and represented that she despised it although one of her close friends was obviously homosexually inclined. In her psychosis she protested that the homosexual advances of another woman were obnoxious to her. It seemed that the patient obtained the most satisfaction from masturbation, which she had begun at the age of three, and through sexual relations with a man old enough to be her father.

The combination in a female homosexual of devotion to the father and hatred of the mother is likely to give rise to violent emotional reactions to either sex. One patient of this type lived with her husband only five weeks, was aggressive toward him and then contemplated murdering him. In a psychosis 10 years later she said she was a man. She was unusually aggressive toward the nurses and without apparent provocation nearly killed another patient old enough to be her mother.

A patient who was devoted to her father and despised her mother married a widower at the age of 22. She did this in rebellion against her mother who had called her a loose woman. Afer marriage she was frigid. In her psychosis 13 years later and after a period of using drugs and drinking to excess, she accused her husband of being a homosexual. She said that she had fooled him about her sexual desires and that she herself was a congenital Lesbian.

An unpleasant homosexual assault in childhood may be related to an aggressive, vindictive attitude. A patient who at the age of four had had her rectum stuffed with paper by another girl is recorded as having thrashed a boy who teased her several years later. In her psychosis she thought she had killed her mother and feared she would kill the nurse.

Whatever the relation of these sexual experiences may be it is reasonably clear that sexual traumata in childhood leave a lasting impression. A timid, self-depreciative woman reared in a home dominated by women was in childhood much under the influence of her brother. They indulged in mutual exposure and attempted intercourse. Before the age of 10 a man had exposed himself to her and she had peeked at her father. At the age of 20 there was a short period of infatuation with a friend of her brother which she terminated because the idea of intercourse seemed terrible. In her psychosis she had fantasies of male and female genitalia and of auto-fellatio—the genitals appeared unattached and were related vaguely to the man who had exposed himself to her in childhood. She had fantasies of her father assaulting children. She wished to have sexual relations with her brother and was afraid to have him visit her. She had fantasies of his penis getting longer and longer and going into her. She wished he were dead so that he would not be around to bother her any more.

Another patient was the favourite of a sexually promiscuous and miserly father. At the age of six she was informed by her grandmother that the father might use her sexually and that he was a beast. She was also warned that she would go crazy if she abused herself. Two years later she was sent by her mother to spy upon her father while he was having an affair with the woman next door. After she had witnessed the scene her mother explained to her that they were practising fellatio. When the patient was 17 the father remarried but she could not tolerate another woman in her mother's place and wanted to die. For several years she had promiscuous heterosexual relationships but with satisfaction from masturbation only. In her psychosis 10 years later she had strong impulses to perform fellatio on an effeminate man to whom she later became engaged.

Undoubtedly homosexual interests often are important factors in the choice of a career. This was observed in a male homosexual who was indifferent to girls and who began masturbation at the age of six. At puberty a camp counsellor introduced him to mutual masturbation and homosexual interests were continued with an instructor in a private school. In this school he was told that sexual desires must be subdued by vigorous exercise. Later he became very popular with boys through his unusual athletic ability.

His illness was precipitated by the engagement of a girl, a distant cousin, to one of his friends. He had not previously shown any interest in this cousin but then declared he was deeply in love with her. He had been working in a bank simply to please his mother but he really wanted to teach in a boys' school and coach athletics. He acted as an usher at this cousin's wedding but was disgusted by the drinking after the ceremony. He would not take a drink himself because he was afraid he would disclose his real feelings if he became intoxicated. Within a few weeks he became very religious and wanted to become a priest. He asked for a pistol and when this was refused he started to run to a nearby monastery. In the hospital he prayed constantly for God's help against the devil and said he must atone for his sins before he could enter the priesthood. He became very much attached to a male nurse, wished to be of service to others and said he would like to be an attendant in this hospital.

When the conflict over homosexuality leads to a psychosis the patient often feels that there is no solution for his problems, becomes desperate and may be driven to acts of violence. The aggressive activity is often directed towards others but it may at the same time be self-destructive. This may be illustrated by the history of a 29-year-old catatonic male whose mother was psychotic and whose father was rather excitable but devoted to him. He was a docile child who before puberty was afraid of his father and thereafter was fond of him. During adolescence the patient lived in a priest's family. He idealized women and although homosexuality was abhorrent to him he was tolerant of those so inclined. His first heterosexual experience at 17 was unsatisfactory and a few years later he sought and was given treatment for syphilis although he had not been infected. At the age of 25 he began a serious love affair with a married woman 15 years his senior and at about the same time he was circumcised. Four years later he was obsessed with the idea that he had contaminated others with syphilis and that for this he would probably be electrocuted. When voices reminded him of homosexual practices he would say, 'Oh! Shut up—I never did such a thing —just a little at the start.' He became aggressive and resistive. He thought his father was against him, that the physician was going to take out his eyes and that he was going to be killed. He called the male nurses murderers and thieves and attacked them whenever they entered his room. On the other hand he asked to be put into packs, to be fed by tube and he made desperate self-destructive dives onto the floor and against the wall.

Uncontrollable self-destructive tendencies associated with a profound sense of guilt and feelings of utter hopelessness and desperation may be observed for weeks and months before the final act is committed. This combination may be illustrated by the histories of two female homosexuals. One of them was the only child of a worrisome, psychotic father and of a nervous, sleepless and devoted mother. As a child the patient did not care to associate with other children and she was watched with unusual care by the mother because of supposed heart trouble. At the age of six she was taught masturbation by a female cousin. During adolescence she preferred the company of girls who were of the intellectual type like herself and this preference caused boys to shun her. Although her mother was her constant companion sex topics were never discussed.

Her first heterosexual interests appeared when she was 27 and during the next five years she indulged in perverted sexual practices with a man whom she expected to marry. Marriage was postponed in order to please the mother and because neither wished to be separated. The patient said that even if she did marry she wanted to continue to live with her mother. At 31 a strong, athletic girl of 19 won her affections. At first the patient represented that she was trying to keep this girl from being sexually promiscuous. Sometimes homosexual relations occurred several times a day and through these experiences the patient began to obtain sexual gratification. This had not been achieved in her heterosexual relations. The man and the girl were jealous of each other and the patient felt guilty because she was not being fair with her fiancé. Within a year she became self-accusative and hypochondriacal. She confessed to her mother that she had been 'wicked' and was no longer her 'darling child'. She felt that the nurses were plotting against her and delighted in making her suffer. They knew all about her homosexual relations and inferred she was having such relations with other patients. They had spread a rumour that she was going to have a baby. (No interest in having a child had been manifested previously.) She insisted that she could never get well, that her bowels never moved and that she was all stuffed up. She begged insistently to be allowed to go home to her mother. Finally she was removed by her mother against advice and three days later in her home she committed suicide with gas.

The second patient was the youngest child and only daughter of an indulgent father. He had had an affair in his 74th year. Her nervous repressed mother had instilled prudish ideas and kept the patient ignorant of sexual matters. She had been a robust, tomboyish girl and was described by her mother as having been unafraid of 'God, man or the devil'. At the age of 10 a man showed her a picture of a nude female statue. She ran away from him, told her mother and thereafter feared she would grow up to be like the statue, with no genital opening. At 13 she was much upset when her brother tried to introduce her to masturbatory activities. While attending dramatic school at 18 she started out with a road company but soon deserted because of nostalgia and her mother's solicitude. Two years later she started a business course but after two months again returned to her mother. For a short time she accepted the attentions of a young man who later told her brother that she was as 'cold as a fish'.

She became psychotic at the age of 34 after a benign cyst had been removed from her vulva. Her mother had died five years prior to this and because the patient refused to do any housework she and her father went to live with a married brother. She spent much of her time smoking and in discussing ultra-modern views of sex with sophisticated spinsters. She also participated in the quarrels with her brother's wife.

About four months after the operation on her vulva she became excited, said the doctor had aroused her sexually and that he had robbed her of her sex. She was greatly upset when this physician mentioned the possibility of an early menopause. She walked about the house nude and frequently said; 'I have to know the truth—is it too late?—Is there something wrong with me?' While still under the influence of an overdose of allonal which she had taken with suicidal intent she said: 'I am still in the dark as to sex—there are two sides to me—my male side and my female side. I must have relations with a man and a woman—must have sexual experience—I must have a full term baby. Sex has been hidden from me.' She also said that she was afraid to die lest she meet her mother.

She exposed herself to her brother, indulged in autoerotic practices with him, entered a neighbour's home and offered herself to two men there. She pursued a 16-year-old neighbour lad with such zeal that for two weeks he was afraid to leave his home. She also attacked a coloured maid and had homosexual relations with her father's nurse. On the day before admission to the hospital it was a problem to keep her from assaulting men sexually and she did attack her brother's wife and the nurse.

After admission she again stated, 'There are two sides to me— a female and a masculine side—it is too late—things could have been made all right for me years ago.' Voices told her that it was too late and they also told her to assault nurses and develop her masculine side. She requested the physician to perform an operation upon her to hasten the growth of hair and the development of a penis so that she would become a man. She also said that a woman physician had tried to take away her masculine side. She made vicious assaults upon the nurses, trying to kiss them and at the same time pulling their hair, clawing them and attempting to bite them. On one occasion she got out of the prolonged bath and tried to drown the nurse. In these assaults she would make rhythmic movements of her body strongly suggesting the masculine role and sexual approach. She said it was too late to have sexual relations with men, and: 'I am going to live with women—the male sexual organs are slowly developing—I will soon be a whole man—Doctor E., who performed the operation (removal of cyst from vulva)—started the male side to develop and I will use it—I am dried up from a female standpoint but I will become a man of the most rotten type.' She admitted that since the early part of her illness voices had commanded her to assault people and had continually said to her, 'It is too late for you, now'. She was transferred to a State hospital and four days later hanged herself.

If we could be sure that the heterosexually adjusted patients had not been exposed to sexual traumata in childhood it might then be possible to conclude that homosexuality is psychogenically determined. It is probable, however, that the heterosexual patients also had to deal with psychosexual problems early in life. Even if these problems were conspicuously less acute than those of the homosexual group the question still arises as to why the heterosexual individual appears to have been unaffected by sexual traumata while in the psychosexual history of the homosexual there is the sequence of events already related. It seems that there must be other factors which contribute to the differences in psychosexual development.

Even the layman is aware of constitutional differences in human beings and it seemed worth while to try to determine what physical traits might be associated with psychosexual development. By paying special attention to the stage of development of the primary and secondary sex characteristics in the patients studied we might be able to arrive at some estimate of the constitutional differences and of the degree of sexual development at a physiological level. There might then be evidence of greater susceptibility to psycho-sexual traumata, especially on the part of individuals who manifest homosexual preferences.

In any case the results of such a study* made upon the group of patients included in this investigation are particularly illuminating.

The combination of constitutional and psychogenic factors is well illustrated in a homosexual male, 37 years old. There were several members of his family showing endocrinopathies. The mother was neurotic and had a depression. Nevertheless she took care of the family finances as the father had no business sense. A younger brother was also neurotic.

At birth the patient weighed only five pounds and during early childhood his health was impaired by severe illnesses. He was described as a sweet, submissive and agreeable child who attended religious services regularly. He was, however, very sadistic toward his younger brother. He used to promise to give this brother a ride in return for being allowed to pinch him or to jump up and down upon him. They never have got along well together.

When he was six years old he asked his mother about the mechanism of reproduction but he was not enlightened by her explanation. At that age he experienced sexual pleasure by climbing up a pole. At 10 he began solitary masturbation, a practice which he has continued. He also enjoyed watching an older boy exhibit his genitals. Mutual masturbation begun with another boy was continued until the patient's marriage.

Although he was intellectually precocious he did only average work at school. He deliberately made mistakes so that he would be punished. He envied another boy who was frequently whipped. Although his mother spanked him, she would not allow him to be spanked at school with the result that he had to write sentences instead.

When he was 12 years old he was surprised on seeing his father's genitals to find that his father was actually not a sexless person. The patient has always worried about his own small penis and envied the large penis of the friend with whom he had mutual masturbatory experiences. He also felt inferior because of his

*I am indebted to Dr. Hugh M. Galbraith for his assistance in making the physical examinations of these patients.

small stature (5 ft. 2¼ ins.) and was jealous of his younger brother whose body as well as his penis was larger.

At the age of 13 he discovered the facts about reproduction while studying physiology. He was disgusted at the thought of sexual contact between his parents. Two years later he fell in love with a girl of 12 but there was no other heterosexual interest of this kind until he was nearly 30.

In college he studied dentistry for two years but then gave it up because the microscope hurt his eyes. As he was able to do any amount of reading at this time it is probable that in discontinuing the study of dentistry he avoided comparison with his father who was a successful dentist.

After being a professor of German for several years, until this language could no longer be taught because of the feeling during the war, he sought a Ph.D. degree in French. At the time of the examinations he suffered from insomnia, had a sense of impending disaster, feared his heart would stop beating and was troubled with nausea, vertigo and with numbness of his left arm.

He was then 33 years of age and had been married two years. He had become very anxious to marry and after being refused by two girls he married a woman four years his senior who had been practically reared by his own mother. Although he had known his wife for 20 years he had seen her only once in the 10 years prior to the wedding. Their courtship was by correspondence. She was of the same physical build, a somewhat masculine type of woman and she was found to have an infantile uterus. She was also suspected of being a homosexual. Both were anxious to have children but conception did not take place. The patient had his semen tested and was found to have plenty of spermatozoa. In vain his wife had four gynaecological operations on his insistence and during this time intercourse was impossible. His physician advised relations with prostitutes but he always suffered from ejaculatio praecox.

After marriage and until a year before he became psychotic he had lived opposite his mother's home and had visited with her daily. He then persuaded his wife to purchase a very expensive house so that his home would be as good as his father's. He spent all of his salary on the mortgage and was dependent upon his wife for other expenses. This worried him as did also the fact that he saw his mother only occasionally.

At this time they adopted a German boy and thereafter in spanking him the patient experienced sexual pleasure. He made plans to go to Germany provided that he could get a position there. His wife would be happier in Europe but his mother violently opposed the plan as she did not wish to be separated from him.

Three days after his salary was reduced and he was told that he could remain at college only as a lecturer, he attended a spiritualistic seance. This occurred at the home of the man with whom he had had homosexual relations. (He had recently had a mutual masturbatory experience with this man.) A message from the spirit world stated that his wife should go to Europe alone. He did not seem to have any reservations regarding messages received and insisted that his wife do as the spirits ordered. He also followed the directions of the spirits to have homosexual relations with his friend and to masturbate every other day. He saw Jesus, thought he was His son and believed that he had been divinely appointed to improve the world and to make everyone anxious to live according to the Golden Rule.

In addition to his diminutive stature this patient had small bones, marked hyperextensibility of the joints, a 'peaches and cream' complexion, deficient hair on the chest and abdomen, excess fat in the breasts, on the abdomen and about the hips, a very high-pitched voice, very small and soft testicles and a very small penis descending from a well marked scrotal fold. The consulting internist referred to the patient as having a remarkably feminine face, voice, manner and behaviour as well as an immature appearance.

Equivalent physical anomalies were observed in the other cases cited but it may be more informative to summarize briefly the findings obtained from a study of the whole group. Observations on the constitutional make-up were made on 228 patients but this paper includes also a detailed investigation of the psychosexual histories of 22 additional patients. All of them had daily interviews over a period of at least three months and in a large proportion of the cases for more than a year.

Out of the total group special physical examinations were made without selection of cases upon 123 male and 105 female patients, regardless of the nature or stage of the illness and before their psychosexual histories were studied. Note was made of those constitutional and physical characteristics which are usually associated with maleness and femaleness. Some of these notations were of precise measurements but most of them were dependent upon direct impressionistic observations.

After these observations had been made the psychosexual history of each patient was obtained from the clinical records. No patient was included in this study who had not been in the hospital at least three months. Information regarding sexual experiences and preferences was obtained from the formal history, the personality study and the records of clinical investigations. These records were made by the various members of the staff of the hospital and independently of this study.

From the data thus obtained it was discovered that 33 patients had conspicuous homosexual experiences and preferences. This group was selected for special study and for comparison with a group of 15 patients whose heterosexual adaptation was reasonably satisfactory. It was of course necessary to subdivide these groups according to sex before any comparative study could be made.

In order to arrive at a general estimate of the physical characteristics of the different groups, somewhat arbitrary values were assigned to the notations in each case. Male characteristics included heavy bones, a carrying angle greater than about 170 degrees, a minimum amount of firm adipose tissue, large and firm muscles, coarse hair on face, chest and extremities and a masculine distribution of pubic hair, low-pitched voice, the usual male genitalia and absence of scrotal fold. Among the female characteristics were light bones, a carrying angle less than about 170 degrees, the usual adipose tissue found in the female breasts, shoulders, girdle and buttocks, small and soft muscles, absence of or not more than a slight amount of fine hair on the face, chest and extremities, the usual feminine distribution of pubic hair, high-pitched and soft voice, and the usual adult female genitalia.

It was found that many of the homosexual males have a feminine carrying angle of the arm, large muscles, deficient hair on the face, chest and back, a high-pitched voice, small penis and testicles and the presence of a scrotal fold. Not uncommonly' they have soft fat in greater amount in the shoulders, abdomen and buttocks. Some have an unusually large penis.

In like manner the female homosexual patients are characterized by firm adipose tissue, deficient fat in the shoulders and abdomen, firm muscles, excess hair on the chest, back and lower extremities, a tendency to masculine distribution of pubic hair, a small uterus, either over or underdevelopment of the breasts, fine hair, excess hair on face and a low-pitched voice.

One of the more common associations with masculinity and femininity is the relative width of the shoulders and hips. The heterosexual male ratios were equally distributed and slightly above or below the average for the whole group while the homosexual male ratios deviated farther from the average. Sixteen out of the 17 homosexuals had broader shoulders* with respect to the pelvic diameter than the average for the whole group of male patients. The same is true of the ratios in the heterosexual and homosexual female patients except that the deviation of the homosexual ratios from the average is less than

*A study of the actual measurements shows that the average biacromial diameter is the same for both the heterosexual and the homosexual males but the interspinal diameter of the heterosexual male averages about 2 cm. longer than that of the homosexual male.

was found with the homosexual males and also the homosexual female ratios are evenly distributed above and below the average ratio for all of the females.

A greater tendency to deviate from the average torso-leg ratio was observed in the homosexual males. There seems to be a distinct tendency to long legs with respect to the length of the trunk. On the other hand the torso-leg ratio of heterosexual females deviates farther than the ratio of homosexual females from the general average female ratio. This greater deviation was due to a tendency to a longer trunk with respect to the length of the legs in heterosexual females. Nevertheless in both sexes the homosexuals tend to have longer legs with respect to the trunk length.

From the measurements of the external conjugates of 123 male patients the average was found to be 18·2 cm. while the average external conjugate of 103 female patients was 17·3 cm. In comparing the measurements of the two groups of patients the homosexual male external conjugate proved to be slightly longer. The difference in the external conjugate measurements of the two groups of female patients was much more marked. The average heterosexual external conjugate was 19·2 cm. while that of the homosexual was only 17·6 cm. In other words, in about one-half of these patients the conjugate vera was probably shortened and with about one-third of them serious interference with normal delivery might be expected because of pelvic contraction.

In regard to the results obtained from the skeletal measurements it is not surprising that the homosexual male has relatively narrow hips and that the boyish form is thus preserved. The tendency to relatively long legs in the homosexual male may be another indication of delayed gonadal development with compensatory pituitary activity. These characteristics, together with a feminine carrying angle, suggest that structurally the homosexual male has remained nearer the species type rather than progressing to the highly differentiated adult masculine form.

Skeletal immaturity in the female homosexuals is most evident in the high percentage of contracted pelves.

In the absence of precise standards for comparison the notation of fat deposition in amount and distribution is entirely impressionistic. Although women are usually fatter than men, the race, heritage and habits of life of the individual are important factors in determining the relation of fat to body contour. Fat deposition is of course dependent upon the function of various ductless glands and both sexes tend to become obese after the period of sexual involution.

None of the patients included in this study had any gross endocrine dysfunction and none were pathologically obese or emaciated. A few had passed the period of sexual involution without presenting obvious corpulency.

Accurate estimations of the musculature were likewise difficult but the observations nevertheless tend to show that the homosexual more closely approximates a species type than the heterosexual. The male homosexual may have larger muscles but he also has excess fat and feminine contours. The female homosexual is often deficient in fat, has small and firm muscles and therefore tends to have more angular and masculine contours.

Although there were no obvious endocrine anomalies in the patients included in this study there were marked differences in the growth of hair. Homosexual males tended to have a deficient growth of hair while the homosexual females were prone to have an excess growth of hair on the face, around the nipples, on the abdomen and the extremities. With regard to the growth of hair, therefore, it may be said that there was much more suggestion of arrested sexual development than was found in the heterosexual patients.

In general, it appears that the homosexual patient tends to have a dysplastic constitution and an arrested sexual development at the physiological level of integration. We may never be able to progress very far beyond speculation in evaluating constitutional and environmental influences contributing to homosexuality but it is obviously necessary to study carefully both aspects of the problem in dealing with any given case.

Assuming that there are constitutional differences, such as have been mentioned, between homosexual and heterosexual individuals, it is not surprising that their psychosexual behaviour should also be different. Insofar as the information gained in this study may indicate the general tendency among individuals with personality disorders, a homosexual adjustment among male patients is more than three times as common as a reasonably adequate heterosexual development. Among the female patients a heterosexual adaptation seems to be less difficult as the excess of homosexual over heterosexual individuals is only 50 per cent.

Among the 16 female homosexuals there were only 8 who had had heterosexual relations. None of these made a satisfactory heterosexual adjustment although 7 of them had been sexually promiscuous. Six of them had masturbated in childhood, continued to obtain sexual gratification through masturbation only and were frigid in their heterosexual relations. One of them left her husband five weeks after marriage and then contemplated murdering him. There was one other homosexual who manifested her heterosexual interest by striking her lover on the eve of their marriage and by urinating in his lap after the ceremony was performed. It is probably superfluous to remark that they never lived together and that marriage was annulled.

When the psychosexual histories of the female homosexuals are compared with those of the female heterosexuals the contrast is astonishing. No member of the heterosexual group has a record of sexual traumata in childhood and there is no history of masturbation before puberty. It is improbable that the members of this group did not have sexual experiences in childhood but whatever these experiences may have been they seem to have made little impression on the patients or the families.

All of the individuals in the heterosexual group married before the age of 25, made a satisfactory heterosexual adjustment and had from one to seven children. Four of them became psychotic within a year after their husbands died and a fifth patient developed a psychosis after her husband became impotent.

Even the psychotic productions of this group bear little resemblance to those of the female homosexual group. The heterosexual psychotic woman usually develops a profound sense of guilt for having indulged in any form of sexuality other than normal heterosexual relations with the husband. One depressed patient felt at times that her dead husband was calling her to join him. Another depressed patient dreamed about being with her husband and that he was affectionate to her. (He had actually been alcoholic and brutal to her and insisted upon fellatio relations. A year before the onset of her illness he was killed while he was drunk.) She also said: 'He is in my thoughts all the time—that's why I dream about him.' None of the heterosexual group had paranoid tendencies.

On the other hand, the psychotic female homosexuals seldom manifested any interest in the opposite sex and they were occupied with homosexuality or incest relationships. Most of them expressed a feeling of attraction for their own sex, some made homosexual advances and others accused nurses or patients of doing something to arouse them sexually. One-fourth of them made violent homosexual attacks and practically all of them expressed paranoid trends.

An equally sharp contrast is observed when a comparison is made of the heterosexual and homosexual male groups. Two-thirds of the male homosexual patients had sexual traumata in childhood and the libidinous preferences thus established usually continued throughout life. All but two of the homosexual males attempted heterosexual relations but none of them succeeded in making a heterosexual adjustment. Failures were due to impotence, ejaculatio praecox or to preference for homosexual or other perverse sexual relationships. A few were actively promiscuous for a short time but usually while partially intoxicated. Some of the heterosexual experiences either were purely platonic or the sexual relations were incomplete. Some were repeatedly seduced by sophisticated women but they soon became inadequate if the heterosexual relations were continued. Not uncommonly heterosexual relations were attended by a feeling of disgust and one of the patients vomited whenever he attempted heterosexual relations.

In the psychotic state all of the male homosexuals manifested their homosexual trends in one way or another. About a third of them made active homosexual advances. As many declared that other people were making them homosexual or were using them for homosexual purposes. A few either feared castration or asked to be castrated. About one-third of them made violent attacks on other males and some of these patients also made desperate attempts to kill themselves, usually by diving head first on the floor or against the wall.

The heterosexual males were throughout life consistently different than the homosexuals. There is no record of sexual traumata in childhood, no violent emotional reactions to parents, and none of them had any apparent difficulty with heterosexual relations. None of them are recorded as having had extramarital relationships. One of them became alcoholic after his homosexual wife refused to take care of their only child. He threatened to kill her when he found that she was unfaithful. The other heterosexual males were depressed when they became mentally ill and some of them were occupied with thoughts of having ruined their families. There were no suggestions of homosexual interests.

When the psychosexual preferences of the individuals included in this study were correlated with their official diagnoses it was found that in the heterosexual group there were 4 patients suffering from involution melancholia, 8 with manic-depressive depression, 2 with agitated depression and 1 with alcoholism. The homosexual group, on the other hand, was composed of 3 manic-depressive, 5 psychoneurotic, 7 psychopathic, 1 paranoic and 17 schizophrenic patients.

In general, it may be said that the psychotic reactions of the whole homosexual group tended to be paranoid and schizophrenic in nature while the heterosexual patients were occupied with feelings of depression and unpleasant sensations associated with bodily processes. They expressed ideas of unworthiness and self-condemnation. None of the heterosexual group manifested paranoid trends. During the periods of life when the heterosexual is not psychotic he is a fairly well-adjusted individual. At least 25 per cent of the homosexuals were psychopathic prior to the onset of mental illness.

It is probable that in this study we are dealing with a kind of homosexual individual, a kind in which the sexual cravings are intolerable and in which the conflict leads to schizophrenic disorganization of the personality. Heterosexual patients were uncommon probably because the psychotic has much less chance to make this adjustment than the average citizen. Civilization's most severe test seems to be imposed upon the heterosexual male.

SUMMARY AND CONCLUSIONS

ON the basis of a study of 250 adult patients grouped according to the predominance of heterosexual or homosexual tendencies, the following general summary and conclusions seem justified:

1. The psychosexual histories in the heterosexual and homosexual groups are conspicuously different. All patients in the heterosexual group were married and had from one to seven children. None of them had been unfaithful after marriage and none of them had been separated or divorced. Only 25 per cent of the homosexual patients were married, none of them made a satisfactory heterosexual adjustment and three-fourths of the marriages were dissolved by separation, divorce or annulment. As a result of these marriages the total number of children born

was only four. The 15 heterosexually adjusted patients, on the other hand, had a total of 38 children.

2. Prolonged, intense emotional reactions to parents, and sexual traumata in childhood are rare in the heterosexually adjusted while these reactions and traumata are frequently noted in the early lives of homosexual individuals. In addition when personality disorders occur the heterosexuals tend to develop benign psychoses while the homosexuals are prone to have chronic paranoic and schizophrenic illnesses. It would seem therefore that any intrusion of adult sexuality in childhood is distinctly unhygienic. It may be an important factor in a perverse psychosexual development and it may be one of the causes of a chronic mental illness.

3. Although environmental influences often are conspicuously active these psychosexual differences are also dependent upon constitutional factors. Homosexual patients were found to have considerably greater constitutional deviations from the general average than those of the heterosexually adjusted.

4. The homosexual male is characterized by a feminine carrying angle of the arm, long legs, narrow hips, large muscles, deficient hair on the face, chest and back, feminine distribution of pubic hair, a high-pitched voice, small penis and testicles and the presence of a scrotal fold. Not uncommonly there is an excess of soft fat on the shoulders, buttocks and at the girdle. Occasionally the penis is very large and the hips are unusually wide.

5. The homosexual female is characterized by firm adipose tissue, deficient fat in the shoulders and at the girdle, firm muscles, excess hair on the chest, back and lower extremities, a tendency to masculine distribution of pubic hair, a small uterus and either over or underdevelopment of the labia and clitoris. There is also a tendency toward a shorter trunk, a contracted pelvis, under-

development of the breasts, excess hair on the face and a low-pitched voice.

6. In general it seems that the homosexual patient tends to have a dysplastic constitution and an arrested sexual development at the physiological level of integration. In addition to the incomplete development of other primary and secondary sex characters the reproductive capacities of pelvic structures remain underdeveloped. This is indicated by relatively narrow hips in the male (a boyish form) and a tendency to contracted pelvis in the female.

Varieties of homosexual manifestation

GEORGE S. SPRAGUE, M.D.

With discussion by DRS. KARL A. MENNINGER,
ISADOR H. CORIAT, CHARLES I. LAMBERT,
ERNEST M. POATE, AND S. W. HARTWELL

FROM the time when Krafft-Ebing drew widespread attention to the problems of homosexuality, the matter has been seen to have increasing significance. At first believed to be a clear-cut relatively rare condition, it was described by Magnus Hirschfeld in a way and a context which made it seem a bizarre anomaly. But as psychiatry has come to see more understandingly into its patients, and as newer viewpoints have been clinically applied, we have come to recognize that far from being any unitary or isolated phenomenon homosexuality is an extremely complicated problem of widely varying manifestations. The purpose of this paper will be to call attention to the manifold aspects of homosexuality and to emphasize the importance of developing a broad concept of the phenomenon if we are to understand the protean clinical material which everywhere presents itself.

In the very definition of the word homosexuality there is occasion to pause, for the old definitions, 'morbid sexual passion towards the same sex', or 'sexual perversion toward the same sex', are not sufficiently inclusive to cover our present-day understanding. The trouble is that only a genital instinctive attitude of mind or behaviour is indicated, as if all there was to homosexuality was gross erotic practice or the mere wish for it. When, however, we attempt to make a more suitable definition of homosexuality, we come upon difficulties. It is hard to offer a definition covering enough territory, because we can look at homosexuality from such different points of view. Shall we consider a fixed instinctive tendency?—or actual gross conduct?

—or constitution and physique?—or personality and sublimated interests?

We should be able and willing to include the overt practice of a tramp and the well-controlled tendency of some happy head of a family. We should have place for the vigorous big shouldered woman with increased hair growth and masculine voice and body build as well as for the motherly teacher in a girls' school, too interested in her work to get married. Then there are other cases to be considered. It is well known that there are changes from time to time in an individual's sexuality both as to intensity and as to quality. Sailors and army men are known to indulge in homosexual activities when heterosexual opportunities are long absent, only to renounce homosexuality when normal conditions are restored. Again, there is a chronological evolutionary progression of sex interest and conduct, in which a homosexual stage intervenes between the child's self-interest and the usual adult heterosexual adaptations. More complicated situations are very frequently met with. There are, for example, persons whose sexuality varies, being at certain periods in their lives quite heterosexually adjusted, but in whom interludes of homosexual activity occur. Again, though probably less frequently, we find persons who seem so ambivalent in their erotism that they desire and actually carry on homosexual and heterosexual relationships simultaneously and with satisfaction.

Attempting to include in one conception such diversified items as those referred to, it is evident that it will be simpler for us to adopt a new form of question about any individual patient. Instead of asking simply: 'Is he homosexual or not?' we should inquire: 'His homosexuality is evidenced in what ways, and under which conditions?' We may find homosexuality in either or both of two forms, the physiological-structural, and the instinctive-psychological with its tendency to produce conduct.

Homosexual expressions then may be constitutional, a matter of configuration, or linked with endocrine variations affecting hair distribution, bony structure, voice quality, and the like. Or they may be shown in the field of genital behaviour, when they are customarily called 'perversions.' Perhaps we have not given enough thought to the comparison of a perversion indulged with a homosexual partner and the same perversion practised with a heterosexual partner. This brings us at once to the conclusion that the mere behaviour of the subject is not the whole matter. It is necessary to note that the individual has and seeks to indulge his present tendencies as the resultant of all that has come before in his personal development. His experiences, his evolution of preferences, his conditionings in a multitude of details—all these have had their effects in building up his present response patterns. One person may have had experiences accenting oral strivings for the gaining of pleasures, while another's conditionings have stressed sadistic tendencies as most satisfying. It need not seem surprising if in a homosexual relationship the former should seek fellatio or cunnilingus and the latter should seek a masochistic partner. We could build up a series of graded levels of homosexual organization by noting the various types of perversions through which homosexuality is expressed in different instances. At one end of this series would stand the most primitive oral pattern, fellatio. At the most advanced level would be the case approaching most nearly to ordinary heterosexual activity—that of pederasty—which might be classed as a pseudoheterogenital level. Thus it seems possible, by considering the wide range of homosexual patterning, to obtain a better evaluation of the individual case. We can form an estimate of his organization which goes beyond the mere declaration of homosexuality and gives us more definite understanding of his problem and of the distance between his and the normal genitality.

An important issue arises as to whether the present status of the individual represents the topmost point in his advancement towards the usual adult patterns, or a retrogression from a former, better matured pattern. And here must be taken into account those evidences perhaps less direct, which are seen in the evaluation of the personality traits of the individual. These are oftenest thought of merely as masculine or feminine without calling attention to any hetero- or homo-sexual significance. It can not escape observation however that aggressive self-assertiveness and initiative are masculine traits, while passivity, suggestibility, and receptivity generally are of feminine colouring whether found in man or woman. If then we note one woman showing a number of the more male personality characteristics, and another whose tendencies are chiefly of female colouring, it may readily be seen that the selection of one rather than the other by some choosing man will be some measure of his interest in more, or less, femininity in his object choice, and hence of less, or more, homosexuality in his own make-up.

We are familiar with personal types which may be described as feminine women, masculine women, effeminate men, and virile men. By selecting our case material, it would be possible to form an entire series of individuals showing a gradation from the extreme of womanliness to the extreme of manliness. This, let it be commented, can be done on a physical basis, or with a psychological criterion. It offers occasion for the observation that a woman who elects to marry a meek, docile husband who allows himself to be dominated, is evidencing a more homo-sexual tendency than is the woman who marries a dogmatic aggressive man.

Let us next consider the individual's own response to whatever homosexual urges within himself are seeking expression. Again, it is striking what a range of variation is to be found. Some of the factors whose variations will modify the total response are the following: The strength of the erotic drive; the amount of its gratification in other than homosexual pathways; the external situation in which the person finds himself; the patterns of self-control, morals, ethics, etc., which characterize his personality; the burden of public opinion and social attitude of his environment. Obvious are the differences of pressure from without and from within, in regard to one's homosexual inclinations in this country with legal penalties up to 20 years in penitentiary, as compared with parts of Syria where homosexuality is openly practised; also, in the instances of a person of extremely rigid religious-moralistic upbringing and the person with few or no scruples of conscience.

The person with homosexual trends has few available possibilities for settling how they shall manifest themselves. He may frankly admit and gratify his tendency. He may so modify its expression as to make it socially acceptable through the process of sublimation. In this case we see certain character traits and certain forms of interest and activity which have a symbolic or displaced homosexual value, as in the case of the teacher in a boys' school, or the professional boxer, or the designer of clothing. And if neither of these courses is followed, there may result a sacrifice in his appreciation of reality, with the formation of a psychosis, or at least a setting aside of his understanding of the actual forces determining the situation. If he gains thus in not being so troubled by unacceptable partial trends within himself, it is at the cost of loss of recognition of important facts about himself and his purposes.

The question may be asked, but not so easily answered, as to whether in a given psychotic case, observed homosexual indications are primary or secondary; that is, whether there is a conflict over homosexuality which has produced the mental disturbance, or whether the impaired mental functioning has failed to manage those trends in the patient's make-up. Such questions arise especially in alcoholic psychoses, in certain of the catatonic schizophrenic cases, and in paranoid patients. In other instances they are definitely secondary and have been released, as it were accidentally, as in the case of homosexual activities in the course of a toxic delirium or an arteriosclerotic confusion. We then are offered clues to better evaluation of the patient's stresses of life adjustment in the nonpsychotic period.

Naturally it is of considerable importance, both for the understanding of the patient's illness and in the rationale of therapy, to determine the presence of homosexual problems as early as may be. Particularly is this true where the patient's conflict and sensitiveness are the greatest, although this very fact may lead to attempts at masking the indications. As examples of clinical findings which may make us think of possible homosexuality, the following are selected from case records at random. In their heterogeneity is evidenced anew the multiformity of homosexual expression—genital, kinesthetic, symbolic, delusional, hallucinatory, etc.

A man became fearful and violent when rectal prostatic examination was made. Another expressed wonder that massage upset him profoundly. Another insisted upon turning his buttocks toward the physician. Another spent all his time for months saying: 'It is not so: I am a perfect gentleman'. Another showed affection for male attendants, saying they were really women in disguise. Another's interest in men was said to be because they were his sons. One could never decide to marry, saying he found no one so worthy as his brother. A delirious minister sought to pull men into his bed. A boy sawed off his ear as proof that he was too courageous to be homosexual. One patient grew angry because he was sure homosexuals were on all sides. One complained of feeling some hard object pressing on his palate and of a strange taste. Another asserted that he was given atropin to make him homosexual against his will. A confused man saw male genitalia all over his bed. A woman with masculine haircut talked loudly and boasted her strength. A deteriorated man talked chiefly of stabbing and shooting. A husband was potent only when intoxicated. One patient refused to use the mouth for any of its usual functions. Another lovingly caressed the nasal tube without interrupting his feeding. Another complained of 'strange scum' in his feeding. Another thought it contained semen. One was worried for years because of a mild homosexual advance offered by a friend. The prospect of marriage caused unrest, hypochondria, or actual panic. One man spoke of magnetic rays entering his body. Another wished seclusion to prevent getting germs in the throat. Another assaulted nurses in the belief they were attacking a fellow patient sexually. Another felt rectal pressures and requested a bullet-proof vest. A paretic heard voices saying he was homosexual. Another was being shadowed by gangs of men. A boy ate a lighted cigarette, and begged castration to cure homosexuality. One suspected his fiancée of having relations with his best friend. Another had numerous affairs with married women and wondered if he was God. Another insisted on sleeping and walking about nude. Another wished seclusion and attacked whenever nurses entered the room. Another sought to wrestle with or playfully to trip the attendants.

In every instance above cited, the cases were definitely found to evidence some form of homosexual problem. Some were concerned to deny the presence of homosexuality in themselves; some sought to escape responsibility for it; some showed variations of the inhibiting factors, with corresponding changes in the frankness of exhibiting homosexual behaviour. Some defended; some welcomed; some worried. The point is that a multitude of clinical evidences confront the psychiatrist through which it is possible to discern a great variety of homosexual issues. But variegated as the individual pictures appear, they may be reduced to certain basic reaction patterns according to the individual's essential type of response.

In a study of such cases in one hospital recently, there have been found no less than 11 different patterns by which men have dealt with their homosexual urges. The simple formula for these types may be stated thus:

1. I want a man homosexually. Here is recognition and acceptance of the homosexual instinct without deviation.

2. I want a man, but on a guarded basis. In this case there is a limitation, a partial suppression of homosexuality.

3. I want a man, but not homosexually. This is another form of denial, less acceptant than type 2, but more so than the following.

4. I don't want a man homosexually. This is a simple denial and repudiation.

5. I want a man, but pretend he is a woman. At the expense of delusional loss of reality, there is here a sparing of any guilt over recognition of one's homosexuality.

6. He and I have similar, heterosexual, interests. Here a disguised interest is shown in the object's sexuality, but displacement prevents a feeling of anxiety.

7. I want many women. These cases are of the Don Juan type which seeks by overcompensation to avoid disquieting self-discovery.

8. A man wants me homosexually. Here is seen a projection upon the outside world, admitting the homosexuality, but avoiding responsibility for it. A variant is: I am made to be homosexual, which disclaims guilt but recognizes homosexuality in oneself.

9. Others are homosexual, but not I. This form of projection gives still more complete protection against the recognition of one's own involvement.

10. Others think I am homosexual. One here partly faces the idea of his own homosexuality, but projects it so as to be better able to defend against it.

11. There are great vague forces at work. This most interesting defence avoids the issue still further, by leaving out of clear focus the concept of homosexuality which is not seen, but often replaced by confused notions about gravitation, electricity, world influence, and the like.

From these various methods of dealing with some of the instinctive forces which motivate people, it can be seen that the problems of homosexuality as they confront the psychiatrist are not by any means simple situations. Instead of being merely a certain status which can be declared to be present or absent in a given patient, there is a mass of habit patterns by means of which certain instinct drives seek expression. If the habit patterns have been established differently in two individuals, then their homosexuality will necessarily follow different courses; and those differences we should be ready to recognize as aids in forming more accurate estimations of patients' problems.

The homosexual impulse might be compared to the bassoon in an orchestra; sometimes it plays solo parts; whenever it speaks at all, it gives distinctive colouring to the music; but often it is quite silent; its driving power, the player's breath, is not so significant to us as is the quality imparted to the concert. Let us suggest then, in closing, that homosexuality may be regarded as a pulsing, fluctuating colouring of an individual's way of living his life, and assert that its expressions in habitus, in personality and character, in genitality, in conflict and in psychosis, constitute an exceedingly challenging province in the field of psychiatric study.

DISCUSSION

DR. KARL A. MENNINGER: I think such a critical summary of certain aspects of homosexuality as Dr. Sprague made is timely as well as important. I was particularly interested in hearing of the 11 types of expression of homosexuality in the latter part of the paper, which I had already read and thought particularly commendable.

I am moved to certain critical remarks which I shall interject now, not only because I feel them, but because I hope they will afford a basis for some fruitful discussion. In the first place, I think the topic is really too big. To talk about homosexuality is like discussing New York City, or love, or political economy, or something of the kind. Perhaps I have a bias in this regard, as I find myself at issue with Dr. Sprague in the illustration at the end of the paper. I think perhaps my whole point of view can be best made clear if I take this illustration: He said that homosexuality might be compared to a bassoon in an orchestra; sometimes it played solo parts, and sometimes it was silent.

Those of us who study the unconscious psychological processes along with the conscious, I mean those of us who have some psychoanalytic convictions, would not be willing to agree to the aptness of that illustration at all. In the first place, homosexuality is never silent, it always expresses itself in everybody's personality in some way or other.

In the second place, it can not possibly be compared to a relatively insignificant single instrument like the bassoon in an orchestra. The illustration might be that it is like the strings in the orchestra, which are not so loud as the horns, maybe, but have a very important part to play in everybody's personality. Psychoanalytically, we do not feel at all that homosexuality is the nasty little part of the individual which crops up now and then and with which some individuals are unfortunately afflicted to a more conspicuous extent. We take the position that everybody has in his personality a very large amount of homosexual demand, along with his heterosexual demand.

Third, I think I might criticize the paper a little, too, because of some confusion that arises out of the author's failure to distinguish between conscious and unconscious homosexuality. You remember that toward the end, Dr. Sprague illustrated 11 ways in which the homosexual urge is handled by different individuals. My point is, that what he listed here is not all homosexuality, but some of these were the various barriers erected by the individual against his homosexuality, against his unconscious urge toward homosexuality. I am sure Dr. Sprague knows this and I think it would lend clarity to the paper if, accepting as much of psychoanalytic theory as he does, he would go, if not the whole way, at least a little further.

Every individual has in him the narcissistic love, homosexual love and heterosexual love. So if I go to a luncheon today with three or four of my friends, unconsciously this is undoubtedly a gratification of homosexual impulses even though I am not aware of sexual feeling in it. Certainly I don't go to lunch with my men friends because I love their wives, or their mothers; I go because I love them, because I like to be with them. To carry out genital activity with them, would be conscious and overt homosexuality, quite a different thing. It is just as necessary to distinguish between them as to distinguish between blood that is flowing out of a wound and blood that is supplying the tissues inside. One is overt and exposed by some disintegration of the fabric, and one is internal and necessary to the organism.

This distinguishing between conscious and unconscious homosexuality is important, because many people think when you say homosexuality that you refer to genital activities with somebody of the same sex. The paper carefully seeks to prevent one from getting that idea, but I do not think this is possible without a clear distinction between conscious homosexual feelings or activity and unconscious homosexual feelings or activity. Otherwise one wonders—Does he mean sublimated oversexuality? inhibited homosexuality? denied and rejected homosexual feelings?—all these various stages in the development of our interest in the outside world.

Therefore, I think if Dr. Sprague would make this distinction a little more clear, I would find great satisfaction in this very nice collection and presentation of some of the forms in which homosexuality is observed.

I want to say again that the one reason for this contentious discussion is to provoke some defence and some support from other discussors in the hopes of a fruitful discussion of this interesting paper.

DR. ISADOR H. CORIAT: I would like to follow up Dr. Menninger's remarks by discussing the question of homosexuality from the dynamic or analytic standpoint. I feel that I must express a different opinion from that of the last reader, in spite of his illuminating paper in which he has shown that homosexuality may manifest itself on different libidinal levels, because I am quite sceptical that homosexuality is ever a physiological or a constitutional difficulty, as he has termed it.

Analytical experience has shown that homosexuality is more instinctive than physiological; it is not a difference in sexuality but in object-choice. If it is physiological, structural or constitutional, then we are dealing more with a somatic hermaphroditic manifestation with homosexual tendencies. Of course, it is well known that in the development of homosexuality and in its various manifestations, whether this homosexuality is conscious or unconscious, the superego plays a great part, in the presence or absence of feelings of guilt. In the original narcissism which lies at the basis of all homosexuality, the individual loves members of his own sex because he loves himself.

In psychoanalytic therapy, the analysis cannot change conscious homosexuality to heterosexuality any more than psychoanalysis can change a heterosexual to a homosexual. What psychoanalysis does is to repress the manifest homosexuality; it then reconstructs the repressed heterosexual drive to form a new object choice. From the purely psychiatric standpoint it is well known that homosexuals occasionally commit suicide and this suicide can be interpreted possibly as a regression to the original mother-matrix, out of which all homosexuality develops on account of the early development of the Oedipus situation. Oral regression in homosexuality is very common, either in the form of active fellatio or in the form of fellatio fantasies or dreams. In those cases which come for analysis because of anxiety, conflicts and depression due to masturbatory activities, as the analysis unfolds the unconscious material, it can be demonstrated that the masturbatory activities are really manifestations or covers of the repressed homosexuality.

Homosexuality is common in both sexes. We know its mechanism in man; we are beginning to understand its mechanism in woman. In both sexes psychoanalysis has shown a very definite relationship of homosexuality to paranoid states. In women, homosexuality seems to be associated not with the feeling of inferiority or the inferiority complex, but rather with a definite characteristic of female psychology, namely, penis envy and the feeling of an illusory penis.

CHAIRMAN HAMILTON: Must we have an entire divorcement between constitution and function?

DR. CORIAT: As far as homosexuality is concerned, I think so.

DR. CHARLES I. LAMBERT: The thing that impresses me about the homosexual is, first, the constitutional make-up. Starting with the obvious bisexual make-up of the hermaphrodite, in which the gonadal structures may show a fifty-fifty distribution of the sexual characteristics, a relative departure toward the extreme, or inverted sex types, may show itself. In consequence of this, homosexuals of either sex may show preponderantly active, aggressive behaviour on the one hand, or passive, submissive conduct on the other, with intergrading varieties between the two extremes; and then the role of dynamic influences in the environment and experience may tend to fix emotional-instinctive reactions in these individuals at early periods in their development, with the result that persistent immature satisfactions will favour the development of a homocentric personality make-up rather than a balanced homoheterosexual character. In my opinion, both constitution and environment have to be considered in estimating the eventual personality make-up of the so-called homosexual. In an individual who is preponderantly aggressive and assertive in his aptitudes we may expect transgressive reactions toward another individual, or society; and, on the contrary, the individual who is more passive, submissive in his make-up is more likely to develop a sense of reproach and guilt, and direct this feeling toward himself with possibly suicidal impulses, as the extreme of his reaction. Only a careful study of the constitution and personality make-up will enable us to estimate and predict the preferred type of response the homosexual will display; and Dr. Sprague, the reader of the paper, has given us this approach in an exceptionally lucid way.

DR. ERNEST M. POATE: It used to be the case that if anybody talked about homosexuality, everybody else kept quiet and looked ashamed. Now, if you talk about homosexuality, everybody else gets up and wants to argue. I want to disagree with Dr. Coriat. I do not believe it is possible to separate function from biological constitution. You cannot say that homosexuality, for example, is purely a matter of psychological urge. That urge must be expressed physically, if at all. We do not know whether it originates in the psyche or in the ductless glands.

I would like to bring out something you probably all know; that at puberty practically every normal boy goes through a phase of conscious homosexuality, which may be merely fantasies, anal or oral, regarding imagined inversions of sex, or may go on to more or less sincere experiments, usually in pederasty. Occasionally there is a phase of quite active homosexuality for several months, which then disappears and usually never recurs.

DR. S. W. HARTWELL: I am sorry that I did not hear all of Dr. Sprague's paper. I may say that my opinion, based on the study and treatment of a considerable number of adolescent boys and girls who were indulging in overt homosexual practices or who very definitely recognized their desire to do so, is that there is little reason from these clinical observations to believe there is a constitutional basis or element in the causation of homosexuality as observed in children or adolescents. These patients do not have glandular dysfunctions clinically demonstrable, nor the physical characteristics of the opposite sex. I have seen also a large number of children who did have glandular dysfunction and contra-sex physical characteristics and in only one case was this condition associated with homosexual manifestations. And this boy had been badly repressed and punished as a very young child for sex acts with his sister largely based on curiosity.

I believe that a large majority of children, both boys and girls, go through a period when homosexual feelings are conscious and in greater or less degree acted upon. The two factors that in my cases have seemed to be most important in the child failing to go on to a heterosexual psychosexual adjustment are first and most important his or her fixation on and an instinctual satisfaction through the parent of the opposite sex that lasts too long or is too important; second, a feeling of guilt about his acts, or more often his desires, that is not liquidated while it is yet conscious.

I have a number of interesting cases demonstrating these mechanisms that I hope some time to present to this society.

DR. GEORGE S. SPRAGUE: I want to thank the gentlemen who have contributed to the discussion, because doing that has accomplished the purpose I had in mind. I wished to accent the fact that homosexuality is many things rather than one thing, and so, was pleased with Dr. Menninger's first criticism that the topic was too big. Dr. Menninger asked whether the tenets of analytical therapy about homosexuality were convincing to me. They are. I did not want to get into a discussion of that topic, because I did not want to raise specific issues, but I would conform with them definitely.

Dr. Coriat brought up the question of doubt as to whether homosexuality was ever constitutional-physiologic, another question that I did not wish to make any attempt to settle, but I am glad that the question was brought before our minds. I was thinking of this subject somewhat in the way one thinks about typhoid fever. Typhoid fever may come to the attention of a clinician because of fever, first, or it may come in some other case because rose spots are discovered, or in the third case because diarrhoea is complained of; but from whatever angle it is first discovered, one traces through his threads and comes finally to the realization that typhoid fever is the question with which we are dealing and which we must treat.

My purpose, then, was to call attention to a number of various ways in which the homosexual problem may confront the clinician, whether an analyst, a constitutionalist, or whoever it may be. I am sure that we may get one of our first clues to the existence of such a problem in a constitutional finding. Whether that be aetiologically related or not, I do not attempt to discuss at this time; but one may find, for example, the masculine body which is practically devoid of hair growth, or the feminine body which is excessively hairy, and such a finding might lead one to consider whether there was a special manifestation.

I would grant, of course, that homosexuality is present in all instances. The bassoon example has been taken as suggesting what I did not mean to suggest, that homosexuality plays a latent part ever, but it may not be the thing that one is consciously most aware of.

Types of male homosexuality

SANDOR FERENCZI, M.D.

TRANSLATED BY ERNEST JONES, M.D.

WHAT we have learned about homosexuality* through psychoanalysis may be put together in a few sentences. The first and
most important step towards a deeper knowledge of this instinct-
aim was the supposition by Fliess and Freud† that really every
human being traverses a psychically bisexual stage in his childhood.‡ The 'homosexual component' falls later a victim to
repression; only a minor part of this component gets rescued in
a sublimated form in the cultivated life of adults, in playing, in
readiness for social help, in friendship leagues, in club life, etc.,
a part that is not to be under-estimated. Insufficiently repressed
homosexuality can later, under certain circumstances, become
once more manifest, or express itself in neurotic symptoms; this
is especially the case with paranoia, concerning which the more
recent investigations have been able to establish that it is really

*'The Nosology of Male Homosexuality,' reprinted in *Contributions to
Psychoanalysis.*
†Freud, Drei Abhandlungen zur Sexualtheorie.
‡On a previous occasion I proposed the use of the expression 'ambisexual'
instead of that of 'bisexual', it being thereby expressed that the child in certain
stage of development feels amphierotically, *i.e.*, can transfer his sexual hunger
to man and woman (father and mother) at the same time. In this way the
contrast between Freud's conception and Fliess' theory of biological bisexuality
would be clearly brought out.

to be conceived as a disguised manifestation of the inclination towards the person's own sex.*

A newer point of view, which renders more easy the understanding of homosexuality, we owe to Sadger and Freud. Sadger discovered in the psychoanalysis of several male homosexuals that intense heterosexual inclinations had been displayed in their early childhood; indeed that their 'Oedipus complex' (love for the mother, attitude of hate towards the father) had come to expression in a specially pronounced manner. He considered that the homosexuality which later develops in them is really only an attempt to restore the original relation to the mother. In the homosexual pleasure-objects of his desires the homosexual is unconsciously loving himself, while he himself (also unconsciously) is representing the feminine and effeminate part of the mother.

This loving of oneself in the person of another human being Sadger called Narcissism.† Freud has shown us that narcissism possesses a much greater and more general significance than had been thought, and that every human being has to pass through a narcissistic stage of development. After the stage of 'polymorphous-perverse' autoerotism, and before the real choice of an external love-object takes place, every human being adopts himself as an object of love, in that he collects the previously autistic erotisms together into a unity, the 'darling ego'. Homosexuals are only more strongly fixed than other people in this narcissistic stage; the genital organ similar to their own remains throughout life an essential condition for their love.

All these pieces of knowledge, however, important as they are in themselves, give no explanation of the peculiarities of the sexual constitution and the special experiences that lie at the base of manifest homosexuality.

I may say at once that, in spite of much puzzling over them, I

*Freud, Jahrb. d. Psychoanalyse, Bd. III. [See also Ferenczi's contributions in the first section of the present book. Ed.].

†(Or, rather, borrowed the term from Naecke. Transl.)

have not succeeded in solving these questions. The aim of this communication is nothing more than to bring forward some facts of experience and points of view that have spontaneously forced themselves on me in the course of many years' psychoanalytic observation of homosexuals, and which may be capable of rendering easier the correct nosological classification of homosexual clinical pictures.

It seemed to me from the beginning that the designation 'homosexuality' was nowadays applied to dissimilar and unrelated psychical abnormalities. Sexual relations with members of a person's own sex are only a symptom, and this symptom may be the form in which the most diverse psychical disorders and disturbances of development, as well as normal life, appear. It was thus *a priori* improbable that everything to which the name 'homosexuality' is now applied would in a simple way yield itself as a clinical unity. The two types of homosexuality, for example, distinguished as 'active' and 'passive' have been up to the present conceived as obviously two forms in which the same condition may appear; in both cases one spoke of 'inversion' of the sexual instinct, of 'contrary' sexual sensation, of 'perversion,' and overlooked the possibility that in this way one might be confounding two essentially different morbid states merely because a striking symptom is common to both. Yet even superficial observation of these two kinds of homoerotism★ shows that they belong—in the pure cases, at all events—to quite different syndromes, and that the 'acting' and the 'suffering' homoerotics represent fundamentally different types of men. Only the passive homoerotic deserves to be called 'inverted', only in his case does one see real reversal of normal psychical— and perhaps also bodily—characteristics, only he is a true 'intermediate stage'. A man who in intercourse with men feels

★The word comes from Karsch-Haack (Das gleichgeschlechtliche Leben der Naturvölker, 1911) and is in my opinion preferable to the ambiguous expression homosexuality, since it makes prominent the psychical aspect of the impulse in contradistinction to the biological term 'sexuality.'

himself to be a woman is inverted in respect to his own ego (homoerotism through subject-inversion, or, more shortly, 'subject-homoerotism'); he feels himself to be a woman, and this not only in genital intercourse, but in all relations of life.

It is quite otherwise with the true 'active homosexual'. He feels himself a man in every respect, is as a rule very energetic and active, and there is nothing effeminate to be discovered in his bodily or mental organization. The object of his inclination alone is exchanged, so that one might call him a homoerotic through exchange of the love-object, or, more shortly, an object-homoerotic.

A further striking difference between the 'subjective' and the 'objective' homoerotic consists in the fact that the former (the invert) feels himself attracted by more mature, powerful men, and is on friendly terms, as a colleague, one might almost say, with women; the second type, on the contrary, is almost exclusively interested in young, delicate boys with an effeminate appearance, but meets a woman with pronounced antipathy, and not rarely with hatred that is badly, or not at all, concealed. The true invert is hardly ever impelled to seek medical advice, he feels at complete ease in the passive role, and has no other wish than that people should put up with his peculiarity and not interfere with the kind of satisfaction that suits him. Not having to fight with any inner conflicts, he can sustain fortunate love-relationships for years, and really fears nothing except external danger and being shamed. With all this his love is feminine to the finest details. He lacks the sexual overestimation, which according to Freud characterizes a man's love; he is not very passionate, and, as a true Narcissus, chiefly demands from his lover the recognition of his bodily and other merits.

The object-homoerotic, on the other hand, is uncommonly tormented by the consciousness of his abnormality; sexual intercourse never completely satisfies him, he is tortured by qualms of conscience, and overestimates his sexual object to the uttermost. That he is plagued with conflicts and never comes to terms with his condition is shown by his repeated attempts to obtain medical help for his trouble. It is true that he often changes his companions in love, not from superficiality, however, as the invert does, but in consequence of painful disappointments and of the insatiable and unsuccessful pursuit of the love-ideal ('formation of series,' as Freud calls it).

It may happen that two homoerotics of different types unite to make a pair. The invert finds in the object-homoerotic a quite suitable lover, who adores him, supports him in material affairs, and is imposing and energetic; the man of the objective type, on the other hand, may find pleasure in just the mixture of masculine and feminine traits present in the invert. (I also know active homoerotics, by the way, who exclusively desire non-inverted youths, and only content themselves with inverts in the absence of the former).*

However simply these two character pictures of homo-erotism lend themselves to distinction, they signify no more than a superficial description of syndromes so long as they are not submitted to the resolving procedure of psychoanalysis, which alone can render their mode of origin psychologically comprehensible.

Now I have had the opportunity of treating psychoanalytically a number of male homoerotics; many for only a short period (a few weeks), others for months, a whole year, and even longer. Rather than narrate any anamneses in this summary, it seems to me more instructive to condense my impressions and experiences

---

*I am conscious that, when I call inverts 'female' and object-homoerotics 'male,' I am using terms the scope of which is not sufficiently sharply defined. It may be just indicated here that by maleness I understand activity (aggressivity) of the sexual hunger, highly developed object-love with overestimation of the object, a polygamy that is in only apparent contrast with the latter trait, and, as a distant derivative of the activity, intellectual talent; by femaleness I understand passivity (tendency to repression), narcissism and intuitiveness. The psychical attributes of sex are, of course, mingled in every individual —although in unequal proportion. (Ambisexuality).

on homoerotism into two psychoanalytical Galton photographs.*

I may at once forestall the final result of my investigations: Psychoanalysis showed me that the subject- and object-homoerotism are really essentially different conditions. The former is a true 'sexual intermediate stage' (in the sense of Magnus Hirschfeld and his followers), thus a pure developmental anomaly; object-homoerotism, however, is a neurosis, an obsessional neurosis.

In both types of amphierotism† the deepest layers of the mind and the oldest memory-traces still bear testimony to the investment of both sexes, or the relationship to both parents, with sexual hunger. In the subsequent development, however, inversion and object-homoerotism diverge far from each other.

We can dig down very deeply into the early history of the subject-homoerotic and find already everywhere signs of his inversion, namely, the abnormal effeminate being. When merely quite a young child he imagined himself in the situation of his mother and not in that of his father; he even brings about an inverted Oedipus complex; he wishes for his mother's death so as to take her place with the father and be able to enjoy all her rights; he longs for her clothes, her jewellery, and of course also her beauty and the tenderness shown to her; he dreams of begetting children, plays with dolls, and is fond of dressing up as a girl. He is jealous of his mother, claims for himself all his father's tenderness, whereas his mother he rather admires as something enviably beautiful. In many cases it is plainly to be seen that the tendency to inversion, which is probably always constitutionally conditioned, is strengthened by external influences as well. 'Only children' who are spoilt, little favourites who grow up in an exclusively feminine environment, boys who, because they made their appearance in the place of the girl

*A further motive for this is consideration for the patients' anonymity, which it is especially important to preserve.

†This word renders, I believe, the psychological character of what is intended better than the term 'ambisexuality,' previously suggested by me.

that was longed for, are brought up in a girlish way, can sooner become inverted, given the corresponding predisposition in their sexual character.★

On the other hand, the narcissistic nature of a boy can provoke excessive indulgence on the parents' part, and so lead to a vicious circle. Bodily attributes also—girlish figure and features, a wealth of hair, and so on—may contribute to the consummation of a boy being treated as a girl. In this way the father's preference and its response may have arisen altogether as a secondary process in relation to the child's narcissism; I know cases in which a narcissistic boy provoked the father's latent homoerotism in the form of excessive tenderness, the latter then contributing not a little to the fixation of the former's own inversion.

Nor can psychoanalysis tell us anything new concerning the subsequent fate of these boys; they stay fixed in this early stages of development, and become finally such personalities as we know well enough from the autobiographies of urnings. I can here lay stress on only a few points. Coprophilia and pleasure in smell are deeply repressed with them, often to the extent of aestheticism; there is a fondness for perfumes, and as a sublimation an enthusiasm for art. Characteristic, further, is their idiosyncrasy against blood and all bloody things. They are mostly very suggestible and can easily be hypnotized; they are fond of imputing their first seduction to the 'suggestion' of a man who stared hard at them or otherwise pursued them. Behind this suggestion there lurks, of course, their own traumatophilia.

★Among boys who grow up without a father homoerotics are to be found relatively often. I imagine that the fixation on the Imago of the father who was lost early or never known results, at least in part, from the fact that under such circumstances the otherwise unavoidable conflict between father and son is absent. ('A man always credits fate twice as highly for something that is lacking as for something that he really possesses; thus my mother's long accounts filled me with more and more longing for my father, whom I no longer knew.' G. Keller, 'Der grüne Heinrich,' Cap. II). In families where the father is alive, but is inferior or insignificant, the son longs exceedingly for a 'strong' man and remains inclined to inversion.

Since analysis of inverts does not really elicit any affects that might result in changing his previous attitude towards the male sex, inversion (subject-homoerotism) is to be regarded as a condition incurable by analysis (or by any kind of psychotherapy at all).* Psychoanalysis does not remain, however, without any influence on the patient's behaviour; it removes any neurotic symptoms that may accompany the inversion, especially the morbid anxiety, which is often by no means slight. The invert acknowledges his homoerotism more frankly after the analysis than before. It must further be remarked that many inverts are by no means quite insusceptible to the endearments of the female sex. It is through intercourse with woman (*i.e.* their like) that they dispose of what may be called the homosexual component of their sexuality.

How differently does the picture of object-homoerotism present itself even after only a superficial analysis. After the very shortest examination those suffering from it prove to be typical obsessional patients. They swarm with obsessions, and with obsessional procedures and ceremonies to guard against them. A more penetrating dissection finds behind the compulsion the torturing doubt, as well as that lack of balance in love and hate which Freud discovered to be the basis of the obsessional mechanisms. The psychoanalysis of such homoerotics as only feel abnormally in reference to their love-object, and are otherwise of a purely masculine type, has shown me plainly that this kind of homoerotism in all its phenomena is itself nothing else than a series of obsessive feelings and actions. Sexuality in general is obsessive enough, but, according to my experience, object-homoerotism is a true neurotic compulsion, with logically irreversible substitution of normal sexual aims and actions by abnormal ones.

The average (analytically investigated) early history of homoerotics of the masculine type is somewhat as follows:

*This position is not universally held by contemporary psychoanalysts. [Editor's note.]

234

They were all very precocious sexually, and heterosexually aggressive (thus confirming Sadger's finding). Their Oedipus phantasies were always 'normal', culminating in sexual-sadistic plans of assault on the mother (or her representative) and cruel death-wishes against the disturbing father. Further, they were all intellectually precocious, and in their impulse for knowledge created a number of infantile sexual theories; this forms also the foundation of their later obsessional thinking. Apart from aggressivity and intellectuality their constitution is characterized by unusually strong anal-erotism and coprophilia.* In the earliest childhood they had been severely punished by one of the parents† for a heteroerotic delinquency (touching a girl indecently, infantile attempt at coitus), and on such an occasion (which was often repeated) had to suppress an outburst of intense rage. Following on this they became especially docile in the latency period (which set in early), avoided the society of girls and women half obstinately, half anxiously, and consorted exclusively with their friends. In one of my patients there occurred several times 'irruptions' of homoerotic affection in the latency period; in another the latency was disturbed through overhearing parental intercourse, after which the previous good conduct was interrupted by a transitory period of naughtiness (revenge phantasies). When the sexual hunger increases at the time of puberty the homoerotic's inclinations again turn at

*The view defended in this essay, that object-homoerotism is an obsessional neurosis, was strengthened when Freud, in his work on 'Die Disposition zur Zwangsneurose,' (this Zeitschrift, Jahrg, I. Heft 6) announced that the constitutional basis of this neurosis is the fixation on a pregenital, sadistic-anal-erotic stage in the development of the sexual hunger. It was precisely sadism and anal-erotism that I found at the basis also of object-homoerotism, a fact that speaks decidedly in favour of the inherent connection of these morbid states. See also Ernest Jones, 'Hass und Analerotik in der Zwangsneurose,' (This Zeitschrift, Jahrg. I. Heft 5).

†It struck me how often it was the mother who administered these reprovals to later homoerotics, but I attached no special significance to this circumstance until Professor Freud called my attention to the importance of this very factor.

first towards the opposite sex, but the slightest reproval or warning on the part of someone they respect is enough to reawaken the dread of women, whereupon there takes place, either immediately or shortly after, a final flight from the female to his own sex. One patient when he was fifteen fell in love with an actress about whose morality his mother passed some not quite flattering remarks; since then he has never approached a woman and feels himself impulsively drawn to young men. In the case of another patient puberty set in with an absolute frenzy of heterosexuality; he had to have sexual intercourse every day for a year, and obtained money for it, if necessary, in dishonourable ways. When he made the house servant pregnant, however, and was called to account for it by his father and vilified by his mother, he applied himself with the same ardour to the cult of the male sex, from which no effort has been able to wean him ever since.

In the transference-relation to the physician object-homoerotics recapitulate the genesis of their trouble. If the transference is a positive one from the beginning then unexpected 'cures' come about even after a short treatment; on the slightest conflict, however, the patient relapses into his homoerotism, and only now, on the setting in of resistance, does the real analysis begin. If the transference is negative from the outset, as it is especially apt to be with patients who come to the treatment not on their own accord, but at their parents' bidding, then it takes a long time to reach any real analytic work, the patient wasting the hour with boastful and scornful narrations of his homoerotic adventures.

In the object-homoerotic's unconscious phantasy the physician can represent the place of man and woman, father and mother, reversals* of the most diverse kind playing a very important

*The dreams of homoerotics are very rich in reversals. Whole series of dreams have often to be read backwards. The symptomatic action of making a slip of the tongue or pen in the use of the gender of articles is common. One patient even made up a bisexual number: the number 101 signified, as the context showed, that for him 'backwards and forwards were the same'.

part in this. It turns out that an object-homoerotic knows how to love the woman in a man; the posterior half of man's body can signify for him the anterior half of a woman's, the scapulae or nates assuming the significance of the woman's breasts. It was these cases that showed me with especial plainness that this kind of homoerotism is only a substitution product of the heteroerotic sexual hunger. At the same time the active homoerotic satisfies in this way also his sadistic and anal-erotic impulses; this holds good not only for the real pederasts, but also for the over-refined boy lovers, those who anxiously shun all indecent contact with boys; with the latter sadism and anal-erotism are replaced by their reaction-formations.

In the light of psychoanalysis, therefore, the active homo-erotic act appears on the one hand as subsequent (false) obedience, which—taking the parental interdiction literally—really avoids intercourse with women, but indulges the for-bidden heteroerotic desires in unconscious phantasies; on the other hand the pederastic act serves the purpose of the original Oedipus phantasy and denotes the injuring and sullying of the man.*

Considered from the intellectual aspect obsessional homo-erotism proves to be in the first place an overcorrection of the doubt concerning the love towards the man's own sex. The homoerotic obsessional idea unites in a happy compromise the flight from women, and their symbolic replacement, as well as the hatred of men and the compensation of this. Woman being apparently excluded from the love-life, there no longer exists, so far as consciousness is concerned, any further bone of con-tention between father and son.

It is worth mentioning that most of the obsessional homo-erotics (as this type might also be called) I have analysed make use

*One patient, whenever he felt himself insulted by a man, especially by a superior, had at once to seek out a male prostitute; only in this way was he able to save himself from an outburst of rage. The supposed 'love' for a man was here essentially an act of violence and revenge.

of the intermediary stage theory* of homosexual tendencies, which is now so popular, to represent their condition as congenital, and therefore not to be altered or influenced, or, to use the expression from Schreber's 'Denkwürdigkeiten', 'in harmony with the universe'. They all regard themselves as inverts, and are glad to have found a scientific support for the justification of their obsessional ideas and actions.

I have naturally also to say something here as to my experience concerning the curability of this form of homoerotism. In the first place I observe that it has not yet been possible (for me, at all events) to cure completely a severe case of obsessional homoerotism. In a number of cases, however, I have been able to record very far-reaching improvement, especially in the following directions: abatement of the hostile attitude and feeling of repugnance towards women; better control of the previously urgent impulse for homoerotic satisfaction, the direction of the impulse being otherwise retained; awakening of potency towards women, therefore a kind of amphierotism, which took the place of the previously exclusive homoerotism, often alternating with the latter in periodic waves. These experiences encourage me, therefore, to expect that obsessional homoerotism will be just as curable by means of the psychoanalytic method as the other forms of obsessional neurosis. In any case I imagine that the fundamental reversion of an obsessional homoerotism that has been firmly rooted for a long time must need whole years of analytic work. (In one very hopeful case I was treating the cure had to be broken off for extrinsic reasons after almost two years.) Only when we have at our disposal cured cases, *i.e.* cases analysed to the end, will it be possible to pass a final judgment on the conditions under which this neurosis arises, and on the peculiarities of its dispositional and accidental factors.

* (About equivalent to what we call the 'third sex' theory in English countries. Transl.)

It is possible, indeed probable, that homoerotism is to be found not only in those here described, but also in other syndromes; with the isolation of these two types I certainly do not mean to exhaust all the possibilities. In making the nosological distinction of subject- from object-homoerotism I only wanted in the first place to direct attention to the confusion of ideas that prevails even in the scientific literature on the homosexuality problem. Psychoanalytic investigation shows further that nowadays the most heterogeneous psychical states are treated alike under the title 'homosexuality'; on the one hand true constitutional anomalies (inversion, subject-homoerotism), on the other hand psychoneurotic obsessional states (obsessional or object-homo-erotism). The individual of the first kind feels himself to be a woman with the wish to be loved by a man, the feeling of the second is rather neurotic flight from women than sympathy towards men.

In designating object-homoerotism as a neurotic symptom I come into opposition with Freud, who in his 'Sexualtheorie' describes homosexuality as a perversion, neuroses on the contrary as the negative of perversions. The contradiction, however, is only apparent. 'Perversions,' *i.e.* tarrying at primitive or prepar-atory sexual aims, can very well be placed at the disposal of neurotic repression tendencies also, a part of true (positive) perversion, neurotically exaggerated, representing at the same time the negative of another perversion.* Now this is the case with 'object-homoerotism'. The homoerotic component, which is never absent even normally, gets here overengaged with masses of affect, which in the unconscious relate to another, repressed perversion, namely, a heteroerotism of such a strength as to be incapable of becoming conscious.

I believe that of the two kinds of homoerotism here described the 'objective' one is the more frequent and the more important socially; it makes a large number of otherwise valuable men

*(Abraham has shown that the same is true of another perversion: exhi-bitionism. Jahrbuch der Psychoanalyse. 1914. Transl.)

(psychoneurotically disposed, it is true) impossible in society, and excludes them from propagation. Further, the constantly increasing number of object-homoerotics is a social phenomenon the importance of which is not to be underestimated, and one that demands explanation. As a provisional explanation I assume that the extension of object-homoerotism is an abnormal reaction to the disproportionately exaggerated repression of the homoerotic instinct-component by civilized man, *i.e.* a failure of this repression.

In the mental life of primitive peoples (as in that of children) amphierotism plays a much greater part than in that of civilized people. But even with certain highly civilized races, *e.g.* the Greeks, it used to be not merely a tolerated, but a recognized kind of way for the satisfaction of desire; it is still so in the Orient of today. In modern European regions of culture, however, and in those attached to them, not only is actual homoerotism lacking, but also the sublimation of it that appeared so obvious to the people of antiquity, enthusiastic and devoted friendship between men. It is in fact astounding to what an extent present-day men have lost the capacity for mutual affection and amiability. Instead there prevails among men decided asperity, resistance, and love of disputation. Since it is unthinkable that those tender affects which were so strongly pronounced in childhood could have disappeared without leaving a trace, one has to regard these signs of resistance as reaction-formations, as defence symptoms erected against affection for the same sex. I would even go so far as to regard the barbarous duels of the German students as similarly distorted proofs of affection towards members of their own sex. (Only slight traces still exist today in a positive direction; thus, in club and party life, in hero worship, in the preference of so many men for boy-girls and for actresses in male parts, also—in attacks of cruder erotism—in drunkenness, where the alcohol reverses the sublimations.)

It looks, however, as if these rudiments of the love for their own sex would not fully compensate the men of today for losing the love of friends. A part of the unsatisfied homoerotism remains 'free floating', and demands to be appeased; since this is impossible under the conditions of present-day civilization, this quantity of sexual hunger has to undergo a displacement, namely, on to the feeling-relationship to the opposite sex. I quite seriously believe that the men of today are one and all obsessively heterosexual as the result of this affective displacement; in order to free themselves from men, they become the slaves of women. This may be the explanation of the 'chivalry' and the exaggerated, often visibly affected, adoration of woman that has dominated the male world since the Middle Ages; it may also possibly be the explanation of Don-Juanism, the obsessive and yet never fully satisfied pursuit of continually new heterosexual adventures. Even if Don Juan himself would find this theory ridiculous, I should have to declare him to be an obsessional invalid, who could never find satisfaction in the endless series of women (so faithfully drawn by Leporello in his book) because these women are really only substitutes for repressed love-objects.*

I do not wish to be misunderstood: I find it natural and founded in the psycho-physical organization of the sexes that a man loves a woman incomparably better than his like, but it is unnatural that a man should repel other men and have to adore women with an obsessive exaggeration. What wonder that so few women succeed in meeting these exaggerated demands and in satisfying, as well as all the other ones, also the man's homoerotic needs by being his 'companion', without doubt one of the commonest causes of domestic unhappiness.

The exaggeration of heteroerotism for the purpose of repressing love towards the same sex involuntarily reminds one of an epigram of Lessing's (Sinngedichte, Buch II):

'The unjust mob falsely imputed love of boys to the righteous Turan. To chastise the lies what else could he do but—sleep with his sister.'

*There also exists a Don-Juanism of unsatisfied heteroerotism.

The reason why every kind of affection between men is proscribed is not clear. It is thinkable that the sense of cleanliness which has been so specially reinforced in the past few centuries, *i.e.* the repression of anal-erotism, has provided the strongest motive in this direction; for homoerotism, even the most sublimated, stands in a more or less unconscious associative connection with pederasty, *i.e.* an anal-erotic activity.

The increasing number of obsessional homoerotics in modern society would then be the symptom of the partial failure of repression and 'return' of the repressed material.

In a brief summary, therefore, the attempt to explain the prevalence of object-homoerotism would run somewhat as follows. The exaggerated repression of the homoerotic instinct-component in present-day society has resulted in general in a rather obsessive reinforcement of heteroerotism in men. If now the heteroerotism is also inhibited or strictly restrained, as is necessarily the case during education, the consequence may easily be—in the first place with those who are predisposed to it for individual reasons—a reverse displacement of the compulsion from heteroerotism to homoerotism, *i.e.* the development of a homoerotic obsessional neurosis.

On homosexuality

I want to report here some cases of homosexuality which I have observed. They will afford us a psychological approach to this important problem. This is, of course, only an initial approach and I do not here intend to 'solve' that problem. I shall begin with the report of a case I had the opportunity of analysing for seven months. The patient came to me with the complaint that he felt attracted only by men and in no way by women and girls. When he was fifteen years old he once had relations with a servant girl but since then he had never succeeded in any sexual contact. Just before he came for treatment he was in a brothel but could not get an erection and felt very much dejected about it. In none of his relations with men has he ever had real sexual intercourse. All of his relations with men have been of the psychic type and are connected with many phantasies.

At the time when he began treatment he had a friend who was of a very virile and masculine type as were all his friends. He is not fond of the so-called typical homosexuals, of homosexuals who make a rather more feminine impression. He prefers friends of the distinctly masculine type and he wants to be superior to them. This superior attitude he achieves by being very amiable, by being necessary to them, by showing them some intellectual superiority. In his relations with these friends he displays a double attitude. On the one hand he wants to take the place their girl friends play in their lives and he sometimes imagines that he has intercourse with his friend and thus takes the place of the latter's girl. He, therefore, never has friends who are really homosexuals. He is attracted only by men who are typical heterosexuals. On the other hand, he wants to make his friend inferior and himself to achieve superiority over this friend. In short, he wants to bring his friend into the feminine position and this is his double attitude.

Now, it was interesting to observe that this double attitude towards his friends was based upon a special attitude he had acquired towards his father. The patient's father was a man of decidedly masculine type. The patient always hated him even from childhood and hates him still. He wants to be superior to his father but he is fearful lest he will not achieve this. His wish is to see his father far beneath him. It goes back to early childhood, but he has always feared his father, always felt that his father was much stronger than he and that he would never become so strong as his father. With this wish, one of the patient's experiences takes on a great importance for his whole sex attitude and for his life. It is important from a theoretical point of view that all his tendencies of superiority and inferiority are based upon sexual scenes that he witnessed when he was a very little child. He slept in bed with his mother and he observed rather frequently that during the night his mother would go to his father's bed after which he would hear noises that made him surmise that something was going on. Once when he was seven or eight years old he went to his father's bed where his father and mother were cohabiting and was promptly sent back by his father. This situation has very likely been of the greatest importance in his life. In puberty he had phantasies of many men and women in intercourse and in these phantasies he himself sometimes played the part of the woman and sometimes the part of the man. He wanted to play the part of the father but he always had the feeling that his father was stronger than he, that he would never approach him, and he therefore began to feel 'if I cannot play the part of my father, then I will play the part of the mother.' He identifies himself with his mother fearing that he will not be able to identify himself with his father.

The patient's father had very often beaten him and had ridiculed him because of his feminine attitude. He, on the other hand, began to despise his father because the latter had had many promiscuous relations. The father had once had a gonorr-heal infection and the patient had observed him in pain during urination. In puberty the patient built up the idea that he did not want to be like his father, he did not want to have sex relations with women. He built up an ascetic ideal and it is very important to note that this ascetic ideal derives partly from the feeling that he is weak in comparison with his father. Neverthe-less he never gave up this fight against his father. He always wanted to be superior to him and he wanted to get this super-iority by being more clever, more educated than the father. And that, too, is his attitude towards his friends. He does not want to be like his father in relations with girls, fearing that he might not be strong enough. This is an important motive in almost every homosexuality, *viz.*, that the heterosexual partner seems somehow too distant, too difficult to reach and therefore the individual decides to take what is apparently the line of least resistance. At the same time, however, he does not want to give up his masculinity and being, as I have described, superior to most masculine men, he still maintains his masculinity. His masculinity is somehow threatened but he retrieves it in a roundabout way, by a detour. This, I think, is one of the deepest rules in many homosexual cases.

As psychoanalysts, however, we cannot believe that events in the seventh and eighth years of life can be of such great impor-tance for the whole of development. We suppose that something must have taken place in an earlier period of life which points in the same direction. The patient's first memories appeared in connexion with a dream which he brought in one of the first hours I had with him—'I am in a grey suit and have a knife in my hand. I press the knife to my heart. The knife is not made of metal, however, but of *papier maché* and collapses slowly and falls together.' The associations to this dream lead very quickly to the fact that the grey suit is a suit of his present friend and the next association was the following memory. When he was about four years old his father once came home drunk and was violent towards his mother. His mother became very excited, was very frightened and made an attempt at suicide, taking the kitchen knife and trying to stab it into her chest. In this dream we see very clearly a hint of the father. The father violent, the father pressing the knife, the phallus, and the mother suffering, the mother falling down. He wants to bring his friend into this same position and he himself also wants to be in the same position; or, in other words, it is very likely that an at early age (before five) he had the opportunity to observe the sex life of his parents, the activity of his father, the passivity of his mother, the feeling that his father might be very dangerous, very violent and that perhaps it might not be possible to do the same as the father does. We can also say that at bottom there is here a double tendency to identification: first and primarily the tendency to take the place of the father but feeling himself too weak, he takes the second course of identification, *viz.*, that with the mother. But that does not satisfy him and so he tries to regain his superiority in a roundabout way, by being superior to the most masculine man, the father.

This patient also had a strong love for his mother as well as for his sister. This is something that we always find in homosexual cases. There is no case of homosexuality in which there is not also a phase where heterosexuality plays a great part. In this patient it appeared in a very clear way. In the quarrels between his mother and his father, he always fought against his father, taking the part of his mother. In an interesting dream which he brought, he dreamed about a man in a parcel with strings around it who is being pulled out of the water. It turned out that in some way that parcel, the package, is a symbol of the mother's uterus, that he was always interested in his mother's uterus and in the operations she had undergone as well as in the womb of his sister who had also been operated on very often. The same hostile attitude that he has towards his father, he also has towards his brother-in-law. As in every other patient of this type, we find in him a very strong heterosexual tendency which appears also very clearly in many little psychic love affairs he had in early puberty. He had completely forgotten these affairs when he began the analysis but he then gave the typical history of homosexuals, *viz.*, that when they were little boys, they were interested only in the things that women are interested in. 'I played only with little girls and I have always had an interest only in men.' It is this sort of history which has caused some psychiatrists to believe that homosexuality is a fate one brings with him from birth and can never lose.

But, in this whole picture, there is one point which is of especial importance and that is, the particular relation this patient had to his phallus. He always had a feeling of inferiority concerning it. We always find that these cases are in despair, that they will never equal the father, never be as strong as the father and, in the more concrete way of childish thinking, never have as big a sex organ as the father has. It is also very important to hear from our patient in this connexion that he was very much concerned at the time of puberty because he felt that he did not have enough hair around his phallus. He masturbated before a mirror and always observing his phallus not having enough hairs, he took cotton and put it around his genitals in order to substitute the pubic hairs. This is indeed an important feature and we see here that the general feeling of inferiority is not really a generalized feeling but is based upon a relation to a special organ, to the phallus. We find this almost invariably in cases of homosexuality.

Some other features did not appear quite so clearly in this analysis although the practical result was satisfactory, but our experiences in other cases make it very likely that these factors were also present in our patient, especially the fact that he wanted a love object possessed of the beloved phallus. The above related parcel dream makes it probable that he saw it in the mother but did not find it there. When our patient is in his masculine attitude, he may find in his friend the mother with the phallus whereas he himself plays the part of the father.

I will pass directly to the second observation, a boy of twenty-two, whom I could not analyse for such a long time as I did the first patient. I can, however, prove in this other case that this patient, too, clearly had a strong interest in heterosexuality. He had a very great interest in his mother, a very great interest during puberty in girls, but he was in fear that he might not be strong enough to maintain this relation to girls and during puberty he built up the fancy that it would be easier to have intercourse with a cow, the introitus of which is not so narrow. We meet again this idea that sexual intercourse is too difficult; that he, the patient, is not strong enough to have such a sex relation. I might add, in connexion with this patient, that at a very early age he already had very strong sex interests. When he was about five years old he gave money to a little girl of four years to induce her to allow him to put his genital into hers. He had a very strong general sex activity.

Now, something very interesting happened in this case. When he was about six years old he went to school and was seduced by a rabbi who, after the lesson, took some of the schoolboys into the classroom and ordered them to touch his erect phallus. It is interesting from the general point of view of the psychology of seduction, to know how this seduction took place. Our patient had heard from other boys that something of the kind was going on. He did not want to go away and arranged it so that he could go to this teacher and be alone with him. When he saw this man's erect phallus, he got a feeling of inferiority, compared his small organ with this big one. His whole childhood is filled with his interest in the phallus of other persons and with an interest in measuring his phallus with that of others. He developed an enormous sex activity and had sex relations with almost everybody in his class. It is interesting to know that at this time he did not have a feeling that these homosexual actions were really sexual and he felt that the heterosexual actions are quite as important but something very different. And this we meet not only in the psychology of homosexuals as long as they are children or as long as they are in puberty, but in some way all their perverse actions are not considered as real sexuality. I have seen female patients who were rather prudish in heterosexual relations but who did not have the fear that the homosexual relation really had something to do with sex. This is of very great importance for the general psychology of homosexuality and perversion.

I want to continue about this boy. In his later life he continued his extensive homosexual activity, always in fear that he was too weak to have relations with girls. His attitude was sometimes active and sometimes passive. In the latter attitude he wanted to receive the phallus of his partner and had passive anal intercourse with others. His passivity is not primarily chosen but is resorted to because he does not feel himself strong enough to be active. This passivity culminated in an interesting delusion which he developed at about eighteen years of age. He believed that by anal intercourse he would get a child and that he would get the Nobel prize because he, as a boy, was able to give birth to a child. He developed this idea at a time when he suffered very much from inflamed hemorrhoids. It is important to see here again a great interest in the phallus, a feeling of inferiority based upon the feeling that the phallus is insufficient and then a consequent regression to passivity which, in this case, is closely related to the anal attitude. In the course of the treatment, he had intercourse with prostitutes but he experienced his sex excitement chiefly through the idea that another man's phallus was in his partner's vagina also having intercourse. Feeling his own semen in the vagina, he immediately got a second emission without withdrawing.

I mentioned, in connexion with the other case, that most homosexuals who come to us, come with the homosexual legend that they have been homosexual from the beginning, that they have never changed and that they always had sex interests only in boys and have never had interest in girls. In both my cases I have demonstrated that the homosexual originally has strong heterosexual tendencies. But there is another part of what I would like to call the homosexual legend and that is that the homosexual is not really interested in the anus of the other man but that he is merely interested in coitus inter femoro and that only a few attempt anal intercourse. That might be true in the consciousness of homosexuals. Indeed, it is true that many homosexuals abhor anal intercourse but not so many as stated in some of those books which plead for homosexuality. If one analyses homosexuals, however, one finds that every one of them has the primary tendency to anal intercourse. This is a matter of course if we consider these things from a psychoanalytical point of view. If we have before us someone with a tendency to passivity, there must be an organ for this passivity, an organ which takes in something. Passivity and anal sexuality must therefore be very closely connected and if we analyse any homosexual, we always find that the feeling of not being strong enough to be active or, to put it more concretely, the feeling of 'My phallus is not strong enough to be active' must be connected with the feeling 'Then I shall be passive, I have the organ for this passivity.' I would say, therefore, that male homosexuality and anal erotism are always connected with each other, but in consciousness the process of repression often makes it appear as if the homosexual abhors anality.

Before I discuss these problems from a purely theoretical point of view, I want to report a third observation of mine. This is a patient whom I could not analyse for a long time. He began treatment when he was about thirty-seven years old. He liked to speak with boys between the ages of twelve and thirteen or fourteen. He was not at all interested in older boys. He did not do very much with the boys he liked. He tried to have a talk with them and during such conversation he ordered them to tell him something about what happened in school and he was especially glad when the boys told him that their teacher had been dissatisfied with them, had punished them, had put them in a corner, etc. Sometimes the patient experienced a desire to beat these boys himself or felt a tendency to pull their ears and at such a time he experienced sexual satisfaction. He never performed real sex actions with these boys.

There was also something else about this patient which was of interest. He was a rather wealthy man and whenever he had met such a boy and had spoken to him, he felt somehow obliged to care for the boy a little more. He would approach the boy's parents, speak with them and very often he arranged to take care of the boy's education or, as he himself put it, he behaved towards the boy like a mother. This is his sex life.

In his manifest sex life, indeed, he has never shown any interest in women, but it appeared in the course of the analysis that he was very much interested in his mother and this relation to his mother was of a special type. He came to this topic in the following way. In the course of the analysis it became clear that the patient had no idea as to what sex life is and that was the more astonishing as he was the owner of an estate where he had cows and bulls, etc. Once he asked me whether the erection were not a sign of shame. He believed that one got an erection only if one were ashamed. In connexion with that, it appeared that he had his first erection when he was about eight years old and had been beaten by his mother and it was therefore that he wanted to hear that the boys were ashamed. He felt that the boys, telling about it, would also have an erection and he himself at such a moment also got an erection. It appeared that in his phantasies as a boy, he supposed that something similar took place with his mother when she was beating him. In other words, this scene that he lived through with his mother, *i.e.* being beaten, getting an erection, and supposing some sex excitement in his mother, has become the scene after which his later sex life has been moulded. When he wants to beat these boys or to pull their ears, he wants to take the part of his mother. In other words, in his sex life he identifies himself with his mother.

Now we understand why this man has the intention of caring for these boys, paying for their education, etc. We can state generally that we have here again the love for the mother and the identification with the mother. We can say that in the first case I reported, the patient identified himself with his mother because he felt himself too weak to identify himself with his father. In the present case the genesis of the identification was different. The patient began to identify himself with his mother when he was about twelve years old. At that time his older brother became schizophrenic and his mother and father (especially the mother) who were very old in comparison with the age of the child, withdrew their affection from our patient. He had never been shown much tenderness by his mother but even that little was taken from him. He felt very lonely, felt that he would not have the love of his mother, and at that time he resolved to take her place. We see this mechanism very frequently, *viz.*, that in the moment of great disappointment, the disappointed person terminates the love relation by identification. It was at such a moment that the patient took the place of his mother, feeling that then he would be loved by boys of this age in the same way that he himself had loved his mother. That is the mechanism of identification. We identify ourselves with other persons in order to gain the love, the esteem, the other persons possess or, as Freud puts it, we identify ourselves with other persons on the basis of the same wish. We identify ourselves with others when we want to get what the others have. In this case that is indeed the cause for the identification and we now understand why the patient plays the part of the mother, why he began to play this part when he was twelve years old and why, throughout his life, he is interested in boys of that age.

I want to stress one point. The patient has had a great number of relations of the type mentioned, in fact two of the patients of whom I speak were very polygamous and my general impression is that perverse persons are for the most part much more polygamous than heterosexuals usually are. I do not underestimate the promiscuity of heterosexuals but still it appears small in comparison with the promiscuity of the average homosexual. That might have something to do with the fact that it is very likely only at the highest, the heterosexual, level that we find that development of tenderness which makes it possible to cling to the love object for a longer period of time.

In returning to our case I want to stress the fact again that an especial interest in his own phallus was also present in this patient. It appeared in the following way. He had a phimosis and had resolved, on the advice of his family physician, to rid himself of the phimosis by operation. It required a long time for him to make such a resolution. On the day before he was to be operated, he caught a cold and could not be operated on the following day. Now, it was interesting that after that, the patient never again had the idea of being operated on. It is of further interest that, during the night before the operation was to have been performed, he dreamed that he broke his leg and that he was very much frightened about it, a rather clear symbolism. In very early childhood, between four and five, our patient had the feeling that it is the most terrible feeling to break one's leg. Along with that the fact came into his mind that he had heard something in old Greek myths of castration, breaking the phallus. This special interest of our patient in his phallus also appeared in the way he cared for this organ. In the winter time he always had a noticeable sensation of cold there and he therefore wrapped his phallus up in order to keep it warm and well cared for. We have found similar attitudes towards the individual's own phallus in the other cases. No psychology of homosexuality can neglect the interest of the homosexual in his own phallus. He does not want a person as a partner in love life who does not have the same valuable organ. Or, we could say that every homosexuality contains some narcissism, some self-love. This self-love centres on the phallus.

To formulate briefly, we may say that the male homosexual identifies himself with the mother. But the identification differs in different cases. There can be a disappointment in the love object (case 3), there can be a feeling that it will be impossible to equal the father and therefore the part of the mother is taken (case 1); or there can be a feeling of insufficiency in regard to the individual's own phallus (case 2). In the last case, the incomplete psychoanalysis pointed to an identification with the mother, but the identification is not absolutely proven. Taking the mother's part does not necessarily lead to passivity. In case 1, the impossibility of equalling the father, leads to roundabout contrivances to become superior to him and to place him in the position of the female; the hated father then takes the place of the mother (with a phallus). It may also be possible that great tenderness on the part of the father forces the boy into an identification with the mother. Besides the identification with the mother in the male homosexual, the love for, and interest in the individual's own phallus and the phallus of the partner play an important part. With the passivity is connected a strong anality, the anus substituting the phallus of the mother. In one of my cases (not analysed), the homosexuality was at least precipitated by the fact that a beloved boyish female teacher used to pull the patient's ears while standing behind him. The picture was marked by anal tenderness. In cases of female homosexuality the idea of not being able to accomplish the female sex function (narrowness of the vagina, ugliness) leads to identification with the father. In Freud's case of female homosexuality,* this identification is reached in another way. In one of my cases, a twenty-six-year-old girl, rough playing with the father instilled in her a desire to be superior to him. His phallus had made a great impression on her when, as a child of four, she had observed him urinating. Her distrust of her female sex ability, on the other hand, drove her into an identification with the beloved father. She therefore chooses more masculine love objects and fights with them for superiority. In another case of female homosexuality, the child feared the severe father. On the other hand, she found in the mother with whom she slept, a fit love object. In a case of schizophrenia, the patient complained that

*See 'A Case of Homosexuality in a Woman' in the following section of the present book [Ed.].

her vagina was being obliterated and that in this way she was being made homosexual. It is not yet clear what part anal erotism plays in female homosexuality. We also do not know enough about the role of self-love and the narcissistic pride in the genitals in these cases. I suppose that the female homosexual would show an exaggerated pride in the care of her body. It seems that the female as well as the male homosexual try to take the masculine part when they want to achieve superiority over their father.

When we consider homosexuality from this point of view, we can never agree with the statement that homosexuality is based on special cells in the testicles, an opinion which Steinach, for example, expressed. We can never expect that homosexuality would be cured if we were to replace the patient's testicles with the testicles of a heterosexual individual. We must say that every case of homosexuality is based on a psychic development and only on such a basis can we understand the great variety in homosexual taste. In one of the cases which I have reported there is, for instance, an interest only in twelve-, thirteen- and fourteen-year-old boys. That cannot be due to a special type of cell in the testicles. We know, for example, that the first patient about whom I have reported is interested only in men of a very masculine type. Others are interested in men of a very feminine type and still others only in men who have reached a certain age, the senile phase, etc. In short, we must also take the psychological development of the individual into consideration and then we shall find that there was first a heterosexual tendency and that by the development of some infantile conflicts, heterosexuality has been replaced by homosexuality. We have here also an instance of the general idea that perversion is due to childhood conflict. This conception is somewhat different from the earlier psychoanalytical construction of perversion. You know that Freud at first expressed the opinion that perversion is merely a persistence of an increased partial desire. It may be that there is a homosexual partial desire but it is not the pure partial desire which persists but rather this partial instinct is increased in potency by what takes place in infantile life; or, in other words, a perversion is the result of an infantile neurosis. What is true for the perversion, generally, is especially true for homosexuality (*Cf.* Rank and Freud).

Now, what is the role of the body in homosexuality? It may be that the constitution plays a definitive part. We would never deny from the psychoanalytical point of view that there is a deviation in the sexual constitution also, but the sexual constitution alone never produces homosexuality if it has not been shaped by what takes place in psychic development.

We may now go a step beyond these formulations on homosexuality and draw some general conclusions about activity and passivity in sex life. We may ask what does homosexuality teach us about the essence of femininity and masculinity. In the instances I have given, it is clear that we can not say generally that the male homosexual is passive or feminine. We find only that in the course of his psychic development the passive, the feminine trends, can be increased and also that with the passivity the anality is increased. In addition to that, we find many active tendencies. But we have to assume that what appears in the homosexual must be present in the normal individual also. It is one of the principles of psychoanalysis that we never find mechanisms in the neurosis which cannot also be found in the normal person. The differences are merely quantitative. We must reckon with passive tendencies, the tendency to anality, in every male individual and a definition of masculinity as activity or of femininity as passivity is therefore wrong to begin with. We must presuppose bisexuality in everyone. We can say that bisexuality is somehow characteristic of the basal constitution of every human being and consequently we must suppose that female, passive and anal characteristics must be present in every male individual just as we must suppose that active tendencies are present in the female, too. K. Schneider has stated that the active attitude is an attitude which somehow consists only in looking down from above, looking down towards the woman in a protecting way, being stronger than she is. I think such a definition is wrong. It is absolutely erroneous to believe that the masculine principle consists in activity. There are active as well as passive tendencies in every individual, but it may be that the manner in which the active or passive tendencies are combined in the male is different from the way in which these tendencies are combined in the female. It is thus perhaps of advantage to consider the psychology of sex action, of intercourse, from a more general point of view. We may reckon with the general principle that the sex organ and the body generally may lead us to a better understanding of what the psychology of these organs may be.

We may say that in the first phase of sex activity the shape and action of the male sex organ show that there is a sadistic active tendency of intrusion into the other person's body; but that is only the first phase of intercourse and in the culmination of intercourse, when the intrusion has taken place, the activity decreases, the organ of activity is, as it were, given away. In other words, male sexuality consists in an initial phase of great activity, the activity being followed by passivity, by the feeling of being given into the power of the female and of the female genitals. Male sexuality can be recorded in a curve in which there is at first activity and then a succeeding passivity. The curve of female sexuality is perhaps the converse. In the first place passivity, receiving, followed by triumph, of having gotten the valuable organ of activity. There is a state of superiority, of holding the man and his organ like holding a child, of having him in her arms helpless, powerless like a child. The female curve is passivity in the beginning and activity towards the end. The shape of the sex organs in both sexes expresses this clearly and we can say that sex psychology reflects itself in the sex organs, as psychology generally expresses itself in the organism. In the male body, on the other hand, there are organs of passivity, or receiving, *i.e.*, the anus; and we could say therefore that also in the male there must be some passivity in the initial phase of sex activity. I believe that in really satisfactory sex life not only the activity but also the passivity of the male has to be gratified.

We can say that what we meet in homosexuality is not something completely new but something which exaggerates only what can also be found in the sex life of the normal male and female. Activity and passivity are characteristic of every human being. Everyone's body is prepared to be not only active, to protrude with something into the other's body; the clitoris, the tongue, the phallus, but everyone's body also has parts which are ready to receive: the mouth, the vagina, the anus. We can therefore say that we may understand the psychology of sex only if we consider it under the double aspect of the desire to intrude, the desire to be given to the body into which we intrude. Intruding and being within, being strong and being weak, these are the two poles of every sexual activity.

Incest and homosexuality

GILBERT V. HAMILTON, M.D.

THERE will be presented here some research findings which point to fear of incest as a major determinant of human homosexuality. Although this factor is of sufficient importance, in my opinion, to justify its separate consideration, I do not present it as a specific or essential 'cause'. In fact, no specific aetiology can be claimed for any of the known psychopathological formations, once we exclude the obvious resultants of injury, infection, chemical intoxication, arterial changes, neoplasms and endocrinopathies. . . .

For about nine years I made systematic observations of the sexual behaviour of monkeys under both captive and non-captive conditions in a live-oak woods near Santa Barbara, California. Twenty different animals—seven females and thirteen males—were used during this period. Three of these, a male and two females, were born in the laboratory woods and survived to the end of the research. Two females and three uncastrated males were acquired before they had reached sexual maturity. Six of these eight young subjects attained sexual maturity while they were under observation. Three castrated males—one adult and two half-grown ones—were acquired. The other nine subjects were sexually mature when purchased. The one unclassified female was larger than any of the other females. There was also one unclassified male. He so far exceeded all the other monkeys in size that impending contact with him invariably precipitated flight on the part of his fellow males. Eighteen of the twenty monkeys were of the familiar rhesus and cynomolgus types, three of them being crosses between these species.

Methods were developed for experimental arrangement of situations which could be fairly well controlled and repeated at will. The research plant in the woods included a primate building which was partitioned off into eleven large cages. Each cage had a door opening into an enclosed common alley, and this in turn opened into a large terminal room, the top and three sides of which were of wire netting. I was thus able to restrict and arrange the social contacts of all the animals whenever they were called in from the woods for experimental purposes.

The results of these studies have been published in detail elsewhere (*Journal of Animal Behavior*, vol. 4: pages 295-318), hence only a brief summary of them will be given here:

Homosexual plays were of daily occurrence among the non-captive immature males, regardless of the availability of the females. The smaller of a pair of copulating males would generally assume the passive (female) position, but at times the larger male would play the female role. Heterosexual behaviour was also observed among immature males.

Any male, mature or immature, was likely to assume the female position for copulation when attacked by a more powerful fellow of either sex if escape by flight was impossible. A typical observation taken from my records will illustrate this:

During one of the studies of defensive homosexuality, all of the animals were kept in the cages. The alley made it possible to sort them out into couples and groups for separate imprisonment. By leaving open the alley doors of two or more cages it was possible to determine whether a given animal would seek escape from or contact with particular groups or individuals. In one experiment, all doors leading into the alley were opened excepting the one in the cage which confined the very large and powerful male already described. He was, therefore, the only animal who did not have free range of ten cages, the alley, and the terminal room.

After the monkeys had fought their way through to some sort of tribal integration, the big fellow was admitted to the alley. All of them fled at his approach excepting the largest of the females. One recently weaned little male darted into an empty cage and crouched in a corner on the floor. The giant followed, leering at him as if about to attack. The little fellow squealed in terror and looked about for an avenue of escape. Finding none, he assumed the female position of copulation. His enemy now displayed only friendliness and mild sexual excitement, but the youngster ducked between his legs and escaped.

Assumption of the female position by a fellow seemed almost automatically to precipitate a copulative (male) reaction in an aggressively hostile monkey of either sex, regardless of the sex of the submissive one. A monkey dashing to a ferocious attack upon a fellow would promptly cease to manifest hostility if the intended victim assumed the female position. If the aggressor was female, she would mount her victim, make a few perfunctory copulative movements, then turn to some new interest.

Mature males would sometimes lure weaker males to them by assuming the female position, only to spring at the intended victim as soon as the homosexual bait brought the latter close enough to make escape impossible. Such behaviour lacked all appearance of sexual motivation on the part of the luring male, who would move to attack before sexual contact occurred. Mature females were also apt to resort to the same trick in luring weaker or more timid female enemies to them.

During all my nine years of research with monkeys, I observed only one episode of homosexual behaviour between two females in which there was definite evidence of sexual excitement on the part of either participant. This occurred when Kate, a mature female, was freed after more than a year's imprisonment and consequent separation from her immature, noncaptive daughter, Gertie. As soon as mother and daughter met, they rushed into a front-to-front embrace, then Gertie dropped on all fours, turned her posterior to Kate, and assumed the female position. The mother promptly mounted her and made male copulative movements. Both animals smacked their lips and displayed sexual excitement. They were never again observed to manifest any sexual interest in each other.

No uncastrated sexually mature male was ever observed to assume the female position unless there was a defensive need of doing so, or an obvious intention of luring a timid enemy to nonsexual combat.

Nursling monkeys of either sex would assume the female position almost reflexly on the approach of any large monkey if the mother was not close at hand, but with obvious manifestations of terror and none of sexual excitement.

The three castrated males were the most timid members of the tribe, and although one of them was of adult size, he disclosed the same preference for homosexual behaviour that was characteristic of the two smaller ones.

When we turn to the well-established fact of human bisexuality we are confronted by a question as to what, if any, normally adaptive expressions it can have in consciousness and behaviour. The bisexuality of infra-human primates offers an experimental approach to this problem which deserves far more attention than has been given to it by comparative psychologists, but such findings as are available seem to me to throw a considerable light on human homosexuality. The research discussed above discloses, in my opinion, certain general adaptive needs which are met by infra-human bisexuality:

During immaturity, the balance between homosexual and heterosexual tendencies is so nearly even in the male monkey that his erotic impulses can find satisfying expression in sexual plays with fellow males. This outlet sufficiently reduces the strength of his heterosexual compulsions to insure him against entering into dangerous competitions with adult males for possession of the females.

Although the balance tips heavily in the heterosexual direction when sexual maturity is attained, the adult male remains sufficiently bisexual to be capable of assuming the female position whenever there is defensive need of doing so. Tribal integration and, in the end, species survival would be impossible if flight were the only defence against the hostile aggressions of stronger fellows. For this reason it is not only important that the male of any age should be ready to play the female role in a defensive emergency, but that the aggressor should respond sexually to the female position, regardless of the sex of the submissive one.

Copulation involves no structural injury to the immature male, but such a danger exists for the immature female. The latter, being under no compulsion to compete with the mature female for male sexual favours, has no need, according to my theory, of engaging in homosexual plays before maturity, and she does not, in fact, engage in such plays. On the other hand, she is sufficiently bisexual to be capable of offering herself for copulation to hostile females at any age, whenever there is a defensive need of doing so. The screaming flight of the female nursling to her mother before sexual contact can occur, when the female position is assumed as a defence against an approaching male or female, gives us valuable evidence on this point.

The readiness of the adult female to accept an invitation to play the role of copulating male, when she has directed a hostile attack against a fellow of either sex, again discloses the adaptive value of retained bisexuality, since it is in the interests of both individual and species survival.

The tendency to lure a timid enemy of the same sex to combat, by feigning readiness to sustain the passive sexual role, discloses another phase of the adaptive value of bisexuality: the individual's standing in the tribe is always enhanced by victory over another fellow.

If, as can be indubitably established by appropriate methods of experimentation, homosexual behaviour is at times resorted to as a purely defensive measure by the infra-human primate, a question arises as to whether defensiveness is a factor in the determination of human homosexuality. My studies of compulsive alcoholism, certain types of the manic-depressive psychosis, and overt human homosexuality have led me to the conclusion that fear of incest is a more important factor in the development of sexual inversion than is generally recognized.

As early as 1908, Abraham called attention to the fact that homosexual tendencies which are usually repressed are likely to become evident when a man is drunk. (Karl Abraham: *Selected Papers*, page 83.) In line with this observation I have found, in common with almost all other psychiatrists, that the periods of prolonged and excessive drinking of the compulsive alcoholic are precipitated by an unconscious need to ease tensions engendered by repressed homosexual urges. An occasional compulsive alcoholic will be frankly, overtly homosexual during his sprees, but as a rule these patients do not go beyond socially allowable verbal expressions of their loyalty to, and admiration of, male friends. Although they are not, as a rule, rated as being anything less than perfectly heterosexual by themselves and their friends, it is easily apparent to the trained observer that only a very thin repressive line separates them from their overtly homosexual brothers.

Two almost unfailing observations led me to study the compulsive drunkard's mother: *a.* her overpossessive love of him during his infancy and early childhood, and *b.* her underlying hatred of his wife, no matter how wise, devoted, and long-suffering the latter may be. I found that the typical mother of such a patient is the kind of woman who obviously, albeit unconsciously, turns to her male child for the emotional satisfactions that are normally found in the spousal relationship. In some cases the early death or defection of the husband, more rarely his impotency or repellent unworthiness as a human being, could be blamed. In the majority of cases the fault lay with the mother's own repressions, which prevented her from developing an adult love-life.

I do not mean to imply that the mother of the future compulsive alcoholic makes conscious overt sexual advances to her male child. She avoids direct genital contact with him and is often quite intolerant of his masturbation, 'unclean thoughts', and anything suggestive of erotic advances on his part toward females of his own age. Her eroticism toward him takes the form of much kissing, fondling, verbal endearments, and a not over-subtle maternal coquetry. Even after he has reached adolescence and has fallen in love with a girl of his own generation, such a mother will reproach him for his infidelity to her, demand assurance that he loves his maternal 'sweetheart' best after all, and display a very real jealousy.

Illness in the family, an unexpected guest, or any other excuse for juggling the family sleeping arrangements are made occasion for occupying the same bed with her son. One victim of a subtly incestuous mother told me that he and his mother slept together all during the winter he came into puberty. Illness in the family was her excuse. In another case the mother of two future drunkards would playfully crawl into bed with them on Sunday mornings, from the time they were little boys until they had reached an age when either of them could have made her pregnant. Examples of this kind could be endlessly multiplied, but in each case the situation described would be essentially the same: a mother's persistent efforts to keep alive and even to augment the incestuous tendencies of her male child.

When we study the victim of the unconsciously incestuous mother we find that the dynamic sequence is fairly simple in its general outlines. The primary direction of his major sexual impulse is heterosexual—with the mother as love-object. This incites fear and repulsion at a functionally higher (*i.e.*, more nearly conscious) level of response, and there is a sharp deflection of the impulse from mother, and femaleness in general, toward maleness. Other important factors enter here, such as the castration-anxiety of the Oedipus period, regression to narcissistic choice of love-object and, in certain cases, endocrine setup; but my observations as a comparative psychologist and, later, as a psychoanalyst, strongly incline me to the opinion that fear of incest is the most important of the factors involved in the over-development of the homosexual tendency.

In the compulsive alcoholic, homosexuality has a demonstrably defensive motivation, but this in turn is feared and repressed. All that comes into consciousness is an urge to ease an intolerable tension and at the same time to obtain a sense of indubitable masculinity. Alcohol satisfies this need, and effects a partial release of primarily heterosexual impulses, thus making it possible for the heavily drinking compulsive to function with prostitutes or other women who are not too easily identifiable with the forbidden mother.

It is an extremely significant fact that the compulsive alcoholic usually becomes sexually impotent for his wife if and when the usual maternal element creeps into their relationship. He will cling to an attractive and devoted young wife and fall into a frenzy of despair when she threatens to leave him, but he will also avoid sexual relations with her. Many of these men are sexually frigid toward all women during their sober intervals. It is only when they are drunk that they seek release in sexual orgies with prostitutes or women of their own class who are merely good playfellows for whom they have no significant affection.

Manic-depressive cycles present some very intricate psychodynamic problems related to the pregenital stages of libidinal development, hence the observations which directly follow have reference to the incest-homosexuality sequence as merely one component of a far more complex determinant-resultant sequence than can be discussed here.

One type of manic-depressive patient is excessively alcoholic during the excited phase, and either very temperate or wholly abstemious at all other times. During the excited phase, after prolonged, excessive drinking, the ordinarily repressed homosexual tendencies break through, either as direct expression in behaviour or as delusions to the effect that enemies are accusing him of homosexuality. When such a patient submits himself to a psychoanalysis during a free interval, the naïvely presented first few dreams disclose a high degree of unconscious preoccupation with incestuous fantasies, but the free associations elicited by the usual analytic instructions cluster around homosexual themes.

In another group of manic-depressives, one finds, instead of alcoholism, a compulsive need of close and ardent friendships with persons of the same sex. This does not ordinarily involve genital or other overtly sexual expressions of love, but it calls for a pathological degree of repression. Here, too, we find that the patient's sexual impulses are primarily directed toward incestuous satisfactions, and that their homosexual trends are merely a defence against incest. Either at the peak of the excited phase, or when the depressed phase reaches a severity which involves serious clouding of consciousness, the deeply repressed incestuous trends find their way to overt verbal expression. The manic patient will either freely express incestuous longings, or accuse a parent or a sibling of the opposite sex of such longings. The confused, hallucinated melancholiac will hear voices accusing him (or her) of incestuous behaviour.

There is a type of manic-depressive patient who never marries, and among these I have found a considerable number of patients who were thrown into a panic by the imminence of marriage or even of a proposal. Whenever it has been possible to make intensive studies of such cases, I have found that the prospective spouse was rejected because he (or she) had acutely acquired the reactive value of an incestuously loved parent or sibling.

One young woman who discovered that she could not marry the man she loved, because 'it would be like going to bed with father', became frantically dependent on the affection of a girl friend directly the engagement was broken. There had been a tranquil, unemotional friendship between the two girls for years, but now my patient demanded that their relationship should move over onto a highly emotional basis.

In another case a girl who had never been conscious of any homosexual longings, attributed each of her three broken engagements to her inability to escape a feeling that, because she loved her fiancé (a different man in each case), it would somehow be unnatural to have sexual relations with him. I was summoned to see her during the height of her third depression. I found an extremely agitated patient who would not talk to me until the nurse was sent out for a walk. The patient then told me that she had an uncontrollable impulse to make sexual advances to the nurse. After some difficulty I persuaded her to admit the nurse to a three-cornered conference about the matter. My reassurances not only calmed the patient, but, as subsequent events proved, gave the nurse courage to yield to her own consciously but timidly held homosexual inclinations. Without any connivance on my part the two effected a permanent homosexual union. The patient got well and has remained free of attacks for more than a decade. The fact that she had three manic-depressive cycles during the third decade of her life, and none thereafter, leads one to suspect that in her case an overt and stable homosexual union was a sufficient prophylaxis. She was predictably in for many subsequent attacks unless a successful analysis could be had, and external circumstances rendered this impossible.

Overt homosexuality has a complex and variable determination, but there is one factor which, I have begun to suspect, may be invariably present: I have not yet made an intensive study of an overt homosexual who has failed to tell me, *without leading or other kinds of suggestive questioning*, that he (or she) was conscious of having been erotically loved by a parent or sibling of the opposite sex. Even the manic-depressive young woman just alluded to, volunteered the information that she had always felt that an element of sexual passion entered into her over-demonstrative father's kissing and fondling, and that her somewhat older brother made definite sexual advances to her when she was approaching puberty.

Another young woman—not a manic-depressive—had copulated with an older brother all during childhood. A year or so before her first menstruation he returned home after a six months' absence. He had come into puberty and his sex organ had greatly increased in size since their last sexual contact. Their first and only copulation, after his return, caused her considerable pain and his emission terrified both of them. Fear of pregnancy, an acutely developed sense of guilt and repulsion, and an antagonistic attitude toward the brother directly followed. During her twenties she was easily seduced by a homosexual woman and was jealously in love with her when the case history was taken.

I have published elsewhere (*Introduction to Objective Psychopathology*, pages 39 45) accounts of sexually maladjusted women for whom heterosexuality had, *per se*, the reactive value of incest, and Fenichel has made a similar observation. When such a reactive value is established for heterosexuality in consequence of overtly incestuous behaviour during childhood, the defensive need of interposing an overdeveloped homosexual tendency between incestuous longings and consciousness seems to be imperative. Freud makes the following sweeping statement concerning overt male homosexuals, and my own case records justify me in making an equally sweeping statement as to the invariability of this finding in the histories of male inverts, and in stressing the defensive value of their inversion.

In all the cases examined, we have ascertained that those who are later inverts go through in their childhood a phase of very intense but short-lived fixation on the woman (usually the mother), and, after overcoming it, they identify themselves with the woman and take themselves as the sexual object; that is, proceeding on a narcissistic basis, they look for young men resembling themselves in persons whom they wish to love as their mother loved them. (Freud: 'Three Contributions to the Theory of Sex', 1915, p. 560 n.)

To this observation I would add that such fixations are almost without exception demonstrably due to the veiled but unmistakable eroticism of 'the woman' in her treatment of the future invert. The incestuous aggressiveness of this kind of mother-love leaves her male child no alternative to incest but homosexuality. He must either go on surrendering to his mother as love-object, or defensively direct his sexual impulses away from femaleness in general.

Psychoanalysis offers the most productive of all research techniques for teasing out the detailed psychodynamic structure of overt homosexuality. Its soundness and adequacy as a theory of mind must be credited with this circumstance, but it is also true that the overdeveloped narcissistic exhibitionism of the invert and the impaired repressive strength of his ego greatly facilitate the exploration of his unconscious processes. For this latter reason the patient's verbal productions on the analytic couch will usually supply a mass of extremely valuable research material before his unconscious resistances require the analyst to add anything to his initial instructions.

Once the homosexual realizes that he must let his stream of consciousness flow through his mind as an unhindered, undirected, uncriticized response to dream components, and that he must hold nothing back from verbalization on the couch, the analyst can play a purely passive role during a prolonged initial period of analysis. For this reason, and because their material is so strikingly uniform, the findings of Freud and his followers can be taken as a collection of scientifically established data.

The male homosexual under analysis unerringly uncloaks that period of infancy which was dominated by incestuously directed impulses. While this is a common denominator of all male infantile experience, it is of abnormal intensity with the homosexual. Its abnormal intensity is due, in my opinion, to a correspondingly intense erotic component in the maternal love to which he is subjected. Freud's already quoted statement as to the future invert's fixation on 'the woman' sums up a finding which no homosexual male patient of mine has ever failed to verify.

Fenichel has brought together (in his *Outline of Clinical Psycho-analysis*, 1934, pages 244–264) a series of generalizations which I have found to be very helpful in my efforts to tease out this one important strand in the psychodynamic tangle presented by overt homosexuality:

1. He states that 'an inner psychological circumstance' excludes woman as a sex object for the male invert.

2. Homosexuality, in his opinion, is 'like a screen memory' against a repressed heterosexuality which is primarily incestuous. I am quoting him out of full context here. He duly stresses the other factors that enter into account in addition to fear of incest.

3. Homosexuality is a special outcome of the Oedipus-castration anxiety. In other words, *the future invert so greatly fears castration as a punishment for his incestuous longings (for his mother) and his consequent death wishes against the father, that he eschews heterosexual gratification as his consciously held erotic aim.* If he copulates with women at all, it is usually for the sake of having children or for his own reassurance: he typically speaks of heterosexual experience as unsatisfying.

Nevertheless, even the male invert who is exclusively homo-sexual unconsciously longs for heterosexual relations. To quote Fenichel literally: 'It is possible to show in all cases of homosexuality . . . the original heterosexual orientation which was rejected as a result of castration anxiety.' Fenichel is unneces-sarily cautious, in my opinion, in a further statement: 'We may, therefore, state as a provisional formulation that for certain individuals, normal sexuality unconsciously means incest and is perceived as entailing dangers of castration.' In my experience this holds true in all cases of overt homosexuality I have studied, and is usually found in those cases of pathologically repressed homosexuality to which one attributes certain types of the compulsion neurosis, psychical impotence, compulsive alcohol-ism, and the manic-depressive psychosis.

The limitations of this article forbid an elaboration of the psychoanalytic material which would have to be taken into account if an attempt were made to trace the dynamic relationship of fear of incest to all the other known factors entering into the determination of homosexuality. It is necessary, however, to make at least a brief allusion to the tendency of the libido to regress to earlier stages of its development when fear, frustration, or the general tendency of the infant to socialize its impulses, interfere with the achievement of heterosexual object-love. This regressive tendency is marked in the overt homosexual who, at maturity, is preponderantly narcissistic, incapable of object-love, still hobbled in his emotional life by the repression of an unresolved Oedipus complex, and more or less fixed at the anal (or oral) level of libidinal development.

In summing up the findings of my own studies in comparative psychology, objective psychopathology, and psychoanalysis, and correlating them with the well-established findings of Freud and his colleagues, I have arrived at two still tentatively held conclusions:

The homosexual tendencies that are a normal component of human bisexuality are apt to be overdeveloped as a defence against incest toward the end of infancy by males who have been too erotically loved by their mothers or mother-surrogates. Female homosexuality is likewise a defensive against incest, but it has a more complex determination, and post-infantile factors, such as the sexual aggressions of brothers or the too erotically tinged affection of fathers, usually play an important role.

The character traits of the overt homosexual are due to regressions from the phallic stage of libido development to earlier stages, and this in turn is a flight from incest. In this sense, the character traits of the homosexual as well as his actual inversion are defensive against incest.

Homosexuality and the Kinsey Report

EDMUND BERGLER, M.D.

... The purpose of the present paper is not to discuss *Sexual Behavior in the Human Male, per se*, its merits and fallacies: I shall concentrate exclusively on one sector, Kinsey's findings on homosexuality.[1]

Kinsey's yardstick as to what constitutes a homosexual is the *quantitative* distribution in the '*heterosexual-homosexual balance.*':

'... many persons who are rated "homosexual" by their fellows in a school community, a prison population, or society at large, may be deriving only a small portion of their total (sexual) outlet from that source. The fact that such a person may have had hundreds of heterosexual contacts will, in most cases, be completely ignored. ...

In assaying the significance of any particular activity in an individual history, or any particular type of sexual behaviour in a population as a whole, it is necessary to consider the extent to which that activity contributes to the total picture (pp. 193–194).

It is imperative that one understand the relative amounts of the heterosexual and homosexual in an individual's history if one is to make any significant analysis of him. Army and Navy officials and administrators in schools, prisons, and other institutions should be more concerned with the degree of heterosexuality or homosexuality in an individual than they are with the question of whether he has ever had an experience of either sort.

Everywhere in our society there is a tendency to consider an individual "homosexual" if he is known to have had a single experience with another individual of his own sex. Under the law an individual may receive the same penalty for a single homo-sexual experience that he would for a continuous record of experiences. In penal and mental institutions a male is likely to be rated "homosexual" if he is discovered to have had a single contact with another male. In society at large, a male who has worked out a highly successful marital adjustment is likely to be rated "homosexual" if the community learns about a single contact that he has had with another male. All such misjudg-ments are the product of the tendency to categorize sexual activities under only two heads, and of a failure to recognize the endless gradations that actually exist (pp. 647, 650).'

Kinsey introduces a 'heterosexual-homosexual rating scale' (p. 638):

0. Exclusively heterosexual with no homosexual.

1. Predominantly heterosexual, only incidentally homosexual.

2. Predominantly heterosexual, but more than incidentally homosexual.

3. Equally heterosexual and homosexual.

4. Predominantly homosexual, but more than incidentally heterosexual.

5. Predominantly homosexual, but incidentally heterosexual.

6. Exclusively homosexual.

Kinsey concludes (pp.650–651):

'From all of this, it becomes obvious that any question as to the number of persons in the world who are homosexual and the number who are heterosexual is unanswerable. It is only possible to record the number of those who belong to each of the positions on such a heterosexual-homosexual scale as given above. Summarizing our data on the incidence of overt homo-sexual experience in the white male population and the distribu-tion of various degress of heterosexual-homosexual balance in that population, the following generalization may be made:

Thirty-seven per cent of the total male population has *at least some overt homosexual experience* to the point of orgasm between adolescence and old age. This accounts for nearly two males out of every five one may meet.

Fifty per cent of the males *who remain single until age 35 have had overt* homosexual experience to the point of orgasm, since the onset of adolescence.

Fifty-eight per cent of the males who belong to the group that goes into *high school* but not beyond, *fifty per cent of the grade school level,* and *forty-seven per cent of the college level* have had homosexual experience to the point of orgasm if they remain single to the age of 35.

Sixty-three per cent of all males *never have overt* homosexual experience to the point of orgasm after the onset of adolescence.

Fifty per cent of all males (approximately) *have neither overt nor psychic* experience in the homosexual after the onset of adolescence.

Thirteen per cent of the males (approximately) *react erotically* to other males *without having overt* homosexual contacts after the onset of adolescence.

Thirty per cent of all males *have at least incidental homosexual experience* or reactions (*i.e.* rate 1 to 6) over at least a three-year period between the ages of 16 and 35. *This accounts for one male out of every three in the population who is past the early years of adolescence.*

Twenty-five per cent of the male population *has more than incidental homosexual experience* or reactions (*i.e.* rates 2-6) for at least three years between the ages of 16 and 55. In terms of averages, one male out of approximately every four has had or will have such distinct and continued homosexual experience.

Eighteen per cent of the males have at least *as much of the homosexual as the heterosexual* in their histories (*i.e.,* rate 3-6) for at least three years between the ages of 16 and 55. This is more than one in six of the white male population.

Thirteen per cent of the population *has more of the homosexual than the heterosexual* (*i.e.,* rates 4-6) for at least three years between the ages of 16 and 55. This is one in eight of the white male population.

Ten per cent of the males are *more or less exclusively homosexual (i.e.,* rate 5 or 6) for at least three years between the ages of 16 and 55. This is one male in ten in the white male population.

Eight per cent of the males are *exclusively homosexual (i.e.,* rate 6) for at least three years between the ages of 16 and 55. This is one male in every thirteen.

Four per cent of the white males are *exclusively homosexual throughout their lives,* after the onset of adolescence.'

Kinsey's conception of the 'hetero-homosexual balance' is augmented by the dictum:

'The *homosexual* has been a significant part of human sexual activity since the dawn of history, primarily because it is an *expression of capacities that are basic in the human animal* (p. 866).'

A series of objections can be raised against Kinsey's conclusions.

The main points of disagreement are the following:

I. UNCONSCIOUS MOTIVATIONS ARE COMPLETELY IGNORED

STATISTICALLY speaking, Kinsey avoids with 100 per cent completeness even the smallest concession to the existence of the dynamic unconscious. According to the 'taxonomic approach,' to which Kinsey adheres, the 'human animal,' as Kinsey calls *homo sapiens,* seems not yet to have developed the unconscious part of his personality. As far as the 'human animal's' sex life is concerned, the latter is propelled by a 'heterosexual-homosexual balance' which is exclusively biologically conditioned:

'Homosexual activities occur in a much higher percentage of the males who became adolescent in an early age; and in a definitely smaller percentage of those who became adolescent at later ages (p. 630).

'As a factor in the development of the homosexual, age of *onset of adolescence* (which probably means the *metabolic drive* of the individual) may prove to be more significant than the much-discussed *Oedipus relation of Freudian philosophy* (p. 315).'

Derogatory remarks about Freudian psychoanalysis are mainly based on ignorance or resistance, or both. When this pair of characteristics occurs in biased *laymen*, one explains it away as typical resistance to acceptance of unconscious facts. The reason for this attitude in biased *scientists* is, of couse, identical, though less defensible.

Kinsey is clearly not informed about the following facts:

a. Psychoanalysis has never denied the *biologic substructure* in human drives; on the contrary, it has stressed it. The *psychologic superstructure*, its interconnexion with biologic facts and their *mutual influence*, form the ABCs of Freudian psychoanalysis.

b. Homosexuality is no longer considered the result of the 'Oedipus relation'. About 1930 Freud discovered the *pre-Oedipal phase*,[2] meaning the precursor of the Oedipus complex. Before the child enters the triangular mother-father-child relationship, it goes through the duality: mother-child.

It is true that psychoanalysis, being an empirical science, passed through different phases. Freud discovered first the more superficial layers of the unconscious, the 'phallic' and 'anal' phases. The deepest regression—the 'oral' one—was discovered only much later. 'Geologic' strata of the unconscious were not discovered in their 'proper order'; one cannot prescribe to a genius the sequence of his discoveries. Thus the *historic* sequence of analytic *discovery*, and the *historic sequence of individual development*, do not coincide.

Hence analytic papers pertaining to homosexuality have been time-bound. They reflect the state of knowledge, or lack of it, at the specific time in which they were published. Thus there are early statements of Freud and his pupils connecting homosexuality with specific aberrations of the Oedipus complex. With strange intuition, however, Freud brought homosexuality into connexion with the pre-Oedipal phase as early as 1910 in his study on Leonardo: 'We will for the moment leave aside the question as to what connexion there is between homosexuality and sucking at the mother's breast.'[3]

And in 1925 Freud declared: 'According to a comment of the old child specialist, Lindner, the child discovers the pleasure-giving genital zone—penis or clitoris—during sucking. I shall leave it undecided whether the child really takes this newly-acquired source of pleasure as a substitute for the recently lost nipple of the mother's breast.'[4]

Kinsey is obviously neither familiar with these statements nor with the work on homosexuality carried out by Ernest Jones (1928),[5] Helene Deutsch (1932),[6] on female homosexuality, nor my own on male homosexuality, starting in 1933.[7] An interesting follow-up study is a recent paper by Major I. Weiss on homosexuality with special reference to military prisoners.[8]

Whether connected with more superficial or deeper layers,[9] psychoanalysis has always considered the homosexual a *frightened fugitive from misconceptions he unconsciously builds around women.* The fact remains that even the later male homosexual had (like every human being) a specific *first* experience in life with his mother. And this very real emotional experience *with a woman* leaves its marks. When later in life he turns to man as sexual object, he does so in a *neurotic elaboration of that first and undigested experience.*

A short genetic survey produces the following picture:[10]

Perversion homosexuality is characterized by conscious accept-ance of sexual gratification derived from a relation with an object of the same sex. Whether feelings of guilt are connected or cynically discarded is immaterial for the diagnosis, though not for the therapeutic prognosis. Homosexuals pretend consciously that they simply imitate the husband-wife relationship. Therefore —in the passive variety—they imitate women, in such things as manner of dressing, movements, talking, walking, and use of perfume and cosmetics. This superficial (consciously desired) impression results in the typical misconception that every 'effeminate' man is a homosexual. Nothing is further from the clinical facts. In accepting the superficial camouflage, the naïve observer plays into the hands of the unconscious 'alibi' of homosexuals. He is in the situation of a detective who takes at face value all the clues planted by the wrongdoer, to hide his real identity.

What is the unconscious situation of a man suffering from the disease-entity 'perversion homosexuality'? He has regressed to the earliest level of psychic development, the 'oral stage'. Every child has to cope with the fact of weaning from bottle or breast. The normal solution is in itself fantastic: The male child overcomes the trauma of weaning by denying its dependence on the mother and by consoling himself that he has on his own body an organ similar to the withdrawn breast or bottle, that is, the penis. Anatomic differences do not bother the child. His problem is to rescue vestiges of childish megalomania. Hence the ridiculous over-valuation of the 'breast substitute', hence the well-marked 'penis pride' of the boy.

One of the many abnormal solutions of that early conflict is encountered in homosexuals. These persons are so angry with the disappointing breast or breast-substitutes that they discard the whole disappointing sex: woman. They run in life after the 'reduplication of their own defence-mechanism'—the penis. Every analysis of homosexuals (the writer has analysed dozens of them) confirms the fact that behind their frantic chase after the male organ the disappointing breast is hidden. How can this seemingly fantastic connexion be proved clinically? Simply by analysing without bias the unconscious conflicts of homosexuals. They all labour under the 'mechanism of orality', as described repeatedly by the writer. The mechanism consists of the following triad:

Act 1. Through their provocative behaviour a situation is brought about in which some substitute of the pre-Oedipal mother is 'refusing'.

Act. 2. Not realizing that they themselves unconsciously manufacture this very disappointment, they become aggressive in 'righteous indignation' and seemingly in self-defence.

Act. 3. Then they indulge in endless self-pity, unconsciously enjoying psychic masochism.

Consciously, these sick persons realize only their 'righteous indignation', leading to self-defence and self-pity. They repress completely the fact of their own initial provocation, which began the sequence, as well as the masochistic enjoyment of self-pity. Thus the ego-strengthening illusion of 'aggression' is maintained, and the dynamically decisive masochistic substructure is hidden. Those neurotics are 'injustice collectors'.

The existence of the 'mechanism of orality' which is operative in homosexuals gives a clue to the fact that these people are orally regressed, and that the Oedipus complex is *not* decisive for them. But the mechanism of orality does not make a homosexual. There are many entirely different neuroses in which that mechanism is visible. The existence of this mechanism in a specific person only proves his oral regression. What is characteristic *specifically* of the homosexual is the fact that the narcissistic structure accentuates the mechanism to the *nth degree*. The truly megalomaniacal superciliousness of homosexuals is unique. Precisely because of their narcissistic substructure, the blow caused by incapacity to maintain the infantile fiction of omnipotence hits children who become homosexuals so severely. They recover only partially from the defeat of weaning, and even then only with narcissistic recompense. It is here that the 'reduplication of their own defence mechanisms' comes into play.

Another proof of the oral substructure of homosexuals is a fact first stressed by the writer. In analysis, nearly all of these patients go through, during the end stages of destruction of the perversion, a period in which they produce the symptom of premature ejaculation with women. And complicated cases of premature ejaculation always show an oral substructure. Such patients refuse the woman pleasure, 'they spill the milk before it can reach the mouth.' They still live on the basis of their alleged hatred toward the sex, woman. So deep is the fright of their own masochistic attachment that pseudo-aggression is their *modus vivendi*.

The amazing degree of unreliability of homosexuals—the combination they show with psychopathic trends—is also one of the end results of the masochistic elaboration of the oral trauma. Superficially, it refers to the revenge fantasy; basically, under this thinly veiled palimpsest, deep self-damaging tendencies are hidden. The broad pseudo aggressive façade covers the self-damage poorly in the majority of homosexuals.

Why do so few homosexuals want to change? The reasons are: Living out the perversion guarantees them pleasure which is felt consciously. This is a very precise distinguishing mark of perversions as contrasted with neuroses, in which the pleasure-gain is without exception on an unconscious level. Moreover, the neurotic symptom is always rejected consciously as a foreign body. There are no impotent men, for instance, who are proud of their impotence. In cases of perversion, the situation is quite different: Some homosexuals accept, and are even proud of, 'being different'. Psychoanalytically, we know today that a complicated inner defence is involved. *Homosexuals approve of their perversion because such acceptance of it—corresponding to a defence mechanism—enables them to hide unconsciously their deepest conflict, oral-masochistic regression.* Since the homosexual who has not been treated has no inkling of the real state of affairs, he clings 'proudly' to his defence mechanism. Only in cases in which a portion of inner guilt is not satiated by the real difficulties (hiding,

social ostracism, extortion) which every homosexual experiences, does the problem of changing come up.

Characterologically, homosexuals are classical *'injustice collectors'*, resulting from the 'mechanism of orality' sketched in the
foregoing.

II. 'ONE MALE IN THREE OF THE PERSONS ONE MAY MEET AS HE PASSES ALONG A CITY STREET HAS HAD SOME HOMOSEXUAL EXPERIENCE'

KINSEY and his collaborators gathered their conclusions by
questioning 12,000 people. I believe that Kinsey's figures are
correctly compiled and presented in good faith. Still, his disregard for psychologic factors has very likely played a trick on
him; he takes his human guinea pigs for idealists who volunteered only for the purpose of further scientific research:

'Thousands of persons have helped by contributing records of
their own sexual activities, by interesting others in the research
. . . Even the scientist seems to have underestimated the faith of
the man of the street in the scientific method, his respect for the
results of scientific research, and his confidence that his own life
and the whole of the social organization will ultimately benefit
from the accumulation of scientifically established data . . . (p. 4).
The chief appeal has been *altruistic* . . . (p. 36).'

Kinsey himself has some doubts about his volunteers, however:
'Still more remarkable is the fact that many of the cases histories
in the present study have come from subjects who agreed to give
histories *within the first few minutes* after they first met the inter-
viewer. *We are not sure that we completely comprehend why people
have been willing to talk to us* (pp. 35-36).'

The chances are that many volunteers who secondarily interested other volunteers, though *consciously* inspired by noble
intentions, had some less altruistic *unconscious* motives. Among
these, one could suspect, were many homosexuals who gladly

used the opportunity of proving, by volunteering, that 'everybody' has homosexual tendencies—thus seeking to *diminish their own inner guilt.*

Moreover, the clinical fact remains that the circle of friends of neurotics consists almost exclusively of neurotics. Hence the second and third 'crop' of volunteers must have consisted of too many neurotics, too.

I believe that Kinsey's figures about homosexual outlet will be revised downward as the present 12,000 interrogated are increased to 100,000, as Kinsey promises in the next twenty years.

One could enlarge on the involuntary selectivity of Kinsey's material by enumerating other unconscious propelling factors in the interrogated persons—for instance, the fact that it sometimes takes trained psychiatrists months to get the facts out of the patient, whereas Kinsey and his collaborators get it in one interview. We 'fire questions' no less than Kinsey's schedule provides for; still, we need more time. Strange—or someone seems to be naïve.

But even assuming the improbable fact that further interrogations will only confirm the published statistics, the complete neglect of unconscious factors renders the results dubious.

III. THE LACK OF GENETIC DIFFERENTIATION AMONG DIFFERENT FORMS OF 'HOMOSEXUAL OUTLET'

THE only differentiation Kinsey advocates among various forms of homosexuality is a *quantitative* one. He is opposed to calling a man a homosexual in whom the 'heterosexual-homosexual balance' is only slightly or temporarily shifted to the homosexual side.

The *quantitative* approach cannot replace the *genetic* one in medicine. Imagine that someone advanced the idea of subdividing headaches entirely according to quantitative principles, rating them from 1 to 6 according to the severity of the headache.

Medically speaking, a headache is only a symptom indicating a variety of possibilities; from brain tumour to sinus infection, from migraine attack to uremia, from neurosis to high blood pressure, from epilepsy to suppressed fury. Instead of the genetic viewpoint, we would have in this new order only six types of quantitatively varying degrees of big, middle-sized, and small headaches.

The quantitative viewpoint is *one* of the necessary criteria, but the genetic approach is indispensable. Not only correct diagnosis but therapy depends on it. Using only the quantitative yardstick leads to erroneous conclusions: It omits differentiation of the underlying diseases. Moreover, in the previously-mentioned rating of headaches, at a specific moment a headache produced by a sinus attack could be more severe than one produced in certain stages of a brain tumour.

The homosexual 'outlet' covers a *multitude of completely different genetic problems*. Hence a genetic yardstick is necessary for the differentiation and cure of the confusing and many-faceted variety of types of the man-to-man relationship. Before arriving at such a differential diagnostic yardstick, let us look at the problem genetically.

1. *Transitory Phase in Adolescence*
The frequent homosexual episode in adolescence does not allow any conclusion as to the future sex life of the boy. The endocrinologically-based sexual 'push' revives, in a 'second edition,' the psychological infantile conflict which was closed at the age of five. Hence pre-Oedipal and Oedipal conflicts arise again. All these conflicts are linked with 'castration fears' connected with women of the nursery days. These fears can, for a time, promote a homosexual intermezzo, which is secondarily rationalized.

The early onset of maturation, stressed by Kinsey as decisive for homosexuality, is but a *somatic* expression of a *psychologic* fact: Inner conflicts influence inner glands no less than inner glands influence inner conflicts. One could assume that *early* puberty is an antedated defence expressed organically. The activity inherent in the sex drive is used as defence against the passivity and *guilt* revolving around reverberations of the infantile conflict. Puberty, in favourable cases, decides the battle of infantile passivity and guilt in favour of activity. Hence people with greater conflicts—such as orally regressed neurotics—try to save themselves with biologic help earlier. Kinsey's revelation of early adolescence speaks, in effect, against his assumption of 'heterosexual-homosexual balance'.

2. *Perversion Homosexuality*

Perversion homosexuality denotes genetically a stabilization on the unconscious defensive level: 'I cannot be masochistically attached to Mother; I have nothing in common with her and am not even interested in a woman.' He singles out the disappointing organ (breast or breast-equivalent), finds on his own body (in his penis) a replica of it, and throughout his life runs after the copy of the replica—the penis of the other man.

Secondarily, a 'philosophy' is created by the homosexual to bolster his unconscious defence. He 'approves' of his homosexuality *because* it camouflages well the facts he runs away from: those of oral-masochistic regression.

He cannot escape, though, other reverberations of that conflict: In his personality, he is the classical 'injustice collector'. Hence he constantly feels 'unjustly treated'.

Sometimes homosexuals assert that they are completely 'happy', the only thing bothering them being the 'unreasonable approach' of the environment. That is a convenient blind. There are no happy homosexuals; and there would not be, even if the outer world left them in peace. The reason is an internal one: Unconsciously they want to be disappointed, as does every adherent of the 'mechanism of orality'. A man who unconsciously runs after disappointment cannot be consciously happy.

The amount of conflict, of jealousy for instance, between homosexuals surpasses everything known even in bad heterosexual relationships.

Imagine a baby wanting to prove that its mother is unjust; imagine further a pathologic mother wanting to harm and refuse the baby's demands—there one has in a nutshell the basic conflict of every homosexual relation. *The homosexual is sick inwardly;* and he shifts the blame, in a convenient process of displacement, to the evil outer world. In a roundabout way he gets once more, in this way, his chief diet: psychic masochism.

It takes a homosexual some time—usually until his late teens—to discover, and take congnizance of, his perversion. The period of fighting against conscious awareness of his defence mechanism—which he misunderstands as his final destiny—is, under typical conditions, concluded in the late teens, or at most, in the early twenties.

Applying these precepts, we can arrive at a *genetic yardstick* for the differential diagnosis: *A male homosexual is a person who predominantly uses the unconsciously based defence mechanism of man-man relationship to escape his repressed masochistic attachment to the mother*—and *who shows predominantly in his personality the mechanism of the 'injustice collector'*. Only the combination of the two ingredients constitutes the homosexual.

Paradoxically the homosexual never 'escapes mother' although his overdimensional inner fears push him into 'another continent' in his frantic flight. His main character trait—'injustice collecting'—belongs genetically and historically to—mother. The penis of the partner for which he allegedly craves is a disguised breast or breast-equivalent of—*mother*. His quick 'turnover' of partners is a pseudoaggressive defence directed intrapsychically against—*mother*.

3. *Spurious Homosexuality: the Innocent Milquetoast*
In a rather grotesque misunderstanding, a specific type of passive man is constantly accused—*and accuses himself*—of homosexual

'tendencies': the Caspar Milquetoast type. In a longer essay,[11] I have tried to vindicate this innocent victim of a miscarriage of rumours and misconceptions.

The genesis of the passive-feminine man runs as follows: The boy develops at the age of two and one-half to give a strong attachment to the Oedipal mother, and a strong aggressive rejection of the father. A typical 'positive Oedipus complex' is built up. By itself, that development is typical for every child, as Freud proved fifty years ago. Normally these transitory wishes of libidinous-aggressive contents are given up—a road which leads to normality.

Parallel with the 'positive' Oedipus, every child develops also (to a quantitatively negligible degree) an attitude called the 'negative' or 'inverted' Oedipus complex. The boy's relation to his father does not consist merely of rejection. He admires his father's alleged strength and power. He identifies also with the mother and wants to enjoy all the mysterious and 'cruel' things father does with mother. Here the father is loved, the mother rejected as competitor. Under normal conditions, these passive trends pass without causing trouble. In hysteric neurotics, fixated on the 'negative' Oedipus, this harmless and transitory phase becomes predominant. Expressed analytically: The hysteric neurotic with the unconscious feminine identification is fixated on the level of the 'negative' Oedipus.

The result spells troubles without end. The inner conscience (superego) objects constantly to the passive wishes. The inevitable result is that the passive-feminine man is forced to build up unconsciously a series of defences, to disprove the accusations of conscience. He produces a compensatory he-man attitude, later becomes a woman-chaser, and speaks disparagingly of women. His potency is weak and full of 'whims'; sometimes it works on a record-breaking level—mostly it refuses to 'behave'.

Not always does the compensatory mechanism embedded in the forced and cramped he-man attitude work so perfectly. In some cases, the defences are weak—and the outer world designates this Mr. Milquetoast as an effeminate man, misjudging him as a homosexual.

The resulting two types—super-he-man and Milquetoast—are genetically carved out of the same wood; it is only the strength of the defence which varies.

How did it come to pass that the poor Milquetoast was unjustifiably accused, even in scientific literature, of homosexuality? This is understandable only by reviewing the development of psychoanalytic science. Freud started his discoveries, not from the deepest level of regression, but from the highest, as was indicated earlier in this paper. He first discovered the Oedipus complex, which plays a decisive role in hysteric and obsessional cases. The oral level was at that time either unknown or neglected. The result was that homosexuals, too, were considered specific aberrations of the Oedipus complex.

The external behaviour of homosexuals and that of the homosexually innocent 'passive-feminine' men, are not only unreliable indicators, but are completely misleading. The effeminate man is not a homosexual; the markedly effeminate homosexual, on the other hand, shows a camouflage, hiding his real conflict. One must distinguish between two forms of unconscious identification, the 'leading' and the 'misleading'. The 'leading' unconscious identification petrifies, as it were, the representation of the decisive wishes of the personality, crystallized as the end result of the infantile conflict. The 'misleading' identification denotes identification with persons chosen for the purpose of denying and rebuffing the reproaches of the superego, directed against the basic neurotic wishes. The passive-feminine man's 'leading' identification pertains to the Oedipal mother; his 'misleading' unconscious identification to the he-man type. The 'leading' unconscious identification of the homosexual pervert pertains either to the pre-Oedipal mother (active variety) or to the baby (passive variety). His 'misleading' unconscious identification is either with the Oedipal father (active) or the Oedipal mother (passive).

A person confusing the two types of identification can blame only himself if the whole problem of homosexuals and 'effeminate men' is full of unsolved contradictions for him. He cannot even explain the active variety of homosexual perverts, since he is blinded by the fallacy of the effeminate man. By the same token he classifies every weakling of a man who is mistreated by an aggressive shrew as a homosexual. Further, poor Milquetoast is apt to accuse himself of homosexuality—unjustifiably.

4. *Homosexual 'One-timers'*

A very large number of men have one or two homosexual experiences but no more. The group constituted by these men is genetically extremely heterogeneous and comprises a variety of unconscious reasons leading to the homosexual interlude. For most part these men are not homosexuals.

a. *Temporary oral regression in specific situation of stress.* Here belong transitory episodes of inductees in the armed services during the war. Loneliness, danger, fear, provoke the unconscious infantile accusation: 'Bad mother is responsible.' Masochistic attachment being revived, the latter is warded off with pseudo-aggression leading to the homosexual act as 'revenge' and reassurance. The whole process is, of course, unconscious.

b. *Allurement of the forbidden.* In some cases the homosexual episode is but an expression of the masochistic wish for a short journey into 'transgression of the forbidden'. In the same way, not all persons who drank during prohibition were drinkers; some were looking for the 'adventure of danger' (psychic masochism).

c. *Shifted guilt.* Frequently guilt pertaining to other inner causes is expressed in single homosexual episodes. This guilt may have its origin in entirely different sources.

d. *The mirage of lack of heterosexual objects.* One of the pillars of the assumption of shifting and exchangeable 'balance' between heterosexuality and homosexuality is the argument that in prisons even previously heterosexual men become 'homosexuals'.

T   289

But a curious oversight is here involved: Most prison inmates are persons who use the 'mechanism of criminosis'[12]—hence an orally-determined solution occurs. The problem cannot be discussed without elaboration of the problems of the genetic factors leading to crime in general.

Using the genetic yardstick advocated in the foregoing, a differentiation between true and spurious cases of homosexuality is possible.

5. Homosexuality as Inner Admission of the 'Lesser Crime'

There are literally dozens of elaborations of the 'mechanism of orality' leading to injustice-collecting. As stressed before, the existence of that mechanism proves oral regression. To this is added a specific mechanism explaining why different clinical pictures result.

There exists, however, one type of orally-regressed man who uses a strange defence in his 'battle of the conscience.'[13] Accused by his superego of masochistic repetition of an infantile conflict with the mother, projected upon a *woman* (he associates regularly with termagants), intrapsychically he denies the attachment by *temporarily* running to the—man. These neurotics use transitory homosexual 'spells' as defences against another 'crime': that of masochistic attachment. They *fortify themselves*, so to speak, *with a dose of homosexuality*. They gain 'immunity' toward women by using the homosexual conflict—temporarily. After a short time, they revert to termagants only to repeat the identical procedure. The whole process is, of course, unconscious.

Very likely this type accounts for Kinsey's observation of *sporadic* homosexuality in specific ages in specific individuals. Kinsey, of course, takes it as proof of the shaky 'heterosexual-homosexual balance'.

6. Homosexuality in Conscious Fantasy Only

There are neurotics who never revert to overt homosexuality, though their masturbatory sex life is concentrated on homo-sexual fantasies.

Using the previously expounded genetic yardstick, we are able to distinguish between homosexuals and pseudohomosexuals in this group. The fact that only fantasy outlet is used does not, *per se*, exclude the fact that homosexuality is involved.

7. The 'Bisexuals'

Some homosexuals are seemingly 'bisexual'—that is to say, slight remnants of heterosexuality can be detected. These remnants guarantee, for some time, erective potency in a lustless coitus. Nobody can dance at two weddings at the same time, not even the wizard of a homosexual. Equal distribution of libidinous drives between homo- and heterosexuality does not exist, simply because homosexuality is not a drive but a defence mechanism. The so-called 'bisexuals' are in reality homosexuals with a slight admixture of potency with unloved women. Frequently they belong in Group 5, the 'lesser crimes' type.

IV. STABILITY OF HETEROSEXUALITY—INNER WISH OR CONCESSION TO SOCIETY

The zoologist Kinsey seems to be of the opinion that the stability of a heterosexual love relationship is only a concession to social customs:

'Long-time relationships between two males are notably few. *Long-time relationships in the heterosexual would probably be less frequent than they are, if there were no social custom or legal restraints to enforce continued relationship in marriage.* But without such outside pressure to preserve homosexual relations, and with personal and social conflicts continually disturbing them, relationship between two males rarely survives the first disagreement' (p. 633).

This curious statement shows grandiose disregard for (or unfamiliarity with) the psychologic fact that the *unconscious*

291

setting in a hetero- and homosexual relationship is *totally different.*

The *homosexual* neurotic is inwardly and constantly in flight from his masochistic attachment to the mother of his pre-Oedipal period. He wards off this attachment with pseudo-aggressive means, by rejecting the woman. Hence his compensatory aggression toward the mother (projected on the homosexual partner) results in the repetitive tendency to discard the partner after using him as a sexual object exclusively. Nowhere is the impersonal part of the *human* relationship so predominant as in homosexuals, as visible in the fact that some of them have masturbatory activities in comfort stations without either knowing or looking at their 'partners'.

As far as homosexuals remaining together for any length of time, their quarrels—especially in jealousy—surpass everything that occurs, even in the worst heterosexual relationship: They simply act out the mechanism of 'injustice collecting'.

Heterosexual relationships are of all kinds, normal and neurotic. The latter are innumerable in variety. With the intuition of a neurotic genius Tolstoy said, 'All happy families resemble one another; every unhappy family is unhappy in its own fashion.'

Relative *normality* results only when the oral phase is passed without mishap, and the Oedipal phase reached *and* relinquished. Since every child goes through the emotional experience of the Oedipus complex, he wants to replace the parent of the same sex. The original objects of attachment are given up—otherwise neurosis results—but the *emotional affinity* to the duality of replaced father and mother respectively, as objects, remains. Hence under normal conditions marriage partners want to remain united.

Moreover, the *tender element* (completely disregarded by Kinsey) plays an important part, especially in its unconscious connotations.[14] How one can describe the phenomenon of human sexual relations and at the same time omit tender love, is not quite comprehensible. It is as if somebody described a sunset without mentioning the colours. The omission is not a small one: the whole description becomes worthless.

V. HOMOSEXUALITY—BIOLOGIC DESTINY OR NEUROTIC DISEASE?

Kinsey pleads in effect for the acceptance of homosexuality as a biologically given fact to which law and prejudice had better adapt themselves.

'Community gossip and reactions to rumours of homosexual activity in the history of some member of the community would probably be modified if it were kept in mind that the same individual may have a considerable heterosexual element in his history as well . . . (p. 669).

'The judge, who is considering the case of the male who has been arrested for homosexual activity, should keep in mind that nearly 40 per cent of all the other males in the town could be arrested at some time in their lives for similar activity, and that 20 to 30 per cent of the unmarried males in that town could have been arrested for homosexual activity that had taken place within that same year. The court might also keep in mind that the penal or mental institution to which he may send the male has something between 30 and 85 per cent of its inmates engaging in the sort of homosexual activity which may be involved in the individual case before him (p. 664).

'The difficulty of the situation becomes still more apparent when it is realized that these generalizations concerning the incidence and frequency of homosexual activity apply in varying degrees to every social level, to persons in every occupation and of every age in the community. The police force and court officials who attempt to enforce sex laws, the clergymen and business men and every other group in the city which periodically calls for enforcement of the laws—particularly the laws against sexual "perversion"—have given a record of incidences and frequencies in the homosexual which are as high as those of the rest of the social level to which they belong. It is not a matter of individual hypocrisy which leads officials with homosexual histories to become prosecutors of the homosexual activity in the community. They themselves are the victims of the *mores*, and the public demand that they protect those *mores*. As long as there are such gaps between traditional custom and the actual behaviour of the population, such inconsistencies will continue to exist (p. 665).

'There are those who will contend that the immorality of homosexual behaviour calls for its suppression no matter what the facts are concerning the evidence and frequency of such activity in the population. Some have demanded that homosexuality be completely eliminated from society by a concentrated attack upon it at every point, and the "*treatment*" or isolation of all individuals with any homosexual tendencies (p. 665).

'The evidence that we now have on the incidence and frequency of homosexual activity indicates that *at least a third of the male population would have to be isolated from the rest of the community, if all those with any homosexual capacities were to be so treated.* It means that at least 13 per cent of the male population (rating 4 to 6 on the heterosexual-homosexual scale) would have to be institutionalized and isolated, if all persons who were predominantly homosexual were to be handled in that way. Since about 34 per cent of the total population of the United States are adult males, this means that there are about six and a third million males in the country who would need such isolation' (p. 665).

Strangely enough, Kinsey sees only the antithesis: acceptance of homosexuality as a biologic fact vs. senseless segregation. He speaks disparagingly of treatment of homosexuality (he puts it ironically into quotation marks). The *third* possibility, namely to declare homosexuality a *neurotic disease*, does not even occur to him.

The facts are that the initial pessimism toward psychoanalytic treatment of homosexuals (maintained by psychoanalysts previously) is completely unjustified. Triumphantly Kinsey states:

'The opinion that homosexual activity in itself provides evidence of a psychopathic personality is materially challenged by these incidence and frequency data. Of the *40 or 50 per cent of the male population which has homosexual experience*, certainly a high proportion would not be considered psychopathic personalities.... As a matter of fact, there is an increasing proportion of the most skilled psychiatrists who make no attempt to redirect behaviour, but who devote their attention to helping an individual accept himself, and to conduct himself in such a manner that he does not come into open conflict with society' (p. 660).*

Kinsey refers here to the outdated attempt, based on therapeutic helplessness, to reconcile a homosexual with his 'destiny' by diminishing his guilt. The attempt is as outdated as treatment of syphilis before the therapeutic acceptance of salvarsan.

On the other hand, endocrinology has nothing therapeutic to contribute to the problem of homosexuality. This fact is best illustrated in the summary of a witty endocrinologist: 'Some psychiatrists claim that the best they can do for a homosexual is to make an unhappy homosexual a "happy" one. This is little, but still more than endocrinology can do for a homosexual: the latter can only make a prosperous homosexual a less prosperous one.'

The most that can be said psychiatrically about the biologic substructure in homosexuality was summarized by P. Schilder:

*It is rather amusing that Kinsey, who is full of antipsychiatric bias, becomes at once a friend of psychiatry where the latter in temporary helplessness (belonging to the past) confirms Kinsey's pet notions. Kinsey's biological one-sidedness goes so far that he denies the existence of the most frequent form of psychogenic potency disturbance, premature ejaculation (p. 580), declares as unjustified the assumption of the mere existence of vaginal orgasm (p. 576), and wants to devote Volume 2 of his series to this denial. If one concentrates on biologic aspects, the whole sex act reduces itself to deposition of sperm, hence duration and pleasure involved in that act become unimportant. Which all goes to show into what dead ends denial of psychological facts leads.

'It has been repeatedly attempted to apply the results of Gold-schmidt's experiments to the problem of homosexuality. His experiments deal with very definite physical characteristics, and to transfer his results to the psychic field has no scientific basis at the present time. As to the experiments of Steinach, who had feminized male guinea pigs which really behaved like females and were sought as females by males, it must be emphasized that there is no proof that in homosexuals changes in the hormones take place similar to those experimentally produced. I agree therefore with Oswald Schwarz that *no proof exists that homosexuality is due to biologic hermaphroditism.* . . .[15]

The fact remains that today homosexuality is a curable neurotic disease, requiring specific therapeutic techniques and prerequisites.[16]

VI. DANGERS OF THE MYTH OF A NEW NATIONAL DISEASE

Let us do some figuring; after all, we are dealing with a statistical study.

According to Kinsey, people using the 'homosexual outlet' comprise '*at least*' 37 per cent of the male population of the United States. According to the last census, 34 per cent of the total population are adult males. The last published report on the population of the United States is one released on March 10, 1948: The total population for 1947 was 145,340,000. Thirty-four per cent of 145 million is approximately 49 million; hence there are 49 million adult males. From these 'at least' 37 per cent use the 'homosexual outlet' part-time, full-time, or sometimes. Thirty-seven per cent of 49 million is approximately 18 million. Hence there are 18 million people whom the unpsychological outer world (though against Kinsey's protests) would consider 'homosexuals'.

Add to these 16 and one-half millions the vast army of Lesbians —the number of which is statistically not yet determined, though frequently assumed (Magnus Hirschfeld) to *double* that of their male confreres.* By simple arithmetic, one arrives at somewhere around *50 million people seated on the homosexual scale of the 'heterosexual-homosexual balance.'* †

If these figures are only approximately correct (Kinsey sticks to percentages and does not translate them into actual numbers), then 'the homosexual outlet' is *the predominant national disease*, overshadowing in numbers cancer, tuberculosis, heart failure, infantile paralysis. Of course, Kinsey denies that the 'homosexual outlet' is a disease in the first place. But psychiatrically, we are dealing with a disease, however you slice it.

Scientific research is interested in truth only, and cannot be responsible for the possible misuse by the laity of these results. But what if the results are erroneous? Then actual damage—otherwise only a painful though unavoidable concomitant—is done for no purpose at all.

I believe that Kinsey's results on homosexuality will do damage without furthering the cause of scientific truth.

*In *Sexual Behavior in the Human Female*, the Kinsey associates give the 'accumulated incidences of overt contacts to the point of orgasm' among females as having reached 13 per cent as compared with the male figure of 37 per cent. Accumulated incidences of homosexual responses reached 28 per cent for females; 50 per cent in the males. The Kinsey report concludes that homosexual responses occurred in 'about half as many' females as males, and contacts to orgasm occurred in 'about a third' as many females as males. Other studies which report a lower incidence for the female are: Hamilton, 1929 (57 per cent male, 37 per cent female); Bromley and Britten, 1938 (13 per cent male, 4 per cent female); Gilbert Youth Research, 1951 (12 per cent male, 6 per cent female). However, the Kinsey report points out that the 'gradation between the casual nonerotic physical contacts which females regularly make and the contacts which bring some erotic response' made it impossible to secure frequency data except where they led to orgasm. [Editor's note.]

†It is possible that one must deduct 10 per cent from all these figures for the unknown homosexual quantity of the coloured population. Kinsey says frequently that he speaks of *white* males, but sometimes his generalizations seem to comprise the *whole* male population.

First, every homosexual will receive tax-free an 'irrefutable', 'statistical', and 'scientific' argument for the maintenance and spread of his perversion without conscious guilt.

Second, 'borderline cases' will be more easily persuaded to enter homosexual relations. The scruples of not a few candidates for homosexuality will be torn down by statistical proofs: 'Who are you to argue with 37 per cent of the male population?'

Third, many impotent neurotics, entirely innocent of the 'homosexual outlet', will suffer, through a grotesque misunderstanding. Women have a simple formula: 'Impotent, *ergo* a fairy.' This, of course, is erroneous. There are dozens of unconscious reasons for psychogenic potency-disturbance, completely unrelated to homosexuality.[17] Still, women cling stubbornly to this silly simplification. Taking into account the fact that men are ignorant on that score, too, men are apt to believe it. I know of cases in which irate wives have first put Jackson's *The Fall of Valor* (which endorses Kinsey's viewpoint in a literary way) on their husband's night tables, followed by Kinsey's book.

Fourth, every neurotic will, in cases of potency disturbance, immediately suspect 'biologically conditioned' homosexuality, though his troubles actually have completely different (and unconscious) reasons. Since there are millions of neurotics and only infinitesimal possibilities of psychiatric help (due to lack of knowledge, money, trained psychiatrists) greater desperation among untreated neurotics will result.

Last but not least, Kinsey's erroneous psychological conclusions pertaining to homosexuality will be politically and propagandistically used against the United States abroad, stigmatizing the nation as a whole in a whisper campaign, especially since there are no comparative statistics available for other countries.

Kinsey attempts to give homosexuals a clean bill of health, and claims, rather emotionally:

'Males do not represent two discrete populations, homosexual

298

and heterosexual. The world is not to be divided into sheep and goats. Not all things are black nor all things white. . . . Only the human mind invents categories and tries to force facts into separate pigeonholes. The living world is a continuum in each and every one of its aspects. The sooner we learn this concerning human sexual behavior the sooner we shall reach a sound understanding of the realities of sex' (p. 639).

'Sound understanding of the realities of sex' is not furthered by creating the myth of a new national disease of which 50 million people are victims. Nor is 'sound understanding' increased by labelling disease as 'health' in the name of an equally mythological 'heterosexual-homosexual balance'.

REFERENCES

[1] Kinsey, Pomeroy, and Martin. Saunders 1948. Italics in the following quotations are mine.
[2] 'On Female Sexuality,' *Int. Z. f. Psychoan.* (1931).
[3] *Ges. Schr.* IX, p. 399.
[4] *Ges. Schr.* XI. p. 12.
[5] *Int. Z. f. Psychoan.* (1928), pp. 11 ff.
[6] *Int. Z. f. Psychoan.* (1932), pp. 218 ff.
[7] The breast complex in the male (in collaboration with L. Eidelberg), *Int. Z. f. Psychoan.* (1933).
[8] *Psychiat. Quart.* (1946).
[9] For a review of the extensive literature, see the author's: Eight prerequisites for the psychoanalytic treatment of homosexuality. *Psychoan. Rev.*, *31*, 286 (1944).
[10] Reference is made to my work on homosexuality, as reported in: 'The breast complex in the male' (with L. Eidelberg), *Int. Z. f. Psychoan.* (1933); 'The present situation in the genetic investigation of homosexuality,' *Marriage Hygiene* (1937); 'The respective importance of reality and fantasy in female homosexuality', *J. Crim. Psychopathol.* (1943); 'Eight prerequisites for the psychoanalytic treatment of homosexuality', *Psychoan. Rev.* (1944); 'Psychology of friendship', *Med. Rec.* (1946); *Unhappy Marriage and Divorce*, International Universities Press, New York, 1946. 'Differential diagnosis between spurious homosexuality and perversion homosexuality', *Psychiat. Quart.*, *21*, 399–409 (1947); 'Facts and fiction about Lesbianism', *Marriage Hygiene*, *1*, 4 (1948). (Lesbians have the identical conflicts as do male

homosexuals, but elaborate them somewhat differently since they do not possess the organ used as compensation.)

[11] Differential diagnosis between spurious homosexuality and perversion homosexuality, loc. cit.

[12] 'Suppositions about the mechanism of criminosis', *J. Crim. Psychopathol.*, V, 215–246 (1943). See also the writer's contribution to Lindner-Seliger's: *Handbook of Correctional Psychology*, Philosophical Library, New York (1947).

[13] See the writer's book: *The Battle of the Conscience*, Washington Institute of Medicine (1948).

[14] For elaboration, see Chapter 1 (The enigma of tender love) of my book: *Unhappy Marriage and Divorce*, International Universities Press (1946), and: *Divorce Won't Help*, Harpers (1948).

[15] *Goals and Desires of Men*, Columbia University Press (1942), p. 159.

[16] For details see: Eight prerequisites for the psychoanalytic treatment of homosexuality, loc. cit. (Truly hormonal cases, if any, are an extreme rarity).

[17] See: 'A short genetic survey of psychic impotence', *Psychiat. Quart.*, 3 and 4 (1945).

Changing concepts in psychoanalysis

CLARA THOMPSON, M.D.

THE term 'homosexual' as used in psychoanalysis has come to be a kind of wastebasket into which are dumped all forms of relationships with one's own sex. The word may be applied to activities, attitudes, feelings, thoughts, or repression of any of these. In short, anything which pertains in any way to a relationship, hostile or friendly, to a member of one's own sex may be termed homosexual. Under these circumstances, what does an analyst convey to himself, his audience, or his patient when he says the patient has homosexual trends? It does not clarify much in his own thinking, nor convey a definite idea to his audience. When he uses the term in talking with the patient, his words—instead of being helpful—often produce terror, for in ordinary speech the word 'homosexual' has a much more specific meaning, and in addition a disturbing emotional colouring.

In view of the general confusion, it has seemed to me worthwhile to review the whole subject, trace the various psychoanalytic ideas about homosexuality, and, finally, describe the status of the concept today.

Freud, in accordance with his libido orientation, considered unconscious homosexuality something basic and causal in neurosis, while more recent analysis has led to the conclusion that homosexuality is but a symptom of more general personality difficulties. Instead of being the basic problem in a given case, it is but one of the manifestations of a character problem and tends to disappear when the more general character disturbance is resolved. From Freud's point of view, unconscious homosexuality is to be found in everyone. It is a part of the original libido endowment. According to him, it may exist in three different forms. There is latent homosexuality, repressed homosexuality, and overt homosexuality. Latent homosexuality apparently exists in everyone, although perhaps the amount varies from one person to another. It is not necessarily pathological. Freud assumes it may either find expression in pathological difficulties or in sublimation. Psychoanalysis has to deal with homosexuality as a problem only in its repressed or overt forms. If the use of the term were limited to these two forms, there would be less confusion, although even here Freud speaks of repressed homosexual trends in situations where the sexual content in the usual limited sense of the term does not exist.

Freud's view of the matter is based on his concept of bisexuality. According to him a part of the original libido endowment is allocated to homosexuality. This libido apparently cannot be converted into heterosexual libido. The two remain distinct and are a part of the original bisexuality. In the course of development, one of the two wins out, and the loser either becomes sublimated or is the foundation for the formation of neurotic difficulties. So in Freud's theory unconscious homosexuality is an important ingredient of basic personality structure. It has never been clear to me under what conditions Freud thought these unconscious tendencies became conscious or overt.

The inverted Oedipus complex is presented as the starting point of homosexual development. In some situations also a regression to narcissism is thought to favour the development of homosexuality, since loving a member of one's own sex may be thought of as an extension of love of oneself. However, even if one accepts Freud's formulation, this description does not explain the dynamics of the process. It is still necessary to know what specific life experiences produced the inverted Oedipus or the regression to narcissism, and why regression to narcissism does not always produce overt homosexuality. Freud suggests that a possible determinant may be varying strengths of original homosexual endowment. Resort to constitution as an explanation very often simply means—the necessary information is not yet available.

One confusion in the literature arises from the fact that cases are sometimes reported as examples of homosexuality where no clear-cut sexual relation existed, but only a strong neurotic dependency on a member of one's own sex was demonstrated. One is left to assume that there is no difference in the dynamics of such a case and one with definite overt manifestations. As far as I know, there has been no analytic data in the classical school on what produces the final violation of cultural taboo when the person accepts an overt homosexual way of life, except the very general idea that such a person has a weak superego, that is, he is unable to control the direction his libido drives.

If Freud's basic theory of personality is questioned, that is, that the character structure is the result of the sublimation of sexual drives, the problem of repressed and overt homosexuality has to be approached differently. When the libido formula is discarded, it is much easier to see that homosexuality is not a clinical entity. There is no clear-cut situation in which it invariably occurs. It appears as a symptom in people of diverse types of character structure. The simple division into active and passive types does not cover the picture, nor are these distinctions always clear-cut. For example, the same person may be active with a younger partner and passive with an older one. The personality type who happens to have made an overt homosexual adjustment in one case may be almost identical with the personality type who under very similar circumstances makes a heterosexual choice in another case. Robbins* describes the competitive and exploitative personalities as characteristic of homosexuals. However, as is well known, competitive and exploitative heterosexual situations are also very frequent. So the specific choice of the sex object is not explained in Robbins's paper.

One can agree with Freud that all people are not only bisexual but polysexual in the sense that they are biologically capable of being sexually roused by either sex, or in fact by a variety of other

*Robbins, Bernard S., 'Psychological Implications of the Male Homosexual "Marriage", *Psychoanalytic Rev.* (1943) *30*, 428–37.

stimulants. Many people tend to form a more or less lasting attachment to the partner in their sexual pleasure. In childhood before the taboos of adults are imposed, a state of uncritical enjoyment of body stimulation exists. When the pleasure is shared, it may be shared with either sex depending to a great extent on propinquity or availability.

On the basis of the early childhood example, it would be interesting to speculate about what might happen if a person could continue his development in a culture with no sex restrictions. It is possible that most children would eventually develop a preference for the biologically most satisfactory type of sexual gratification and that that would prove to be found in the union of male and female genitals. If it should be found that heterosexual activity eventually became the preferred form of sex life, would this mean that the other forms had been repressed? If the culture were truly uncriticizing, repression would be unnecessary. Homosexuality would disappear when more satisfactory gratifications were available. It might reappear if the heterosexual possibilities were withdrawn. In other words, it is probable that on the physiological level uninhibited humans would get their sex gratification in any way possible—but if they had a choice, they would choose the most pleasurable. However, most sexual relationships, in addition to the physiological gratification of lust, have meaning also in interpersonal terms. The relationship as a whole has significance. The value of the relationship in turn affects the satisfaction obtained from the sexual activity. Except in some situations, to be described presently, in which the choice of a homosexual love object is determined by environmental limitations, it would seem that the interpersonal factors—that is, the type of relationship, the nature of the dependency, the personality of the love object—cannot be overlooked in determining whether the choice is a heterosexual or a homosexual way of life. Before discussing this in detail, it would be well to look at some of the varying degrees of acceptability of homosexuality in our own society.

Some form of sexual restriction is found in most cultures. There is a preferred and acceptable form of sexual behaviour while other forms of sexual gratification are in varying degrees of disrepute—some being absolutely forbidden and punishable, others simply less acceptable. It is obvious that under these circumstances no individual is free to choose. He has to cope with the danger of ostracism if he is driven towards a culturally unacceptable form of sexual behaviour. This is definitely one of the problems associated with overt homosexuality in our culture, especially in the case of men.

Freud believed one important distinction between a repressed and an overt homosexual was that the former had a stern superego and the latter a weak superego. This is too simple a statement of the problem, for among overt homosexuals one finds, in addition to the psychopaths who answer to Freud's description, those people who suffer from (stern or severe) superegos and are genuinely unhappy about their condition; others who accept their fate with resignation but feel handicapped; and still others who have lost all sense of self-esteem and think of their sexual behaviour as but another evidence of their worthlessness. Also some more fortunate cases through protected circumstances have not happened to come in contact with the more criminal psychopathic elements in homosexual groups, especially in large cities, and because of their isolation or discreet living have not been made acutely aware of society's disapproval. These homosexuals do not feel great conflict about their relationship, although in other respects they are not lacking in a sense of social responsibility, that is, they do not have weak superegos, to use Freud's term.

Women are most frequently found in the last named situation. This brings us to a consideration of the difference between male and female homosexuality, at least in this culture. Women in general are permitted greater physical intimacy with each other without social disapproval than is the case with men. Kissing and hugging are acceptable forms of friendly expression between women. In America a father is often too self-conscious to kiss his own son, while mother and daughter have no such inhibitions.

Ferenczi* pointed out that in our culture compulsive heterosexuality is one outgrowth of the taboo on even close friendship
with one's own sex. It is obvious that in the case of women there
is a much more permissive attitude about friendship with one's
own sex and therefore about overt homosexuality. Until recent
times there was a much stronger taboo on obvious nonmarital
heterosexual situations. Two overt homosexual women may live
together in complete intimacy in many communities without
social disapproval if they do not flaunt their inversion by, for
example, the assumption of masculine dress or mannerisms on
the part of one. Sometimes even if they go to this extreme they
are thought peculiar rather than taboo. On the other hand, two
men attempting the same thing are likely to encounter marked
hostility.

Perhaps this difference in the attitude of society has a deep
biological origin, to wit: two women may live together in
closest intimacy with kisses, caresses, and close bodily contact
without overt evidence of sexual gratification; two men in the
same situation must know that they are sexually stimulated.

Whether this biological factor contributes to the increased
tolerance for female homosexuals or not, there are other factors
which definitely contribute to making the situation more normal
in women. Earlier in the discussion I pointed out that in situations
of limited choice a person makes the best of the sexual partner
available. If there is a wide range of choice, a person chooses the
most desirable. Circumstances producing privation—such as
army life in remote places—may make strange creatures attractive as sex objects. However, in general, men encounter fewer
external causes of deprivation than women. So when a man
becomes an overt homosexual it is almost always because of
difficulties within himself. Of these society is not tolerant. It tends
to label the man as weak. Women are more frequently in an
isolated situation with regard to heterosexual possibilities than

*Ferenczi, S., *Sex in Psychoanalysis*. Boston, Richard G. Badger, Gorham
Press (1922).

men. Age and physical unattractiveness handicap women more. More conventions surround her search for a partner so that even when young and attractive she may find herself for long periods without socially acceptable means of meeting men. Thus strong external difficulties often lead relatively mature women into homosexual relationships, whereas overt homosexuality in the male is usually an expression of grave personality disorder. I do not wish to imply that there are no severely disturbed homosexual women, but rather that society's tolerance may be traced to the greater proportion of fairly healthy homosexual women.

The different cultural attitudes toward the sissy and the tomboy again show society's greater tolerance for the female homosexual type. When a boy is called a sissy, he feels stigmatized, and the group considers that it has belittled him. No such disapproval goes with a girl's being called a tomboy. In fact she often feels considerable pride in the fact. Probably these names get their value from childhood ideas that courage and daring are desirable traits in both sexes. So the sissy is a coward, a mamma's boy, and the tomboy is a brave girl who can hold her own with a boy her size. These attitudes probably become a part of later attitudes toward homosexuality in the two sexes.

The attitude toward homosexuality in Western society may be summed up as follows: In most circles it is looked upon as an unacceptable form of sexual activity. When external circumstances make the attainment of a heterosexual choice temporarily or permanently impossible, as with women or with men in isolated situations, society is more tolerant of the homosexual situation. Also character traits usually associated with the homosexual affect the degree of disapproval of the individual invert. Thus the tomboy receives less contempt than the sissy.

People who for reasons external to their own personality find their choice of love object limited to their own sex may be said to be 'normal' homosexuals, in the sense that they utilize the best type of interpersonal relationship available to them. These people are not the problem of psychopathology.

The question which concerns psychotherapists is what kind of inner difficulty predisposes a person to the choice of overt homosexuality as his preferred form of interpersonal relationship. When no external limitations are in evidence, is there any one predisposing factor or may it appear in a variety of interpersonal difficulties? Is it an outgrowth of a definite personality structure or do accidental factors add it to an already burdened personality? Or are there in each case definite tendencies from early childhood leading in the direction of homosexuality? It is possible that each of these situations may occur as a predisposing background, and that in each case the meaning of the symptom of homosexuality is determined by the background. In short, homosexuality is not a clinical entity, but a symptom with different meanings in different personality set-ups. One might compare its place in the neurosis to that of a headache in various diseases. A headache may be the result of brain tumour, a sinus, a beginning infectious disease, a migraine attack, an emotional disturbance, or a blow on the head. When the underlying disease is treated successfully, the headache disappears.

Similarly, overt homosexuality may express fear of the opposite sex, fear of adult responsibility, a need to defy authority, or an attempt to cope with hatred of or competitive attitudes to members of one's own sex; it may represent a flight from reality into absorption in body stimulation very similar to the autoerotic activities of the schizophrenic, or it may be a symptom of destructiveness of oneself or others. These do not exhaust the possibilities of its meaning. They merely represent situations which I have personally found in analysing cases. The examples indicate the wide scope of difficulties which may find expression in the symptom.

The next concern is to determine if possible why this symptom is chosen as a solution of the difficulty. Can one invariably show in a given person tendencies which can clearly be traced from childhood, predisposing to homosexuality?

In many cases this seems to be true. In our culture, most children grow up in very close relationship to two people of opposite sexes. It is clear that a child has a distinct relationship to each parent and that sexual interest and curiosity play some part in this, although there are usually more important factors. The relationship is to a great extent moulded by the role of that parent in the child's life. For example, the mother is usually more closely associated with the bodily needs than is the father. The father's function varies more widely. In some families he stands for discipline, in others he is the playmate, in others he shares the care of the child with the mother. These facts influence the child's reaction to the parent. In addition, the child has a relationship to the parent in terms of the kind of person the parent is. He early learns which parent wields the power, which loves him more, which is the more dependable, which one can be manipulated best by his techniques, and so on. These facts determine which parent the child prefers and where his allegiance lies. A very important determining influence in the development of homosexuality is the child's awareness that his sex was a disappointment to his parents or to the more important parent, especially if their disappointment leads them to treat the child as if he were of the opposite sex. However, none of these considerations invariably produce homosexuality in the adult. Girls whose parents wished them to be boys may grow up without any special interest in their own sex. Boys with gentle motherly qualities often marry and find satisfaction in mothering their own children without ever having gone through a struggle against homosexuality. If the father happened to be the strongest, most loving and constructive influence in a boy's life and the mother failed him badly, the boy may become a homosexual, but it is equally probable he will seek a woman of his father's personality type; or if he is more seriously damaged, he will be driven to marry a woman with a destructive influence on him somewhat in the pattern of his mother, or he may even become involved in a homosexual relation with a destructive man. In the same manner one can take up all the possible personality combinations found in parents and show that they in themselves do not predetermine the choice of the sex of the later partner.

Sexual relationships seem to be determined along two main lines. There is the constructive choice where mutual helpfulness and affection dominate the picture, and there is the destructive choice where one finds himself bound to the person whom he fears and who may destroy him—the moth and flame fascination. There are of course many in-between situations where, for example, the partnership is on the whole constructive but has some destructive elements, and so on. This distinction cuts across sex lines. There are both types of heterosexual relationships and both types of homosexual ones.

It is therefore necessary to look further for definite predetermining factors in the formation of the symptom of homosexuality. Two other considerations are important in this respect—the degree of personality damage and the role of accidental factors. People who have been greatly intimidated or have a low self-esteem and therefore have difficulties in making friends and being comfortable with other people have a tendency to cling to their own sex because it is less frightening. They feel understood by people like themselves. There is not the terrifying unpredictability of the unknown. Moreover, relationship with the opposite sex makes greater demands—the man is expected to support the woman, a woman is expected to have children. Also the frightened woman fears to test whether she is sufficiently attractive to win a man, and the frightened man fears he may not be sufficiently successful to attract a woman. However, the above considerations do not invariably produce homosexuality, for the fear of disapproval from the culture and the need to conform often drive these very people into marriage. The fact that one is married by no means proves that one is a mature person.

A homosexual way of life also attracts people who fear intimacy and yet are equally afraid of loneliness. As already mentioned, one's own sex is less frightening because it is familiar. The relationship looks less permanent, less entrapping, as if one could get away at any time. To be sure, the appearance of freedom often proves deceptive, for neurotic attachments with either sex have a way of becoming binding through neurotic dependencies. Among men the fear of the struggle for existence tempts a certain number to become dependent financially as well as otherwise on another man.

Thus far I have shown that various personality problems may find partial solution in a homosexual symptom, but nothing has been shown as specifically producing homosexuality. Some writers have laid great stress on the importance of early seduction by homosexuals, and many homosexuals attribute their way of life to such experiences. However, many people have such experiences without becoming homosexual. It is probable that a homosexual experience to a boy who is already heavily burdened, fears women, and feels unequal to life may add the decisive last touch to his choice of neurosis. Yet a similar seduction of a boy not afraid of life is but an incident in the process of investigation of life, and he simply goes on to master new experiences. Homosexual play is known to be very frequent in preadolescence and causes no serious disturbance in the majority of children.

Perhaps because of Freud's great emphasis on the sexual origin of neurosis and perhaps also because of the strong cultural disapproval, therapists are likely to think of homosexuality as a more fundamentally significant symptom than it really is. It seems certain from analysis in recent years that it is a problem which tends to disappear when the general character problems are solved.

Even as a symptom, homosexuality does not present a uniform appearance. There are at least as many different types of homosexual behaviour as of heterosexual, and the interpersonal relations of homosexuals present the same problems as are found in heterosexual situations. So the mother-child attachment is sometimes found to be the important part of the picture. Frequently competitive and sadomasochistic feelings dominate the union. There are relationships based on hatred and fear and also relationships of mutual helpfulness. Promiscuity is possibly more frequent among homosexuals than heterosexuals, but its significance in the personality structure is very similar in the two. In both the chief interest is in genitals and body stimulation. The person chosen to share the experience is not important. The sexual activity is compulsive and is the sole interest. In fact, in much activity carried on in movies, the partner is not even clearly seen and often not a word is exchanged.

At the other extreme is the homosexual marriage, by which I mean a relatively durable, long-term relationship between two people—a relationship in which the interests and personalities of each are important to the other. Here again we may find all of the pictures of a neurotic heterosexual marriage, the same possessiveness, jealousies, and struggles for power. The idea may be at least theoretically entertained that a homosexual adult love relationship can exist. Adult love seems to be a rare experience in our culture anyway and would doubtless be even more rare among homosexuals, because a person with the necessary degree of maturity would probably prefer a heterosexual relation unless external circumstances in his life made this impossible.

So the actual choice of homosexuality as the preferred form of interpersonal relations may have different origins in different cases, as I have indicated. If it is caused by some one specific situation or combination of circumstances, that has not yet been discovered.

Even though the specific cause for homosexuality can not be found, the specific needs which it satisfies can be examined. Obviously it gives sexual satisfaction, and for a person unable to make contact with the opposite sex, this is important. Also, because it requires a partner, it helps cope with the problem of loneliness and isolation. The very fact of belonging to a culturally taboo group has its satisfactions. One can feel defiant, brave, and strong, and as a member of a band united against the world, lessen the feeling of ostracism. I have spoken earlier of other satisfactions, such as financial support—especially in the case of some male homosexuals—and freedom from responsibility.

An overt homosexual way of life can play a constructive or destructive role in the personality. It may be the best type of human relation of which a person is capable and as such is better than isolation. This would apply especially to the mother-child type of dependencies found in homosexuals of both sexes. Or it may be an added destructive touch in a deteriorating personality. In no case will it be found to be the cause of the rest of the neurotic structure —the basic origin of the neurosis—although after it is established, it may contribute to the problems. As in the case of other symptoms in neurosis, psychoanalysis must deal primarily with the personality structure, realizing that the symptom is a secondary development from that.

A case of homosexuality in a woman

SIGMUND FREUD, M.D.

TRANSLATED BY BARBARA LOW AND R. GABLER

I

HOMOSEXUALITY in women, which is certainly not less common than in men, although much less glaring, has not only been ignored by the law, but has also been neglected by psychoanalytic research. The narration of a single case, not too pronounced in type, in which it was possible to trace its origin and development in the mind with complete certainty and almost without a gap may, therefore, have a certain claim to attention. If this presentation of it furnishes only the most general outlines of the various events concerned and of the conclusions reached from a study of the case, while suppressing all the characteristic details on which the interpretation is founded, this limitation is easily to be explained by the medical discretion necessary in discussing a recent case.

A beautiful and clever girl of eighteen, belonging to a family of good standing, had aroused displeasure and concern in her parents by the devoted adoration with which she pursued a certain lady 'in society' who was about ten years older than herself. The parents asserted that, in spite of her distinguished name, this lady was nothing but a *cocotte*. It was said to be well known that she lived with a married woman as her friend, having intimate relations with her, while at the same time she carried on promiscuous affairs with a number of men. The girl did not contradict these evil reports, but neither did she allow them to interfere with her worship of the lady, although she herself was by no means lacking in a sense of decency and propriety. No prohibitions and no supervision hindered the girl from seizing every one of her rare opportunities of being together with her beloved, of ascertaining all her habits, of waiting for her for hours outside her door or at a tram-halt, of sending her gifts of flowers, and so on. It was evident that this one interest had swallowed up all others in the girl's mind. She did not trouble herself any further with educational studies, thought nothing of social functions or girlish pleasures, and kept up relations only with a few girl friends who could help her in the matter or serve as confidantes. The parents could not say to what lengths their daughter had gone in her relations with the questionable lady, whether the limits of devoted admiration had already been exceeded or not. They had never remarked in their daughter any interest in young men, nor pleasure in their attentions, while, on the other hand, they were sure that her present attachment to a woman was only a continuation, in a more marked degree, of a feeling she had displayed of recent years for other members of her own sex which had already aroused her father's suspicion and anger.

There were two details of her behaviour, in apparent contrast with each other, that most especially vexed her parents. On the one hand, she did not scruple to appear in the most frequented streets in the company of her questionable friend, being thus quite neglectful of her own reputation; while, on the other hand, she disdained no means of deception, no excuses and no lies that would make meetings with her possible and cover them. She thus showed herself too brazen in one respect and full of deceitfulness in the other. One day it happened, indeed, as was sooner or later inevitable in the circumstances, that the father met his daughter in the company of the lady. He passed them by with an angry glance which boded no good. Immediately after, the girl rushed off and flung herself over a wall down the side of a cutting on to a railway line. She paid for this undoubtedly serious attempt at suicide with

315

a considerable time on her back in bed, though fortunately little permanent damage was done. After her recovery she found it easier to get her own way than before. The parents did not dare to oppose her with so much determination, and the lady, who up till then had received her advances coldly, was moved by such an unmistakable proof of serious passion and began to treat her in a more friendly manner.

About six months after this episode the parents sought medical advice and entrusted the physician with the task of bringing their daughter back to a normal state of mind. The girl's attempted suicide had evidently shown them that the instruments of domestic discipline were powerless to overcome the existing disorder. Before going further it will be desirable, however, to deal separately with the attitude of her father and of her mother to the matter.

The father was an earnest, worthy man, at bottom very tender-hearted, but he had to some extent estranged his children by the sternness he had adopted towards them. His treatment of his only daughter was too much influenced by consideration for his wife. When he first came to know of his daughter's homosexual tendencies he flared up in rage and tried to suppress them by threatening her; at that time perhaps he hesitated between different, though equally painful, views—regarding her either as vicious, as a degenerate, or as mentally afflicted. Even after the attempted suicide he did not achieve the lofty resignation shown by one of our medical colleagues who remarked of a similar irregularity in his own family, 'It is just a misfortune like any other.' There was something about his daughter's homosexuality that aroused the deepest bitterness in him, and he was determined to combat it with all the means in his power; the low estimation in which psychoanalysis is so generally held in Vienna did not prevent him from turning to it for help. If this way failed he still had in reserve his strongest countermeasure; a speedy marriage was to awaken the natural instincts of the girl and stifle her unnatural tendencies.

The mother's attitude towards the girl was not so easy to grasp. She was still a youngish woman, who was evidently unwilling to relinquish her own claim to find favour by means of her beauty. All that was clear was that she did not take her daughter's passion so tragically as did the father, nor was she so incensed at it. She had even for a long time enjoyed her daughter's confidence concerning the love affair, and her opposition to it seemed to have been aroused mainly by the harmful publicity with which the girl displayed her feelings. She had herself suffered for some years from neurotic troubles and enjoyed a great deal of consideration from her husband; she was quite unfair in her treatment of her children, decidedly harsh towards her daughter and overindulgent to her three sons, the youngest of whom had been born after a long interval and was then not yet three years old. It was not easy to ascertain anything more definite about her character, for, owing to motives that will only later become intelligible, the patient was always reserved in what she said about her mother, whereas in regard to her father she showed no feeling of the kind.

To a physician who was to undertake psychoanalytic treatment of the girl there were many grounds for a feeling of discomfort. The situation he had to deal with was not the one that analysis demands, in which alone it can demonstrate its effectiveness. As is well known, the ideal situation for analysis is when someone who is otherwise master of himself is suffering from an inner conflict which he is unable to resolve alone, so that he brings his trouble to the analyst and begs for his help. The physician then works hand in hand with one part of the personality which is divided against itself, against the other partner in the conflict. Any situation but this is more or less unfavourable for psychoanalysis and adds fresh difficulties to those already present. Situations like that of a proprietor who orders an architect to build him a villa according to his own tastes and desires, or of a pious donor who commissions an artist to paint a picture of saints, in the corner of which is to be a portrait of himself worshipping, are fundamentally incompatible with the conditions of psychoanalysis.

It constantly happens, to be sure, that a husband informs the physician as follows, 'My wife suffers from nerves, so that she gets on badly with me; please cure her, so that we may lead a happy married life again'. But often enough it turns out such a request is impossible to fulfil, *i.e.*, that the physician cannot bring about the result for which the husband sought the treatment. As soon as the wife is freed from her neurotic inhibitions she sets about dissolving the marriage, for her neurosis was the sole condition under which maintenance of the marriage was possible. Or else parents expect one to cure their nervous and unruly child. By a healthy child they mean one who never places his parents in difficulties, but only gives them pleasure. The physician may succeed in curing the child, but after that it goes its own way all the more decidedly, and the parents are now far more dissatisfied than before. In short, it is not a matter of indifference whether someone comes to analysis of his own accord or because he is brought to it, whether he himself desires to be changed, or only his relatives, who love him (or who might be expected to love him), desire this for him.

Further unfavourable features in the present case were the facts that the girl was not in any way ill—she did not suffer from anything in herself, nor did she complain of her condition—and that the task to be carried out did not consist in resolving a neurotic conflict but in converting one variety of the genital organization of sexuality into the other. The removal of genital inversion or homosexuality is in my experience never an easy matter. On the contrary, I have found success possible only under specially favourable circumstances, and even then the success essentially consisted in being able to open to those who are restricted homosexually the way to the opposite sex, which had been till then barred, thus restoring to them full bisexual functions. After that it lay with themselves to choose whether they wished to abandon the other way that is banned by society, and in individual cases they have done so. One must remember that normal sexuality also depends upon a restriction in the choice of object; in general, to undertake to convert a fully developed homosexual into a heterosexual is not much more promising than to do the reverse, only that for good practical reasons the latter is never attempted.

In actual numbers the successes achieved by psychoanalytic treatment of the various forms of homosexuality, which, to be sure, are manifold, are not very striking. As a rule the homosexual is not able to give up the object of his pleasure, and one cannot convince him that if he changed to the other object he would find again the pleasure that he has renounced. If he comes to be treated at all, it is mostly through the pressure of external motives, such as the social disadvantages and dangers attaching to his choice of object, and such components of the instinct of self-preservation prove themselves too weak in the struggle against the sexual impulses. One then soon discovers his secret plan, namely, to obtain from the striking failure of his attempt the feeling of satisfaction that he has done everything possible against his abnormality, to which he can now resign himself with an easy conscience. The case is somewhat different when consideration for beloved parents and relatives has been the motive for his attempt to be cured. Then there really are libidinal tendencies present which may put forth energies opposed to the homosexual choice of object, though their strength is rarely sufficient. It is only where the homosexual fixation has not yet become strong enough, or where there are considerable rudiments and vestiges of a heterosexual choice of object, i.e., in a still oscillating or in a definitely bisexual organization, that one may make a more favourable prognosis for psychoanalytic therapy.

For these reasons I declined altogether holding out to the parents any prospect of their wish being fulfilled. I merely said I was prepared to study the girl carefully for a few weeks or months, so as then to be able to pronounce how far a continuation of the analysis might influence her. In quite a number of cases, indeed, the analysis divides itself into two clearly distinguishable stages: in the first, the physician procures from the patient the necessary information, makes him familiar with the premises and postulates of psychoanalysis, and unfolds to him the reconstruction of the genesis of his disorder as deduced from the material brought up in the analysis. In the second stage the patient himself lays hold of the material put before him, works on it, recollects what he can of the apparently repressed memories, and behaves as if he were living the rest over again. In this way he can confirm, supplement, and correct the inferences made by the physician. It is only during this work that he experiences, through overcoming resistances, the inner change aimed at, and acquires for himself the convictions that make him independent of the physician's authority.

These two stages in the course of the analytic treatment are not always sharply divided from each other; this can only happen when the resistance maintains certain conditions. But when this is so, one may institute a comparison with two stages of a journey. The first comprises all the necessary preparations, today so complicated and hard to effect, before, ticket in hand, one can at last go on to the platform and secure a seat in the train. One then has the right, and the possibility, of travelling into a distant country, but after all these preliminary exertions one is not yet there—indeed, one is not a single mile nearer to one's goal. For this to happen one has to make the journey itself from one station to the other, and this part of the performance may well be compared with the second stage in the analysis.

The analysis of the patient I am discussing took this course of two stages, but it was not continued beyond the beginning of the second stage. A special constellation of the resistance made it possible, nevertheless, to gain full confirmation of my inferences, and to obtain an adequate insight on broad lines into the way in which her inversion had developed. But before relating the findings of the analysis I must deal with a few points which have either been touched upon already by myself or which will have roused special interest in the reader.

I had made the prognosis partly dependent on how far the girl had succeeded in satisfying her passion. The information I gleaned during the analysis seemed favourable in this respect. With none of the objects of her adoration had the patient enjoyed anything beyond a few kisses and embraces; her genital chastity, if one may use such a phrase, had remained intact. As for the lady who led a double life, and who had roused the girl's most recent and by far her strongest emotions, she had always treated her coldly and had never allowed any greater favour than kissing her hand. Probably the girl was making a virtue of necessity when she kept insisting on the purity of her love and her physical repulsion against the idea of any sexual intercourse. But perhaps she was not altogether wrong when she vaunted of her wonderful beloved that, aristocrat as she was, forced into her present position only by adverse family circumstances, she had preserved, in spite of her situation, a great deal of nobility. For the lady used to recommend the girl every time they met to withdraw her affection from herself and from women in general, and she had persistently rejected the girl's advances up to the time of the attempted suicide.

A second point, which I at once tried to investigate, concerned any possible motives in the girl herself which might serve to support a psychoanalytic treatment. She did not try to deceive me by saying that she felt any urgent need to be freed from her homosexuality. On the contrary, she said she could not conceive of any other way of being in love, but she added that for her parents' sake she would honestly help in the therapeutic endeavour, for it pained her very much to be the cause of so much grief to them. I had to take this as a propitious sign to begin with; I could not divine the unconscious affective attitude that lay behind it. What came to light later in this connexion decisively influenced the course taken by the analysis and determined its premature conclusion.

Readers unversed in psychoanalysis will long have been awaiting an answer to two other questions. Did this homosexual girl show physical characteristics plainly belonging to the opposite sex, and did the case prove to be one of congenital or acquired (later developed) homosexuality?

I am aware of the importance attaching to the first of these questions. Only one should not exaggerate it and obscure in its favour the fact that sporadic secondary characteristics of the opposite sex are very often present in normal individuals, and that well-marked physical characteristics of the opposite sex may be found in persons whose choice of object has undergone no change in the direction of inversion; in other words, that in both sexes *the degree of physical hermaphroditism is to a great extent independent of the psychical hermaphroditism.* In modification of this statement it must be added that this independence is more evident in men than women, where bodily and mental traits belonging to the opposite sex are apt to coincide in their incident. Still I am not in a position to give a satisfactory answer to the first of our questions about my patient; the psychoanalyst customarily forgoes thorough bodily examination of his patients in certain cases. Certainly there was no obvious deviation from the feminine physical type, nor any menstrual disturbance. The beautiful and well-developed girl had, it is true, her father's tall figure, and her facial features were sharp rather than soft and girlish, traits which might be regarded as indicating a physical masculinity. Some of her intellectual attributes also could be connected with masculinity: for instance, her acuteness of comprehension and her lucid objectivity, in so far as she was not dominated by her passion; though these distinctions are conventional rather than scientific. What is certainly of greater importance is that in her behaviour towards her love-object she had throughout assumed the masculine part: that is to say, she displayed the humility and the sublime overestimation of the sexual object so characteristic of the male lover, the renunciation of all narcissistic satisfaction, and the preference for being lover rather than beloved. She had thus not only chosen a feminine love-object, but had also developed a masculine attitude towards this object.

The second question, whether this was a case of inherited or acquired homosexuality, will be answered by the whole history of the patient's abnormality and its development. The study of this will show how fruitless and inappropriate this question is.

II

After an introduction which digresses in so many directions, the sexual history of the case under consideration can be presented quite concisely. In childhood the girl had passed through the normal attitude characteristic of the feminine Oedipus complex* in a way that was not at all remarkable, and had later also begun to substitute for her father a brother slightly older than herself. She did not remember any sexual traumata in early life, nor were any discovered by the analysis. Comparison of her brother's genital organs and her own, which took place about the beginning of the latency period (at five years old or perhaps a little earlier), left a strong impression on her and had far-reaching after-effects. There were only slight hints pointing to infantile onanism, or else the analysis did not go deep enough to throw light on this point. The birth of a second brother when she was between five and six years old left no special influence upon her development. During the prepubertal years at school she gradually became acquainted with the facts of sex, and she received this knowledge with mixed feelings of fascination and frightened aversion, in a way which may be called normal and was not exaggerated in degree. This amount of information about her seems meagre enough, nor can I guarantee that it is complete. It may be that the history of her youth was much richer in experiences; I do not know. As I have already said, the analysis was broken off after a short time, and therefore yielded an anamnesis not much more reliable than the other anamneses of homosexuals, which there is good cause to question. Further,

---

*I do not see any progress or advantage in the introduction of the term 'Electra-complex', and do not advocate its use.

the girl had never been neurotic, and came to the analysis without even one hysterical symptom, so that opportunities for investigating the history of her childhood did not present themselves so readily as usual.

At the age of thirteen to fourteen she displayed a tender and, according to general opinion, exaggeratedly strong affection for a small boy, not quite three years old, whom she used to see regularly in a playground in one of the parks. She took to the child so warmly that in consequence a permanent friendship grew up between herself and his parents. One may infer from this episode that at that time she was possessed of a strong desire to be a mother herself and to have a child. However, after a short time she grew indifferent to the boy, and began to take an interest in mature, but still youthful, women; the manifestations of this in her soon led her father to administer a mortifying chastisement to her.

It was established beyond all doubt that this change occurred simultaneously with a certain event in the family, and one may therefore look to this for some explanation of the change. Before it happened, her libido was focused on motherhood, while afterwards she became a homosexual attracted to mature women, and has remained so ever since. The event which is so significant for our understanding of the case was a new pregnancy of her mother's, and the birth of a third brother when she was about sixteen.

The network of causes and effects that I shall now proceed to lay bare is not a product of my gift for combination; it is based on such trustworthy analytic evidence that I can claim objective validity for it; it was in particular a series of interrelated dreams, easy of interpretation, that proved decisive in this respect.

The analysis revealed beyond all shadow of doubt that the beloved lady was a substitute for—the mother. It is true that she herself was not a mother, but then she was not the girl's first love. The first objects of her affection after the birth of her youngest brother were really mothers, women between thirty and thirty-five whom she had met with their children during summer holidays or in the family circle of acquaintances in town. Motherhood as a 'condition of love' was later on given up, because it was difficult to combine in real life with another one, which grew more and more important. The specially intensive bond with her latest love, the 'Lady', had still another basis which the girl discovered quite easily one day. On account of her slender figure, regular beauty, and offhand manner, the lady reminded her of her own brother, a little older than herself. Her latest choice corresponded, therefore, not only with her feminine but also with her masculine ideal; it combined gratification of the homosexual tendency with that of the heterosexual one. It is well known that analysis of male homosexuals has in numerous cases revealed the same combination, which should warn us not to form too simple a conception of the nature and genesis of inversion, and to keep in mind the extensive influence of the bisexuality of mankind.[*]

But how are we to understand the fact that it was just the birth of a child who came late in the family, at a time when the girl herself was already mature and had strong wishes of her own, that moved her to bestow her passionate tenderness upon her who gave birth to this child, *i.e.*, her own mother, and to express that feeling towards a substitute for her mother? From all that we know we should have expected just the opposite. In such circumstances mothers with daughters of about a marriageable age usually feel embarrassed in regard to them, while the daughters are apt to feel for their mothers a mixture of compassion, contempt and envy which does nothing to increase their tenderness for them. The girl we are considering, however, had altogether little cause to feel affection for her mother. The latter, still youthful herself, saw in her rapidly developing daughter an inconvenient competitor; she favoured the sons at her expense, limited her independence as much as possible, and kept

[*]Cf. J. Sadger, *Jahresbericht über sexuelle Perversionen*.

an especially strict watch against any close relation between the girl and her father. A yearning from the beginning for a kinder mother would, therefore, have been quite intelligible; but why it should have flamed up just then, and in the form of a consuming passion, is not comprehensible.

The explanation is as follows: The girl was just experiencing the revival of the infantile Oedipus complex at puberty when she suffered a great disappointment. She became keenly conscious of the wish to have a child, and a male one; that it was her father's child and his image that she desired, her consciousness was not allowed to know. And then—it was not she who bore the child, but the unconsciously hated rival, her mother. Furiously resentful and embittered, she turned away from her father, and from men altogether. After this first great reverse she forswore her womanhood and sought another goal for her libido.

In doing so she behaved just as many men do who after a first painful experience turn their backs forever upon the faithless female sex and become woman-haters. It is related of one of the most attractive and unfortunate princes of our time that he became a homosexual because the lady he was engaged to marry betrayed him with a stranger. I do not know whether this is true historically, but much psychological truth lies behind the rumour. In all of us, throughout life, the libido normally oscillates between male and female objects; the bachelor gives up his men friends when he marries, and returns to club life when married life has lost its savour. Naturally, when the swing-over is fundamental and final, we suspect some special factor which has definitely favoured one side or the other, and which perhaps only waited for the appropriate moment in order to turn the choice of object finally in its direction.

After her disappointment, therefore, this girl had entirely repudiated her wish for a child, the love of a man, and womanhood altogether. Now it is evident that at this point the developments open to her were manifold; what actually happened was the most extreme one possible She changed into a man, and took her mother in place of her father as her love-object.* Her relation to her mother had certainly been ambivalent from the beginning, and it proved easy to revive her earlier love for her mother and with its help to bring about an overcompensation for her current hostility towards her. Since there was little to be done with the real mother, there arose from the conversion of feeling described the search for a mother substitute to whom she could become passionately attached.†

In her actual relations with her mother there was a practical motive furthering the change of feeling which might be called an 'advantage through illness'. The mother herself still attached great value to the attentions and the admiration of men. If, then, the girl became homosexual and left men to her mother (in other words, 'retired in favour of' the mother), she removed something which had hitherto been partly responsible for her mother's disfavour.‡

*It is by no means rare for a love-relation to be broken off by means of a process of identification on the part of the lover with the loved object, a process equivalent to a kind of regression to narcissism. After this has been accomplished, it is easy in making a fresh choice of object to direct the libido to a member of the sex opposite to that of the earlier choice.

†The displacements of the libido here described are doubtless familiar to every analyst from investigation of the anamneses of neurotics. With the latter, however, they occur in early childhood, at the beginning of the love-life; with our patient, who was in no way neurotic, they took place in the first years following puberty, though, by the way, they were just as completely unconscious. Perhaps one day this temporal factor may turn out to be of great importance

‡As 'retiring in favour of someone else' has not previously been mentioned among the causes of homosexuality, or in the mechanism of libido-fixation in general, I will adduce here another analytical observation of the same kind which has a special feature of interest. I once knew two twin brothers, both of whom were endowed with strong libidinal impulses. One of them was very successful with women, and had innumerable affairs with women and girls. The other went the same way at first, but it became unpleasant for him to be trespassing on his brother's beat, and, owing to the likeness between them, to be mistaken for him on intimate occasions, so he got out of the difficulty by becoming homosexual. He left the women to his brother,

The attitude of the libido thus adopted was greatly reinforced as soon as the girl perceived how much it displeased her father. Once she had been punished for an overaffectionate overture made to a woman she realized how she could wound her father and take revenge on him. Henceforth she remained homosexual out of defiance against her father. Nor did she scruple to lie to him and to deceive him in every way. Towards her mother, indeed, she was only so far deceitful as was necessary to prevent her father from knowing things. I had the impression that her behaviour followed the principle of the talion: 'Since you have betrayed me, you must put up with my betraying you.' Nor can I come to any other conclusion about the striking lack of caution displayed by this otherwise ingenious and clever girl. She *wanted* her father to know occasionally of her intercourse with the lady, otherwise she would be deprived of satisfaction of her keenest desire—namely, revenge. So she saw to this by showing herself openly in the company of her adored one, by walking with her in the streets near her father's place of business,

---

and thus 'retired' in his favour. Another time I treated a young man, an artist, unmistakably bisexual in disposition, in whom the homosexual trend had come to the fore simultaneously with a disturbance in his work. He fled from both women and work together. The analysis, which was able to bring him back to both, showed that the fear of the father was the most powerful psychic motive for both the disturbances, which were really renunciations. In his imagination all women belonged to the father, and he sought refuge in men out of submission, so as to 'retire from' the conflict in favour of the father. Such a motivation of the homosexual object-choice must be by no means uncommon; in the primeval ages of the human race all women presumably belonged to the father and head of the primal horde.

Among brothers and sisters who are not twins this 'retirement' plays a great part in other spheres as well as in that of the love-choice. For example, an elder brother studies music and is admired for it; the younger, far more gifted musically, soon gives up his own musical studies, in spite of his longing, and can not be persuaded to touch an instrument again. This is one example of a very frequent occurrence, and investigation of the motives leading to this 'retirement' rather than to open rivalry discloses very complicated conditions in the mind.

and the like. This maladroitness was by no means unintentional. It was remarkable, by the way, that both parents behaved as though they understood the secret psychology of their daughter. The mother was tolerant, as though she appreciated the favour of her daughter's 'retirement' from the arena; the father was furious, as though he realized the deliberate revenge directed against himself.

The girl's inversion, however, received its final reinforcement when she found in her 'Lady' an object which promised to satisfy not only her homosexual tendency, but also that part of her heterosexual libido still attached to her brother.

III

Consecutive presentation is not a very adequate means of describing complicated mental processes going on in different layers of the mind. I am therefore obliged to pause in the discussion of the case and treat more fully and deeply some of the points brought forward above.

I mentioned the fact that in her behaviour to her adored lady the girl had adopted the characteristic masculine type of love. Her humility and her tender lack of pretensions, '*che poco spera e nulla chiede*,' her bliss when she was allowed to accompany the lady a little way and to kiss her hand on parting, her joy when she heard her praised as beautiful—while any recognition of her own beauty by another person meant nothing at all to her—her pilgrimages to places once visited by the loved one, the oblivion of all more sensual wishes: all these little traits in her resembled the first passionate adoration of a youth for a celebrated actress whom he regards as far above him, to whom he scarcely dares lift his bashful eyes. The correspondence with the 'type of object-choice in men' that I have described elsewhere, whose special features I traced to the attachment to the mother,* held good even to the smallest details. It may seem remarkable that

Collected Papers, vol. iv.

she was not in the least repelled by the evil reputation of her beloved, although her own observations sufficiently confirmed the truth of such rumours. She was after all a well-brought-up and modest girl, who had avoided sexual adventures for herself, and who regarded coarsely sensual gratification as unaesthetic. But already her first passions had been for women who were not celebrated for specially strict propriety. The first protest her father made against her love-choice had been evoked by the pertinacity with which she sought the company of a cinema-actress at a summer resort. Moreover, in all these affairs it had never been a question of women who had any reputation for homosexuality, and who might, therefore, have offered her some prospect of homosexual gratification; on the contrary, she illogically courted women who were coquettes in the ordinary sense of the word, and she rejected without hesitation the willing advances made by a homosexual friend of her own age. The bad reputation of her 'Lady', however, was positively a 'condition of love' for her, and all that is enigmatical in this attitude vanishes when we remember that in the case of the masculine type of object-choice derived from the mother it is also an essential condition that the loved object should be in some way or other 'of bad repute' sexually, one who really may be called a 'light woman'. When the girl learned later on how far her adored lady deserved to be called by this title and that she lived simply by giving her bodily favours, her reaction took the form of great compassion and of phantasies and plans for 'rescuing' her beloved from these ignoble circumstances. We have been struck by the same endeavours to 'rescue' in the men of the type referred to above, and in my description of it I have tried to give the analytical derivation of this tendency.

We are led into quite another realm of explanation by the analysis of the attempt at suicide, which I must regard as seriously intended, and which, by the way, considerably improved her position both with her parents and with the lady she loved. She went for a walk with her one day in a part of the town and at an hour at which she was not unlikely to meet her father on his way from his office. So it turned out. Her father passed them in the street and cast a furious look at her and her companion, whom he had by that time come to know. A few moments later she flung herself on to the railway cutting. Now the explanation she gave of the immediate reasons determining her resolution sounded quite plausible. She had confessed to the lady that the man who had given them such an irate glance was her father, and that he had absolutely forbidden their friendship. The lady became incensed at this and ordered the girl to leave her then and there, and never again to wait for her or to address her—the affair must now come to an end. In her despair at having thus lost her loved one for ever, she wanted to put an end to herself. The analysis, however, was able to disclose another and deeper interpretation behind the one she gave, which was confirmed by the evidence of her own dreams. The attempted suicide was, as might have been expected, determined by two other motives besides the one she gave; it was a 'punishment fulfilment' (self-punishment), and a wish-fulfilment. As a wish-fulfilment it signified the attainment of the very wish which, when frustrated, had driven her into homosexuality—namely, the wish to have a child by her father, for now she 'fell'* through her father's fault.† The fact that at this moment the lady had spoken to the same effect as the father, and had uttered the same prohibition, forms the connecting link between this deeper interpretation and the superficial one of which the girl herself was conscious. From the point of view of self-punishment the girl's action shows us that she had developed in her unconscious

---

*(In the text there is a play on the word *niederkommen*, which means both 'to fall' and 'to be delivered of a child.' There is also in English a colloquial use of the verb 'to fall,' meaning pregnancy or childbirth.—Trans.)

†That the various means of suicide can represent sexual wish-fulfilments has long been known to all analysts. (To poison oneself=to become pregnant; to drown = to bear a child; to throw oneself from a height = to be delivered of a child.)

strong death-wishes against one or other of her parents: perhaps against her father, out of revenge for impeding her love, but, more likely, also against her mother when she was pregnant with the little brother. For analysis has explained the enigma of suicide in the following way: probably no one finds the mental energy required to kill himself unless, in the first place, he is in doing this at the same time killing an object with whom he has identified himself, and, in the second place, is turning against himself a death-wish which had been directed against someone else. Nor need the regular discovery of these unconscious death-wishes in those who have attempted suicide surprise us as strange (any more than it need make an impression as confirming our deductions), since the unconscious of all human beings is full enough of such death-wishes, even against those we love.* The girl's identification of herself with her mother, who ought to have died at the birth of the child denied to herself, makes this 'punishment-fulfilment' itself again into a 'wish-fulfilment.' Lastly, a discovery that several quite different motives, all of great strength, must have co-operated to make such a deed possible is only in accord with what we should expect.

In the girl's account of her conscious motives the father did not figure at all; there was not even any mention of fear of his anger. In the motivation laid bare by the analysis he played the principal part. Her relation to her father had this same decisive importance for the course and outcome of the analytic treatment, or rather, analytic exploration. Behind her pretended consideration for her parents, for whose sake she had been willing to make the attempt to be transformed, lay concealed her attitude of defiance and revenge against her father which held her fast to her homosexuality. Secure under this cover, the resistance allowed a considerable degree of freedom to the analytic investigation. The analysis went forward almost without any signs of resistance, the patient participating actively with her intellect, though absolutely tranquil emotionally. Once when I expounded

*Cf. 'Reflections upon War and Death.' *Collected Papers*, vol. iv.

to her a specially important part of the theory, one touching her nearly, she replied in an inimitable tone, 'How very interesting,' as though she were a *grande dame* being taken over a museum and glancing through her lorgnon at objects to which she was completely indifferent. The impression one had of her analysis was not unlike that of an hypnotic treatment, where the resistance has in the same way withdrawn to a certain limit, beyond which it then proves to be unconquerable. The resistance very often pursues similar tactics—Russian tactics, as they might be called*—in cases of the obsessional neurosis, which for this reason yield the clearest results for a time and permit of a penetrating inspection of the causation of the symptoms. One begins to wonder how it is that such marked progress in analytic understanding can be unaccompanied by even the slightest change in the patient's compulsions and inhibitions, until at last one perceives that everything accomplished had been admitted only under the mental reservation of doubt,† and behind this protective barrier the neurosis may feel secure. 'It would be all very fine,' thinks the patient, often quite consciously, 'if I were obliged to believe what the man says, but there is no question of that, and so long as that is not so I need change nothing.' Then, when one comes to close quarters with the motivation of this doubt, the fight with the resistances breaks forth in earnest.

In the case of our patient, it was not doubt, but the effective factor of revenge against her father that made her cool reserve possible, that divided the analysis into two distinct stages, and rendered the results of the first stage so complete and perspicuous. It seemed, further, as though nothing resembling a transference to the physician had been effected. That, however, is of course absurd, or, at least, is a loose way of expressing it; for some kind of relation to the analyst must come about, and this is usually transferred from an infantile one. In reality she transferred to me the deep antipathy to men which had domin-

*[A reference to the European War, 1914–18.—Trans.]

† (*I.e.*, believed on condition that it is regarded as not certain.—Trans.)

ated her ever since the disappointment she had suffered from her father. Bitterness against men is as a rule easy to gratify upon the analyst; it need not evoke any violent emotional manifestations, it simply expresses itself in rendering futile all his endeavours and in clinging to the neurosis. I know from experience how difficult it is to make the patient understand just this mute kind of symptomatic behaviour and to make him aware of this latent, and often exceedingly strong, hostility without endangering the treatment. So as soon as I recognized the girl's attitude to her father, I broke off the treatment and gave the advice that, if it was thought worth-while to continue the therapeutic efforts, it should be done by a woman. The girl had in the meanwhile promised her father that at any rate she would not communicate with the 'Lady', and I do not know whether my advice, the motive for which is evident, will be followed.

Only once in the course of this analysis did anything appear which I could regard as a positive transference, a greatly weakened revival of the original passionate love for the father. Even this manifestation was not quite free from other motives, but I mention it because it brings up, in another direction, an interesting problem of analytic technique. At a certain period, not long after the treatment had begun, the girl brought a series of dreams which, distorted as is customary and couched in the usual dream-language, could nevertheless be easily translated with certainty. Their content, when interpreted, was, however, remarkable. They anticipated the cure of the inversion through the treatment, expressed her joy over the prospects in life then opened before her, confessed her longing for a man's love and for children, and so might have been welcomed as a gratifying preparation for the desired change. The contradiction between them and the girl's utterances in waking life at the time was very great. She did not conceal from me that she meant to marry, but only in order to escape from her father's tyranny and to follow her true inclinations undisturbed. As for the husband, she remarked rather contemptuously, she would easily deal with him, and besides, one could have sexual relations with a man and a woman at one and the same time, as the example of the adored lady showed. Warned through some slight impression or other, I told her one day that I did not believe these dreams, that I regarded them as false or hypocritical, and that she intended to deceive me just as she habitually deceived her father. I was right; after this exposition this kind of dream ceased. But I still believe that, beside the intention to mislead me, the dreams partly expressed the wish to win my favour; they were also an attempt to gain my interest and my good opinion—perhaps in order to disappoint me all the more thoroughly later on.

I can imagine that to point out the existence of lying dreams of this kind, destined to please the analyst, will arouse in some readers who call themselves analysts a real storm of helpless indignation. 'What!' they will exclaim, 'so the unconscious, the real centre of our mental life, the part of us that is so much nearer the divine than our poor consciousness, so that too can lie! Then how can we still build on the interpretations of analysts and the accuracy of our findings!' To which one must reply that the recognition of these lying dreams does not constitute an astounding novelty. I know, indeed, that the craving of mankind for mysticism is ineradicable, and that it makes ceaseless efforts to win back for mysticism the playground it has been deprived of by the *Traumdeutung*, but in the case under consideration surely everything is simple enough. A dream is not the 'unconscious' itself; it is the form into which a thought from the preconscious, or even from waking conscious life, can, thanks to the favouring conditions of sleep, be recast. During sleep this thought has been reinforced by unconscious wish-excitations and thus has experienced distortion through the 'dream-work', which is determined by the mechanisms valid for the unconscious. With our dreamer, the intention to mislead me, just as she did her father, certainly emanated from the preconscious, or perhaps even from consciousness; it could come to expression by entering into connexion with the unconscious wish-impulse to please the father (or father-substitute), and in this way it created a lying dream. The two intentions, to betray and to please the father, originate in the same complex; the former resulted from the repression of the latter, and the later one was reduced by the dream-work to the earlier one. There can therefore be no question of any devaluation of the unconscious, nor of a shaking of our confidence in the results of our analysis.

I will not miss this opportunity of expressing for once my astonishment that human beings can go through such great and momentous phases of their love-life without heeding them much, sometimes even, indeed, without having the faintest suspicion of them: or else that, when they do become aware of these phases, they deceive themselves so thoroughly in their judgment of them. This happens not only with neurotics, where we are familiar with the phenomenon, but seems also to be common enough in ordinary life. In the present case, for example, a girl develops a devotion for women, which her parents at first find merely vexatious and hardly take seriously; she herself knows quite well that her feelings are greatly engaged, but still she is only slightly aware of the sensations of intense love until a certain disappointment is followed by an absolutely excessive reaction, which shows everyone concerned that they have to do with a consuming passion of elemental strength. Even the girl herself had never perceived anything of the conditions necessary for the outbreak of such a mental upheaval. In other cases we come across girls or women in a state of severe depression, who on being asked for a possible cause of their condition tell us that they have, it is true, had a little feeling for a certain person, but that it was nothing deep and that they soon got over it when they had to give up hope. And yet it was this renunciation, apparently so easily borne, that became the cause of serious mental disturbance. Again, we have to do with men who have passed through casual love affairs and then realize only from the subsequent effects that they had been passionately in love with someone whom they had apparently regarded lightly. One is also amazed at the unexpected results that may follow an artificial abortion which had been decided upon without remorse and without hesitation. One must agree that the poets are right who are so fond of portraying people in love without knowing it, or uncertain whether they do love, or who think that they hate when in reality they love. It would seem that the knowledge received by our consciousness of what is happening to our love instincts is especially liable to be incomplete, full of gaps, or falsified. Needless to say, in this discussion I have not omitted to allow for the part played by subsequent failures of memory.

IV

I now come back, after this digression, to the consideration of my patient's case. We have made a survey of the forces which led the girl's libido from the normal Oedipus attitude into that of homosexuality, and of the paths thus traversed by it in the mind. Most important in this respect was the impression made by the birth of her little brother, and we might from this be inclined to classify the case as one of late acquired inversion.

But at this point we become aware of a state of things which also confronts us in many other instances in which light has been thrown by psychoanalysis on a mental process. So long as we trace the development from its final stage backwards, the connexion appears continuous, and we feel we have gained an insight which is completely satisfactory or even exhaustive. But if we proceed the reverse way, if we start from the premises inferred from the analysis and try to follow these up to the final result, then we no longer get the impression of an inevitable sequence of events which could not be otherwise determined. We notice at once that there might have been another result, and that we might have been just as well able to understand and explain the latter. The synthesis is thus not so satisfactory as the analysis; in other words, from a knowledge of the premises we could not have foretold the nature of the result.

It is very easy to account for this disturbing state of affairs. Even supposing that we thoroughly know the aetiological factors that decide a given result, still we know them only qualitatively, and not in their relative strength. Some of them are so weak as to become suppressed by others, and therefore do not affect the final result. But we never know beforehand which of the determining factors will prove the weaker or the stronger. We only say at the end that those which succeeded must have been the stronger. Hence it is always possible by analysis to recognize the causation with certainty, whereas a prediction of it by synthesis is impossible.

We do not, therefore, mean to maintain that every girl who experiences a disappointment of this kind, of the longing for love that springs from the Oedipus attitude during puberty, will necessarily on that account fall a victim to homosexuality. On the contrary, other kinds of reaction to this trauma are probably commoner. Then, however, there must have been present in this girl special factors that turned the scale, factors outside the trauma, probably of an internal nature. Nor is there any difficulty in pointing them out.

It is well known that even in the normal person it takes a certain time before a decision in regard to the sex of the love-object is finally achieved. Homosexual enthusiasms, unduly strong friendships tinged with sensuality, are common enough in both sexes during the first years after puberty. This was also so with our patient, but in her these tendencies undoubtedly showed themselves to be stronger, and lasted longer, than with others. In addition, these presages of later homosexuality had always occupied her conscious life, while the attitude arising from the Oedipus complex had remained unconscious and had appeared only in such signs as her tender fondling of the little boy. As a schoolgirl she was for a long time in love with a strict and unapproachable teacher, obviously a mother substitute.

A long time before the birth of her brother and still longer before the first reprimand at the hands of her father, she had taken a specially keen interest in various young mothers. From very early years, therefore, her libido had flowed in two streams, the one on the surface being one that we may unhesitatingly designate homosexual. This latter was probably a direct and unchanged continuation of an infantile mother fixation. Possibly the analysis described here actually revealed nothing more than the process by which, on an appropriate occasion, the deeper heterosexual libido-stream was also deflected into the manifest homosexual one.

The analysis showed, further, that the girl had suffered from childhood from a strongly marked 'masculinity complex'. A spirited girl, always ready to fight, she was not at all prepared to be second to her slightly older brother; after inspecting his genital organs she had developed a pronounced envy of the penis, and the thoughts derived from this envy still continued to fill her mind. She was in fact a feminist; she felt it to be unjust that girls should not enjoy the same freedom as boys, and rebelled against the lot of woman in general. At the time of the analysis the idea of pregnancy and childbirth was disagreeable to her, partly, I surmise, on account of the bodily disfigurement connected with them. Her girlish narcissism had betaken itself to this refuge,* and ceased to express itself as pride in her good looks. Various clues indicated that she must formerly have taken great pleasure in exhibitionism and scoptophilia. Anyone who is anxious that the claims of environment in aetiology should not come short, as opposed to those of heredity, will call attention to the fact that the girl's behaviour, as described above, was exactly what would follow from the combined effect in a person with a strong mother fixation of the two influences of her mother's indifference and of her comparison of her genital organs with her brother's. It is possible here to trace back to the impression of an effective external influence in early life something which

*Cf. Kriemhilde's confession in the *Nibelungenlied*.

one would have been ready to regard as a constitutional peculiarity. But a part even of this acquired disposition, if it has really
been acquired, has to be ascribed to the inborn constitution. So
we see in practice a continual mingling and blending of what in
theory we should try to separate into a pair of opposites—
namely, inherited and acquired factors.

An earlier, more tentative conclusion of the analysis might
have led to the view that this was a case of late-acquired homosexuality, but deeper consideration of the material undertaken
later impels us to conclude that it is rather a case of inborn
homosexuality which, as usual, became fixed and unmistakably
manifest only in the period following puberty. Each of these
classifications does justice only to one part of the state of affairs
ascertainable by observation, but neglects the other. It would
be best not to attach too much value to this way of stating the
problem.

Publications on homosexuality usually do not distinguish
clearly enough between the questions of the choice of object,
on the one hand, and of the sexual characteristics and sexual
attitude of the subject, on the other, as though the answer to
the former necessarily involved the answer to the latter. Experience, however, proves the contrary: a man with predominantly
male characteristics and also masculine in his love-life may still
be inverted in respect to his object, loving only men instead of
women. A man in whose character feminine attributes evidently
predominate, who may, indeed, behave in love like a woman,
might be expected, from this feminine attitude, to choose a man
for his love-object; but he may nevertheless be heterosexual, and
show no more inversion in respect of his object than an average
normal man. The same is true of women; here also mental
sexual character and object-choice do not necessarily coincide.
The mystery of homosexuality is therefore by no means so
simple as it is commonly depicted in popular expositions, e.g.
a feminine personality, which therefore has to love a man, is
unhappily attached to a male body; or a masculine personality,

irresistibly attracted by women, is unfortunately cemented to a female body. It is instead a question of three series of characteristics, namely—

Physical sexual characteristics (*physical hermaphroditism*)
Mental sexual characteristics (*masculine, or feminine, attitude*)
Kind of object-choice

which, up to a certain point, vary independently of one another, and are met with in different individuals in manifold permutations. Tendencious publications have obscured our view of this interrelationship by putting into the foreground, for practical reasons, the third feature (the kind of object-choice), which is the only one that strikes the layman, and in addition by exaggerating the closeness of the association between this and the first feature. Moreover, they block the way leading to a deeper insight into all that is uniformly designated homosexuality by rejecting two fundamental facts which have been revealed by psychoanalytic investigation. The first of these is that homosexual men have experienced a specially strong fixation in regard to the mother; the second, that, in addition to their manifest heterosexuality, a very considerable measure of latent or unconscious homosexuality can be detected in all normal people. If these findings are taken into account, then, to be sure, the supposition that nature in a freakish mood created a 'third sex' falls to the ground.

It is not for psychoanalysis to solve the problem of homosexuality. It must rest content with disclosing the psychical mechanisms that resulted in determination of the object-choice, and with tracing the paths leading from them to the instinctual basis of the disposition. There its work ends, and it leaves the rest to biological research, which has recently brought to light, through Steinach's* experiments, such very important results concerning the influence exerted by the first factor mentioned above on the second and third. Psychoanalysis has a common basis with biology, in that it presupposes an original bisexuality

*Cf. A. Lipschütz, *Die Pubertätsdrüse und ihre Wirkungen.*

in human beings (as in animals). But psychoanalysis cannot elucidate the intrinsic nature of what in conventional or in biological phraseology is termed 'masculine' and 'feminine': it simply takes over the two concepts and makes them the foundation of its work. When we attempt to reduce them further, we find masculinity vanishing into activity and femininity into passivity, and that does not tell us enough. In what has gone before I have tried to explain how far we may reasonably expect, or how far experience has already proved, that the elucidations yielded by analysis furnish us with the means for altering inversion. When one compares the extent to which we can influence it with the remarkable transformations that Steinach has effected in some cases by his operations, it does not make a very imposing impression. Thus it would be premature, or a harmful exaggeration, if at this stage we were to indulge in hopes of a 'therapy' of inversion that could be generally used. The cases of male homosexuality in which Steinach has been successful fulfilled the condition, which is not always present, of a very patent physical 'hermaphroditism'. Any analogous treatment of female homosexuality is at present quite obscure. If it were to consist in removing the probably hermaphroditic ovaries, and in implanting others, which would, it is hoped, be of a single sex, there would be little prospect of its being applied in practice. A woman who has felt herself to be a man, and has loved in masculine fashion, will hardly let herself be forced into playing the part of a woman when she must pay for this transformation, which is not in every way advantageous, by renouncing all hope of motherhood.

Analysis of two homosexual dreams

C. G. JUNG, M.D.

... I must first introduce you to the personality of the dreamer, for without this acquaintance you would hardly be able to feel yourselves in the peculiar mental atmosphere of the dreams. There are certain dreams that are like poems, and consequently can be understood only as a sort of expression of the dreamer's entire mental condition.*

The dreamer of whom I shall speak is a youth just above twenty years of age, and quite adolescent in his general bearing. There is, in fact, something girlish in his appearance and in his modes of expression. We can infer from the latter that he is a person of good education and artistic tendencies. His artistic interests are definitely in the foreground of his personality. We perceive his good taste immediately, just as we do his fine appreciation of all forms of art. His emotional life is tender and soft, slightly dreamy, that is, of the type characteristic of puberty, but of a feminine nature. A marked preponderance of the feminine is undeniable. There is no trace of the usual clumsiness of the age of puberty. He is obviously too young for his age, and clearly therefore an example of retarded development. This is corroborated by the fact that he has come to me on account of his homosexuality. The night preceding his visit to me he had the following dream:

'I am in a large cathedral wrapped in a mysterious dusky light. I have been told that it is the Cathedral of Lourdes. In the middle of it is situated a deep, dark well into which I ought to go.'

*From 'The Significance of the Unconscious' in *Contributions to Analytical Psychology*.

343

The dream is clearly a connected expression of a mood. The dreamer added the following remarks: 'Lourdes is the mystic fount of healing. Yesterday I very naturally thought of the fact that I was going to seek a cure. There is supposed to be such a well at Lourdes. Presumably it is not very pleasant to plunge into the water. The well in the church was very deep.'

Now what does this dream tell us? On the surface it seems clear enough, and we might conceivably be content with interpreting it as a kind of poetic formulation of an expectation. We should, however, never allow ourselves to be satisfied with an obvious interpretation, for it is a fact of experience that dreams are much deeper and more significant than they appear at first sight. Such a dream might lead us to believe that the dreamer had come to the doctor in a very poetical frame of mind; that he was entering into his treatment as though it were a consecrated religious act to be performed in the mystical half-light of an awe-inspiring sanctuary. But this in no way corresponds to the actual situation.

Our patient has come to the physician in connexion with a very disagreeable matter; namely, to be treated for homosexuality. That is anything but poetic. In any case, from the actual mood of the preceding day it would hardly be intelligible as to why he should dream so poetically, if we are to assume a direct causation for the origin of the dream. But we may perhaps assume that it was the impression produced by the very unpleasant matter in hand that was the direct occasion of the dream. We might, for instance, hazard the supposition, that it was just because of the unpoetic nature of his mood that he dreamed in such a poetic manner; just as a person who has fasted in the daytime often dreams of sumptuous meals at night. We must admit that the idea of the treatment, and of the unpleasant procedure connected with it, recurs again in the dream, but in a poetical disguise, that is, in a form which corresponds most effectively to the vivid aesthetic and emotional requirements of the dreamer. He is inevitably lured on by this attractive picture, in spite of the fact that the well is dark, deep, and cold. Something of this dream mood is likely to survive the dream, and to persist well into the morning of the day on which he has to submit to his unpleasant and unpoetic duty of visiting me. The pale light of reality may thus perhaps become embellished through the golden afterglow of the dream feelings.

Is this perhaps the object of the dream? This is quite possible, for according to my experience, the vast majority of dreams are of a compensatory nature. They stress the other side in each particular instance, and thus they tend to preserve the psychic equilibrium. But this compensation of mood is not the only purpose served by the dream. It also serves to correct one's understanding of the actual situation. In this case the patient had of course formed no adequate conception of the nature of the treatment to which he was on the point of submitting himself. The dream, however, furnished him with a picture in which the essence of the treatment was defined in terms of a poetical metaphor. This is clearly apparent if we bear in mind the supplementary associations that came up in connexion with the image of the cathedral. They were as follows: 'The word "cathedral" brings to my mind,' he said, 'the cathedral at Cologne. I had already been deeply interested in it in my earliest youth. I remember that it was my mother who first told me about it. I also call to mind that, as a child I used to ask my mother, whenever I saw a village church, whether that was the Cologne Cathedral. I hoped to become a priest in such a cathedral.'

The patient is here describing a very important experience of his youth. As in most cases of this kind there exists an especially intimate connexion with the mother. We must not, however, picture to ourselves any conscious tie to the mother of a particularly warm and intensive character, but a secret one rather, expressing itself consciously perhaps, only in the retardation of character development and a relative amount of infantilism. In its development, the personality strives to break away from such an unconscious, infantile tie, for nothing hinders development so much as the persistence of an unconscious, one might almost say embryonic, psychic condition. Therefore the earliest opportunity is instinctively taken to substitute some other object for the mother. This object must bear some analogy to the mother if it is to serve as a substitute for her. In the case of our patient this holds true in the fullest sense. The intensity with which his childish phantasy seized upon the symbol of Cologne Cathedral corresponds to his strong unconscious need for finding a substitute for his mother. This unconscious need is naturally intensified in a case where the infantile tie threatens to become a danger. There is necessity in the way his childish phantasy eagerly seizes upon the image of the church, for the church is in the fullest sense, and from every point of view, a mother. Not only do we speak of 'Mother Church', but even the 'womb of the church'. and in the ceremony of the '*benedictio fontis*' of the Catholic Church the baptismal font is even called the '*immaculatus divini fontis uterus*'. We naturally think that these meanings must be consciously known if they are to become operative in a person's phantasy, and that it is inconceivable that they should take hold of a child who is manifestly unacquainted with their significance. Of course these analogies do not operate through consciousness, but in an entirely different manner.

The church here represents a higher spiritual substitute for the merely natural, and in a way, 'carnal' tie to the parents. It is an image therefore that can release an individual from his unconscious natural bonds, which strictly speaking are no bonds at all, but simply a condition of primordial unconscious identity. This state of identity, because of its unconsciousness, possesses tremendous inertia and offers the most determined resistance to all higher mental development. It would indeed be hard to say how such a condition differs from mere animal existence. It is by no means the special prerogative of the Christian church to aim at, and also make possible, the freeing of an individual from his initial animal-like state. The Christian church simply represents the modern, and specifically western European form of an instinctive striving which, presumably, is as old as man. We are dealing here with a precisely similar urge that is found in the most varied forms among all primitive peoples who are in any way developed, and have not again degenerated. It corresponds to the men's initiation ceremonies. At the age of puberty a youth is taken, either to the bachelor house, or to some other place of initiation, and systematically estranged from his family. At the same time he is initiated into the religious secrets of the tribe, and acquires in this way, not merely new kinds of relationships, but finds himself placed in a new world, he himself having become 'quasi modo genitus' a changed and renewed personality. Frequently the initiation is connected with all sorts of tortures, circumcision and similar rites being by no means unusual at this time. These customs are undoubtedly extremely old, and, like many other primitive experiences, have left their imprints upon our unconscious. They have almost become instinctive mechanisms, so that they even recur without any external need, as for example, the initiations into student societies of German universities, or the more exaggerated types of initiation found in the American university fraternities. They have become deeply engraved upon the unconscious in the form of a primordial image, an archetype, as St. Augustine calls it.

When the mother spoke to her small son about the Cologne Cathedral, this primordial image was activated and called into life. But no priestly educator was at hand to develop it further, and the child remained in his mother's care. The boy's longing for male direction, however, continued to develop, unfortunately in the form of homosexuality, a crippled development that might perhaps not have resulted, had some man taken a hand in the further elaboration of his childhood phantasy. The deviation toward homosexuality has, to be sure, numerous historical antecedents. In ancient Greece, as among certain primitive groups, homosexuality and education were in a sense identical. From this point of view the homosexuality manifested at adolescence, although disastrously misunderstood, is nevertheless a purposive reaching out toward the man. According to the dream context, the patient's submission to treatment signifies the fulfilment of the meaning of his homosexuality, in other words, his entrance into the world of mature men.

All that we have been forced to express by difficult and circuitous detail the dream has condensed into a few expressive metaphors; and therewith it creates a picture that influences the phantasy, feeling, and understanding of the dreamer, infinitely better than a learned disquisition could do. By his dream, the patient came to his treatment far better and more ingeniously prepared than he would have been by the largest collection of medical and pedagogical dogmas. It is for this reason that I regard the dream not merely as a valuable source of information, but also as an unusually effective instrument for education and therapeutic treatment.

I shall now give you the second dream that the patient dreamed on the night following his first visit to me. His previous dream is here completed in a very interesting way. Let me add that during his first visit I paid no attention to the dream. He did not even mention it, nor was the slightest word said that could possibly be brought into any connexion with what we have discussed above.

The second dream was as follows: 'I am in a large Gothic cathedral. At the altar stands a priest. My friend and I stand before him. I hold in my hand a small Japanese ivory figure and I have the feeling as though it had to be baptized. Suddenly an elderly lady appears, takes the ring off my friend's finger and puts it on her own. My friend is afraid that he might be regarded as being bound by it. At this moment, however, the most wonderful organ music is heard.'

Unfortunately I cannot enter into all the details of this exceedingly ingenious dream in the short space allotted to me. I shall therefore only mention here those points that continue and complete the previous dream. This dream is clearly connected with the first one, for the dreamer finds himself again in a church, that is, in a condition suitable for initiation. Now, however, we encounter a new figure, the priest, whose absence in the earlier situations has already been commented upon. The dream thus corroborates the fact that the unconscious meaning of the homosexuality has been fulfilled, and that a new development can be started. The actual initiation ceremony, that is, the baptism, may now begin. In the symbolism of the dream my previous statement is thus corroborated, namely, that it is not the prerogative of the Christian church alone to bring about such transitions and psychic transformations, but that behind them there looms a primordial image which, under the right conditions, can actually compel such transformations. The object that is to be baptized, according to the dream, is a small ivory figure. In this connexion that patient gave me the following: 'The figure was that of a small grotesque looking manikin, that reminded me of the male organ. It is certainly strange that it is this organ that has to be baptized, and yet among the Jews circumcision is a kind of baptism. Doubtless this refers to my homosexuality, for the friend who is standing near me at the altar is the person with whom I have the homosexual connexion. He is in the same student society with me. The ring apparently symbolizes this connexion.'

As you of course realize, the ring in ordinary usage is regarded as the symbol of a bond or tie, as for instance the wedding ring. We may therefore regard the ring in this case as a metaphor for the homosexual relation, just as the same meaning is to be given to the fact that the dreamer appears together with his friend.

The malady to be cured is, we know, homosexuality. The dreamer is to be brought out of this relatively infantile condition into a more mature stage of development by means of a kind of circumcision ceremony directed by the priest. These ideas correspond exactly to my comments upon the first dream. Up to this point the development has taken place logically and consistently, and in conformity with the archetypal images. But now a disturbing factor seems to enter. An elderly lady suddenly possesses herself of the ring. In other words, she transfers to herself what has hitherto been a homosexual relationship, and by her act causes the dreamer to fear that he has now fallen into a relationship implying new obligations. Since the ring is now on the finger of a woman, a type of marriage has been consummated, that is, the homosexual relationship has been transformed into a heterosexual one. But it is a heterosexual relation of a very peculiar kind, for the lady in question is an elderly woman. 'She is', my patient added, 'the friend of my mother. I am very fond of her, she is in fact a motherly kind of friend.' This statement allows us to understand what has happened in the dream. Through his initiation, his homosexual tie has been dissolved, and a heterosexual relation has been substituted for it, in this case a warm kind of friendship for a woman resembling his mother. In spite of her resemblance to his mother, this woman is in fact not his mother, and so his relation to her is a step forward. It leads him beyond the mother in the direction of masculinity, towards a freeing of himself from the mother and an overcoming of adolescent sexuality.

The fear of the new bond is easily understood as the fear that the woman's resemblance to his mother might naturally arouse. It might be argued, for instance, that through the dissolution of the homosexual tie there had been a complete regression to the mother, due to the fear of the new and unknown factors of the mature heterosexual condition with such possible obligations as marriage, etc. That we are dealing here not with a regression but with a progress seems to be corroborated by the sudden peal of the organ. Our patient is musical, and he is particularly susceptible to the awe-inspiring influence of organ music. Music therefore signifies for him a positive feeling, in this instance an intimate termination of the dream that is well adapted to leave a beautiful, almost holy feeling for the coming morning.

If now the fact be considered that up to that moment the patient had seen me only during one consultation in which very little had been said beyond the general medical anamnesis, it must surely be admitted that these dreams disclose very remarkable anticipations. On the one hand, they throw an exceedingly peculiar light upon the unconscious situation of the patient, and a stranger one still from the point of view of consciousness. On the other hand, an aspect is given to a very banal medical situation that allows us, in a way that nothing else could, to understand the whole psychic peculiarity of the dreamer, and moreover this aspect is pre-eminently fitted to activate the patient's aesthetic, intellectual, and religious interests. Thus the best possible conditions for treatment are obtained.

The meaning of the dreams almost seems to suggest that the patient entered into the treatment with the greatest expectation and hopefulness, and that he was quite prepared to discard his adolescence and become a man. But this was absolutely not the case. Consciously, he was filled with trepidation and resistance, and in the subsequent course of the treatment he always showed himself antagonistic and difficult to handle, and always ready to fall back into his earlier infantilism. Accordingly his dreams are in definite contrast with his conscious behaviour. They move along a progressive line, and are on the side of his instructor. In my opinion, they permit the unique function of dreams to be clearly recognized. This function I have called compensation. The unconscious progressive tendency of dreams, when linked to the conscious regressive tendency, forms a contrasting pair of opposites which, so to speak, balance each other. The influence exerted by the instructor represents the balancing wheel. Hence, dreams can afford an effective support to our educational efforts, and, at the same time, they make a more profound insight possible into the intimate phantasy life. Thus the conscious attitude becomes gradually more understanding and receptive to new influences.

Transvestism

CHRISTIAN HAMBURGER, M.D., GEORG K. STURUP, M.D. and E. DAHL-
IVERSEN, M.D.

TRANSVESTISM has been defined as the desire to appear in the clothes of the sex to which the person in question, according to his or her external genitalia, does not belong. The word is derived from *trans:* opposite, and *vestitus:* dress, and was coined by the German sexologist, Magnus Hirschfeld.[1] In the English-speaking countries the term eonism is sometimes applied. As with 'sadism' and 'masochism', it is derived from the name of an actual person; in this case a French diplomat, Chevalier d'Eon (born 1728, in Bourgogne, died 1810, in London). There have been a number of reports on transvestism.[2]

Transvestism, in the widest sense of the term, must be regarded as a symptom that may appear in a number of conditions, and only by thorough clinical analysis it is possible to distinguish between these various states. There are fetishists, who, as a consequence of neurotic obsession, concentrate on one or more articles of dress, thereby developing an interest in partial or complete cross dressing. Not frequently, homosexual men of the passive type develop a desire to wear jewellery, to use perfumes, and to dress in feminine clothes. In both these categories the transvestic urge is sexually caused to a pronounced degree and is usually of secondary importance only. Transvestism in women will not be dealt with in the present report. There remains, then, the category of transvestic men in whom the desire is so dominant as to justify the designation 'genuine transvestism' or 'psychic hermaphrodism'; there may be reason to reserve the term eonism for this group. On the basis of the literature, our own observations, and personal letters, the present report sets out to outline the characteristic features of eonism (or genuine transvestism).

Eonists are persons with a fundamental feeling of being victims of a cruel mistake—a consequence of the female personality in a male body. They experience an extremely pronounced desire to wear women's clothes; this, however, must be understood as only one of the many means through which the person attempts to identify himself with the female sex, to be regarded as a woman by society, to be called by a woman's name, and to occupy himself with womanly tasks. Men's clothes are felt to be an intolerable disguise and manly occupations a severe burden. The person conceives it to be against his nature to have to live and act as a man, with never a possibility of being able to follow the spontaneous inclinations of his own 'self'; this entails a continual mental stress that may lead to more or less intense neurotic conflicts and possibly to suicidal attempts. When male transvestites wear feminine clothes and appear as women, they experience mental relaxation, balance, and inspiration, and the enjoyment of life.

The wearing of women's clothes in these cases does not aim at, and does not involve, any sexual satisfaction, and it is a characteristic feature that the dress is respectable and in no way provocative. On the whole, the sexual life generally plays but a minor part. Attraction to normal, heterosexual men is no infrequent phenomenon, but the genuine transvestite is disgusted by relationship with homosexual men. Attraction toward the female sex is generally on a higher plane, but only rarely, and possibly never, is such attraction of a direct erotic nature. The dominant feature is the urge toward attaining the 'ideal of perfection', and here is the cause of marriages in these cases, possibly in many instances coupled with the hope of suppressing the transvestic tendencies through a normal married life. Most marriages between normal women and transvestites will grow disharmonious and be dissolved, but it is no rare occurrence for the wife to accept the tendencies in her husband. If children are born of the marriage,

z

the husband frequently will feel deep attachment and love toward them. Married sexual intercourse is generally rare, and the husband considers himself the passive partner. The feeling of 'being in reality a woman' will often lead to dislike of, disgust of, or veritable hatred against the person's own sexual organs, with the logically consequent wish for castration or demasculinization. Attempts at self-castration are by no means rare.

DEVELOPMENT AND COURSE

Eonism may, in most cases, be traced back to early childhood: an intense wish to be a girl; preference for playing with dolls; sympathy, mixed with envy, toward girls; and the satisfaction of wearing girls' clothes. The years of puberty bring no change, beyond the consciousness of the abnormal state. The young man will become separated from his friends, feeling rootless, divided, and lonely. The lack of understanding he encounters will cause isolation from his fellow men; he will disguise his tendencies and take up the futile battle to conquer them. Hereafter, the feeling of being a woman who has to act as a man will be the all-dominant factor in the patient's life. In his earlier adult years he may try to overcome his tendency through hard masculine work, through normal intercourse, and possibly through marriage. A certain, but definitely limited, number will try—but in vain—to enlist medical assistance. The urge will be unconquerable, and the fight against it will have to be abandoned. Some patients become resigned and satisfy their transvestic tendencies in loneliness, hidden from everyone else, and it is an obvious supposition that many genuine transvestites have gone to their graves without anyone suspecting their abnormality. Others take up the fight against society; they wish to persuade the community to acknowledge their right to live as women. It is impossible to say with any degree of certainty to what advanced age the tendencies persist; but we have proof that the problem is alive in men almost aged 60. They are willing to sacrifice anything to live a short term of years as women, even as 'elderly women'.

CAUSES

It can not be denied that eonism may be psychically conditioned. But a number of sexologists and psychiatrists who know these patients and classify them as distinct from homosexuals with transvestic tendencies consider it likely that the affection is constitutionally conditioned (Hirschfeld[1]). So far as we know, no psychiatrist or psychoanalyst has succeeded in tracing a satisfactory explanation of the cause of the affection. It is probable that physical factors may play a decisive role, as evidenced by the frequent appearance of more or less pronounced feminine physical appearance. On the other hand, there are eonists having completely normal masculine habitus. It is reasonable to suppose that the more feminine the physical features in a man the more likely are the chances of sexual difficulties (impotence, homosexual tendencies, and possibly transvestic tendencies). Determinations of the urinary excretions of hormonal substances will probably be of little value for the demonstration of endocrine disturbances as causal factors in transvestism. This can be no matter for wonder when one considers that assays of the urinary metabolites of the gonadal and adrenocortical hormones (e.g., oestrogenic and androgenic substances and 17-ketosteroids) do not permit of determining, with any certainty, whether a specimen of urine originates from a normal man or a normal woman.

The eonist's feeling of being a woman is so deeply rooted and irresistible that it is tempting to seek deeper somatic causes of the disease. We have considered the possibility that some of the most pronounced transvestites might be intersexes (sex intergrades) of the highest degree, i.e., *Umwandlungsmänner*, according to Goldschmidt's intersex theory. It must be considered an established fact that women are homogametic and men hetero-gametic and also that the sex chromosomes are not the sole sex determining factors. According to Goldschmidt,[3] all, or at any rate the majority, of human intersexes should be gametically female, i.e., possess two x-chromosomes in their body cells. The degree of intersexuality was thought to depend on the time at which the disturbance of the sex determination occurs (*Drehpunkt*). By *Drehpunkt* at a very early stage in the foetal development, the gonads are supposed to develop as testes, and the secondary sex organs will be male. The male organs in these persons, who according to their chromosomes are women, must be regarded as malformations. The possibility of the existence of human *Umwandlungsmänner* can by no means be disregarded. Future investigations into the genetics and chromosome distribution in transvestites will decide the possible validity of this working theory.

TREATMENT

As far as is known, all attempts at treating genuine cases of transvestism have been futile, provided treatment is taken to mean attempts at curing the affection. It is acknowledged that psychotherapy does not lead to the desired end; in practice it is impossible to make a genuine transvestite wish to have his mentality altered by means of psychotherapy, thereby bringing it into harmony with his physical appearance. Experience concerning the effect of treatment with male sex hormones (testosterone) is limited. In the cases in which such treatment has been administered, the effects have not been up to expectations. Many patients, however, categorically refuse such attempts; they have no wish to be 'cured' of their transvestism; they feel it is in agreement with their 'true selves' and wish only to be deprived of the detested masculine component. Thus they regard attempts at increasing the maleness as breaches of the laws of nature.

356

The object of the medical profession, therefore, is to bring about—as extensively as possible—conditions that may contribute toward the patients' mental balance and a certain sense of 'purpose of life'. A number of patients are able to handle these problems by themselves, by occasionally putting on women's clothes when they are alone. Others feel the necessity, now and again, of wearing women's clothes in public. In certain countries the authorities may permit such conduct, provided a medical certificate can be obtained to the effect that such conduct is necessary in view of the mental condition of the patient. A great proportion of Hirschfeld's patients had such facilities.[1] In Denmark and Sweden similar permissions have been granted in recent years, in extremely rare cases. Two British patients have informed us that the authorities in question have shown understanding to the degree of having 'legally registered' the patients as women despite the presence of normal male genitals.

In patients with a deeply rooted aversion against their own genitals, the possibilities of treatment are considerably limited by the legislation governing castration in each country. As a rule, castration will have to be sanctioned by the authorities unless pathological processes in the sexual glands necessitate the operation. In certain countries, e.g., Denmark, Norway, and Sweden, the law makes voluntary castration possible when the patient's sexuality makes him prone to commit crimes, thereby making him a danger to society, or when it involves mental disturbances to a considerable degree, or social deterioration.* These legislative measures make it possible to remove in transvestites those organs the presence of which seriously impair their mental health. Surgico-plastic measures in respect of the genitals of castrated persons (including amputation of the penis) have not been foreseen by the law.

*Danish Sterilization and Castration Act, No. 176, May 11, 1935; cf. Danish Sterilization Act, No. 130, June, 1, 1929. In Holland and in certain parts of Switzerland this operation is also possible.

HOMOSEXUALITY

FREQUENCY AND OCCURRENCE

Genuine transvestism is certainly an exceedingly rare affection, although it may occur more frequently than generally supposed. It will hardly be possible to state exact figures. The affection seems to occur in all races and on all levels of society, even among ethically, culturally, and socially highly developed persons. We are in personal contact with five Danish transvestites in a population of nearly 4 million inhabitants.

REPORT OF A CASE

The patient, a man aged 24, approached us in August, 1950, and was subjected to treatment until December, 1952. He was the younger of two children in the family. His sister was some years older, and he had never felt any deep affection for her. The parents were healthy and there is no information of the patient having any exceptional feelings toward them. As a child he was very quiet and reserved, and he had but few friends. As long as he could remember he had had a very strong desire to be a girl, and he had to fight his urge to play with girls' toys. He was highly interested in girls' clothes, and himself wanted to be dressed as a girl. He found it difficult to join in with other boys. The years of puberty did not change his feeling of being 'different' from other boys, but he was unable to take anyone into his confidence, and during the following years he figuratively set up a wall around himself to conceal the knowledge of his peculiarity from those around him. His school achievements were average, but he felt that he would have done better had he been able to concentrate—and without the feeling of isolation. He had to continually occupy himself with new things in order to avoid thinking of himself.

It became more and more evident to him that he would never be able to fit into society as a man; he felt himself to be a woman,

358

and he could not escape the idea that 'nature had made a mistake' in giving him the appearance of a man. Later he yielded to his pronounced transvestic tendencies. He acquired a complete set of women's clothes and secretly put them on. This relieved the psychic pressure he invariably felt when in men's clothes.

He would in no circumstance enter into any homosexual relationship; this not for lack of opportunities. On the whole, his sexual libido appears to have been but slight. He felt a pronounced distaste toward his own genitals and toward his male physical features. Thus, he had shaved his pubic hair, giving it a female upper delineation. According to his own statement he never showed this to anyone, but he experienced an inner satisfaction in this slight alteration toward femaleness. At all times, however, the patient was concerned with the one problem 'man or woman', and his interest in sexual biological problems induced him to seek training in laboratory technique, and he studied the endocrine literature available to him. During this period he consulted a number of physicians, including psychiatrists. However, they viewed with a considerable degree of scepticism the possibilities of helping him by means of psychotherapy, and at all events an exceedingly protracted and immensely expensive treatment was predicted. For a period he administered of his own accord oestrogenic substances orally, the doses being, however, too small to produce any marked effect.

The patient approached us (August, 1950) and explained his case history. Evidently he was severely depressed and felt it impossible to continue life as a man. We thought his mention of possible suicide was sincere. Primarily he wanted, by castration, to be relieved of the essential source of the detested masculine component of his body; further, he hoped with medical assistance to be able to obtain permission to live on 'as nearly a woman as possible'.

Physical Examination: The patient was 170 cm. tall. The width of his chest was 78 cm., and the width of his abdomen 70 cm. His legs (trochanter to floor) were 88 cm. long, and his arms (acromion to the tip of the third finger) were 74 cm. long. He weighed 55 kg. He was of the asthenic type with a feminine habitus. There were fairly pronounced fat deposits in the hip region. There was pigmentation of the nipples and a slight increase of the mammary parenchyma (possibly artificially induced by previous administration of oestrogens), but no gynaecomastia proper. Hair on the arms and legs were sparse. The upper edge of the pubic hair was of feminine configuration; this was stated by the patient to have been artificially produced. There was medium muscle strength. The voice was natural. The non-erected penis was 9 cm. long, and the testes were somewhat under average size but of normal consistency. Rectal exploration revealed normal size, consistency, and surface of the prostate. Examination of sperm and biopsy of the testes was not carried out. The blood pressure was 120/75 mm. Hg.

Personality: The patient was intellectually extremely gifted. His mode of expression tended toward sentimentality. He was slightly affectionate, with feminine voice production and movements. The impression he made through his eccentric choice of men's clothing was odd; the colours were too varied for a man, and his clothes were evidently always 'in the way'. Sexually he was undoubtedly comparatively passive and was obviously embarrassed by having been frequently taken for a homosexual. He was self-reproaching to a considerable degree and probably had a number of well-hidden, unsolved personality problems but no acute neurotic complaints. He did not want a psychotherapeutic solution of the problem, and the desire for it could not be aroused. This was particularly due to his having been previously refused treatment of this kind and partly due to his feeling that it would offend against what he himself felt to be his 'true self' to accept such a scheme, which, moreover, would have met with unsurmountable difficulties, if accepted, as there was no suitable therapist and he had no financial resources.

Hormone Analysis: Two 24-hour urine specimens (Aug. 2 and 10, 1950) were assayed, with the following results:

	1.	2.
Gonadotropic substances	<50 M.U./24 hr.	<50 M.U./24 hr.
Oestrogenic substances	<20 M.U./24 hr.	>50 M.U./24 hr.
Androgenic substances	13 I.U. /24 hr.	28 I.U. /24 hr.
17-ketosteroids	15.1 mg./24 hr.	15.4 mg./24 hr.

These figures are normal for a man of the patient's age, with the exception of a rather high oestrogen level in specimen No. 2 and a rather low androgen level in specimen No. 1. It must be admitted, however, that the technical variation in these biological assays is so great that the figures do not allow of any definite conclusions.

Treatment: Our suggestion of treatment with testosterone preparations in an attempt to alter his mentality in a masculine direction was firmly refused. The patient felt it would be of no help, rather the contrary. We clearly pointed out to him that any irrevocable step should be taken only after careful consideration, but on the other hand we did not think we were in the position—despite all difficulties—to decline an attempt at giving the patient medical aid. All possibilities were thoroughly discussed with the patient, and it was decided to provoke hormonal castration by means of oestrogenic substances. The administration of oestrogenic substances, moreover, served another purpose, i.e., an examination of the effect of oestrogens on the adrenocortical function, as reflected in the urinary excretion of 17-ketosteroids and reducing corticoids. An account of the results has been given in a previous publication,[4] and we shall confine ourselves to summarizing the main results here. After the administration of oestrogens, the excretion of 17-ketosteroids was reduced to half the amount of pretreatment level, whereas no significant changes in the excretion of corticoids occurred. This observation points to the fact that the production of testis hormone, but not the production of corticosteroids, was inhibited. Furthermore, it was found that the 17-ketosteroids reached pretreatment level in the course of 26 days after discontinuation of the oestrogen administration, despite the fact that the period of hormonal castration had lasted four to five months. The inhibition of the testicular function was thus found to be reversible.

In the course of the first 10 months' period of observation the total doses of oestrogenic substances were 95 mg. of oestradiol monobenzoate, administered in oily solution (three intramuscular injections of 15 mg. each and 10 intramuscular injections of 5 mg. each), and 13·9 mg. of ethinyl oestradiol, administered orally. The testicular inactivity could be maintained by as small a daily dose as 0·10 mg. of ethinyl oestradiol, taken orally. Simultaneously with the depression of the 17-ketosteroids, marked atrophy of the testes was observed, together with swelling of the breasts. According to the statement of the patient, the sexual libido and erections disappeared during the same period, and this was also true of the mental pressure that he had previously experienced. The patient was now in a state of mental balance, psychically at ease; he was freed from his mental stress and worked with increased vigour and inspiration at his job. On the basis of his state, the patient was able to say during what periods he had low excretion of 17-ketosteroids, before being informed of the analysis reports.

The very thorough continuous psychiatric investigation showed the improvement in the mental state to be stable and genuine. Since the patient adhered to his wish for operative castration, this procedure was preferable to continued oestrogen administration. Consequently, an application for permission to castrate was submitted to the Danish Ministry of Justice. After the application had been considered by the Medico-Legal Council, permission to operate was granted. The operation was performed at the Köbenhavns Amtssygehus (Copenhagen County Hospital). The patient was then 26 years old. During a period of four months preceding the castration, no oestrogenic substances had been administered. Microscopic examination of the testes showed atrophic tubules but well-preserved interstitial cells.

Post-operatively, the 17-ketosteroid excretion was diminished to the same extent as during oestrogen administration, the excretion of reducing corticoids being uninfluenced. As might have been expected, an injection of the oestradiol monobenzoate (15 mg.) had no effect on the 17-ketosteroids after the operation. Shortly after the castration, administration of very small quantities of ethinyl oestradiol (0·02 to 0·05 mg. per day, orally) was resumed, mainly in order to maintain the gynaecomastia. It could not be decided whether the oestrogen treatment had any influence on the growth of hair. The patient underwent treatment by electrolysis to prevent the growth of beard, which had never been remarkable; he also let his hair grow freely. The former feminine features were accentuated to such a degree that only the presence of the penis and scrotum revealed that he was not a girl. The behaviour, gait, and voice production were all strongly feminine.

The patient had one final ardent wish: to have the last visible remains of the detested masculinity removed. This wish persisted one year after castration, and amputation of the penis and plastic surgery of the scrotum had to be considered, since their presence meant a mental load on the patient. The patient was admitted to the surgical department of the Copenhagen University Hospital. After it had been established that no legal complications would follow the operation as planned, the penis was removed, with implantation in the perineum of the urethra dissected from the corpora cavernosa. By plastic skin surgery the scrotum was transformed into labia-like formations. There was no intention of creating an artificial vagina by inlay grafting according to the technique of McIndoe, nor was this a wish of the patient, in whom the sexual requirements were subordinate to the transvestic impulses. The operation was without complications, and the genital region now had a completely feminine appearance.

The goal was attained; by hormonal feminization and operative demasculinization the patient's soma harmonized with the pronounced feminine psyche. The sympathetic attitude shown by the authorities in issuing papers that enabled the patient to appear as a woman gave to the results obtained by medical treatment an importance of wider practical application. The patient will be able to move about freely among other persons, without anyone suspecting that this is not a normal young woman but a male transvestite whose highest wishes have been fulfilled by the assistance of the medical profession and by society. It is impossible, however, to say what future chances this patient will have.

COMMENT

As a social problem, eonism is of very slight importance, as it is an exceedingly rare affection, but from the patient's point of view it is the all-dominant problem, depriving him of any possible happiness from childhood to old age. A number of factors contribute toward the deterioration of the fate of the victims of this affection. The medical profession, on an average, knows too little about the nature of this disease; it is often confused or identified with homosexuality,* from which it follows that society has not been able to grasp properly the problems of transvestites. To this must be added the fact that there is no available means to cure transvestism.

It is understood in medical ethics that if a disease cannot be cured an attempt should be made to improve the stress and inconvenience of the patient in order to make his life as tolerable as possible, having, naturally, due regard to the interests of society. We are unable to agree with Cawadias,[2] who wrote that while male transvestites 'live unhappily and commit suicide when

---

*The authors take a position here which is in opposition to one held by many psychoanalysts who hold that latent homosexuality is apparent in all cases of transvestism. Stekel, for example, wrote: 'The transvestite projects his wish into the future and anticipates the great miracle of sexual metamorphosis.' Without entering into the merits of the controversy, it should be pointed out that Dr. Hamburger himself felt that the case in question had a place in the present volume [Ed.].

thwarted, overwhelming social considerations oblige the physician to ignore their will and thus their pragmatic sex.' Following are the various possibilities available to facilitate the eonist's life and existence.

1. Permission to Wear Women's Clothes in Public: Permission for men to wear women's clothes in public was extensively granted in Germany at the time of Magnus Hirschfeld, provided the authorities were satisfied that such permission was necessary for the mental well-being of the patient. If the permission is made subject to the patient's not outraging public decency, no social inconveniences are attached to it. A number of patients will be able to adjust in this way; in other cases the method will prove inadequate.

2. Legal Recognition and Registration as a Woman. Legal recognition and registration of the patient as a woman has been adopted in some cases. The procedure has the advantage that the patient can always appear as a woman, with a woman's name, without others knowing the true sex, and in this instance no social interests are violated.

3. Administration of Oestrogenic Substances: The aim of administration of oestrogenic substances is the inhibition of the testicular function and the development of feminine features, e.g., gynaecomastia, or the enhancement of pre-existing feminization. Prolonged administration of oestrogens should be avoided because of possible prostatic changes and the faint possibility of encouraging malignant tumours. If the presence of the testes is a threat to the mental balance of the patient, castration may have to be considered. As already mentioned, we consider it a *sine qua non* that administration of oestrogenic substances be carried out (e.g., for a six months' period) before operative castration can be performed.

4. Castration: Legislation as regards castration varies considerably

365

from one country to another. In most countries castration is not allowed unless indicated by pathological changes in the sex glands. The sex glands must, in the eyes of society, be protected at any price. It is not immediately evident with what right society compels persons to tolerate the presence of these organs, if their presence is felt to be an intolerable burden, in some cases poisoning the patient's life from youth to old age. It is possible that the authorities are afraid that a number of homosexual and otherwise sexually abnormal persons might attempt to obtain castration, pretending to be transvestites. It is very unlikely that this would happen to any appreciable degree; the majority of homosexual, like heterosexual, men regard castration as a definitely undesirable measure. At any rate, from a eugenic point of view it would do no harm if a number of sexually abnormal men were castrated and thus deprived of their sexual libido. It might be feared that the patients would later regret the operation. This is a weighty consideration, but if an adult man of sound mind, after having been told the risks of the operation and after careful consideration, himself accepts the responsibility and persists in his wish, it is unreasonable that society should act as a guardian endowed with a superior wisdom. Moreover, the danger of regret on the part of the patient may be considerably reduced if operative castration is preceded by hormonal castration during a sufficiently long period, with careful observation of the patient by skilled psychiatrists.

5. *Demasculinization:* If operative castration has been carried out (and in certain cases the patient may have obtained permission to appear publicly in women's clothes) there can be no serious objection to amputation of the penis and plastic surgery of the scrotum in order that the patient's external genital region may appear to be purely feminine. In many instances this will be a natural and logical wish on the part of the patient, and the risk involved is so negligible that this is no contra-indication against the operation.

366

6. *Formation of Artificial Vagina:* Even if McIndoe's method is applied, the technical difficulties in this operation may perhaps exceed those in women with aplasia of the vagina. In cases of genuine transvestism the question will only rarely arise, because the need of sexual contact is usually of very minor importance. Furthermore, such operation may be undesirable from an ethical point of view.

These measures aim at making life tolerable for the transvestite, but they must not be applied as hard and fast rules, since in this affection there can never be any standard and routine treatment. Each step must be very carefully considered by a team of medical specialists, and it may not always be possible to comply with the patient's wishes. One of the major points to be considered is the patient's habitus. The chances that a man with pronounced masculine proportions, strong and dark growth of beard, considerable growth of body hair, etc., should be able to appear as and resemble a woman are slight; in such cases it is far more difficult to attain the object of the treatment— to create a harmonious balance between soma and psyche —than in persons who have already pronounced feminine habitus.

After having treated the present patient we have discovered an analogous case in Germany, in which operation was performed in 1943. In this case, reported by Huelke,[5] the patient was a man of 35 who had appeared as a woman from his seventeenth year. Castration and amputation of the penis were carried out, and at a post-operative examination six months later the patient was still satisfied with life as a woman.

We would like to add that after the beginning of December, 1952, we have received hundreds of letters, even from the remotest parts of the world, from patients seeking help in their sexual difficulties. Among these there are about 60 writers who are very probably victims of genuine transvestism. Their reports and letters make extremely reliable impressions; many are thorough and factual case histories, often accompanied by photographs. It has been an exceedingly depressing experience to learn the degree to which these persons feel they have been let down by the medical profession and by their fellow men. In loneliness and misery they have had to fight their own tragic fate. It would be desirable if the medical profession and the authorities concerned showed, in future, a more positive attitude toward the efforts at easing and facilitating the daily life of the victims of genuine transvestism.

SUMMARY

On the basis of previously published reports, personal observations, and letters from patients, the symptoms, course, and possible origin of transvestism are discussed. It is emphasized that, among the patients with transvestic tendencies, a fairly small group of men can be singled out. Their feeling of being a woman is so rooted and irresistible that it is reasonable to apply a special term in these cases—that of 'genuine transvestism' or 'eonism'. It is highly probable that eonism is constitutionally conditioned, and the working theory is put forward that some eonists, at any rate, are intersexes of the highest degree, i.e., *Umwandlungsmänner*, according to Goldschmidt's intersex theory. It is recognized that there exist no available means to cure eonism, and all efforts must, therefore, be concentrated on making life easier for such persons.

A case of genuine transvestism in a young man is reported. His psyche was definitely, and his physical appearance moderately, feminine. Besides the transvestic tendencies he had a pronounced aversion for his own genitals. After hormonal castration, brought about by administration of oestrogens (with the patient under careful psychiatric surveillance), operative castration and, later amputation of the penis and plastic surgery of the scrotum were performed. The patient obtained official permission to appear publicly in women's clothes. The various 'therapeutic' measures to create for transvestites a tolerable existence are discussed. It is emphasized that several of these measures could be brought into use in suitable cases without violating the interests of society.[6]

REFERENCES

[1] Hirschfeld, M.: *Sexualpathologie, in Der Transvestitismus,* Bonn, A. Marcus & Weber (1918), chapter 3, p. 139.

[2] Cawadias, A. P.: *Hermaphroditos: The Human Intersex,* William Heinemann, Ltd. (1943); Ellis, H.: *Studies in Psychology of Sex,* (1928), vol. 7; Forel, A.: *Die sexuelle Frage,* München, E. Reinhardt (1909), vol. 12; Hirschfeld, M.: *Geschlechtskunde auf Grund dreissigjähriger Forschung und Erfahrung,* Stuttgart, Püttmann (1926), vol. 1, p. 585; London, L. S. and Caprio, F. S.: *Sexual Deviations,* Washington, D. C., Linacre Press (1950); Hirschfeld, *op. cit.*

[3] Goldschmidt, R.: *Die sexuellen Zwischenstufen, in Gildemeister, M., and others:* Monographten aus den Gesamtgebiet der Physiologie der Pflanzen und der Tiere, Berlin, Julius Springer (1931).

[4] Hamburger, C., and Sprechler, M.: *Influence of Steroid Hormones on Hormonal Activity of Adenohypophysis in Man,* Acta endocrinol. 7, 167 (1951).

[5] Huelke, H. H.: *Ein Transvestit: Der Fall Heinrich B.,* Kriminalistik, *3,* 91 (1949).

[6] Since the article was submitted for publication in *Journal of American Medical Association,* our attention was called to previous cases of tranvestism treated with demasculinization or 'feminization', operations. The pertinent references and discussions may be found in: Aubert, G.: *Trois cas de désir de changer de sexe,* Tavannes, Lausanne (1947); Bürger-Prinz, H. et al.: *Zur Phänomenologie des Transvestitismus bei Männern,* Ferdinand Enke, Stuttgart (1953); Dukor, B.: *Probleme um den Transvestitismus,* Schweiz, med. Wchnschr. *81,* 516 (1951); important discussions in: *Psyche* 4, Nos. 4, 7 and 8 (1950).

An analytic session

HENRI FLOURNOY, M.D.

TRANSLATED BY VERA DAMMAN

x, a bachelor aged thirty, is undergoing analysis for various neurotic difficulties. He is physically normal and is successfully following a liberal profession. But he has suffered since puberty from sexual instability, oscillating between heterosexual and homosexual tendencies.

During the session of Thursday 15th, X reported the following incidents which had occurred since the preceding session of Saturday 10th. On Sunday afternoon he had gone for a walk with his friend Charles, a man younger than himself, with whom he had often practised manual masturbation on some pretext or another. But on this particular day he forced himself to conform to a decision he had made to abstain from any physical contact with his friend, and in spite of strong temptation, nothing sexual occurred between them.

On Sunday evening he happened to see a café waiter walking in the street with his wife. He had noticed this waiter before because of his aloof, haughty and distinguished bearing.

During the night of Sunday he had the following dream:

I saw the waiter . . . and masturbated him . . .   :

The following night, between Monday and Tuesday, X had a dream in two short episodes, as follows:

(a) I was spending the evening at the house of a friend of my own age. His father, Mr. R., gave me the same specially warm welcome that he does in real life and which I find very flattering. Then I found myself sitting at a table with a charming unknown girl eating a 'pêche melba' while Mr. and Mrs. R. looked on.

(b) I was in the home of Mr. and Mrs. S. whose son is also one of my friends and contemporaries. They too received me with great kindness and I was very moved.

X noted that since Tuesday—and as a result of these dreams, as he rightly thought—he was freed from his homosexual desires and once more turned quite naturally toward women.

Let us consider these incidents in their sequence. X, having repressed his sexual desires toward his friend Charles, satisfied them with the waiter in his dream of the following night, and in exactly the same manner as he was accustomed to with Charles. Curiously, he had never before been attracted by the waiter. The latter was a married man, much older than himself, who had waited on him some weeks previously when he was in the café with Charles. On that day the haughty waiter had evidently looked at X in a severe and disapproving way, as if he suspected the relations between the two friends.

When it is known that the waiter's characteristics—a distinguished appearance, a cold and haughty manner, a severe and disapproving expression—are all equally typical of X's father, we realize that in his dream the waiter is a father substitute. We also gain insight into the compensating, reassuring dreams of the following night, both of which, as we shall see, have the same purpose: to propitiate the father and obtain his forgiveness.

To take first the role of Mr. and Mrs. R., X had actually been invited to spend the evening of Saturday 10th at their house but was unable to go. He had been disappointed, because Mr. R. had always taken a most friendly and fatherly interest in him. In the dream he finds himself with this family he likes so well; Mr. and Mrs. R. welcome him most kindly; then under their benevolent eye he shares with a young woman a delicious and flavoursome dessert, a 'pêche melba'—obviously a symbol of sexual pleasure, as he said himself. Having tasted this dish, a fresh pardon is needed. This time the role of benevolent and protective authority is assumed by Mr. S., a distinguished public figure. Let us give his associations to this man.

He had recently seen Mr. S. mentioned in the newspapers and recalled having been invited to his house several months before. During the course of the evening Mr. S's son, a friend of his own age, made an extremely witty remark, a *bon mot*. X failed to get the point and felt embarrassed in front of the other guests. Mr. S. noticed his embarrassment and came to his rescue by saying, doubtless out of kindness, that he too had missed the point. Thus it is quite clear that Mr. S., like Mr. R., is a protective and benevolent father image, ready to forgive.

Oedipus complex and transference. The two-part dream with Mr. R. and Mr. S. came as a sort of neutralizer of the dream of the preceding night in which X had made a sexual attack on the waiter, also father substitute. Here the Oedipus complex was expressed not only as an aggression against the father but also as a seizure of his virility and even of total identification, since at the culminating point of the orgasm the dreamer had felt as if his whole self was fused with his partner's.

What about the other component of the Oedipus complex, the incestuous tendency? This had continuously, though obscurely at times, revealed itself during a series of preceding sessions. He had just passed through a period of several weeks of exclusive interest in his mother, an impressionable, intuitive woman and an overfond mother. During this period of maternal fixation X's natural inclinations toward women had as usual completely disappeared. He recovered them quite spontaneously on the Tuesday, after the liberating effect of the dreams in which he placed himself under the benevolent protective authority of Mr. S. and Mr. R., the fathers of his two friends. Stated in terms of the structure of the psyche: the ego, having yielded to the instinctual drives of the id could only regain its equilibrium by satisfying the demands of the superego, after which normal, heterosexual tendencies again become dominant.

As a general rule X's transference toward me was positive; but in this particular session it suddenly assumed a negative form. After giving his associations to the above incidents and making his own interpretations of them without difficulty—for he had already made considerable progress in his analysis—he suddenly began to criticize me violently and with strong sarcasm, because, as he said, I had not the slightest understanding of the situation.

He accused me of never having recognized that his attachment to his mother could provoke guilt feelings sufficiently strong to be the sole cause of his desire to propitiate his father. He claimed that the dream in two parts was merely a reaction against the long period of mother fixation he had just passed through and that there was no need to bring in the erotic dream with the waiter as a guilt factor, as I had so superficially done.

In reality I had never denied that his mother fixation, entailing unconscious incestuous fantasies, was a sufficient cause for guilt feelings. But I did not think we could disregard the erotic dream when dealing with the analytic material of this particular session. For it furnished the essential link between Sunday, when he had successfully suppressed his homosexual desires in conformance with his ideal, and the dream of Monday night when he nevertheless felt the need to appease the severe superego. (If we accept his theory, why would he feel such a need?) I maintained that the dream was an important element in that it provided the guilt motive in the sequence of events. X, however, denied its relevance and took the occasion of this difference of opinion to attack me for my lack of comprehension.

This sudden outburst of negative feelings could quite well be explained as a new method of defence; in his counter-explanation, X sought to suppress the element which very clearly betrayed his homosexual desires toward his father. Several times already during the course of the analysis his contradictory attitudes toward me (for or against homosexuality) had been fairly transparent in his abrupt shifts in transference feelings.

Psychosexual development of a female

MORRIS W. BRODY, M.D.

IT is our aim to study and trace the psychosexual development of a female in reference to those factors which lead to homosexual maladjustment. The patient, hereafter referred to as C, has been under psychoanalytic treatment for more than eighteen months. C has never had any heterosexual experiences, but on various occasions was the passive partner in sexual relations with other women.

We do not propose to draw any conclusions or to make any generalizations concerning homosexuality. The instinctual drives, the ego capacities and environmental factors differ widely quantitatively and qualitatively, so one cannot say that in this or that type of family constellation this or that type of personality will develop. This does not mean, however, that the study of a single individual is interesting and valuable only for the understanding of that particular person, for often the study of the individual can be helpful in appreciating the problems of others. We will elucidate and stress only those factors which prevented our patient from leading a physiological heterosexual existence and why homosexuality was more acceptable to her, although even here she was not successful.

C was a nice looking girl. There was nothing masculine in her appearance, although she was tall and angular. At the first interview she impressed us as being a seducing sort of person. There was no real foundation for this impression, but perhaps we were influenced by her selection of clothing, dresses for example that were rather tight and tended to accentuate the contour of her thighs. At the age of 20 she entered a hospital for a nurse's training. Her years there were very unhappy. She felt that every nurse was either homosexual or a prostitute.

Numerous sexual advances were made to her by the other girls but the patient pretended ignorance and acted as though she did not know what was expected of her, thus leaving the would-be seducer bewildered. Prior to the completion of her training course she entered into a love affair with another girl. C played the same passive role, did absolutely nothing herself, while kisses and caresses were showered upon her. In the three years following her training, there were two more homosexual love affairs. C took no active part in the sex play. Our patient intensely disliked these affairs, finding it all very revolting. The object choice was always a woman who engineered C into the homosexual affair, the patient apparently powerless to resist. One prolonged affair continued for more than two years, and the last of her homosexual experiences ended at the age of 26 when she began to keep company with a man. Although she saw this man for several years she scarcely realized that she was being courted. To her, it was merely a matter of some convenience. During the last year of this courtship when C was unable to obtain satisfaction for her supposed sex urges she began to suffer severe dysmenorrhea and metrorrhagia so that she had to wear a sanitary pad continuously. Later we will explain the psychological significance of these occurrences. When this courtship finally terminated the patient was more unhappy than ever before and this was the exciting factor that caused her to seek psychiatric help.

In eliciting the history at the first interview the patient offered the following chief complaints. She had been suffering severe headaches during the past year for which thorough somatic examination yielded no efficient cause. She complained of being dissatisfied with herself and felt that she had not made sufficient advancement in her work. She had no friends, felt herself to be unloved, feared being alone, and lastly hinted that the termination of this affair with her male friend disturbed her considerably. The anamnesis revealed itself slowly because the patient was never sure of the facts. She recounted long detailed

375

stories of her development only to discover that she had made some error and would start the story all over again. We ascertained that when the patient was 7 years of age her mother died and a relative R came to care for the family. The patient met R with open hostility, would tell lies about her and did everything to create dissatisfaction with her, not only in the immediate household but also among the neighbours and more distant relatives. The feeling of rivalry with R was quite open. She felt that R was not much older than herself, although in actuality R was many years older than C. Our patient clung to the belief that she was as educated as R, that both read the same books, and that R could not run the household without her assistance.

Despite this obvious rivalry and hostility, R was accepted under a show of complete obedience. The patient immediately began referring to R as mother and she maintained this pattern throughout her adult life and even through the early months of analysis. She would not permit herself to have a single thought of her own mother as this would be disloyal to R. She bore in silence the many difficulties and abuses arising in the household, to make sure R would not leave her. R was regarded as the pinnacle of intelligence, capability and perfection, and apparently R was an individual not adverse to being treated in this manner. The patient believed it quite proper that she should act as a servant to this very superior being, and often referred to herself as R's feeble-minded child.

Concerning her real mother, C could scarcely remember anything. There was an amnesia for the first seven years of her life, *i.e.*, for the years she lived with her mother. C did recall that the mother had died in childbirth. The patient felt this was shameful and fabricated the story that the mother's death had been due to tuberculosis. C was able to recall, however, that she was unmoved by the mother's death and failed to shed a tear at the funeral. Early in the analysis the patient would use the expression 'When there is a parting in the curtain, when I can see beyond this seven year line, I will get well.' Much later in the analysis we had reason to believe that the mother had little affection for the patient but preferred an older brother. C also resented the birth of a sister S who was one year younger than herself. The patient was resentful toward the mother, who was reported to have been a slovenly, ignorant person, socially inferior to the father. This resentment, however, later was understood as an expression of C's feeling of rejection by the mother who preferred the older brother, replaced her with a younger sister, and added the final climax by dying and thus leaving her completely deserted.

The father was a cruel, abusive, psychopathic individual who was frequently intoxicated. He committed all sorts of atrocities toward R and his family. He compelled R to live an incestuous life with him. The patient, however, changed her story so frequently that it was difficult to know exactly what did happen. C talked at length that her father also used her sexually but finally after many months confessed this was not so, although in all probability he did have incestuous relations with C's younger sister S. Secretly, C felt that her father was really a kind man and that he behaved badly only because of R. The home life was indescribably chaotic, and the father was finally ousted from the family group, when the patient was 13 years old and he has not been seen nor heard of since.

For the first months of analysis C talked dutifully and continuously throughout each interview, but without any emotion. The patient talked unceasingly, and if words failed her for a moment she became panicky, obviously fearful that a spontaneous emotion might escape. A great part of each hour was consumed in reporting long dreams, previously reviewed in her mind. The news of the day was monotonously stated, or she gave long varying accounts of her life. Often anxieties arose that she may have made some error or given an incorrect day, and then she would repeat the accounts of her development. Most significant to note was that almost daily she would ask R's confirmation of these accounts. C would often say there was no need for discussing certain subjects in analysis since she had already discussed them with R.

After three months of analysis one could detect the development of positive transference. The patient would complain of feeling miserable over the week end. She felt she longed for something and was anxious to return to the analysis, but on her arrival words left her. She talked at length of other analysands who fell in love with their analysts. She was bitter towards these people saying it was all stupid, and boasted that when thoughts of the analyst occurred to her she immediately erased them from her mind. Occasionally an amorous thought concerning the analyst would escape. At these times the patient would become angry and say 'It means nothing; it is only natural for a patient to have a thought concerning her analyst.' In these instances the patient, who always stammered under emotional stress, would stammer most intensely. The analysis progressed slowly. My office was to her a torture chamber. About the sixth month of analysis her dreams became rather different. She dreamed of obtaining food from the analyst. We began to notice that the patient would rush from the room the moment the hour was over. She explained this behaviour in saying she was allotted a certain amount of time and therefore could not take a second more. Her associations (toward the analyst) indicated clearly that there was a definite feeling of friendship which she still preferred to deny. Later the patient had a dream that she was lying on the couch long past her hour, keeping all the other patients waiting. She became extremely anxious and apprehensive. It seemed as though she could no longer ignore the fact that certain emotional feelings toward the analyst existed.

The following day she failed to keep her appointment. I was informed by telephone that while at work the patient had become ill. She had developed chills and her temperature was recorded 102° F., the pulse being 110. She was sent from work and was seen several hours later by her family physician. At that time the physical examination was negative, temperature and pulse normal. The next day the patient felt well and telephoned saying she would be in the following day. However, on that third day she developed severe pain in the right chest, cough, and a feeling of prostration. Her physician was again called. He found the patient looking very pale, ill, and markedly prostrated. Her temperature, pulse, and respiration were recorded as 103 °F., 110, and 28, respectively. There was pain in the right chest on respiration. Examination of the chest yielded no further information other than bronchovesicular respiration over the right lobe. Voice and whispered sounds seemed to be increased in that area, with some fine rales. Her physician, although fully cognizant of the fact that a strong emotional element was present, was alarmed because of the severe prostration. He hospitalized the patient, his clinical impression being that she had an active broncho-pneumonia. X-ray films of the chest and other laboratory findings were found to be physiological. The temperature fell to 98° 6 within 12 hours. The cough continued for 3 days and the patient was discharged on the fourth day of hospitalization.

When the patient returned to analysis she said that on the first day of her illness she felt depressed. In her own words she said, 'I felt all my defences had slipped out from under me; the props were down. I knew I could no longer control my thoughts. I wanted so much to see you. It made me sick all over. I went home. I knew that if I could see you I would be all right, but R refused to allow me to come. Instead she put me to bed and called the doctor. The following day I felt better. On the third day of my illlness when I thought of coming here I feared I could not control my thinking. Thousands of thoughts and fantasies began to rush through my mind. I was in agony. I wanted so badly to see you but my mother would not permit it. I felt my sickness to be neurotic. I was sent to the hospital but I did not wish to go. I prayed that you would call on me. I had so many dreams and they all seemed about you. I dreamed that we were dancing together. Well, my illness served at least one purpose. R is never home on week ends, so she had to spend at least that one week end with me.' The illness served the purpose of preventing further awareness of friendly feelings toward the analyst and gave C the opportunity to re-establish her attachment to R. To determine why this state of affairs was so necessary to the patient became our problem.

In her early formative years C had real reason to fear and dislike men. The father and R teased, threatened, and scolded her whenever she talked to a boy, so that she became so frightened of boys that she would avoid them whenever possible. R herself never married and favoured a sadistic attitude toward men; and in reality the father was a very cruel person. Since this bad environment had a great deal to do in conditioning the patient's attitude of aversion to men, we felt it would be less of a task to modify her outlook than if the aversion was based solely on disturbed internal emotional conflicts. This proved to be true and at least partially accounted for the excellent progress made in analysis by the patient. More important, however, was the internal conflict, e.g., an extremely ambivalent attitude toward the father whom she constantly stated to hate and yet in the same breath would say that he was a good man who behaved badly only because of R. She was also unconscious of her tendency to identify all men with this father whom she feared. In her youth the father one time slashed C's arm with a knife. C fabricated the story that she had accidentally cut herself while playing with the father's sword. Throughout the analysis in dreams and associations, men were always thought of in relation to swords, daggers, and knives. In one dream the story of Mayerling was depicted. Here the king's son (the father was said to have been of royalty) following a love scene killed his sweetheart. Immediately following these ideas the patient would have thoughts of sexuality with women. This turning to women was not because of love for them but because she had less fear of women than of men.

Despite this fear of the father the patient was, as we shall see, not repelled but was actually attracted to him. C's mother died at the time the patient was struggling with the Oedipus complex. Since C already felt herself rejected she had little regret when the mother died. C was really pleased, for she now had the opportunity to become father's little wife, but this wish was shattered when R entered the household. Cautiously C tried to belittle R, saying that she would make a poor wife and mother, and that she herself was the one best suited for the responsibility. The belief that the father slept with her and not with R or the younger sister was obviously wishful thinking. The patient's frequent statement that she would get well when there was a penetration or parting of the curtain behind the seven-year line referred to her secret desire of having her own hymen penetrated by the male parent. This later assumed a transference meaning as though the patient said she would be cured when she lived out with the analyst her fantastic wish. C was vaguely conscious of her wish for the father but was quite unconscious of the fact that it was her own fear that made fulfilment of the wish impossible. When the mother died the fear of being left alone with the father was so intense that the patient attempted to deny the mother had died by immediately replacing her with R. This behaviour was also motivated by her guilt in having had sexual ideas toward the father. There was also the idea of atoning for the wrong done by a complete renunciation of the father and exaggerated feelings of attachment to R, the mother surrogate. It was as though the patient said 'I love mother so much it proves that I never had any sexual ideas toward my father'.

During the first year of analysis the patient never expressed a single hostile thought toward R. When the analyst offered an interpretation the patient would seek its confirmation from R and then treat it as though the analyst had failed to comprehend her problem and that R had guided her to the proper understanding. It was as though the patient feared that if the analyst helped her R would desert her, and if she was so deserted all would be lost for then there would be no one to protect her from the analyst. R and most women were regarded as efficient, strong, and masculine, as persons more dependable than men. In her early years the patient attempted to cope with the father but failed. It was an extreme disappointment to C that she had failed to attain a penis where R had succeeded. The disappointment was more intense for she must have realized that it was her own fear that prevented attainment of a penis from the already morally delinquent father. She repressed into the unconscious her need to cling to R but rationalized that R was so very powerful that it was impossible for anyone to resist her. Then arose the complaint that R dominated her and treated her as a feeble-minded child.

In the early months of analysis the analyst always appeared in the patient's dreams as a youth, a lad or a feeble-minded boy, i.e., men were regarded as people similar to herself. The patient being unable to relinquish her desire for a penis, and unable to identify herself with the mother surrogate to conceive a child by a man, had identified herself with the father. This inability of C to satisfy her desire for the father and make peace with R was considered the crucial point in her failure to attain full sexual development. Her identification with the male parent was not a simple desire to play the male role in the sex act, but also contained the thought of making herself strong like R and thereby capable of having the father. C would have dreams of stealing money from R, and during childhood in actuality did steal from R. It was as though C felt that in order to have sexual intercourse with a man it would be necessary first to have a phallus like a man, and to attain this phallus she would be compelled to take something from a woman.

This chaos in the phallic phase of development caused a regression in the psychosexual development. Genital matters were regressively translated into pregenital urges. After the eighth month of analysis, and then persisting for more than a year the patient began to complain of two distressing symptoms. The first was described as the 'oral fantasy'. She could never fully describe this. The second symptom was referred to as the 'nursing sensation'. This was described as an unpleasant sensation in the breast. We interpreted the oral fantasy as a biting castrating hatred of the male penis. The pattern for this hatred had its roots in the hatred directed at the mother, the agent who prevented the fulfilment of the wish for the paternal penis. The constellation for hate toward the male penis was derived from the primary source of hate toward mother's breast. The nursing sensation was an expression of C's efforts to attach on herself a breast-penis symbol bitten off from the mother and father. Had the patient a better relation with her mother or with R she probably would have never had such a sadistic attitude toward men. Our patient expressed an oral sadistic attitude toward both sexes and thus was not able to make a satisfactory adjustment to either men or women. It was as though she felt herself without anything, breast or genital with which to give, and if she could acquire something then she could give something.

The first dream brought to analysis was revealing. It ran as follows: '*I seemed to see babies—holy babies. One child seemed to be sitting on a mule. The child had large breasts and was feeding someone. When I awoke I told the dream to R.*'

The dream revealed the patient's desire to possess the father, or be like the father, while the holy baby denies this thought. The huge breast is her genital with which she will feed R. During this hour the patient made a slip of the tongue referring to herself as the best man at a wedding.

After approximately eight months of analysis a constantly recurring association between the words *breast, milk,* and *urine* became prominent. Dreams concerning urination were frequent. The desire to urinate was common during the analytic hour and often the patient would be compelled to leave the room in order to void. The significance of urine in association with breast and milk became more clear with an understanding of the patient's life at the age of 11, that is, when she was approaching puberty. At the age of 11 the patient recalled that once when lying in bed with her father she was consciously aware of the fact that he had an erection and in spite of the fact that she hated him and was repulsed by him she was erotically excited and had erotic desire. She began to suffer dribbling and frequency of urination so that she had to wear a sanitary pad constantly for almost 2 years. The urination was an expression of erotic excitement expressing desire for the father. It symbolized the ejaculating penis which in reality failed to exist, and thus at the same time it was the bleeding wound. C presented the following dream: '*I saw beer. Lots of beer, Dark and light beer. Beer overflowing from a container.*' The patient had the following associations: 'Beer is a stimulating fluid—a pouring out of emotions—I think of breast, of milk—of father, oral, tongue—the fluid which lubricates the vagina.'

One of the patient's dreams shows the relationship of the oral hatred and urethral desire. The dream went as follows: '*I was in bed with father, I was sexually aroused and yet I ought to dislike him. R was there. I could not overcome my desire. I suddenly became conscious of R's nudity. There were 3 glasses on the bureau. Two of the glasses were full of toothbrushes but my glass was empty.* (I just had that nursing sensation again.)' With this dream the patient had the following associations: 'I recall when I was 11, I slept with father. I was aroused but he did not realize it. It was pleasurable to me. It was at that time that I became troubled with frequent voiding and had to wear a pad. The dream means I am frustrated. R comes to mind.' It is as though the patient says to the father, I hate you because you fill mother's glass and leave mine empty. The phallic symbol is the toothbrush, something placed in the mouth. The associations concerning the nursing sensation and the frequent voiding indicate the attempt of C to emphasize that she too had desire (milk and urine), that she now had a breast and was ready to receive the penis.

In everyday life the patient maintained a cold distant attitude toward men, avoiding them whenever possible. One short love affair with a man hastily terminated when the patient received a noncommittal reply from R after requesting her permission to sleep with the man. C kept company with another man for almost 5 years but scarcely realized that she was being courted. During the last year of this acquaintanceship she claims to have pleaded with him to have intercourse with her but he refused. She was constantly aware of the fact that although she was sexually aroused by the man she simultaneously hated him. C began to suffer severe dysmenorrhea and metrorrhagia for which no irreversible organic cause could be found. Her feeling toward this man was identical to her feelings toward her father, and associations seemed to indicate that the dribbling of blood was analogous to the dribbling of urine. C here again expresses the identity of the man with father and refuses to respond as though to deny her experience with the male parent. Although C complained that a penis was denied her, it was her own fear and over-consciousness of her bleeding wound that made sex relations for her impossible. The dysmenorrhea and metrorrhagia ceased under analysis.

Her daily relationships with women were scarcely better than with men. Some women she regarded with contempt, e.g., regarding them as homosexual or prostitutes. Other women, whom she considered superior to herself, were taken down from their high pedestal by means of the patient's act of ignorance. When women approached her genitally, C's pretence of ignorance left the would-be seducer bewildered. In the sex act with women, the extreme passivity or lack of action on the part of the patient again was surely a cloak for her sadism. In the homosexual act the patient played a double role. She was not only the passive one who was penetrated by the partner's finger or tongue, but she was also the one who had injured the partner, i.e., the one who had penetrated. The overt homosexual acts with C, however, did not result from a driving need to hurt women, but rather it was an act of desperation for some human contact.

Our findings concerning homosexuality are not startling but compared to the findings of other authors, Deutsch,[1] Horney,[2] and others who have reported as we have found in our case that difficulties in the Oedipal stage, rivalry with the mother, and predominance of castration feelings always lead to a more or less marked tendency toward homosexuality. Inversion is nourished by the fact that the patient persists with the idea that it is mother who gets the child and not I. Thus fresh fuel is provided for the old fire-Oedipal aggression with further intensification of guilt which is relieved only by means of a new overcompensatory renunciation of the father and definite persistence in the mother attachment. The pre-Oedipal aggression is oral sadistic and its intensification is considered by Jones[3] as the central characteristic of homosexuality in women. Unwilling to relinquish her desire for a penis the homosexual woman forms an identification with the male parent as though to believe the incestuous deed may happen in the future or has already happened in the past. The unconscious attitude toward the parents is strongly ambivalent and has been described as a characteristic of homosexual women.[4] In the sexual act the homosexual woman plays a double role. She is the one who suckles and is at the same time suckled. Not only is the oral system highly charged but also urethral erotism plays a powerful part in the homosexual picture. Brierley[5] has stated that if oro-urethral nucleus is overdeveloped in relation to the oro-vaginal and oro-anal, and particularly where it is highly charged with sadism, it predisposes to homosexuality. This seems to be the case with our patient. Throughout the analysis there was little reference to the anal material although in the dream of the dark and light beer, association indicated that the dark beer may have reference to some anal matter. In homosexual people who present themselves for psychiatric treatment one finds that the disturbance in sexuality is a symptom, an expression of disturbance in the infantile psychosexual development. We are fully in accord with Ferenczi who does not like the biological term 'homosexuality', but prefers a term such as 'homo-erotism' to emphasize the psychic aspect of the impulse.

Homosexuality is a poor term when used in a narrow sense to mean object choice. Homosexuality is a syndrome, a mode of behaviour. Such people are driven to self-degradation expressed obviously or more subtly, and to a more or less marked degree. Unable to tolerate the degraded self, they rationalize that they are so superior there is no need for them to compete with others (healthy people). The rationalization continues: other (healthy people) are so weak and degraded, so afraid of their position in life they are driven to compete. Homosexual people never show their capabilities and at the same time they are enraged that their talents are not recognized. Embittered that they have failed to receive due recognition (for traits they have never shown themselves to possess) they retaliate by refusing to respond or to show their capabilities. The homosexual person as seen by the psychiatrist is not an individual who presents himself for treatment because he and society differ as to what mode of sexuality is preferable, but he is a neurotic with a deep rooted character disturbance. These people would not be healthy persons even if they lived in a society where sexuality with the same sex was socially acceptable.

We have attempted to trace those factors in the psychosexual development of a girl which lead to homosexual maladjustment. A mother who rejected her, a domineering mother surrogate who warned the patient against men, and a cruel father were the dominant environmental factors which reinforced the innate personality toward arrest in development. The internal conflict was characterized by a poorly resolved Oedipus complex, a markedly ambivalent attitude toward both parents, and a complicated returning to the mother attachment. Blindly, reproaching the father that he denied her, the patient was unconscious of her fear of the father which made friendly relations with him or sexual relations with men impossible. Likewise, the patient constantly reproached R for her overwhelming attitude, but was unaware of her own need to establish R as the strong person capable of coping with father. Unable to overcome her desire for the father, and unable to make a satisfactory adjustment to the mother which might lead to having a child by the man, the patient regressively translated genital drives into pregenital urges. The resentment toward the parents was now expressed in oral terms while desire for a penis was expressed in oral, urinary or breast symbols. The anal erotic components have not been analysed and it may be that our patient has yet to express and elaborate a considerable amount of anal sadism before making a last renunciation of urethral-phallic aims to attain normal heterosexuality.

REFERENCES

[1] Deutsch, H.: 'Homosexuality in Women', *Psychoanalyt. Quart.*, 1, Oct· 32, pp. 484–510.
Freud, Sigmund: 'The Psychogenesis of a Case of Female Homosexuality', *Int. Jour. of Psychoanalysis* (1920), Vol. 1, p. 125.

[2] Horney, K.: 'On the Genesis of the Castration Complex in Women', *Int. Jour. of Psychoanalysis* (1924), Vol. V, p. 50.

[3] Jones, Ernest: 'The Early Development of Female Sexuality', *Int. Jour. of Psychoanalysis*, VIII, Oct. 27, p. 459.

[4] Ferenczi, S.: *Contributions to Psychoanalysis.*

[5] Brierley, Marjorie: 'Specific Determinants in Feminine Development'. *Int. Jour. of Psychoanalysis*, XVII, April, 26, pp. 163–180.

A case of male homosexuality

MOSHE WULFF, M.D.

THE reasons which lead me to publish this case of homosexuality are its unusual development and structure. As the reader will see for himself, the structure agrees with none of the patterns that have hitherto been put forward. But this is not the only reason for being interested in the psychological structure of the case. Closely connected with that question is another, which has never yet been settled although it is an essential one, namely, the relative importance and significance of the two factors, physical-constitutional and psychological, in the genesis of homo-sexuality. The present case contributes interesting material in relation to this question as well.

The subject of this case history was a young man of twenty-seven, who presented himself for psychoanalytic treatment on account of psychical impotence. He came to the preliminary interview with his young and beautiful wife. Both complained that throughout the two years of their married life he had proved to be completely impotent, in spite of their good relations and their genuine love for one another. In the course of the two years they had made many attempts at cure and the man had been having one kind of treatment or another almost the whole time, but without result. The appearance of the patient was completely masculine. He was short, it is true, but strong and sturdy. He worked on the land and was a countryman by origin. Physically he was healthy in every respect.

In the very first session he disclosed his great and oppressive secret, namely, that he was markedly homosexual. He was quite indifferent to women; but men, particularly simple, robust, strong men in top-boots, such as peasants, or the ignorant, dirty fellaheen of Palestine, aroused strong sexual excitement in him, with accompanying erections, even when he merely saw them in the street. He would also often see Arabs or peasants of this kind in dreams and would masturbate with them or carry out some other sexual practice; and these dreams were accompanied by emissions. In waking life too he was often obliged to think of such men and produce various phantasies about them, which were accompanied by strong sexual excitement.

The patient came from a modest, but comfortably-off, *petit-bourgeois* family in the South of Russia. He was the only son and youngest child; besides him, there were only two girls. His mother died when he was scarcely four years old and his only memory of her was the scene of her death. In this he pictured himself as a small boy sitting by her bed. She was lying in bed and holding his hand in hers while she stroked his head and hair with her other hand. His father and older sister were sitting a little way off crying quietly, while he sat by the edge of the bed almost entirely detached from it all and not grasping or under- standing what was happening before his eyes. Then his mother suddenly cried out, fell back and lay still. His father and sister wept aloud and said that his mother was dead. It is true that he remembered the whole scene quite clearly, yet he could not recol- lect feeling either agitation or sorrow; it seemed to him that he remained quite quiet and unconcerned. After this he was taken away from home.

As I have said already, he had no other memories of his mother. He only knew from what he had been told that she suffered from severe tuberculosis. She spent most of her time in hospitals and sanatoriums, coming home occasionally for short periods, when she was mostly in bed. His maternal aunt and his two sisters ran the house and did the work. Besides this, he had a dim memory of his wet-nurse, who lived in the same small town and had a large family with whom he spent most of his time until he was three years old. Strange to say, all he could tell about his father was restricted to the time after his mother's death. His father had a great deal of business outside the town and stayed away from the house for almost the whole of the week, returning home towards the end of the week, usually on a Friday, to stay until the Saturday evening, leaving again early on the Sunday morning. But, as he remembered it, the two days which his father used to spend at home had been days of suffering and terror for him and the other members of the family. His father was a very severe, brutal man, and beat the children mercilessly for the smallest offence, even the grown-up sister. The patient remembered that as a boy of 8 or 9 he had not only been beaten by his father very brutally for some offence, but had even been knocked down and kicked, so that his stepmother had literally to save him.

His anger and hatred against his father were boundless. He could go on telling me for hours about his father's merciless beatings and ill-treatment, his heartlessness and brutality. The patient spent three whole months of the analysis almost entirely in complaints about his hard and unhappy childhood, without a mother's love and tormented by his father. His sole comforter and protector was his sister, eight years older than himself, who, though she suffered as much as he did from his father, was not so helpless.

Nor were things much better for the patient at school. The teacher, who usually treated the children quite kindly, was very strict with him at the special request of his father, and used often to beat him, too, for the slightest faults, while other children went unpunished. But it is worth noting that the patient, notwithstanding, was very fond of the teacher and was one of his best pupils.

The patient's first homosexual memories, too, dated from his school days. He recalled the fact that one day (when he was 7 or 8) he had practised mutual masturbation with another boy at school. Besides this, he told of many scenes of a sexual kind of which he had been a witness and which he had observed in a way that was characteristic of him. Peasants from the surrounding villages used to come into the town on market days, and many of them spent the night in their large carts in the streets and market place. On these evenings erotic scenes, which were not limited to kisses and caresses, used to take place between young men and women in the streets. The boy had watched these scenes with the greatest of interest, and, as he clearly remembered, his interest was directed chiefly towards the men. He strove to picture to himself what the woman felt and experienced. The big, coarse, strong farm hands, with their heavy boots, were at that time the most important object of his sexual curiosity and sexual phantasies.

At the same time, however, heterosexual impulses were not absent either. He recalled that as a seven-year-old boy he had imitated coitus with a neighbour's child, and had been caught by his father and terribly punished. On another occasion, when he was ten years old, he was seized by such strong sexual excitement at the sight of an older girl of 14 or 15 in the street, that he suddenly fell on the girl from behind and caught hold of her breasts. The girl screamed and he ran away in terror. Another time he was sent to a shoemaker and when he entered the house found the shoemaker and his wife in bed and, as he thought he remembered it, saw the man's uncovered and erect penis. This scene had stimulated him sexually to a high degree and when he met the woman in the street a short time afterwards, he fell on her from behind in a state of great excitement and caught hold of her breasts. The woman screamed and he ran away.

He was about twelve years old when the revolution in Russia broke out. His sister left home and moved to a large town in South Russia. After some time she arranged for him to join her. There he had to live with an aunt, who, however, had been very reluctant to take him in. He found a job at a wholesale confectioner's, where he had to work hard; and there he came into contact with the drivers who took the goods around to the retailers. They made him acquainted with the sexual life of a big town. The behaviour of the prostitutes which he could observe in the streets greatly excited him sexually. He was particularly excited by observing a middle-aged man accosting a prostitute and disappearing with her into the doorway of a house. But in this case, also, it was primarily his thoughts about the man's part that excited him.

Meanwhile his stay in the town was becoming more and more difficult. His aunt kept him very unwillingly and made this plain to him on every possible occasion. The town was visited by famine; he lost his job and decided to return to his parents' house.

But in the meantime his father had left the original town and had moved to a town in the Ukraine. The fourteen-year-old boy was very ill when he reached his parents' house. He was suffering from typhus. After about two months he recovered sufficiently to leave the house. There was famine and unemployment in the town. In order to manage somehow or other, he got a position, with the help of his sister, as a clerk in the secretariat of the military garrison. He then moved out of the town along with the garrison and was quartered in a village not far away. He lived in a state of continual sexual excitement; he made repeated attempts to approach women but was prevented by strong inhibitions. And when a hospital nurse fell in love with him and pursued him with offers of love, he reacted to it with strong anxiety and in the end gave up his position with the army in order to return once more to his parents.

His father's family made preparations to emigrate to Palestine. At that time this was no light undertaking; indeed it was a dangerous one. It was necessary to smuggle oneself across the frontier into Poland secretly and illegally. The rest of the journey was not much easier and it took months. Having reached Palestine, the patient left his father and went on the land to live in a *kibbutz*.

The homosexual phantasies, in which he indulged from childhood onwards and which now accompanied his masturbation, had undergone an outward change in Palestine; in the place of Russian peasants, Arabs now appeared, or rather the simple fellaheen of the Arab village.

Meanwhile he had reached the age of seventeen years. In the *kibbutz* he soon developed a friendship with two young men; they all lived together in one room. He fell passionately in love with one of his two companions, but since the object of his love, who was a stranger to all homosexual impulses, did not respond to his extremely timid approaches, the patient had to take the greatest care to hide his secret and passionate love. The situation soon became still more complicated owing to the appearance of a beautiful young girl, with whom the patient also fell in love; she, however, would have nothing to do with him and loved the friend. Soon afterwards the friend married and thus the patient was left deserted and separated from all that he loved, depressed and in despair. In this condition of mind he met his future wife, a beautiful, intelligent and well-educated girl who offered him love, comfort and solace. At first he rejected her and remained cold. After much hesitation he gave in and a genuine feeling towards the girl awoke in him. They were married—and then his impotence manifested itself.

This is my patient's somewhat obscure and contradictory life history, given in rough outline. Many details have been omitted and, as so often in analysis, it cost many weeks of work before the picture given here was obtained. Weeks then passed in which the patient indulged in abuse of his hated father. He became furious as he described the unkind treatment, the brutal beatings and torments which he had suffered from him. This certainly relieved him, but the analysis gained little from it and there was not much progress: the condition remained unchanged.

To give a picture of this condition I will sum it up briefly as follows. In spite of his outspoken homosexual tendencies, at all periods of his life he had had heterosexual impulses as well, and he had moreover made attempts to approach women. The homosexual tendencies had already appeared when he was 7 or 8, at which age, as has already been mentioned, he had carried out mutual masturbation with a school friend of his own age, in which he was the seducer and played the active role. At this time, however, his luxuriant sexual phantasies had an interesting characteristic feature: they were not phantasies about sexual activities à *deux* with a youth or man, but a woman was always present too, and the patient always played the part of an onlooker and identified himself with the woman. He tried to imagine the feelings and experiences of the woman, principally when she touched the man's penis. This remained so until puberty, with the onset of which the patient once more stepped out of the situation of onlooker and took up an independent role. The man persisted throughout his phantasies, always with the same characteristics—brutal and primitive. And there was another striking fact: the contradiction between the homosexual tendencies of the patient and his burning hatred of his father.

One day a singular memory occurred to the patient. During the long journey, which had been full of hardships, on the flight from Russia to Palestine, the family came one day to a small Polish town and stayed the night at an inn. The place was by no means a first-class hotel but was so small that they all had to spend the night together in one room. The patient saw the bed prepared for his parents (that is, for his father and stepmother) with its clean white linen, and was suddenly seized with a strange and powerful excitement which he could not account for at all. Gradually, with the overcoming of strong resistances, memories came of the evening of his father's marriage, when his stepmother came to the house for the first time. At that time, too, a bed had been prepared in the same way in his father's bedroom, with white linen sheets, and this seems to have made a similarly strong impression on the little boy.

There followed a chain of interesting memories relating to the time after his father's marriage. The appearance of his stepmother in the house and in particular the sexual relations between

her and his father made a strong impression on the boy, who
believed that, owing to his mother's illness, he had not seen
anything of the same kind in his early childhood, and it stirred
his sexual curiosity to the highest degree, as well as his desire to
look, and most particularly his imaginative activities. For hours
at a time, with all the strength of his imagination, he visualized the
scenes which might be taking place in the bedroom between his
father and his new wife, and his phantasy revelled in these sexual
thoughts. In consequence he found himself in a state of constant
and undiminishing sexual excitement, and at the same time his
sexual curiosity turned specially to his stepmother, towards
whom he felt attracted both sensually and affectionately. In a
certain sense he was successful, at the beginning, in winning her
love, and the relations between them were fairly good up to
the time when the stepmother's daughter, a girl of the same age
as himself, came into the house.

The pathogenic significance of these childhood experiences,
which had been completely repressed and only now emerged
again in memory, was clear. The phantasies of the peasants in
the market, in which a third person, the woman, appeared,
were founded on his father's wedding and the appearance of
his stepmother—a fact which was established for the first time
at this period of the analysis. And there was no difficulty now in
showing that it was precisely these experiences and phantasies
concerning the relations between his father and stepmother
that had led to the development of his sexual interest in the
peasants and their wives. It was now quite possible to relate to
his father the ideas and phantasies of the brutal primitive, strong
man—the peasant. But how are we to link his strong sexual
interest in his father, as a sexual object, with his burning hatred
of him? It is true that his sensual homosexual relation to his
father has remained in the unconscious, while his hatred of him
dominated his conscious thoughts and feelings—though indeed
it was this supposition which had now to be confirmed or
refuted in the analysis.

The working through of this problem brought about a change in the patient. One day he brought an important contribution to the question of why the sight of the beds prepared for his parents had made such a strong impression on him. He remembered that, until the evening on which his stepmother had come to the house for the first time, the patient himself had slept in his father's bedroom and even in the same bed with him; since that evening, however, he had had to sleep alone in the children's bedroom. His stepmother had therefore separated him from his father.

After strong resistances had been overcome, there emerged in the patient, slowly and with hesitation, memories of a very early time, before he was six, when he had been his father's favourite. His father had spoiled him and always brought him home presents, sweets, pretty things and clothes, when he came back from a journey. And at night his father used to take him into bed with him, and on those occasions the patient had often had an opportunity of observing his father's erect penis, and even of playing with it while his father was apparently fast asleep. Then the patient recalled that this had made a strongly attractive and at the same time frightening impression on him and that he had always made every possible effort, whenever he was with his father, somehow, without being noticed, to touch and feel his penis. Thus he succeeded again and again in sitting on his father's knee or standing between his father's legs and in pressing close against the region of his father's genitals with some part or other of his own body. The relation between father and son retained this character until the evening on which the stepmother came into the house.

After these memories had emerged and been worked through, the patient's homosexual impulses and phantasies disappeared completely and in their place there appeared a marked indifference to men and the penis. When he met his favourite type (the fellaheen) in the street, the patient remained quite indifferent and undisturbed; nor did they excite the activity of his phantasy. But now something remarkable became evident; this visible effect of the treatment had as its result that sexual impulses of every kind disappeared in the patient and an almost complete sexual frigidity and indifference towards his wife too took possession of him. This was a great disappointment to him and was the reverse of what he had hoped for. He had expected that liberation from his homosexual tendency would of itself bring an improvement in and strengthening of his heterosexual relations with his wife.

As a result of this, his relations with his wife now came into the foreground of psychoanalytical interest. There is much to report about these relations, but I must first interpose a comment, which has a certain technical interest and is at the same time indispensable to an understanding of the further description of the case. Freud's recommendation that patients should live in abstinence during treatment is often very difficult to carry out, particularly if the patient is married. On the other hand situations exist, particularly in the case of marital conflicts, sexual disturbances such as impotence, perversions, etc., in which the carrying out of this rule is particularly important and is very beneficial to the course of the analysis. So it was in this case. For external and economic reasons even more than from therapeutic considerations, the patient was obliged to stay at Tel-Aviv, separated from his wife, while she lived elsewhere with her parents. It was only from time to time that he visited her, usually on Saturdays, but even then not every week. And in this way every visit, each meeting with her, acquired a special significance and a special value, both therapeutic and elucidatory.

At the beginning of the relationship it was his wife who had played the active part and had been in love, whereas he had remained more or less indifferent and had had the feeling that she wished to force him to approach her. Once even, he made an attempt to withdraw from her entirely and broke off all contact with her for a few months, but then gave way again on a chance encounter, though with a decided feeling that he was being compelled to do so. Already shortly after their marriage, scenes such as this used to take place between the young couple. He would lie down in bed beside his wife at night but would remain indifferent and cold, and would quickly fall asleep. This would irritate his wife and she would launch out into reproaches, grow angry and even hit him. He would then get out of bed quietly and quite indifferently and lie down somewhere else to go to sleep again. In doing this he would often be aware of hatred of his wife. When he noticed his wife's despair and tears, he would feel sorry for her and begin to comfort her and to fondle her, and strong sexual excitement would overcome him. But coitus never took place, because complete impotence set in when he attempted it. A further characteristic detail occurred to him in this connexion: only the upper part of his wife's body, her breasts, or perhaps her buttocks as well, made him feel sexually excited, while the lower part of her body and the genital region hardly affected him at all.

At the outset of the treatment his visits to his wife were suspended until such time as he should feel a desire to make one. On his first visit the familiar pattern repeated itself. When they met and first saw one another, and throughout the whole of the day, their relations were very happy and affectionate. At night, when they were together in bed, there was complete indifference, at which his wife became furious and which led on her side to tears and complaints and bitter reproaches. To these he reacted first with dull indifference, and then with actual hatred, and eventually left the bed. Then followed remorse and pity on his side, apologies, reconciliation, strong sexual excitement with an erection —and impotence when he attempted coitus. The next evening before he went to bed he felt depression, headache, sensations of cold and trembling in his whole body—a condition the significance of which he somehow vaguely surmised. The same sequence of events was repeated in approximately the same form during his next visits. Once he had the following dream. He came into a room, in which his sister was sitting. She was crying, and complained that she was in love with a young man and wanted to marry him, but that her father would not allow it and beat her because of it. Then the menacing figure of his father appeared. The patient went into the street, where it was thundering and there was a great noise—and suddenly he was given a box on the ear, so hard that he saw stars before his eyes. At the same time he thought: 'that was father.' The first association was that the day before when he was going to bed he had trembled just as he used to in his childhood when his father had threatened to hit him. So his father had forbidden him marriage and sexual life with a woman, just as he had forbidden it to his sister.

I will take this opportunity to underline the remarkable frankness of the patient's dreams, which often seemed like daydreams or memories and of which I will give one or two further examples.

'I was going along the street not far from my house and met three or four men; they were Jews and, what is more, devout ones. One of them came up to me and showed me that he was fond of me, and I wanted to go nearer to him too. I became sexually excited, but this soon passed off and the men also disappeared. I then approached our house. I saw a Jew sitting there in a cheerful, festive mood, as though he had been drinking wine. He went into a room with me. Then I found myself in bed with him.' To this he added an association: 'That reminds me of an incident when I was about 5, when I experienced exactly the same thing with my father.'

After the visit to his wife which I have described, the patient brought me an important dream which contributed greatly to the elucidation of his marriage relationship. The dream ran: 'I passed through a great many streets and round corners and over roofs without meeting any Arabs or anyone else. Suddenly I was in a strongly lighted room and saw in front of me a girl of about 12 or 13 in a white dress. I became sexually excited and wanted to go up to her and to put my arms around her. At that moment I saw my father at my side, making a sign to me with his finger, forbidding me to go near the girl and I obeyed him at once. I woke up in a state of great sexual excitement and had a strong erection, and I was obliged to masturbate.'

The first association showed that the girl in the dream was the daughter of the patient's stepmother, who came into the house a few months after his father's marriage.

This girl, who has already been mentioned, had been given a hostile reception by him. He had felt anger and disgust at every chance contact with her, and particularly when he had to sleep in the same bed with her. The reason for this hatred, moreover, seemed quite clear to him: he had a feeling that the girl had stolen his father's love from him, that she was one of the causes of his being treated badly, of the beatings and of his father's hatred of him. In this connexion the patient now remembered that he had had the same feelings and thoughts, immediately after his marriage, about his own wife, when they lay beside one another in bed—but with the difference that, in place of his father, he had to think of one of his friends, of some man or other.

The analysis of the last mentioned dream provided the explanation of his relation to the girl, for it transpired that when his stepsister first came the relation between the children had been a good and affectionate one. They liked playing together and got on quite well with one another. But their games soon took on more and more of a sexual character; they played 'husband and wife', and in this game he embraced the girl, kissed her, touched her genitals and made an attempt at something like coitus. But one day the girl complained to her mother about the patient doing this. He was severely punished and beaten. Incidents of this kind were repeated several times and were always ended by his father administering severe corporal punishment to him. The girl apparently got enjoyment out of seducing the patient into some sort of forbidden activity and then denouncing him, so as to be present while his father beat him. The patient then developed a burning hatred towards the girl but also a feeling of disgust at every contact with her. He recalled a picture of the girl standing naked in front of him, laughing, exciting him in every possible way, stroking her body, showing her breasts and her genitals and turning round before him, making seductive gestures. This excited him sexually and made him want to touch her and catch hold of her, but he did not dare for fear of the denunciation and the beating which would inevitably follow. He remembered feeling strong sexual excitement, as far back as his seventh year, while playing with this girl accompanied by erections and even by sensations resembling an orgasm, and at that time it was the lower part of the female body and the female genitals which had chiefly excited him.

After the failure with his stepmother's daughter he turned to the girls in the neighbourhood and played the same games with them. But one day his father caught him at it, beat him severely, forbade him to have any contact with girls and threatened that there would be terrible consequences for him if he were ever again caught committing a similar misdemeanour. In the end his fear of his father prevailed and he avoided all contact with girls. Then came the incident with the boy at school and he turned finally to the male object.

We are confronted here with a case of homosexuality, which, in its psychological structure, its development and its final clinical picture, is unlike any of the three familiar types. It is characteristic of this case that it was precisely at the time of the Oedipal phase that the part played by his mother, or anyone else standing for her, was extremely small. At that time, moreover, his relation to his father was very strong and often assumed undisguisedly sensual and sexual forms. The death of his mother made almost no impression on the patient and, consciously, he did not experience it as a loss. Some attachment to his sister was present, but it was not strongly felt by him. Only in later childhood, after his father's second marriage, did he feel this relationship more intensely. On the other hand it is important to emphasize that precisely during the phallic phase the boy's chief and ardently loved object was his father, and in particular his father's penis. This apparently led to a quite special overvaluation of the male genital. Freud (1922)[3] has already mentioned the significance of this: 'Behind this factor (narcissistic object-choice) there lies concealed another of quite exceptional strength, or perhaps it coincides with it: the high value set upon the male organ and the inability to tolerate its absence in a love-object. Depreciation of women, and aversion from them, even horror of them, are generally derived from the early discovery that women have no penis. We subsequently discovered, as another powerful motive urging towards the homosexual object-choice, regard for the father or fear of him; for the renunciation of women means that all rivalry with him (or with all men who may take his place) is avoided. The two last motives, the clinging to the condition of a penis in the object as well as the retiring in favour of the father, may be ascribed to the castration complex. Attachment to the mother, narcissism, fear of castration—these are the factors (which by the way have nothing specific about them) that we have hitherto found in the psychical aetiology of homosexuality; and on them is superimposed the effect of any seduction bringing about a premature fixation of the libido, as well as the influence of the organic factor favouring the passive role in love.'

As this analysis shows, we find here only a few of the aetiological factors of homosexuality brought forward by Freud. The first factor mentioned by him, which is usually the most important one, an attachment to the mother, appears to have been altogether absent. But in its place there was a very strong homosexual attachment to the father, to which the significance of a seduction might also in a sense be attributed. Some unimportant narcissistic character traits were, it is true, to be observed in the patient, but there can be no question of any outspoken narcissism in his case. But there is another striking feature in the patient's reactions, which possibly stands in a certain relation to narcissism. Twice in his life his love relations underwent a strong, or one might even say, a complete repression: towards his father and towards his stepmother's daughter. In both cases the same mechanism of repression was at work, namely, the transformation of an affect into its opposite, the transformation of love into hate. As is well known, this mechanism is characteristic of paranoiacs. A person with a wounded narcissism, with feelings of inferiority, usually reacts to a slight, to a disappointment in love or to a rejection, with depression, with an increase in his sense of inferiority and with self-reproach, as we see particularly in the case of melancholia. People with a heightened narcissism, on the other hand, react with delusions of grandeur, as for example in mania; but the paranoiac, over and above this, reacts with an increase in hate. It was striking that in the present patient, in spite of his impotence, almost no feelings of inferiority were to be observed. He regarded his impotence simply as a fact, without really worrying about it. In fact, one often had the impression that he felt a certain satisfaction about his impotence because it protected him from his wife's demands. This behaviour must, however, be attributed chiefly to disdain and contempt for woman as a sexual object, particularly as he had had no occasion to complain of a lack of potency in regard to his more important sexual object, man.

But in this connexion there was a further significant fact: the typical expressions of castration-anxiety, which are usually found in connexion with impotence, such as anxiety before coitus, fear of failing in coitus, fear of having no erection, fear of the *vagina dentata*, etc., were absent in the patient. Generally speaking, there were almost no anxiety symptoms at all to be observed in him and none of the typical expressions of castration-anxiety. He certainly talked about his great fear of his father, but this did not develop fully at the typical age, between four and five, but later, when he was about seven, after his father's marriage. By this I do not mean to say that no castration- anxiety at all existed in the patient, but if it was present it was in such a small degree that it is impossible to attribute to it the importance of a decisive aetiological factor. The patient no longer had to fear castration, for he had accepted it and had resigned himself to the female role in relation to his father.

It will be gathered from this that, of the triad mentioned by Freud as being factors in the psychical aetiology of male homosexuality—attachment to the mother, narcissism and fear of castration—not one is to be found to the full in my patient. On the other hand, apart from his strong attachment to his father, there is another factor to be found which was emphasized by Freud—regard for the father and fear of him—and lastly the factor of narcissistic overvaluation of the penis, which, however, can not be included among the aetiological factors proper. And there is yet another thing to be learned from this case: it demonstrates that the importance of the constellation of the Oedipus complex in judging the causes of homosexuality is perhaps greater than might be supposed according to the theories hitherto put forward.

It must further be remarked that his father's marriage and the change in his attitude towards the patient were a severe disappointment to the latter. His reaction to it was a fresh move in the direction of normal development, that is, towards heterosexuality: he identified himself with his father and tried to carry out sexual games with his stepmother's daughter, and later with other girls as well, and in these games he took the male role and made attempts at coitus. But this development too came to grief, in the first place because of his partner's betrayal, and secondly (according to the patient) because of his father's harshness and punishments. The patient attributed this setback to his great fear of his father; but this must be questioned, since it seems hardly credible that even repeated beatings at the age of 8 or 9 could have such serious results as the diversion of the sexual impulse into homosexuality—particularly since, from what Freud tells us, it appears that avoidance of rivalry with the father is also present in other cases with quite other constellations and under other conditions. It is much more likely that these results should be attributed to his strong attachment to his father, which brought about a condition of psychical subjugation such as was shown by the patient later towards his friend. Nevertheless this attempted move in the direction of normal development had an important consequence, for it was followed once more by an identification with the female object which had been abandoned; a woman appeared in the patient's phantasies with whom he identified himself, so that he experienced her longing for the male organ. This condition continued until after puberty and indicated a repetition from early childhood, when the psychologically motherless boy had assumed the role of his mother in relation to his father.

And there is another consideration. How are we to explain the patient's curiously undisguised and open type of dream? I believe that it is to be related to the peculiarity of the mechanism of repression so strikingly employed by him, in which the work of repression was accomplished not so much upon the ideational material as by a change of the affect into its opposite. A weakening of the affect in the dream was then enough to enable only slightly modified repressed material to obtain representation in the manifest content of the dream.

There is the further question of why precisely this mechanism was employed by the patient. In this connexion it may be remarked that ordinarily the superego should not be able to offer any objection even to an exaggerated love towards the father. In normal development, and in that of neurotics too, the grossly sensual and sexual elements are repressed, while the affectionate current of feeling is retained in consciousness and often even overemphasized. That this was not the case with our patient was owing essentially to the change in affect on the part of the object, the father. The patient's ego, which had been spoilt by his father's former love, and which had therefore been intensified in its self-esteem, reacted now to his bad treatment by his father with strong hatred, which sought to efface the traces of the former love from his consciousness and recollection. The anticathexes responsible for the carrying out of the process of repression were mobilized not merely by the superego but by the ego-contents also; the repression was set in operation not only by the superego but by the ego as well—and principally by purely affective forces. This also increased the resistances in the analysis, which were maintained by both departments of the mind alike.

It only remains now to report that the treatment was brought to a successful conclusion and led to the complete recovery of the patient. When it came to an end his wife was in the third month of pregnancy.

It seems appropriate to raise the question whether we may not be dealing here with a case in which the development to homosexuality took place according to the pattern described by Freud (1920)[2] in his paper on a case of female homosexuality. There, disappointment with regard to the love-object of the opposite sex led to its abandonment and to an identification with it, so that a person of the subject's own sex was then made the sexual object. In our case the love-object was from the beginning a person of the subject's own sex. The disappointment then led to a move in the direction of normal development, towards heterosexuality. This development broke down, however, precisely because of the subject's strong attachment or subservience to the original homosexual love-object.

The second pattern for the development of homosexuality, that proposed by Sadger (1909)[5]—normal primary object-choice of the mother identification with the mother at puberty and narcissistic object-choice of a person of the subject's own sex— fails entirely (as is shown from the case history) to fit my patient.

The same must be said of the third structural pattern of the possible development of homosexuality, described by Freud (1922)[3]: a situation of rivalry between two children of the same sex (brothers), the development of hatred in one of them towards his rival and finally the overcoming of this hatred by a hyper-cathexis of the homosexual love-relation to the rival.

Nunberg (1936)[4] believes that he has found yet another type of homosexual development. What is typical of these cases, according to Nunberg, lies in the fact that 'the aim of the homosexual represents a compromise—a compromise between aggressive and libidinal impulses.' He believes further 'that aggression plays a part of importance not only in the object-choice of the paranoiac but in homosexuality in general, and is at least to be regarded as characteristic of a certain type of homosexual.' But he goes on: 'Even the aggressive type displays certain masochistic traits *also*, even though these are not always well marked. We may therefore speak of a sadistic type when sadism predominates; of a masochistic, when masochism predominates and leaves its impress upon the homosexual.' Actually, therefore, *two* new types are proposed by Nunberg—a sadistic homosexual and a masochistic homosexual.

I find it difficult to concur with these arguments of Nunberg's or with the creation of these new types. In the types set up by Freud and Sadger it is a question of a particular direction of the development of sexual object-choice, of a particular structure and organization of the libidinal object-relation. That is the basis of the whole classification. Nunberg now puts forward an entirely new classification, that of the preponderance in the object relation of a single component instinct. But on what principle, we must ask, was the object-choice made in Nunberg's case? The answer is given by Nunberg himself when he writes of his patient: 'He projects his ideal of a handsome, strong, tall man. This ideal he loves, and he searches for it in the external world.' This means, then, that the object-choice in this case was made according to the narcissistic type. ('A person loves . . . what he would like to be.' Freud, 1914)[1]. But Nunberg's patient had taken over this ideal from his mother. We may therefore say that Nunberg's case is an interesting variety of the Sadger type, a variety in which what is chosen as object is not the subject's own ego (which had been loved by his mother) but his mother's ego-ideal.

In the case which I have described, we are concerned with a peculiar situation in the constellation of the Oedipus complex; for, at the time at which object-choice occurred, the parent of the subject's own sex was alone present and had from the very first taken the place of the parent of the opposite sex. The only object-choice which could be brought out by rivalry was therefore, as a result of this constellation, a homosexual one.

About four years after the conclusion of the treatment I visited the place where the patient lives and met him there. He took the opportunity of introducing his three-year-old daughter to me. His wife was again pregnant. In other respects, too, he felt, as he told me, quite normal, free from any kind of disturbance and happy.

REFERENCES

[1] Freud, S. (1914). (*Trans.* 1925). 'On Narcissism: an Introduction', *Collected Papers*, IV, 47.

[2] ——(1920). (*Trans.* 1924). 'The Psychogenesis of a Case of Homosexuality in a Woman', *Collected Papers*, II, 202.

[3] ——(1922). (*Trans.* 1924). 'Certain Neurotic Mechanisms in Jealousy, Paranoia and Homosexuality', *Collected Papers*, II, 241.

[4] Nunberg, H. (1936). (*Trans.* 1938) 'Homosexuality, Magic and Aggression', *Int. J. Psycho-Anal.*, 19, 1.

[5] Sadger, I. (1909). 'Zur Aetiologie der konträren Sexualempfindung', *Med. Klinik*.

Notes on the contributors

CHARLES BERG, M.D. F.B.PS.S D.P.M.. is Consultant Psychiatrist to the British Hospital for Functional Nervous Disorders. He is the author of *Clinical Pyschology, Deep Analysis, The Unconscious Significance of Hair* and *The First Interview with a Psychiatrist*, and *The Case Book of a Medical Psychologist, Being Lived by My Life.*

EDMUND BERGLER, M.D. is a practising psychoanalyst in New York City. Formerly Assistant Director of the Vienna Psychoanalytic Institute and lecturer at the New York Psychoanalytic Institute, he has contributed to numerous journals. Among his books are *Unhappy Marriage and Divorce, The Basic Neurosis, The Battle of Conscience, Kinsey's Myth of Female Sexuality* (with W. S. Kroger, M.D.).

MORRIS W. BRODY, M.D. is a psychoanalyst and a psychiatrist of wide experience who is Associate Professor and Chairman of the Psychiatric Clinic, Temple University Hospital, Philadelphia.

FRANK S. CAPRIO, M.D. is a practising psychiatrist in Washington, D.C. He has been on the staff of Walter Reed Hospital and is the author, among others, of *Sexual Deviations* (with L. S. London, M.D.), *The Adequate Male, Marital Infidelity, Living in Balance.*

E. DAHL-IVERSEN, M.D. is professor of Surgery at the University Hospital, Copenhagen, Denmark.

ROBERT LATOU DICKINSON, M.D. was known as the dean of American sexologists. A president of the American Gynaecological Association, he was the author of numerous important works on sex anatomy and education including *Topographical Atlas of Human Sex Anatomy, The Single Woman,* and *A Thousand Marriages* (both with Lura Beam).

LUDWIG EIDELBERG, M.D. practises psychoanalysis in New York City. Formerly Chief of the Psychiatric Clinic at Mount Sinai Hospital, he is on the faculty of the New York Psychoanalytic Institute and is the author of *Take Off Your Mask* and *Studies in Psychoanalysis.*

SANDOR FERENCZI, M.D. was a Hungarian neurologist and physician of note before he joined Freud, in 1907, to become one of the most original psychoanalytical theorists. His many classic papers are collected chiefly in *Contributions to Psychoanalysis* and *Theory and Technique of Psychoanalysis.* His paper, 'The Nosology of Male Homosexuality,' was delivered at the Third Congress of the International Psycho-Analytical Association at Weimar, October, 1911.

410

HENRI FLOURNOY, M.D. is a Swiss psychoanalyst who practises in Geneva.

NANDOR FODOR, PH.D., the Royal Hungarian University of Science, now practises psychoanalysis in New York City. A member of the New York Academy of Sciences and an Associate of the Association for the Advancement of Psychotherapy, he is the author of *The Search for the Beloved* and *New Approaches to Dream Interpretation*.

SIGMUND FREUD, M.D. was the discoverer of psychoanalysis. In addition to his monumental books, Freud's *Collected Papers* are published in a five volume English edition. 'The Psychogenesis of a Case of Homosexuality in a Woman,' first published in *Zeitschrift*, Bd. VI, 1920, is found in Volume II of *Collected Papers*.

BENJAMIN H. GLOVER, M.D. is Assistant Professor of Neuropsychiatry at the University of Wisconsin, University Hospitals. His paper reporting the nonjudicial treatment of homosexuality in connexion with the Department of Student Health and Preventive Medicine at the University was presented before the Midwest Association of College Psychiatrists, October 9, 1948, at Madison, Wisconsin.

CHRISTIAN HAMBURGER, M.D. is a leading Danish endocrinologist associated with the Hormone Department, Statens Seruminstitut, Copenhagen. Together with Dr. Stürup and Professor Dahl-Iversen he has done considerable research on the problem of transvestism. The paper printed here was read in part before a joint meeting of the Danish Society for Endocrinology, at the University Hospital, Copenhagen, February 1, 1953.

GILBERT VAN TASSEL HAMILTON, M.D. was a specialist in comparative psychology, psychiatry and psychoanalysis. In addition to many years as a practising psychiatrist, Dr. Hamilton was Director, Division of Psychobiological Research, Bureau of Social Hygiene, Inc. He was the author of *A Study of Perseverance Reactions in Primates, Introduction to Objective Psychopathology, A Research in Marriage, etc.*

GEORGE W. HENRY, M.D. is Attending Psychiatrist, New York Hospital. He has been Associate Professor of Psychiatry, Cornell University Medical School. The results of his research undertaken for The Committee for the Study of Sex Variants has been published in *Sex Variants*. Dr. Henry is also the author of *Essentials of Psychiatry*, etc. The paper reprinted here was first read at the meeting of the New York Psychiatric Society, May 3, 1933.

MAGNUS HIRSCHFELD, M.D. was probably the most eminent sexologist of his time. Founder, in 1918, of the Institute for Sexual Science in Berlin, he was the author of over two hundred titles dealing with sexual knowledge.

C. G. JUNG, M.D. is a Swiss psychoanalyst whose theoretical differences with Freud led to the establishment of analytic psychology. An eighteen volume English edition of Jung's *Collected Works* is being published by The Bollingen Foundation.

PAUL SCHILDER, M.D. came from his native Vienna at the request of Adolph Meyer to become Clinical Director of Bellevue Psychiatric Hospital, New York. He was also on the faculty of New York University Medical School. Dr. Schilder's writings include *Medical Psychology, Brain and Personality, Introduction to Psychoanalytic Psychiatry,* and *The Image and Appearance of the Human Body.* The paper, 'On Homosexuality,' was read before the Washington Psycho-Pathological Society, January, 28, 1929.

OSWALD SCHWARZ, M.D. was an eminent urological surgeon as well as a medical psychologist in Vienna and London. He was the author of several works on sex pathology including *The Psychology of Sex* and *Diagnosis and Treatment of Organic Symptoms of Mental Origin.*

GEORGE S. SPRAGUE, M.D. practises psychiatry and psychoanalysis in Philadelphia. In addition to broad experience on the staffs of a number of hospitals, he has been Assistant Professor of Psychiatry at Temple University Medical School. The paper reprinted in this volume was first read at the ninetieth annual meeting of The American Psychiatric Association, New York City, May 28-June 1, 1934.

WILHELM STEKEL, M.D. was an original member of Freud's Vienna circle who, like Alfred Adler, diverged from the orthodox psychoanalytic movement. Stekel wrote extensively on the question of homosexuality. Among his translated works are *The Homosexual Neurosis, The Beloved Ego, Frigidity in Women, Technique of Analytical Psychotherapy* and *Auto-Erotism.*

GEORG K. STURUP, M.D. is Chief Physician of the Institute for Psychopaths, Herstedvester, Denmark.

CLARA THOMPSON, M.D. is a practising psychoanalyst in New York City. She is Executive Director of the William Alanson White Institute, and author of *Psychoanalysis: Evolution and Development.*

MOSHE WULFF, M.D. practises psychoanalysis in Tel Aviv, Israel. The paper printed here is credited with being one of three detailed studies in psychoanalytic literature reporting a cure in a case of male homosexuality. It was originally published in German, *Imago,* 1941.

Index

GEORGE ALLEN & UNWIN LTD
London: 40 Museum Street, W.C.1

Auckland: 24 Wyndham Street
Bombay: 15 Graham Road, Ballard Estate, Bombay 1
Calcutta: 17 Chittaranjan Avenue, Calcutta 13
Cape Town: 109 Long Street
Karachi: 254 Ingle Road
New Delhi: 13-14 Ajmeri Gate Extension, New Delhi 1
São Paulo: Avenida 9 de Julho 1138-Ap. 51
Sydney, N.S.W.: Bradbury House, 55 York Street
Toronto: 91 Wellington Street West

For Product Safety Concerns and Information please contact our EU
representative GPSR@taylorandfrancis.com
Taylor & Francis Verlag GmbH, Kaufingerstraße 24, 80331 München, Germany